CULTURE REPORT
EUNIC YEARBOOK 2016

CULTURE REPORT
EUNIC YEARBOOK 2016

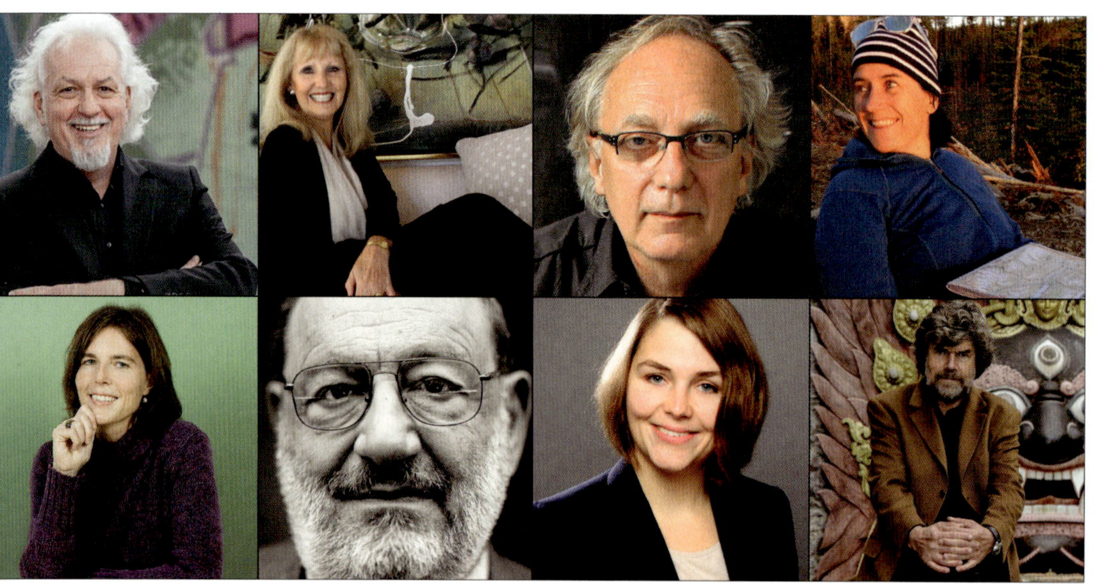

The integration of refugees, conflict resolution, human rights, emancipation and the fight against racism – these are just some of the areas where sport can have a positive role to play. To what extent can global sport act as a strategic instrument of cultural diplomacy and a role model for civil society? Can it help to achieve development policy goals? Does it still make any sense to use mega sports events for the purposes of nation branding? And what can we as normal citizens learn from an extreme mountaineer? These and other questions are addressed in the Culture Report and EUNIC Yearbook 2016 by authors as diverse as Umberto Eco, Reinhold Messner, Dave Eggers, Serhij Zhadan, Beqë Cufaj and Claus Leggewie.

CHAPTER 2: Sport around the world – Emancipation, fair play or curse?

CHAPTER 3 The hand of God or part of our DNA?
Sport is more than a cultural phenomenon

CHAPTER 4: EUNIC and the national institutes for culture –
Promoting trust and understanding worldwide

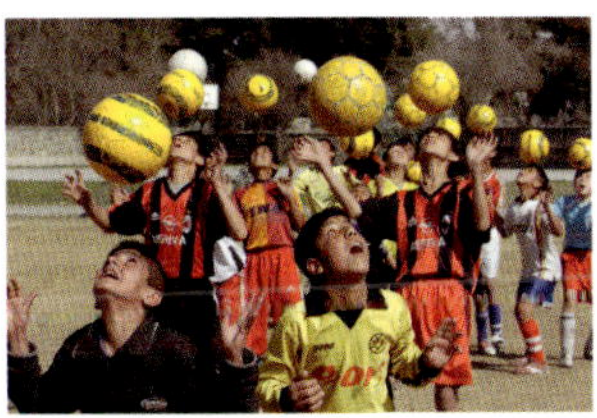

This edition features photographs of kids from all over the world playing football. They are from the NGO Streetfootballworld and other partner organisations around the globe. They are all committed to using football to create change, in the belief that: 'Football has the unique potential to make the world a better place. Our aim is to allow this potential to unfold.'

More than a game – The global language of sport

If we were to take Umberto Eco at his word when, in his charming way, he tells us that he simply doesn't know where to start when it comes to 'sports chatter', then we may as well put this book down right now. His disgust at how openly sporting spectacles and – even more so – 'chatter' about sporting spectacles seek to manipulate people, along with the all-too-obvious parallels between the Roman gladiatoral contests of the past and the enthusiasm of today's dictators for mega sports events, led him to turn his back on organised sports. But he still considered individual sporting activity to be healthy, celebrating its 'recreational waste' as a way of 'freeing ourselves from the tyranny of work'. But the world-renowned author and semiotician Eco would not have wasted his precious time on writing this article – which we unfortunately have to publish posthumously – if he had not been very aware of the importance of the sporting stage for humankind.

'Sport is more than a game, it is potential influence', stresses Grant Jarvie, a sports sociologist at the University of Edinburgh. Sport can create the opportunity for people, cities, countries and associations to connect and allow a nation to have an impact on the political world map. Sport will not solve the world's problems, but it can make a contribution. Precisely how sport makes this contribution to international relations is the focus of this edition of the EUNIC Yearbook.

Major sporting events such as the football World Cup or the Olympic Games are the world's largest transnational media events, of any kind. They bear witness to the way communication is no longer restricted by borders, and at the same time they bring the world together by focusing on cultural differences, and 'lay the foundation for an understated, still fragile cosmopolitanism', to quote political scientist Claus Leggewie. This is because sport has long moved from being simply 'The Beautiful Game' to being the focus of political decisions involving national prestige and economic success. Sport is attractive, it crosses linguistic and cultural borders, gets into the hearts of people all over the world and promotes the acceptance of social rules. For nations, it can provide a showcase or have an internal, integrative effect. The articles by Heather Cameron and Cora Burnett show how the social power of sport can be used for development, integration and peace work. American sociologist Andrei Markovits reminds us how modern sport is inextricably linked to parliamentarism. In the same way that democracy accepts the existence of opposition as a part of its construct, sport also has a tolerance for losing. Losers always have the right to a second chance, a return match, a comeback.

But the authors in this volume also highlight how sport can be toxic for society. Doping, corruption, human rights abuses and the destruction of the environment – the negative side of sport is all too well known. Frank Vogl, a former senior World Bank official and co-founder of Transparency International, looks at the money involved in the global sports business. According to estimates by Price Waterhouse Coopers, this was in the region of US$145 billion in 2015 alone. He considers how the rules of fair play can easily be ignored in light of these vast sums.

Sports scientists also warn of the risk of abuse: Jonathan Grix, Head of the Sports Policy Centre at Birmingham University, looks at how the invention of gigantism at the 1936 Olympics in Berlin led to an organisational arms race (finding its apogee at the Winter Olympics in Sochi). The terror attacks in Munich in 1972 led to a major tightening of security. These, along with the systematic doping carried out by the GDR, represent the extremes of how elite sport can be manipulated for political ends and provides many examples of how sport has been misused. The 2006 Football World Cup improved Germany's image, at least temporarily, because of the festive fan atmosphere that attracted large numbers of women, and it remains a role model for future hosts. But, according to Grix, many countries underestimate the resources that are required to stage such an event, and particularly the need to win the support of the public. Everyone simply hopes for a positive impact, rather than specifically and strategically spending money on achieving this.

Serhij Zhadan, Ukraine's most popular poet, remembers how the football European Championships were held in his country in 2012. What did the tournament leave behind for Ukraine? Nothing. Nothing but the abandoned stadiums that stand as a memorial to times gone by. Looking back, the poet says the Euros were nothing more than an expensive toy bought by the country's wealthy oligarchs – just because they could. Not because they had any expectation of gain, but simply because they felt like it, just as when they buy football clubs in England and elsewhere. Yet the football still brought people together in Ukraine. Everyone supported the national team; they were playing for all Ukrainians.

This edition of the EUNIC Yearbook marks ten years since the establishment of this network. Andrew Murray, Director of EUNIC Global in Brussels, and Rafael Rodríguez-Ponga, Secretary-General of the Instituto Cervantes and the current EUNIC President, look back at the hurdles that have been overcome, review where we are now and anticipate the challenges that lie ahead. Both of them stress the heterogeneity of the members and how the level of collaboration among the network's more than one hundred clusters around the world often puts to shame the lack of collaboration at headquarters. But they both also stress that there has been significant progress in key areas and that EUNIC members have been particularly successful in defining the role of culture in Europe's external relations. The fact that the European Union is currently working on a global strategy for the EU's external relations offers a unique opportunity for EUNIC members to not only significantly increase the visibility of culture, but also their own. In their new strategy, EUNIC members agree that it will also be necessary to focus more on research and monitoring effectiveness alongside their usual cultural and informational activities.

I would like to thank everyone who has contributed to this Yearbook for their productive collaboration: the authors and translators, and particularly our sponsors, the Austrian Foreign Ministry, the Portuguese Camões cultural institute, the Spanish EUNIC presidency and the team at EUNIC Global.

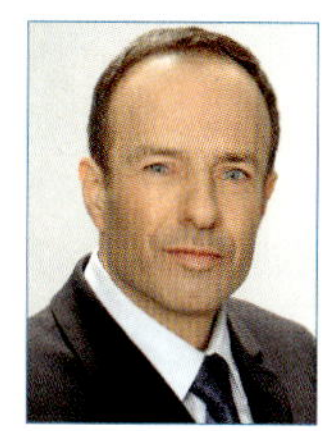

Sebastian Körber is Deputy Secretary-General and Head of the Media Department at the Institute for Foreign Cultural Relations.

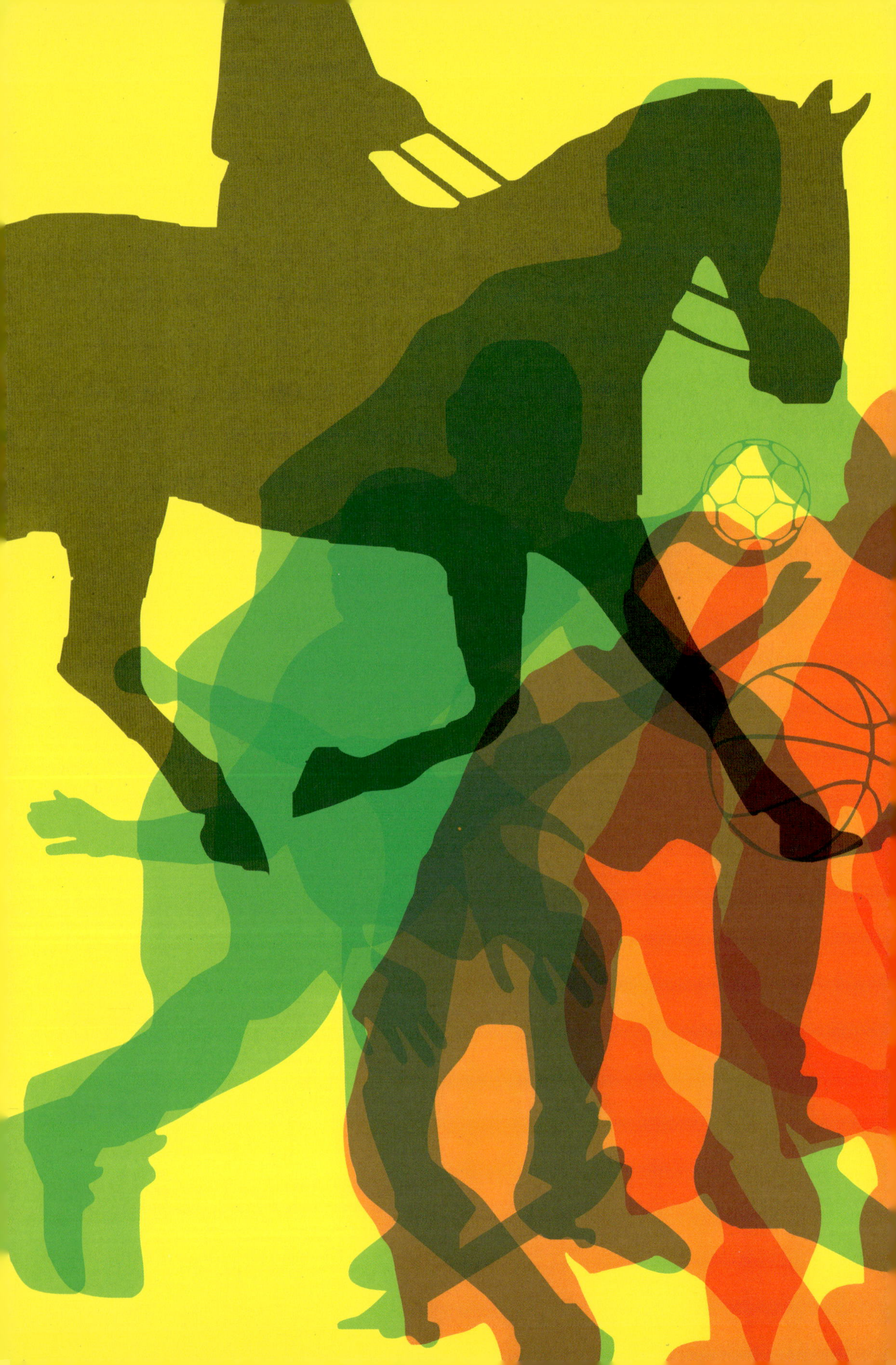

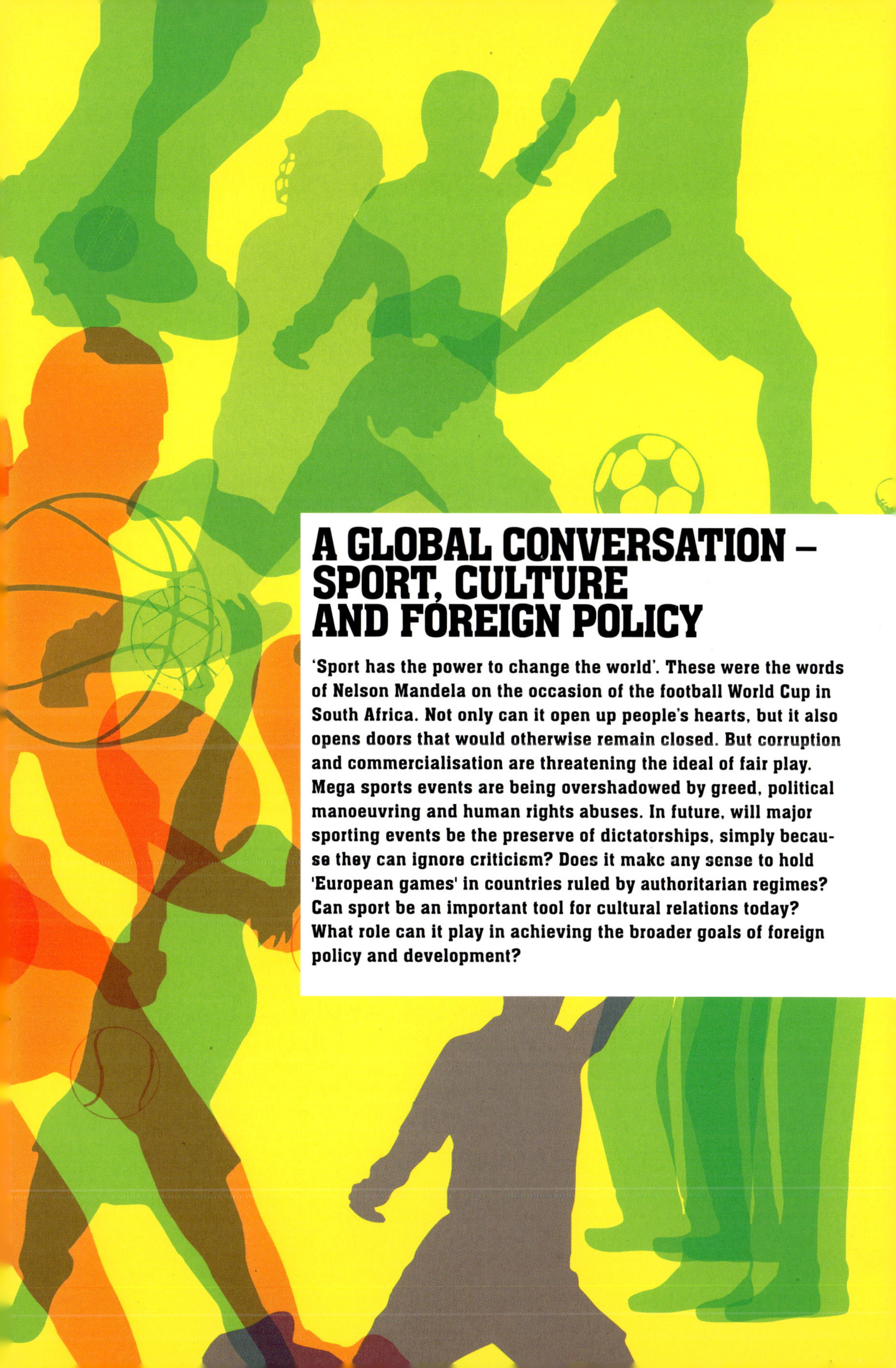

A GLOBAL CONVERSATION – SPORT, CULTURE AND FOREIGN POLICY

'Sport has the power to change the world'. These were the words of Nelson Mandela on the occasion of the football World Cup in South Africa. Not only can it open up people's hearts, but it also opens doors that would otherwise remain closed. But corruption and commercialisation are threatening the ideal of fair play. Mega sports events are being overshadowed by greed, political manoeuvring and human rights abuses. In future, will major sporting events be the preserve of dictatorships, simply because they can ignore criticism? Does it make any sense to hold 'European games' in countries ruled by authoritarian regimes? Can sport be an important tool for cultural relations today? What role can it play in achieving the broader goals of foreign policy and development?

A tool for cultural relations

A tool for cultural relations Sport has a universal appeal that crosses linguistic and cultural borders. It has the potential to win the hearts of people worldwide and open doors that may otherwise remain closed. A real opportunity exists to make the case that sport is part of the essential toolbox for anyone involved in contemporary cultural relations. But to what degree can global sport play a part in achieving wider foreign policy goals? *By Grant Jarvie*

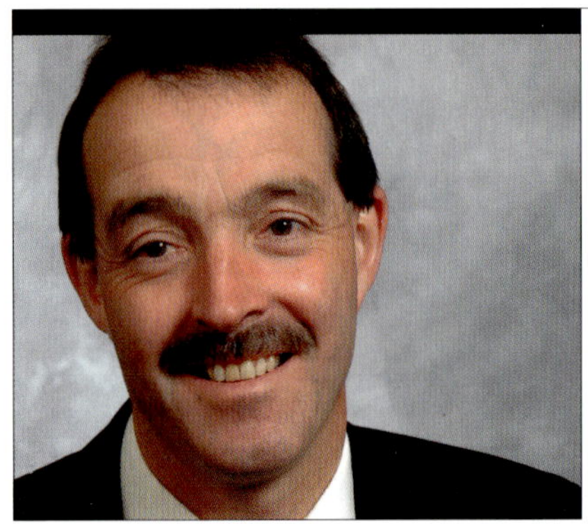

Sport is not a solution in and of itself but its importance in helping with contemporary cultural relations should not be underestimated. We need to continue to press the case for a better understanding of what sport can and cannot do, and what it should do. In a fragmented, tense and increasingly divided world there is a growing need for effective cultural relations. More effective cultural relations would reduce the risk of major conflicts due to a misunderstanding or no understanding between different countries, communities and/or groups and sport should be part of every diplomat's or civil servant's toolbox. A real opportunity exists to make the case that sport is part of the essential toolbox for anyone involved in contemporary cultural relations. We should use any means at our disposal to strive to make the world a less tense and better place.

Whatever the differences between European cultural partners and agencies may be, we are stronger working together than apart. The real opportunity and challenge is whether the European collective expertise, will and effort is strong enough to marshal our evidence and expertise to demonstrate how sport does and can influence cultural relations and foreign policy.

Making the art of the possible possible

I will make the case that sport is capable of making the art of the possible possible. Cultural relations and foreign policy can at times seem remote from our everyday lives. Sport, on the other hand, connects with people from all walks of life and we cannot afford to ignore anything that can contribute to better international cultural relations now, today.

It would be a wrong to suggest the interest in sport, culture and foreign policy is new. There is a considerable body of work that supports and questions the role of sport. It is just about 50 years since the British politicians Christopher Chataway and Philip Goodhart penned their account of international sport in 'A War without Weapons' (1968). They described the place of sport in the Cold War, in South Africa, in the American Civil Rights struggle and in brokering diplomatic relations between the USA and China. More recently Victor Cha, the former Director of Asian Affairs for the White House, provided in 'Beyond the Final Score' (2009) one of the few inside accounts of sporting diplomacy and argued that sport matters because it can provide opportunities for interventions, and it can be less aloof than some forms of diplomacy.

The UK House of Lords report on 'Persuasion and Power in the Modern World' (2014), pointed to the necessity of balancing hard and soft power tactics, and acknowledged the role that sport could play. There is a plethora of distinguished works from which we can learn. They demonstrate that sport matters because it has (i) universal appeal that crosses linguistic and cultural barriers; (ii) the capacity to develop feel-good factors – even temporarily; (iii) the ability to foster conversations between countries that take place around sporting events and (iv) the capacity to reduce crime and suicide rates. Broadly speaking, there are three propositions on sport, culture and foreign policy: one is outward looking, and claims sport contributes to broader goals of cultural and foreign policy. One is inward looking and points to how sports organisations, agencies, clubs and institutions manifest and negotiate their own internal cultural and foreign

Sport can open doors for people, communities and universities, and I would argue that it can help countries communicate. It is a language in its own right.

policy within and across sport. And one is a mixture of both.

Sport is a fantastic area to work in because it can reach out to so many people. It can take you into many interesting areas of discovery. Sport can open doors for people, communities and universities, and I would argue that it can help countries to communicate. It is a language in its own right.

The role of the arts has long been recognised and celebrated in European culture as a valuable social tool. Sport should be awarded the same status as European cultural relations. It should not be considered to be less important than art or music, which are often prioritised in European cultural debates and practice. Sport can be a social, cultural, political and popular force, but we need to know more about what works where, and when, and under what circumstances.

The language around sport, culture and foreign policy is a crowded area. Too crowded, in my view. We hear about hard power, soft power, cultural diplomacy, cultural relations, cultural policy, foreign policy, and public diplomacy. We need a new language around cultural relations, if not a new modus operandi.

As the name suggests, cultural relations seek to create a relationship. The medium of exchange is culture, and what is created is a relationship: something that should be but is not always mutual. Much has been written about sport's contribution to soft and hard power. Evolving evidence acknowledges the existence of cultural relations within this 'hard and soft power spectrum', but in this context we need to understand what works, what tools are available, and how we might get better at using sport and other aspects of culture.

Governments can make countries more attractive to others through policies, diplomacy, and the deployment of resources, including development assistance for sport. This also applies to a host of non-state institutions and agencies working below the level of formal government. If we consider hard and soft power to be what one country does to another, I would contend that effective international cultural relations go well beyond that.

Sport as potential influence

Sport is more than a game – it is potential influence. Sport can help win friends, be a resource of hope and, like other aspects of culture, can help develop human capital. I recently interviewed a UK shadow international development minister on the whole issue of football, poverty and international development. He told me tale after tale about the relevance of sport in some of the most war-torn countries in the world.

He pointed to the crowds during the Arab uprisings, many of whom were wearing football shirts from European football clubs. He told me how football had broken down barriers in Afghanistan, and in a Palestinian refugee camp in Lebanon. The refugees had not wanted to talk to him until he joined in the football game.

He said: 'The young boys were kicking a football around. Now, it was a football by name only it didn't look much like a football, because there was no air in it. But I joined in their kick-about. And, immediately, the families are happy to talk about their situation, their circumstance, their predicament, as Palestinian refugees in Lebanon. So football immediately broke down that barrier.'

In Afghanistan his experience was much the same. He watched members of the then new Afghan security forces, who had taken a break from taking on the Taliban in the dust and the danger of Afghanistan, and were playing in football strips from 30 different European football clubs There they were, with British soldiers at their side guarding the match from attacks from the Taliban.

So here were people who were taking a break from the supreme danger. And what did they do with their time? They had put on the football strip of a club that they had perhaps only heard of by word of mouth. Those sorts of things show the cultural penetration and influence of football. So, despite recent revelations surrounding its world governing body FIFA, football and sport in general can create influence.

Norwegian international development ministers tell similar stories, and have often talked about the role that the Norwegian Football Cup has played in fostering internationalism and co-operation between Norway and other countries. The aim of this tournament is to create bonds between children from different nations at a young age and win friends for Norway. It is perhaps surprising then that Norway comes behind Denmark in the global league table of sporting influence. Denmark is an example of a state that has deliberately set out to plan, evaluate and compare what exactly its sporting influence should and could be.

The Global Sports Political Power Index [http://www.dif.dk/en/om_dif/power-index] was founded in 2013 and attempts to measure the influence that nations have and should have in world sport. Denmark invented and manages the scheme because it wishes to establish an evidence-based assessment of the number of international positions that Denmark should strive to hold in international sport, identifying which nations have the greatest influence on the international scene and which countries Denmark should co-operate with. Analysis of the data shows that, amongst the Scandinavian countries, Denmark comes second behind Sweden but ahead of Norway and Finland. Amongst other European nations, Denmark was placed 12th. Great Britain was top, with Italy, Germany, France and Spain taking the other top five positions. In the international league of sporting nations Denmark was placed 36th, with the top 5 positions being held by the USA, Great Britain, Italy, France and Russia. Australia was 8th, Germany 9th and China 10th.

Denmark was seeking to co-operate in sport with countries that valued a similar approach to democracy. That is to say, the Danish sports federations were seeking to develop mutuality and co-operation with other countries in and through sport. They wanted to build alliances with like-minded countries while diminishing the influence of less democratically inclined countries.

The Danes undertook the analysis in order to better equip themselves to enter international discussions on democracy in sport. But creating further influence in sport is not the same as creating influence through sport where sport is a means to an end.

It is perhaps surprising then that Norway comes behind Denmark in the global league table of sporting influence. Denmark is an example of a state that has deliberately set out to plan, evaluate and compare what exactly its sporting influence should and could be.

The impact of the World Cup in Brazil

Much has been written about the impact of the 2014 FIFA World Cup in Brazil. Brazilian authors remind us that sport has increasingly figured in Brazil's foreign policy agenda since 2003. While the specific foreign policy outcomes have still to be evaluated, winning the right to host major sporting events was planned as a mechanism for giving the country increased recognition and symbolic power in the international arena.

Brazilians wanted to 'sustain the profits of a remarkable level of soft power by using the 2014 World Cup and the 2016 Olympic and Paralympic sport events', as one author puts it. It is clear that such events supported the intention of many Brazilian political officials to increase the status of Brazil in the international sphere through major sporting events.

Much has been written about the way in which sport is used as an aspect of soft power. In 2015 Jonathan Grix from the University of Birmingham and others published their work on the use of sporting events as part of a nation's soft power strategy. In 2013 Robert Huish from the University of Halifax, Canada, and others published work on the place of sport in Cuba's soft power strategy. A group of American researchers have also published a study on street soccer and the building of social and human capital through sport.

The work that provides evidence of sport's capacity to build human capabilities is important because of the link between human capital, economic growth and the reduction of the inequality gap. This aside, the general point that is being made is that we should recognise the way in which countries use sport as a tool to gain influence both within sport and through sport.

I would add that universities also have a huge role to play through sport and other means. My own university, Edinburgh, argues that it has been influencing the world since 1583. Sport has its part to play in this as well, as does the work of different universities who work with others across borders and between nations.

It is not as if the world has not always had its problems. What is new is the contexts in which we live today and the tools at our disposal to resolve these problems and issues. The World Economic Forum has identified the top four international trends as: worsening income inequality; unemployment; rising geo-strategic competition, and intensifying nationalism. Additional concerns include rising population levels; weakening of democracy; climate change, health, and increasing water stress.

No simple solutions

With each world problem there is a temptation to simplify matters, find a quick solution, and identify – sometimes wrongly – aggressors, transgressors and/or victims. But humanity, like power politics, is not that simple. The issues we must confront may be imposing in their scale and expansive in their reach, but they must be faced with fortitude and with a co-operative, collaborative spirit.

Consequently, foreign diplomats, ambassadors, civil servants, cultural agencies, communities and countries need to have a wide variety of tools at their disposal in order to win friends and maintain and foster relationships and understanding. As I said earlier, sport should be one of these tools.

We need to take advantage of sport's global currency, and further the part that sport can play in winning friends for countries. We need to find an effective framework, language, and set of principles through which international cultural relations can and should operate through sport and other facets of culture today. Good cultural relations are a two-way process, but if we are to forge long-standing, meaningful international cultural relation we have to work on issues of mutuality, reciprocity, trust and co-operation.

The role played by a host of non-state institutions and agencies working below the level of government is crucial. These include sports institutions, clubs, agencies, universities and more. Sport has a role to play in making the art of the possible possible. Making sports policy, sports investment, sports research, sports advocacy, commitment, alignment, and the power of universities and civil society working for people, places and communities.

So I hugely value the role of sport and the contribution it can make, and I hugely value the contribution of universities. But I firmly believe that if we are to make them more effective we need to develop new ways of thinking about international cultural relations. Resistance to this might come from traditional theorists or orthodox practitioners, but of course it is the case that coun-

> **With each world problem there is a temptation to simplify matters, find a quick solution, and identify – sometimes wrongly – aggressors, transgressors and/or victims. But humanity, like power politics, is not that simple.**

tries are already facing a million different global challenges.

We may still be lacking a complete philosophy of international cultural relations, but we can demonstrate how good practice works on the ground. We have plenty of examples and evidence of the way in which sport works in developing human, social, and cultural capital. Economists tell us that it is this development of human, social and cultural capital that may help to close the inequality gap and create growth.

I would now like to suggest a few principles that we might like to think about as necessary for more effective international cultural relations, and also propose some of the work that needs to be done.

Connectivity

Connectivity happens at all levels and sport can create the opportunity for people, cities and countries to connect and communicate. From the social events and meetings that take place around an Olympic or Commonwealth Games and other international sports events, to the analysis of sports conversations through social media, we need to map an understanding of what works where, when and how. I am sure Edinburgh is not alone, but some of the work that Edinburgh

We need to find an effective framework, language, and set of principles through which international cultural relations can and should operate through sport and other facets of culture today. Good cultural relations is a two-way process.

Informatics has carried out in analysing Twitter conversations about sport is truly illuminating.

Relationships

Relationships are formed through sport and because of sport. Sport helps foreign leaders to meet and form relationships, often in more informal settings. However, such relationships are built up over time, may not be transactional, and may not even be mutual or trusting, but they can still help. Building sustainable relationships allows countries to talk to each other at a multitude of different levels.

Mutuality and Trust

It may be a normative proposition that sport can help with building mutuality and trust, but there is enough evidence to support the argument that involvement in and through sport can lead to higher levels of social capital. Morrow's work on the mutual ownership of sports clubs is a fine example of this.

Influence

This is the soft power, public diplomacy route where sport can facilitate, and procure-ase outcomes, usually in a one-directional manner, and usually guided by a country's foreign policy or the key messages it wants to convey at a particular time. It is about reducing risk through listening and influencing the risk levels of conflict or increased tension.

Inter-cultural skills and perceptions

Effective international cultural relations are also about perception and projection. Sport helps us to understand the impact of globalisation on culture and culture on globalisation. We need to ask how the language of sport or the inter-cultural tool that is sport helps you to talk to the other and the other to talk to you. How does sport project an image of a place and how do others see and act upon that image?

The City of Glasgow's 2014 message was of the friendly Commonwealth Games, while the Commonwealth's message through Glasgow was one of humanity, diversity and equality. Cultural relations are also about foreign policy. What do foreign diplomats need to know today in order to do their jobs effectively, and are they equipped to understand what sport can and cannot deliver?

I want to mention the work of one Welsh writer and academic, and one Canadian activist and humanitarian. The Welshman is no longer with us, but Raymond Williams penned an important intervention in the 1990s called 'Resources of Hope' (1991), in which he championed the need for commitment. He argued that artists, writers, academics had to balance their freedoms with a duty to strive to help others – what he called the art of the possible. Sport can make the art of the possible possible in so many ways, and we should exploit it to the full.

The Canadian activist Samantha Nutt is one of the most intrepid voices in the humanitarian arena. She is the founder of War Child and author of 'Damned Nations' (2013), a book of uncommon power that aims to raise education levels and looks at the role of women in some of the most challenging circumstances in the world. Nutt's work covers decades of searching for answers to what can and should be done to help communities and countries caught up in conflict, and she describes the well-intended interventions that went wrong.

She reminds us that there is a great resilience, courage and strength in countries and communities where none ought to exist because of the atrocities they have suffered, and that for those seeking to make a difference it is not about interventions paved with good intentions but about making the art of the possible possible and sustainable.

Apart from this, there is an impressive body of work that points to the role of sport in providing a degree of normality in the lives of asylum seekers, when all around seems strange and insecure.

Or a former UN Secretary General for Europe who asserted that 'The hidden face of sport is also the tens of thousands of enthusiasts who find in their football, rowing, athletics and rock climbing clubs a place for meeting and exchange but above all the training ground for community life.'

The fact is, sport has undoubtedly a part to play in culture and foreign policy. But this is not new, and whether sport is viewed as a war without weapons, an agent of hard or soft power, or a tool that the United Nations

There is an impressive body of work which points to the role of sport in providing a degree of normality in the lives of asylum seekers, when all around seems strange and insecure.

can draw upon to help with conflict resolution and rebuilding resilience, we need a new way of framing not just the part played by sport in international cultural relations but international cultural relations per se.

Sport will not solve the world's problems but it can make an effective contribution. The global balance of power is tense, in a state of flux, and countries and cities need effective international cultural relations. This should include sport. Sport has a part to play in helping with global tensions and, perhaps more importantly, winning friends in a mutually supportive way.

I have tried to suggest that the framing of international cultural relations should think about matters of mutuality, trust, and co-operation, and that today's foreign diplomats, civil servants, activists and universities should use sport to the full. We need to re-think and continually evaluate what international cultural relations means today and how such relations can help with making the art of the possible possible. I believe sport has a huge part to play in this.

Grant Jarvie is a professor at the University of Edinburgh and a former vice-principal and acting principal. He is the author of *Sport, Culture and Society*, to be published by Routledge in 2016 (co-authored by Hector Macki).

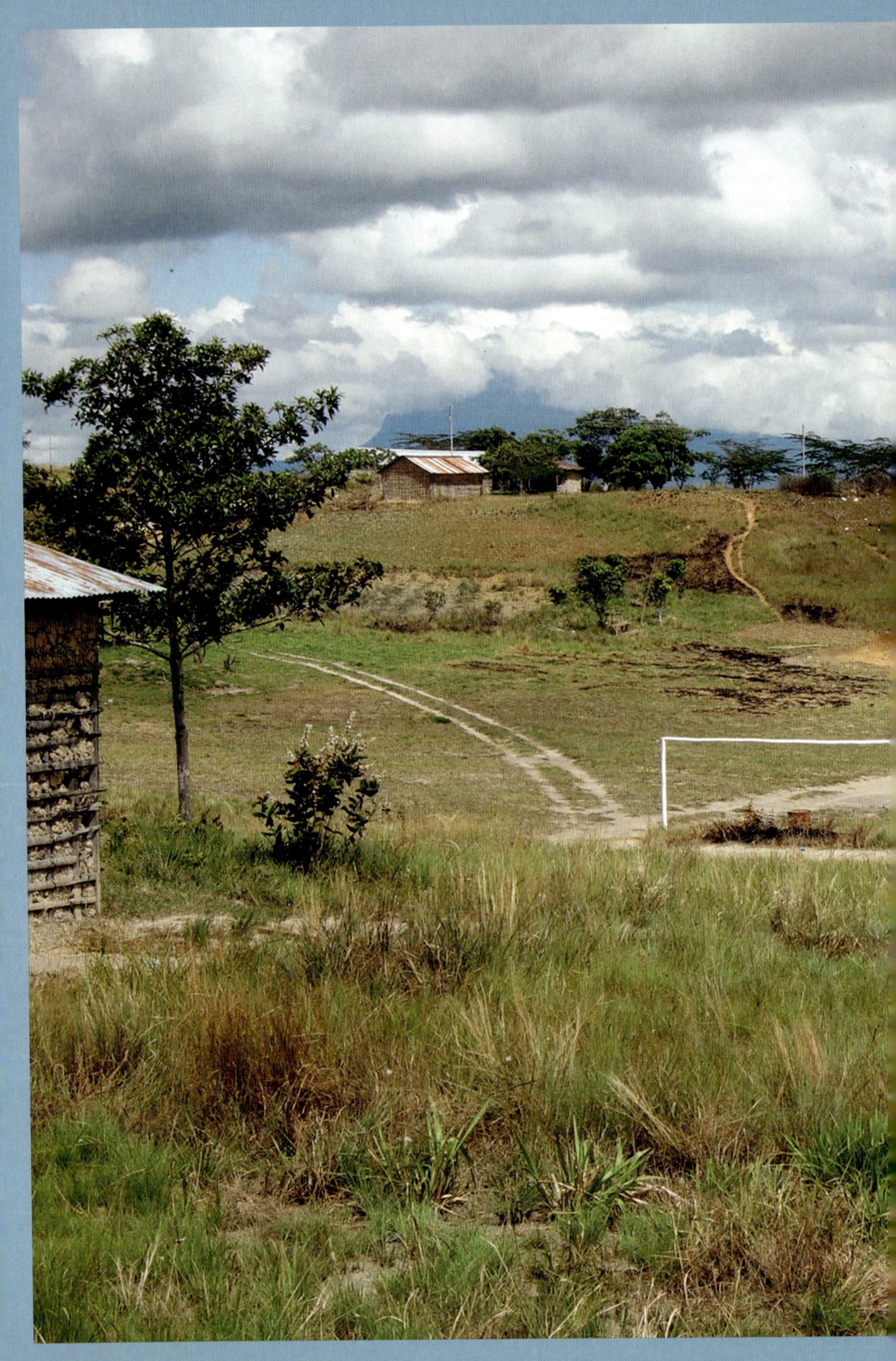

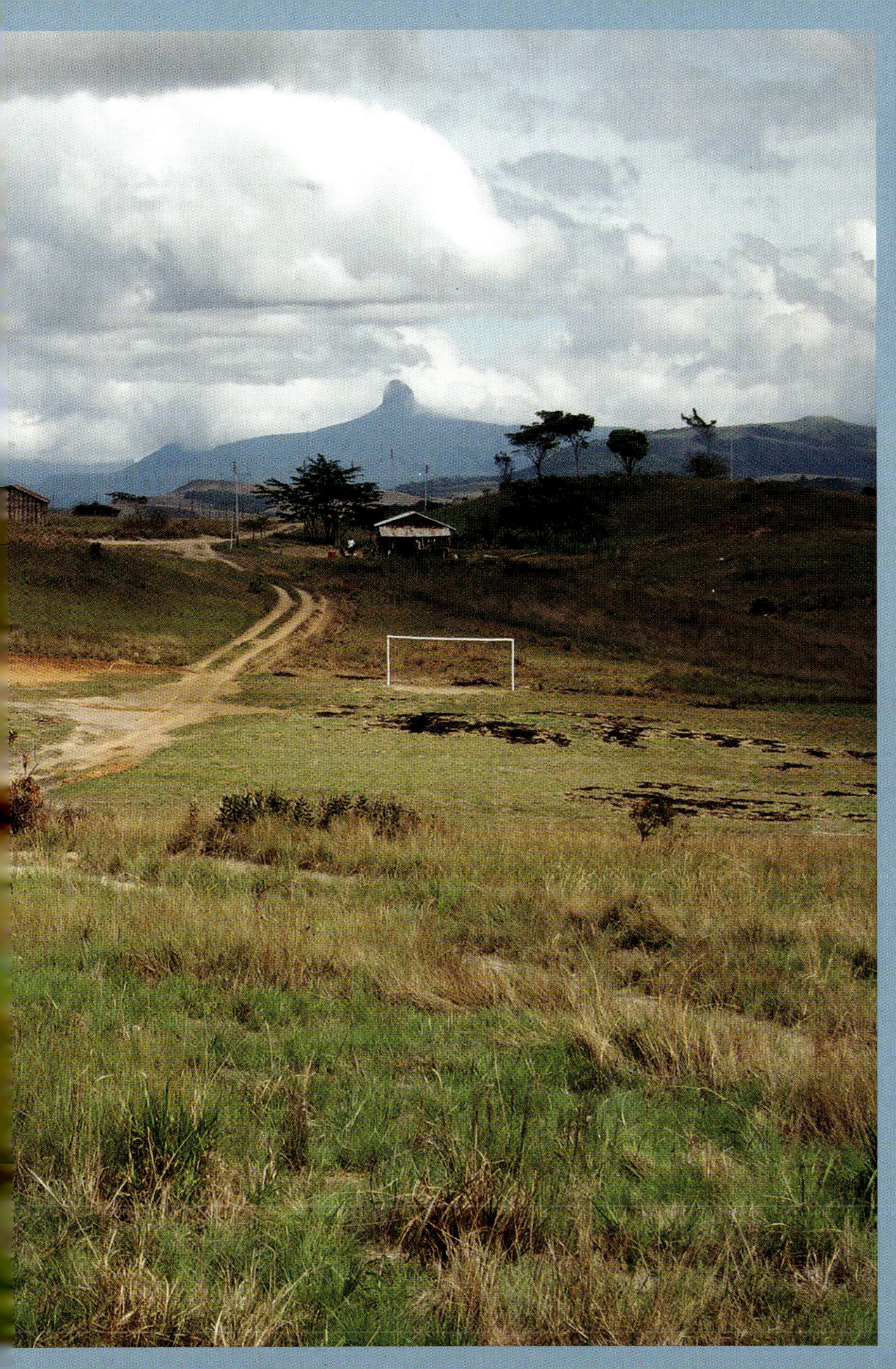

The politics of sport

The politics of sport China has enjoyed unprecedented bilateral relations, despite the Beijing Olympics fore-fronting their abuse of human rights. Qatar continues to blossom, despite the global exposure of its human rights abuses relating to the 2022 Football World Cup. Ukraine came under intense media scrutiny as a result of hosting the 2012 European Football Championships. How do sports mega-events influence the image of a country? What are the future challenges of sport and politics? *By Jonathan Grix*

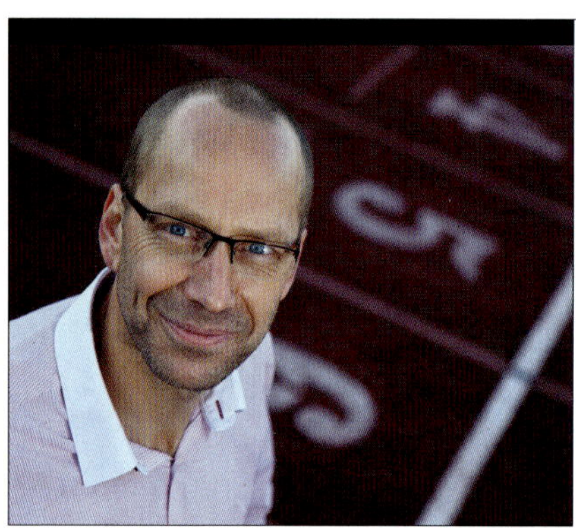

Twenty or thirty years ago an essay on sport and politics would have had to spend a few pages justifying why both concepts were being discussed together. Politicians, sports administrators and athletes themselves regularly lament how sport and politics are, and should be kept, separate. Writing today, however, against a backdrop of widespread doping in sport, corruption, misuse of public money, large-scale infrastructural projects developed in the name of sport and a spiralling 'sporting arms race' there is little space to waste on pondering the political in sport.

The challenge today is a different one: where to begin. Almost all aspects of sport are political – especially if we take the basic meaning of politics to be about the distribution of resources or, as the American political scientist and communication theorist Harold D. Laswell put it back in 1936, 'who gets what, when and how?' Sport has become a commodity, while the sport industry itself brings much-needed revenue to state coffers; elite sport is used as a vehicle to enhance a state's image on the international stage or as a chance for athletes to 'hop' from one nation to another and compete under a foreign flag, usually for financial gain.

Here I want to discuss some of the challenges facing global sport today and some of the historical precedents of those challenges. It begins by drawing on four important examples from German sport history that I believe are relevant to, and have shaped, the challenges facing global sport today. A subsequent section then develops some of the key themes further, including politicians and the discourse of 'legacies' from sports mega-events (SMEs). My conclusion is not that sport needs to be less political, but that we need to try to instrumentalise sport more for social good and less for financial gain.

Germany has played a much understated, yet central, role in the manipulation of sport for political purposes. The first example is what could be considered the start of 'mega' sports events – the so-called 'Hitler Olympics' of 1936. This is widely recognised as the first and most blatant use of sport for political purposes. The Nazis also introduced the torch relay.

The difference between the original political motives for instigating the relay and its use nowadays is enlightening. Whereas the Nazi regime used it to propagate their regime, it has now become an integral part of community engagement by the Olympic movement, in an attempt to whip up enthusiasm for the event rather than the hosts themselves. The torch relay is now a target for protest groups seeking to draw attention to their cause, as was the case in the build-up to the Beijing Olympics and the highlighting of Chinese human rights abuse by Tibetan monks.

Another impact of the 1936 Games on today's use of sport is its gigantism: the extravagant show put on by the Nazis – including 10,000 dancers performing a play and a 3,000-strong choir – has led to an exponential growth in bombastic showcasing during both the opening and closing ceremonies of the Olympics. Today, the host nation often attempts to improve its international image by being seen to be able to stage such a complex, multi-faceted and commercial event and the increase in costs associated with putting on a good show is a 'sporting arms race'.

The second German example is rooted in the tragic events of Munich in 1972, which saw the first political and calculated use of a major sporting event by terrorists and greatly influenced the manner in which subsequent sports mega-events are now 'securitised'. After the

The torch relay is now a target for protest groups seeking to draw attention to their cause, as was the case in the build-up to the Beijing Olympics and the highlighting of Chinese human rights abuse by Tibetan monks.

meticulous planning and considerable effort Germany put into preparations for the 1972 Games, political terrorism intervened and 11 Israeli Olympic team members and one West German policeman were killed during a kidnap attempt by the Palestinian group Black September.

Had the Games finished a few days earlier, when a 16-year-old German had surprisingly won the Olympic high jump, despite being the third choice for her national team, Munich is likely to have gone down in sport history as Germany's post-war re-integration.

The 'securitisation' of mega-events

What Munich does do is it reminds us of the risks involved in staging a major sport event; one of the key legacies of these Games is the 'securitisation' of sports mega-events, which reached its apogee at the recent London 2012 Games. In London, measures taken to prevent a Munich-type security disaster included surrounding the Olympic park with an 11-mile, £80 million, 5,000-volt electric fence – the UK even stationed anti-aircraft missiles on residential roofs close to the Olympic park. The 'securitisation' of such major events is now even more challenging since the 'war on terror' post-9/11 and after the Paris terrorist attacks in 2016. This type of terrorism is likely to impact the way in which such events are run, consumed and enjoyed.

A third German example is that of East Germany, in which the manipulation of elite sport for political gains resulted in arguably the most successful sports system ever known. East Germany's political instrumentalisation of sport for international recognition and legitimacy remains unparalleled. Their success in elite sport has had far-reaching and unintended consequences – the sports model developed and refined in the GDR continues to shape modern-day elite sports in advanced capitalist states.

The legacy continues

There is a certain irony that East Germany collapsed, yet its sporting legacy continues to influence its erstwhile opponents. A majority of today's best sporting nations have a system that is not too dissimilar to East Germany (many with widespread doping too). The consequences of a focus on elite sport success and specific sport disciplines at the expense of support for some sports and grass-roots sport are obvious, yet there appears to be a consensus that elite sport success is 'good' for a state, despite a lack of evidence to suggest why this should be the case. The usual chestnut that 'elite sport success' or a 'sports mega-event' leads to higher rates of sport participation among the masses has not been borne out in research.

A fourth and final German legacy is the use of sports mega-events to change a nation's image. It is fair to say that the 2006 FIFA World Cup (FWC) was an unmitigated success. As a country that had suffered from a poor image abroad for over 60 years, Germany set out to use the FWC to improve it on a global scale.

Of the key factors that made up the German strategy, the (unintended) creation of a feelgood factor around the four weeks of the tournament are of interest. Their fan-centred approach to the event led to the creation of unique fan-zones and fan-miles, where those people without tickets could watch the games live on very large screens. Over 20 million people joined in the party-like celebrations around the large viewing screens which were set up in the 12 host cities in Germany with no major public disorder reported.

The 'Fan Fests' served a number of purposes: first and foremost, they offered a street-party atmosphere to fans and bystanders who did not have tickets or who did not want to watch the football in the stadium(s). These innovative 'spaces' also provided an arena within which fans and people, mostly women, who would not usually follow football, could enjoy a good party atmosphere. The well-functioning fan zones, excellent signage, trained personnel and first-class transport system provided an unintended by-product in the creation of a feelgood factor and carnival-like atmosphere among those outside the stadiums.

In the current post-Paris climate it is unlikely that such a carnivalesque atmosphere will accompany a major sports event again because of terrorist threats, as security measures will, perhaps necessarily, work against the boundary-breaking communitas developed by experiencing sport together. Ironically, perhaps, one of sport's most powerful side-effects – the ability to allow consumers to transcend cultural, religious and even class boundaries – is very likely to be nipped in the bud by the menace and threat of terrorism. The reason? For communitas to develop you need mass congregations, spontaneous gatherings of people before and after the sporting event, all factors that are likely to be discouraged, as the new terrorist threat seeks out innocent crowds of people.

Post-2006 it is clear that Germany's attempt to alter its negative national image abroad was successful. I believe that this has influenced a number of so-called 'emerging' states to host major sporting events. However, most do not have the resources or know-how to undertake long-term planning prior to the event as Germany did; many do not have or are unconcerned about whether their population is behind the event; this then leads to them not having a clear strategy for the event, but rather a 'hope' that the event itself will simply lead to an improvement in their image.

The latter is all they share in common with Germany: a tarnished image in need of improving. Unfortunately, for such states hosting a sports mega-event might be the worst thing to do, as the media tend to focus hard on the reasons why a state has a poor reputation in the first place. Examples include Ukraine and the European football championships in 2012 (joint hosts with Poland), Qatar, South Africa and China. The jury is out on whether bidding for or hosting a sports mega-event has actually improved the image of the above states.

Impact on ability to trade internationally

Arguably, Ukraine, Qatar and China came out worse in terms of how their image is perceived by citizens across the world; the extent to which this impacts on their ability to trade internationally and develop bilateral relations is, however, questionable. China has enjoyed unprecedented bilateral relations and agreements with the UK, despite the Beijing Olympics fore-fronting their abuse of human rights;

There appears to be a consensus that elite sport success is 'good' for a state, despite a lack of evidence to suggest why this should be the case. The usual chestnut that 'elite sport success' or a 'sport mega-event' leads to higher rates of sport participation among the masses has not been borne out in research.

Qatar continues to blossom, despite the global exposure of its human rights abuses, especially of foreign workers building the sporting infrastructure for the 2022 Football World Cup; Ukraine came under intense media scrutiny following its (joint) hosting of the 2012 European Football Championships.

There has been a recent trend of 'emerging' states bidding for and hosting sports mega-events, while, at the same time, many 'advanced capitalist states' have held referenda in which the public have rejected the idea of hosting.

The recent bid for the 2022 Winter Olympics is indicative of this trend and the problems that come with it. After voters in Munich, Stockholm, Krakow, and Graubünden, Switzerland, said no to the spiralling costs, hollow 'legacy' promises and security concerns, it was a race between Beijing – an area with very little snow – and Almaty, Kazakhstan. Both China and Kazakhstan do not fare well in lists on upholding human rights and on corruption – two factors that run counter to the fundamental Olympic ideals.

If the spiralling costs associated with hosting sports mega-events are left unchecked, it is conceivable that those states which care little about the views of their citizenry will be the only place in which such spectacles take place. Sochi is a case in point here – around US$55 billion was spent on the Winter Olympics, making it the most expensive Olympics ever (summer or winter). The usual post-event scenario of under-utilised, inflated sporting infrastructure is likely to be even more pronounced in Russia. Such a use of taxpayer's money is no longer viable in a democratic state.

Yet politicians of all political hues love a sporting spectacle – generally in the hope of raising people's spirits, improving their own popularity and in the hope of generating an economic return on their (that is the public's) investment. They are also part of what could be termed a 'coalition of beneficiaries' – that is, those who seek to bring SMEs to their states and cities.

They are also responsible for the discourse that surrounds such sporting spectacles, often promoting the many 'benefits' or 'legacies' that will befall society should they choose to host. Research on the prospects of such 'legacies', however, suggests that the coalition of beneficiaries are likely to benefit from large-scale sports events, whereas the general population is not.

And here we return to Harold D. Lasswell – if people are to be persuaded to invest in elite sport programmes or the hosting of sports mega-events, then the case for post-event legacies needs to evidenced. At present, would-be legacies are generally hoped-for rather than specifically and strategically aimed for. The perennial sports mega-event question is not 'what happened to the legacy', but rather 'why do states not learn from previous events'? The answer to this is that the coalition of beneficiaries does learn – usually firms involved in construction, event stakeholders, politicians, hospitality trade and so on; it is in their interests to host.

Sport is very big business

If there is any doubt left remaining, a final example of sport's political nature will suffice to show how closely politics and sport are linked. If ever anybody needs convincing of such a link, they can do no worse than consider the role of the key international sporting organisations. We have arrived at the absurd situation whereby undemocratic international sporting organisations such as FIFA and the IOC are able to demand changes to laws in sovereign, democratic states to be able to host their showcase events. Thus, Brazil's economic governance of state capitalism had to tweak many laws to do with employment and procurement to meet the requirements of both FIFA and the IOC.

The net result, one could surmise, is that in order to receive such prestigious events, states need to become just a little more neoliberal. The Olympics has developed into the most commercial sporting event on the planet and is probably about as far from Pierre de Coubertin's revival of the modern Games

Sochi is a case in point here – around US$55 billion was spent on the Winter Olympics, making it the most expensive Olympics ever. The usual post-event scenario of under-utilised, inflated sporting infrastructure is likely to be even more pronounced in Russia. Such a use of taxpayer's money is no longer viable in a democratic state.

in 1896 as you can get. Sponsorship and commercial rights – including the Olympic brand itself – have become far more important than the actual sport and to safeguard top Olympic sponsors and allow them generous tax breaks, hosting state need to adjust their laws.

The latter is indicative of how far we have come – sport is very big business; athletes are prepared to go to any lengths to succeed in this 'win at all costs' culture, so we should not be surprised at revelations of widespread corruption and the use of performance enhancement drugs. While it would be ludicrous to advocate sport without politics, there is reason to believe that we have reached a tipping point at which more effort is needed to turn the tide so that politics no longer dominates sport, but rather uses it to achieve common goods.

Jonathan Grix is Reader in Sport Policy and \ Politics in the School of Sport, Exercise and Rehabilitation Sciences and Director of the Sport Policy Centre at the University of Birmingham. He has authored or edited twelve books and published over 40 referred articles in sport studies and political journals. Topics covered in his latest books and articles include sport under communism, the Sochi Winter Olympics, Russia's unique soft power strategy, public health policy and walking in England.

An expanded space for communication

An expanded space for communication Sport is much simpler than many other social activities, and of course it has fewer boundaries. Matches between the world's top 20 teams in football and basketball, major events in tennis, golf, ice hockey and baseball, sailing, rugby and triathlon – all these beautifully illustrate the phenomenon of the dissolution of borders. Teams studded with international stars give the impression of being global corporations. *By Claus Leggewie*

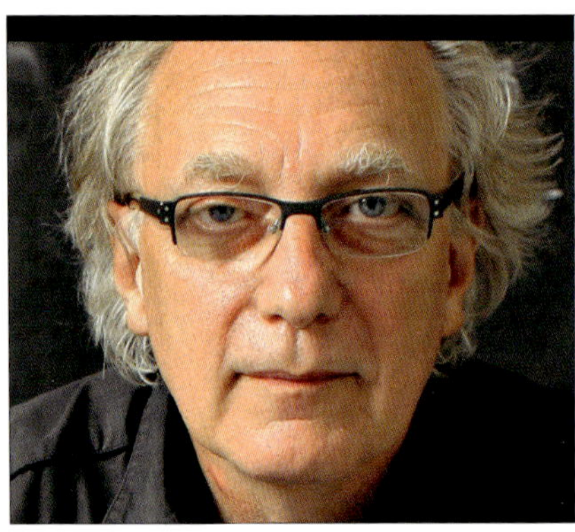

The current refugee crisis may be manifesting the opposite trend, but over recent decades national borders have lost their significance, or to be more precise, they have changed in nature. The dissolution of borders throws into question the use of the nation state as the ultimate unit of analysis for modern political thought and action. We are now in need of additional global governance mechanisms.

Even people who never travel to far-flung destinations for business or pleasure still have an unprecedented connection to the rest of the world: via their televisions – perhaps by watching a major sporting event – the internet or in the workplace. A consequence of the dissolution of borders is that national cultures no longer provide the undisputed foundation and substance of the political feelings of 'us' that are at the root of most nations' collective identity. Culturally mixed or hybrid entities are gaining significance in a global context and new, unexpected phenomena are springing up in transnational interstices.

Businesses have also lost their distinct borders; with their blurred, shifting edges they are now more like magnetic fields or clouds. Transnational corporations have emerged – conglomerates that are simultaneously active in many countries and that go far beyond the traditional dealings between parent companies and foreign subsidiaries.

The transnational nature of such relationships does not revolve around the bilateral or international trading that has been the norm for so long. Now a space for business and culture has emerged that is free from national considerations and where nationality in terms of citizenship is losing significance. Today, the reference system for such operations is most definitely global society, even if mobility in today's global market is still less widespread than is theoretically possible.

So globalisation is not restricted to corporate mergers, internet communications and financial transactions. Cultural communities also span the globe, not only in the way it is done by large companies within large organisational frameworks, but more particularly as decentralised movements, as an unofficial, heterodox, self-justifying civil society.

Cultures create borders that other systems – such as economic systems – ignore or tear down; at the same time they enable the kind of communication that does not exist between economic and ethical systems. Intercultural communication unlocks new spaces for communication that allow the development of new culture.

The public sphere is also experiencing a dissolution of borders: its experience of the world is opening up and its self-awareness is becoming 'globalised'. By 'public sphere' we mean everything that is not confidential or private, more specifically an actual or imagined place that is basically open to all and where the res publica, affairs that concern everyone, can be debated and potentially decided.

For a long time – and still today – political public spheres have often been limited to national or regional communication, although news from far-off countries and corners of the earth has for centuries been afforded a particular significance. So transnational media events have existed for many years, as was demonstrated by the earth-shattering news of the earthquakes that destroyed Lisbon in 1755

Cultures create borders that other systems – such as economic systems – ignore or tear down; at the same time they enable the kind of communication that does not exist between economic and ethical systems.

and San Francisco in 1906. However, the creation of nation states was the result of successfully pooling and focusing communication in a particular entity based on language and culture, which produced an effective distance and hierarchy between one's own nation and other nations.

In this sense we can describe global society as an expanded space for communication and the dissolution of borders with regard to nations, the environment, politics and business is a consequence of the expansion in information and communication. The different regions and peoples that make up global society have really 'discovered' each other through communication and today – not only in the rich countries – they are more connected than ever before via post, telephone, satellite TV and the internet.

Transnational media events

Major transnational media events include the World Cup; live concerts; televised conflicts such as the Gulf War in 1991 and later wars in Yugoslavia and Afghanistan; and ceremonies such as the funerals of Princess Diana and Pope John Paul II. These events have given a more precise shape to the previously rather hazy phenomenon of a 'global public', namely as a 'community of peoples', a virtual 'global conscience' and also as a global playing field and entertainment arena.

The universalism of human rights has been joined by the post-colonial need to respect different cultural mores and indeed to ensure that this right to be different is universally accepted, leading to today's global society recognising that diversity is a universality. Such demands are advanced and at times manipulated by an electronic media audience that has expanded globally in terms of topics and reach. Electronic and digital media allow viewers and listeners to travel through time and space without having to get up from the couch.

This is not mainly about reports on events that metaphorically interest 'the whole world'; specialist channels such as CNN can literally capture the attention of the whole world by screening major events, and viewer figures are the global indicator of media attention. Media with a global reach are not the guardians of our universal morals, but they do integrate global society by highlighting cultural differences and standards. Through this stimulus they lay the foundation for an understated, still fragile cosmopolitanism that allows an unprecedented sense of solidarity with strangers.

Cultural fragmentation

As a result of all this, we now have a cultural fragmentation that cuts across normal distinctions in global society according to functional areas. Secondly, social spaces are being deterritorialised and virtualised so that now, less than ever before, we cannot assume that cultural communities correspond to national borders. Thirdly, transnational communities and identities are being created that transcend nations and nation states. The diversification of social affiliations throws into question the nation state as a political leitmotiv and guiding principle for collective action. Since the 19th century the nation, together with the state as a bureaucratic institution, and democratic representation have also been a fixed point of personal identity and a condition for social affiliation. But today there are new, flexible forms of affiliation and community that challenge the representativeness and legitimacy of democratic government.

Against this general backdrop we can now take a look at the specific contribution of sport to the process of breaking down borders. Sport is much simpler and of course has fewer boundaries than many other social activities. Matches between the world's top 20 teams in football and basketball, major events in tennis, golf, ice hockey and baseball, sailing, rugby and triathlon – all these beautifully illustrate the phenomenon of the dissolution of borders.

In Germany, for example, on the one hand people identify with the national team, and on the other with club teams that include players of many different nationalities. Free movement in the player market means that top European teams have long been dominated by foreign, often black, players from 'third world' countries. And now this trend is making itself felt among managers and trainers: top European managers are taking non-European national teams to the top, while foreign managers are being appointed to run league clubs.

It's not only the world's top 20 teams that are active in the transfer market. A few examples from the German league over recent years include the 'cross-border traffic' that brings Belgian and Dutch players to Schalke in Gelsenkirchen and Slovakian players to FC Nuremberg; Rostock's links to Swedish teams; and Bayern Munich's ties with the Red Bulls in Salzburg. Another example is the way stars who are reaching the end of their careers help to develop the game, as happened in the

USA in the late 1970s, Japan in the 1990s and is currently the case in Qatar. Spectacular transfer deals involving top players preoccupy the world's media for weeks on end, and the centrifugal effect of this rotation has an effect as far down as the third divisions.

Creolisation of national teams

But there's one snag: national teams are not in a position to recruit talented young players unless foreign players gain citizenship and are eligible to play for them. This is known as 'creolisation', but it does not generally affect local patriotic support for football clubs. However, some fans have been heard complaining about a 'squadra globalizzata'. This is the name that was given by the Italian newspaper La Repubblica to the elite Inter Milan team when none of its squad came from the Lombardy region.

Some years ago, football's dominant Real Madrid came up with the Zidanes Y Pavones solution. This aimed to keep its fans happy by providing a mix of world travellers (such as Zinedine Zidane) and locally grown talent (such as Francisco Pavon). Rivals Manchester United followed a similar route, while Borussia Dortmund had to bow to financial pressures and focus on developing young local talent – much to the delight of the fans at the Rote Erde stadium, which has since then also seen it change its name.

Free movement in the player market means that top European teams have long been dominated by foreign, often black, players from 'third world countries.

Teams studded with international stars give the impression of being global corporations. Of course the performance and reputation of clubs (which no longer make the bulk of their income from the playing side) still leave much to be desired. Many professional clubs in Italy and Spain have lost control of their finances. But this also happens in Germany, for example when the Berlin club Hertha BSC asked the city authorities for financial and moral support (despite the fact that the city was also in dire financial straits).

This recourse to public money is interesting because the system does not allow companies to pursue American-style mergers, where for example a powerful top team such as Bayern Munich could afford to run a second team in the capital, or AC Milan could consider a hostile takeover of local rivals Internazionale. The guiding principle behind European sports policy is still to maintain competition between existing teams and to shift the overall picture through the promotion and relegation of teams.

In this respect, in Europe it is also possible to identify an anti-globalisation movement. In 2003 Manchester United was taken over by Malcolm Glazer, an American businessman with no links to football. The fans protested angrily, stayed away from games and some were involved in setting up a new club, which now plays in the seventh tier. A similar thing happened a few years ago when FC Wimbledon left its home ground and attempted to uproot its supporters.

Although nationality is clearly a relative concept when it comes to sport, the national teams have lost none of their fascination. It

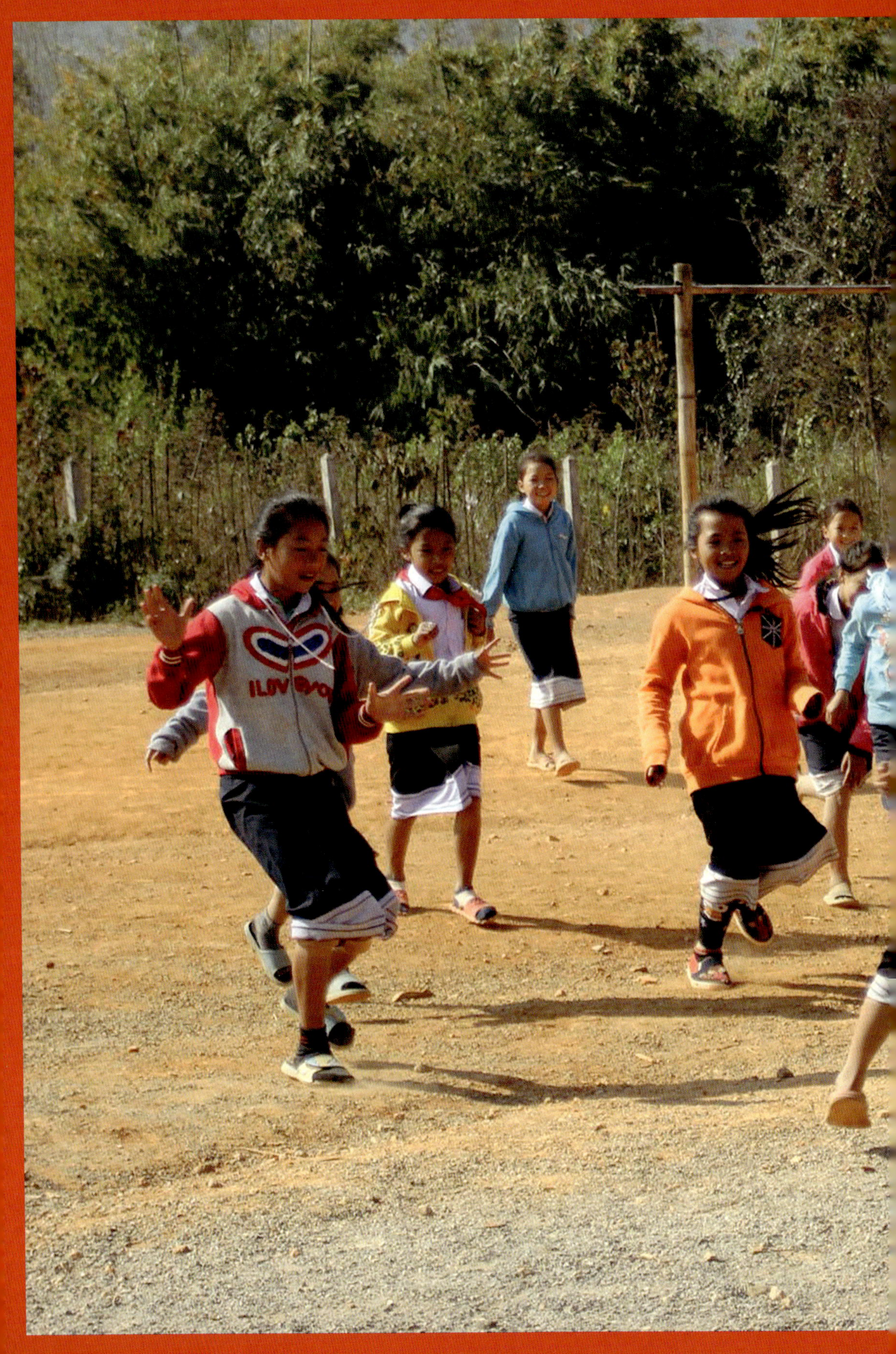

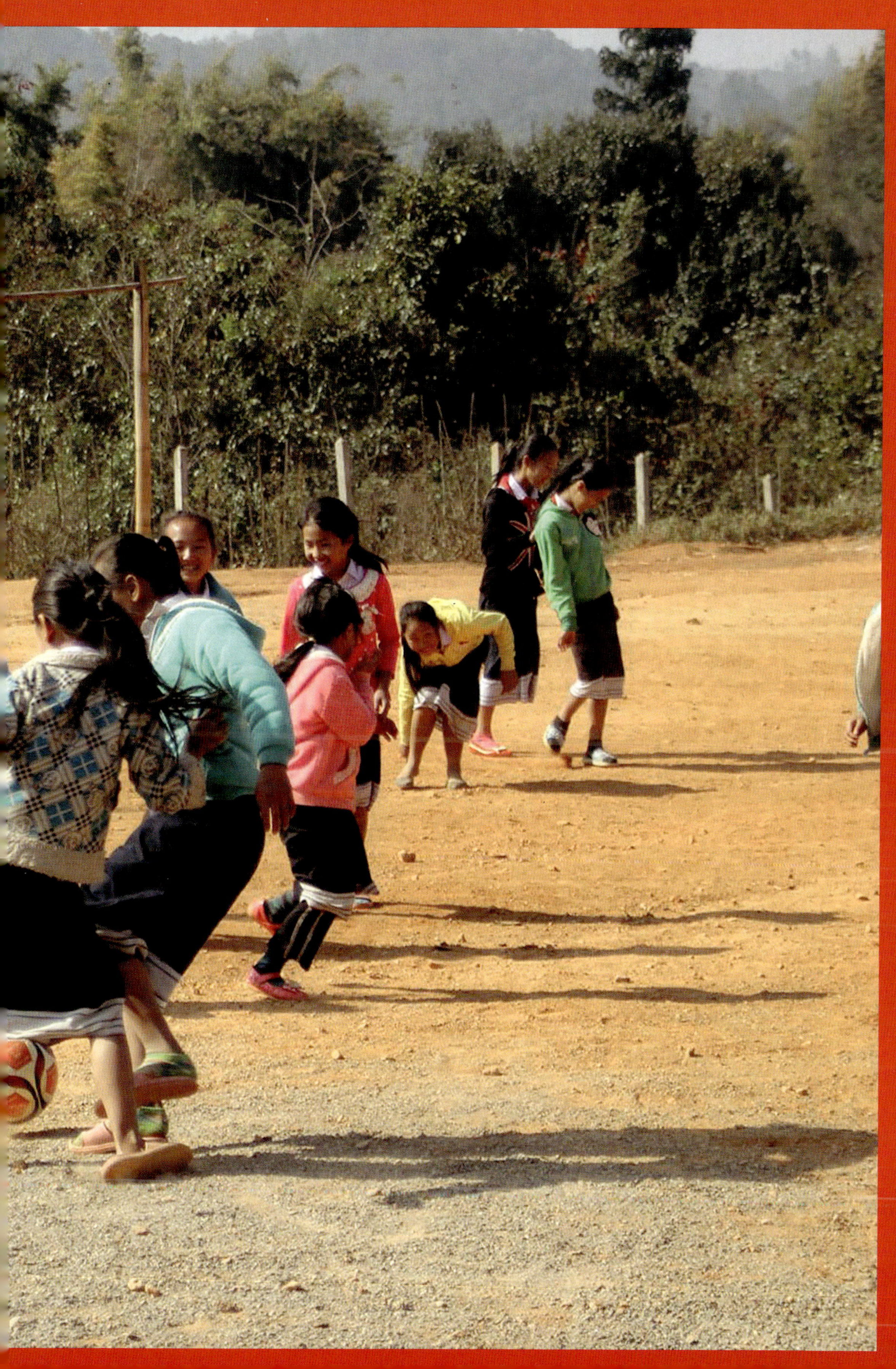

comes to the fore every time there are major world or continental competitions that reveal the close ties between sport, politics and the media. These tournaments provide a prime example of transnational media events that, despite all the standardisation imposed by the rules of the game, the duration of competitions and particular types of sport, create a setting that stands out from the routine of everyday life and the expectations of the actors.

Combining the expected and unexpected

Clearly, a special feature of sports broadcasts is that they are particularly adept at combining the expected and the unexpected. Sports events are also perfectly suited to collective discourse, so to communicative actions in which the actors and viewers first agree on the criteria for recognising the happening as an event.

What constitutes a good or bad game is of course only decided after much debate on the stands and afterwards when it is picked apart on the radio, TV, in the major newspapers and online – and even after many years these assessments can change. The debates and controversies voiced in the electronic media present events in a dual way: they describe the events but are also events in themselves.

In this way, sports events trigger changes in the media: on the part of producers, who work to ensure their technical systems reach more people, provide better quality, improved animation and so on; and on the part of the audience, who are encouraged by these media events to buy new equipment with more features for improved reception and entertainment. Sport and media are linked together in a very special way. They need or generate technology for mass dissemination, which increasingly intensifies social communication.

We have mentioned that in modern times the original 'communication space' was the nation or nation state; today socialisation is no longer solely linked to this historical form. To a certain extent, the readers of reformatory or revolutionary pamphlets founded a nation almost in passing. In the same way, people who watch the first moon landing, a Rolling Stones concert or the World Cup form a (fleeting) transnational community. What borders can be drawn, and where, is not determined by the event or the medium, but by the act of communication itself.

Communication itself is constantly creating borders that go beyond borders, a kind of 'virtual geography'. So sport as a transnational media event boosts globalisation. Spatial distance is overcome and relativised in a 'playful' way, and at the same time the audience displays a particularly high level of receptiveness, which also shows their openness to temporary socialisation. This is how the social memory of the emerging global society is constructed.

In terms of a sociology of the extraordinary, media events respond to the question: how is it possible to keep people's attention in an era when they are bombarded with information? Television in particular is able to combine events and their media staging via live broadcasts. For example, during a global sports broadcast media artefacts are created that also turn the medium and the type of media presentation into an event. Major sporting events become drivers of cultural change and catalysts for building knowledge that transcend borders and are no longer aimed at the people of a single nation. This is because sport has long moved from being simply 'The Beautiful Game' to being the focus of political decisions involving national prestige and economic success.

In Europe, politics is clearly having a growing influence in and on sport, despite the fact that its autonomy is still emphasised. Unlike in the USA, sport is an area that involves government intervention and the welfare state, and it is most decidedly viewed as a social and cultural activity. Its commercial dimension has also become increasingly recognised and encouraged in the Old World, with public investment being designed to produce a 'sports dividend'. This involves a nation increasing its prestige through excellent performances in international competitions, as reflected in Olympic medal tables or preeminent athletes and teams who make the finals of tournaments.

Despite the way that the sports business now goes beyond national borders, it is still a characteristic of transnational sports policy that it symbolically always reverts to a sense of local or national patriotism. So sport is displa-

In Europe, politics is clearly having a growing influence in and on sport, despite the fact that its autonomy is still emphasised. Unlike in the USA, sport is an area that involves government intervention and the welfare state, and it is most decidedly viewed as a social and cultural activity.

ying a certain degree of resistance to the egalitarianism and the loss of a sense of homeland that is entailed by the 'one world' approach, and it is probably the task of sport to tap into these reserves of patriotism in transnational interactions.

However, the 'transnational society of sport' does not only have a compensatory function, but it is also a driving force behind the dissolution of borders in the above-mentioned media/business complex. National sports and business organisations, known as SINGOs and BINGOs, are the key stakeholders involved in preparing for and hosting the Olympic Games and the World Cup. They work with leading companies and associations and a plethora of firms in the fields of travel, merchandising, insurance, law, PR and so on. There is constant friction between traditional, bureaucratic interest groups such as the National Olympic Committee and, in Germany, the Deutsche Sportbund (DSB) on the one hand and the management culture of transnational corporations on the other.

This power struggle is illustrated by arguments about ticket sales, the list of speakers at the World Cup opening ceremony and countless protocol issues.

The key interactions of transnational sports policy can be outlined as follows: there is a synchronous but not identical "logic" in the sub-systems of sport, politics and business, which all together are directed towards competition, staging and profitability. Here the media system plays an intermediary role by elevating a star or prominent personality to a symbolic figurehead, which – even in the case of active athletes – focuses less on their sporting performance than on the part they play in the discourse as part of the struggle to capture the public's attention.

As far as the viewers are concerned, they are also less interested in getting involved than in passive attendance at the 'real virtuality' of broadcast sport, which evens out the normal differences relating to gender, education, income, place of residence and local sports tradition. A striking example of this is the success of women's soccer in the USA, which runs counter to the system.

A common factor is the motif of the commercialisation of sport, which is served by sports policy and sets boundaries to ensure competition. This dovetails with the fixation on sports stars and idols, which we could call the culture of celebrity; in the past leading sports personalities such as Franz Beckenbauer and Michel Platini were able to play key roles in politics, the media and business (now they have been weakened by allegations of corruption); they could even display a certain autonomy in the face of senior ministers such as Wolfgang Schäuble, administrators such as FIFA's Sepp Blatter (who is suspended at the moment), and the DFB. Between the sub-systems there is another distinction, as was shown by the 2006 World Cup: sports policy is privatised in the form of Public Private Partnerships, top-level sport adapts to the imperatives of media coverage, and this is no longer limited to the illustrative function of traditional sports reporting but, like leading corporations, it gets involved in the sports event itself as a sponsor and advertiser. This leads to the emergence of an industrial sports complex that is symbolically held together by media celebrities.

A fatal challenge

Whether it's Vladimir Putin at the Olympic Games in Sochi or the Brazilians at the World Cup and Olympics: governments are constantly trying to benefit from the prestige of hosting major sporting events. For interior and sports ministers, these events present a fatal challenge, as they could lead to promotion – or spectacular failure. This challenge, along with the performance of the national team, affects the mood and morale of the political and economic system, and finally a major sports event plays an important role in the host country's global ranking.

So a major sporting event can never totally divest itself of patriotic and nationalistic connotations, which is why racist attacks against black athletes and multicultural teams are not uncommon, and why international competitions also regularly lead to so-called 'substitute wars'. An example of this is the conflict that escalated between Honduras and El Salvador after the World Cup in July 1969, which caused the deaths of 3,000 people and injured another 6,000. There was also the time when the Swiss put the Turkish team out of

This leads to the emergence of an industrial sports complex that is symbolically held together by media celebrities.

the 2006 World Cup; and the threats arising from the proposed visit of Iranian President Mahmoud Ahmadinejad to the Iranian team in Germany.

A compromise between national/state forms of organisation and transnational sport business may lie in the 'brand'. Host countries of the World Cup or Olympics are presented via extensive image campaigns run by PR agencies. Brand awareness and branding involve residual elements of national identity, but at the same time are compatible with the identity figures of a transnational society and economy.

Germany as a sporting brand that regularly provides memories of the 'great moments' of 1954, 1990, 2006 and 2014 is a clever business and sports-related attempt to make cultural differences and economic standardisation mandatory in a form that is remote from politics. Whether sport is still suited to making this cultural differentiation depends essentially on its ability to perform. Or as footballers put it: it's all decided on the pitch.

Claus Leggewie is Director of the Institute for Advanced Study in the Humanities in Essen and Professor of Political Science at the University of Giessen. Since 2012 he has been Co-Director of the Käte Hamburger Collegium 'Political Cultures of World Society' at the University of Duisburg-Essen. This article is an amended version of a talk that was broadcast in Germany by the Südwestrundfunk radio station.

A matter of governance There is an understanding among policymakers that participation in sport and club membership fosters feelings of belonging. There is also evidence that social support and networking contribute to building a sense of identity and strong self-image across diverse ethnic and cultural groups. What responsibilities and benefits does global sport bring to society as a whole? *By Cora Burnett*

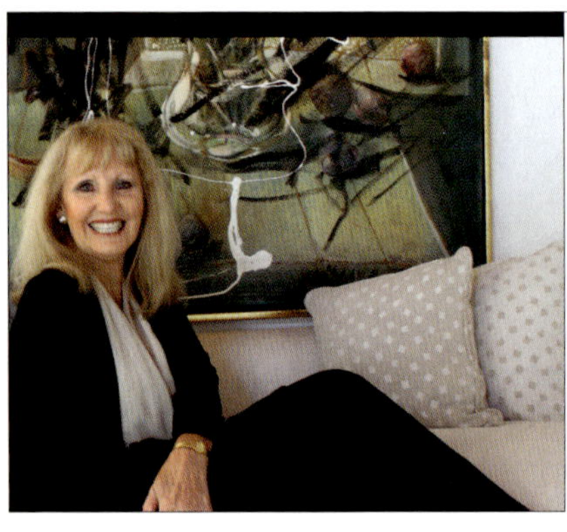

It is now a decade since former UN Secretary-General Kofi Annan declared 2005 to be the International Year of Sport and Physical Education, which provided the impetus for incorporating sport into UN policies and programmes. A plethora of stakeholders took up the challenge of placing sport at the centre of a global agenda of societal transformation. Guided by the Millennium Development Goals and then by the Sustainable Development Goals, sport featured prominently on the post-2015 Development Agenda.

It became such an influential social movement and impetus for social enterprise development that civic society mobilised to get a piece of the cake. In this way, sport emerged as a low-cost way of fixing society's problems, with the world's youth earmarked as change agents. Sport captured the imagination of the public, and publications, conferences and academics joined in studying this emerging phenomenon. Critical voices remained very much on the periphery as politicians, development agencies and non-governmental organisations made persuasive evangelical claims and engaged in an increasingly crowded policy space.

Academics and agencies came up with ways of mapping the field in order to bring some order and understanding, but they made little headway as research evidence mushroomed in all corners of the globe. Implementing agencies contracted impact assessors and evidence poured in at an astounding pace. In his book 'Sport for Development. What Game are we Playing?' Fred Coalter was sharp in his criticism and warned that 'hope is not a plan'. He questioned the value of sport as a stand-alone strategy to meaningfully address deep-seated social issues and discriminatory systems.

Few researchers and practitioners paid serious attention. I was one of a number of critical sociologists, including Grant Jarvie, Jay Coakley, Simon Darnell, John Sugden and Tess Kay, who interrogated the perpetuation of neo-colonial structures, global north (donor) domination and unequal power relations translating into support-dependent practices. Despite issues around 'sustainable development' the floodgates remained open as global sport organisations claimed ownership of sport in its metamorphic role as an agent for change at all levels of society. Global sport organisations came on board to shape a new development agenda for the host cities of mega-events.

Host cities and governments proclaimed a wide range of socio-economic benefits associated with sport. They framed human legacy projects as meaningful contributors to human justice by providing access to sport as part of a human (and children's) rights agenda. The 2010 FIFA World Cup, the planned 2022 Commonwealth Games in South Africa and the 2016 Rio Olympic Games in Brazil are outstanding examples in this regard. The shift in rhetoric from national to global can also be discerned in the difference between the 2004 (Athens) and 2008 (Beijing) Olympic Games, which focused strongly on national development and nationalism and the 2012 London Olympics, which promised global access to sports participation through its International Inspirations legacy programme.

Going beyond the often confusing and intertwined public discourses, many sport-for-development programmes remained donor-controlled and dependent. Unequal access to power and resources remained at the core of many programmes, and the results were neatly mediated in response to preconceived indicators.

Following the agreement between the

In this way, sport emerged as a low-cost way of fixing society's problems, with the world's youth earmarked as change agents.

IOC and United Nations (and UN observer status since 2009), the IOC positioned itself on behalf of the International Olympic and Sport Movement to continue to 'harness the power of Sport for Peace and Development' (agreed upon by the International Working Group and published by Right to Play in 2008). With this background in mind, the question arises: what is the responsibility of global sport towards society as a whole?

To answer this question, global pledges and partnerships are, once again, providing direction and leadership. The IOC's position statement about delivering on the Post-2015 Development Agenda identified six Sustainable Development Goals in which sport (from grassroots to elite levels) is used to make a difference. It advocated the use of sport in different ways and in different settings to:

- Ensure healthy living and promote well-being for all at all ages (Goal 3);
- Ensure inclusive and equitable quality education and promote life-long learning opportunities for all (Goal 4);
- Achieve gender equality and empower all women and girls (Goal 5);
- Make cities and human settlements inclusive, safe, resilient and sustainable (Goal 11);
- Promote peaceful and inclusive societies for sustainable development, provide access to justice for all and build effective, accountable and inclusive institutions at all levels (Goal 16); and
- Strengthen the means of implementation and revitalise the global partnership or sustainable development (Goal 17).

Global and national sports organisations responded and set a different pace. For instance, the Commonwealth Games Federation developed 'The Commonwealth Guide to Advancing Development through Sport' – a project funded by the Commonwealth Youth Programme in partnership with UK Sport. This publication was undertaken by the Commonwealth Secretariat in 2013 and authored by Tess Kay and Oliver Dudfield. In the foreword, Bruce Kidd (Chair of the Commonwealth Advisory Body on Sport) urged governments, non-governmental organisations and sports bodies within the Commonwealth to use grass roots sport-based approaches to meaningfully contribute to education, employment, health, gender equity and the safety of children and youth.

FIFA's Football for Hope project, as well as the IOC's Sport for Hope programme was launched. The latter programme entails establishing two Olympic Youth Development Centres in Zambia and Haiti (see the IOC Agenda 2020) and funding programmes for Olympafrica centres situated in socio-economically vulnerable communities to provide open access to sports participation for disenfranchised children and youth. Such centres inevitably provide additional community-driven programmes in addition to the (IOC) Solidarity-funded Olympic education initiatives.

A strategic priority

Within a human rights framework, the accessibility of sports participation, leadership positions and the empowerment of girls and women became a strategic priority within the sports fraternity. Governments emphasised the contribution made by sport and physical activity to the health of its citizens.

They generally follow a top-down approach to ensure that priority sports and recreation facilities and activities are provided through physical education, school sport and/or community-based facilities. They articulate policy frameworks and visions to deliver on a broad spectrum of aims to be a 'winning' and 'healthy nation'.

Governments are the custodians who ensure the equitable delivery of sports in accordance with their official mandate and pro-poor approaches.

In many African countries, the aftermath of colonialism provided politicians and government machinery with the mandate to redistribute resources. For instance, the hosting of international and national events in addition to democratic representation (in terms of race, class and/or gender) is assumed to play a significant role in social cohesion and nation-building.

At the macro-level social cohesion translates into nation-building and profiling the country which carries a high level of symbolism, and socio-political advocacy and agency. At the community or micro-social level actions are directed by and through social institutions like schools with penetration into civic society, whilst meso-level actions play out at the provincial and district levels within an inter-community perspective. There is a common understanding among policymakers that participation in sport and club membership fosters feelings of belonging, with evidence that social support and networking (social capital) contribute to building a sense of identity and strong self-image across diverse ethnic and cultural groups.

Sport alone cannot prevent violence and conflict or facilitate peace-building, but it has a role to play as part of an integrative approach. For children and young people who are affected by the trauma of conflict or war, participating in sport in safe spaces contributes to normalising their lives as part of a healing process.

Many programmes have cut-across benefits relating to participation in sport and recreational activities. This represents a holistic approach and inter-related effects such as improvements in health and education levels, building social capital, addressing inequities, improving community safety and environmental aspects.

Measuring the impact of crime reduction interventions is no easy feat as the effects of many programmes are not scientifically scrutinised. However, there is evidence that demonstrates the positive effects of sport and physical activity on antisocial behaviour by targeting underlying risks, protective factors and/or explicit behaviour.

Various programmes and practices that

Going beyond the often confusing and intertwined public discourses, many sport-for-development programmes remained donor-controlled and dependent. Unequal access to power and resources remained at the core of many programmes, and the results were neatly mediated in response to preconceived indicators.

address social ills include behaviours relating to issues such as crime, substance abuse, suicide/self-harm, homelessness, unemployment, mental health, truancy and early school leaving. These types of behaviour are considered deviant compared to existing social (ideal) and widely accepted norms within a societal context.

Governments are concerned about public health costs and the negative effects of poor health and lifestyle on human productivity, economic growth and development. Over the last two decades, physical activity has received global recognition as an important health behaviour that significantly reduces all-cause morbidity and chronic diseases of lifestyle (CDL). Physical activity has become an important pillar in the primary and secondary prevention of non-communicable diseases (NCDs), with the well-documented severe consequences of physical inactivity listed as one of the four key risk factors that cause them.

For money invested in sport there are multiple returns in terms of improved health and reduced demand for health services, particularly among older people; improved productivity; economic regeneration; better employment opportunities; and, most importantly, national, regional and local GDP. In view of the potential savings to the economy from the health gains associated with increased physical activity, it makes good business sense to promote an active lifestyle from a young age.

The quantifiable evidence in support of the perceived, and often widely propagated, benefits of mega-events is relatively weak and often unsubstantiated – especially in terms of economic development. The positive effects of hosting international sporting events relate to sport-specific, economic, social and cultural benefits. Sport-specific benefits include attracting resources to particular sports and providing learning opportunities and experiences for athletes, officials, coaches and volunteers. Economic spin-offs entail job creation, regional development, tourism, exports, infrastructure and tax revenues, whilst social benefits relate to access to training and participation. Cultural gains include the portrayal of a unique cultural identity and gaining global recognition.

Not all economists are convinced of the sustainable effects of regenerating host cities due to relatively short-to-medium-term assessments. An event may be a valuable trigger for leveraging regeneration funding, but if it is to have a meaningful impact, it has to be part of a long-term development strategy and wider vision for city regeneration and plans for the sustainable after-use of venues.

Under-utilised facilities and climbing maintenance costs may burden taxpayers for many years after an event. Lessons from the 2000 Sydney Olympic Games and 2004 Athens Summer Olympics relating to costly infrastructure development were well learned by the organisers of the 2012 London Olympics.

Growing importance of the global South

As hosts of the 2010 FIFA World Cup, South Africa and Africa were acknowledged as sporting powers and as evidence of the growing importance of the global South. It was a symbolic award and proof of the host country's closeness to the world's top nations. Some metropolitan municipalities built spectacular stadia and infrastructure, and by doing so, improved the positive image of their cities.

The multiplier effect of economic benefits is often questioned. Cost-benefit studies conducted at city, regional and national level revealed that spending by foreign visitors and visitors from in-country regions is difficult to calculate in terms of what is event-related spending, minus leakages of profits being transferred out of the area. Inflated prices during the event may stretch existing capacities for accommodation, transport and other vital services. Also, prices may go up artificially without sustainable economic benefits for operators within host cities.

The crowding out effect of people leaving the area during mega-events, the limited air transport capacity and the critical analysis of multiplier coefficients all need to be considered when calculating the economic effects. Despite criticism of the 'real' economic impact of major sporting events, visitor-orientated (sport tourism) seems to produce the most tangible economic impacts. It seems that the length of stay and consumer satisfaction play a key role in the decision of foreign participants to stay on in host countries and cities.

For local and mega-events, thousands of volunteers create significant cultural capital, which in turn may have economic and social benefits, although it has not been sufficiently measured to provide substantiated longer-term benefits at individual and city level. An additional effect at sport-for-development events is the development of social capital among the volunteers through building relationships, staying motivated and working for social change with increased reciprocal engagement in sport after the event.

Hosting events does not automatically translate into increased levels of sports participation (mass participation) or sustainable elite sporting success. There is no conclusive evidence that hosting mega sporting events has lasting effects on broad-based sports participation. Increased mass participation may be the result of particular sports gaining greater media exposure or recruiting current participants to a particular sport. It does not seem that watching sport converts individuals into active participants.

Sport as part of the socialisation process

One of global sport's key contributions is in the field of education and training: education within and through sport takes place in both formal and informal settings.

Formal education mostly deals with a specifically designed curriculum, as in the case of physical education at schools, learning centres or tertiary education institutions. Informal learning in and through sports participation forms part and parcel of the socialisation process whereby values, attitudes, skills and knowledge are transferred. This can happen in a wide variety of educational settings.

A sports education environment with the

For local and mega-events, thousands of volunteers create significant cultural capital, which in turn may have economic and social benefits.

inclusion of social skills also makes a tangible contribution to learning about fair play and key life skills and values, which contribute to a decrease in harmful (anti-social) behaviour. Exposure to teamwork improves social interaction, communication and leadership. Exposure to multi-activity sport with half of the lesson time being devoted to moderate to vigorous physical activity translates into positive health and fitness as well as psychosocial benefits.

Although longitudinal studies have reported improved academic performance due to improved behaviour, health and discipline, such results are questioned because of the methodological difficulties of proving causality. Research studies tracing the relationship between improved academic performance and sports participation are relatively diverse and report contradictory results.

Global sport is not democratic. Sport at all levels is a differentiator and shows socially stratified patterns in terms of participation and ownership. Even at grassroots level, girls often need (male) gatekeepers to facilitate their participation in traditionally male sports. Safety issues and entrenched patriarchal ideology make it difficult for girls and women to freely participate in sport at all levels. Policymakers have limited ability to ensure that boys and girls have equal access to sport at all levels.

It is also clear that the situation is often exacerbated when athletes need access to specialist coaching, training facilities and sport science services. Gender and lower socio-economic status tend to provide a double bind that negatively affects access to participation and decision-making positions within the sports fraternity and in the broader spheres of society as a whole.

Racial stacking patterns

Certain ethnic populations experience a similar disenfranchisement in contexts where the face of poverty ties in with a particular racial profile. This is also behind the over-representation of certain racial groups (e.g. Afro-Americans) in basketball or boxing, and of white participants in sports like sailing and swimming. Racial stacking patterns further perpetuate stereotypes, with white players being favoured as decision-makers and black players for their speed and athletic ability in team sports like rugby.

Another pattern of social stratification relates to the concept of 'ability' versus 'disability'. The latter refers to a physical impairment causing functional limitations. Classifying people as 'disabled' or as 'athletes with disabilities' involves an ability-based ranking system that cuts across all sports, but it also relates to the comparison of people with and without 'able' or 'normative' bodies. In societies where young and able bodies are held up as the ideal, less able bodies within a normative category such as older and disabled persons may experience marginalisation and discrimination.

The inception of the Paralympic Games in 1948 led to global perceptions changing so that people began viewing different abi-

lities in a more positive light. The amazing feats of Paralympians changed the medical model (focus on impairments) to cross into the realm of the 'normal'. Successful media campaigns popularised Paralympians and events in such a way that London's 2012 Paralympics sold more tickets than the Olympics themselves. South African athletes such as Natalie du Toit and Oscar Pistorius also broke down barriers by competing against able-bodied athletes. The differently-abled body set its own norms and standards and led to attractive events during the 2014 Glasgow Commonwealth Games.

The Special Olympics that hosts sports for people with intellectual disabilities has become a global enterprise that sponsors research, builds support communities and offer different educational programmes. It sponsors about 50,000 competitions yearly and hosted 7,500 athletes from 185 nations at the 2011 World Summer Games in Athens, Greece. The human stories from the Special Olympics and the amazing physical feats of the athletes with disabilities, including their use of technological advancements (e.g. specially designed race chairs, and prosthetic 'blades') captured the imagination and did a great deal to change perceptions about ability.

Sports participants and elite athletes project an image of youthfulness and optimum sporting ability compared to older people, who are assumed to be incapable of full participation in mainstream activities. Studies

Global sport is not democratic. Sport at all levels is a differentiator and shows socially stratified patterns in terms of participation and ownership.

of sports participation among people over the age of 50 are relatively rare despite the fact that people over the age of 60 are the fastest-growing segment globally.

Sport-related impacts do not happen automatically. They have to be carefully planned, socially engineered and professionally managed. Therefore, governance issues have become a top priority for global sports bodies to ensure high ethical standards, combat corruption and professionalise sporting careers and organisations. Global sports organisations are increasingly being scrutinised and questionable practices (and individuals) exposed, but such scrutiny is less apparent in organisations at national and local level where political agendas are particularly influential.

The impact of sport in wider society is directly dependent on the effective and focused delivery of programmes, with the understanding that positive effects are possible under certain circumstances, for certain populations, and in certain contexts. Sport provides the scope for change to happen and has inherent characteristics that can be 'harnessed', but in itself it is no miracle worker. With development as a contested and complex phenomenon, global sport agencies have yet to develop impactful social strategies and programmes.

Cora Burnett is a professor at the University of Johannesburg, lecturing in the field of the Sociology of Sport and Research Methodology in the Department of Sport and Movement. Her studies include national community and school mass participation projects, indigenous games research, and the status of women and girls in South Africa's democracy.

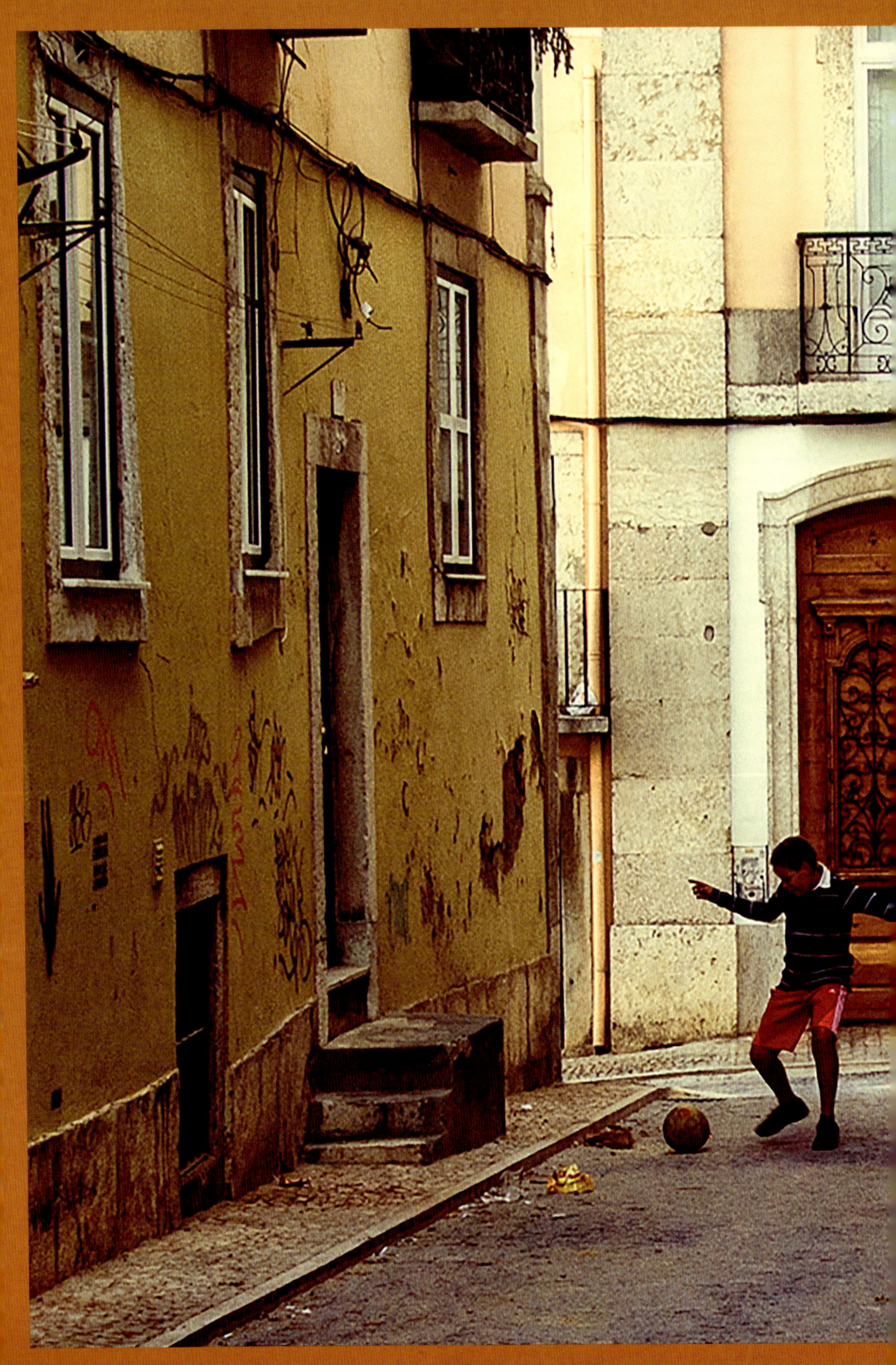

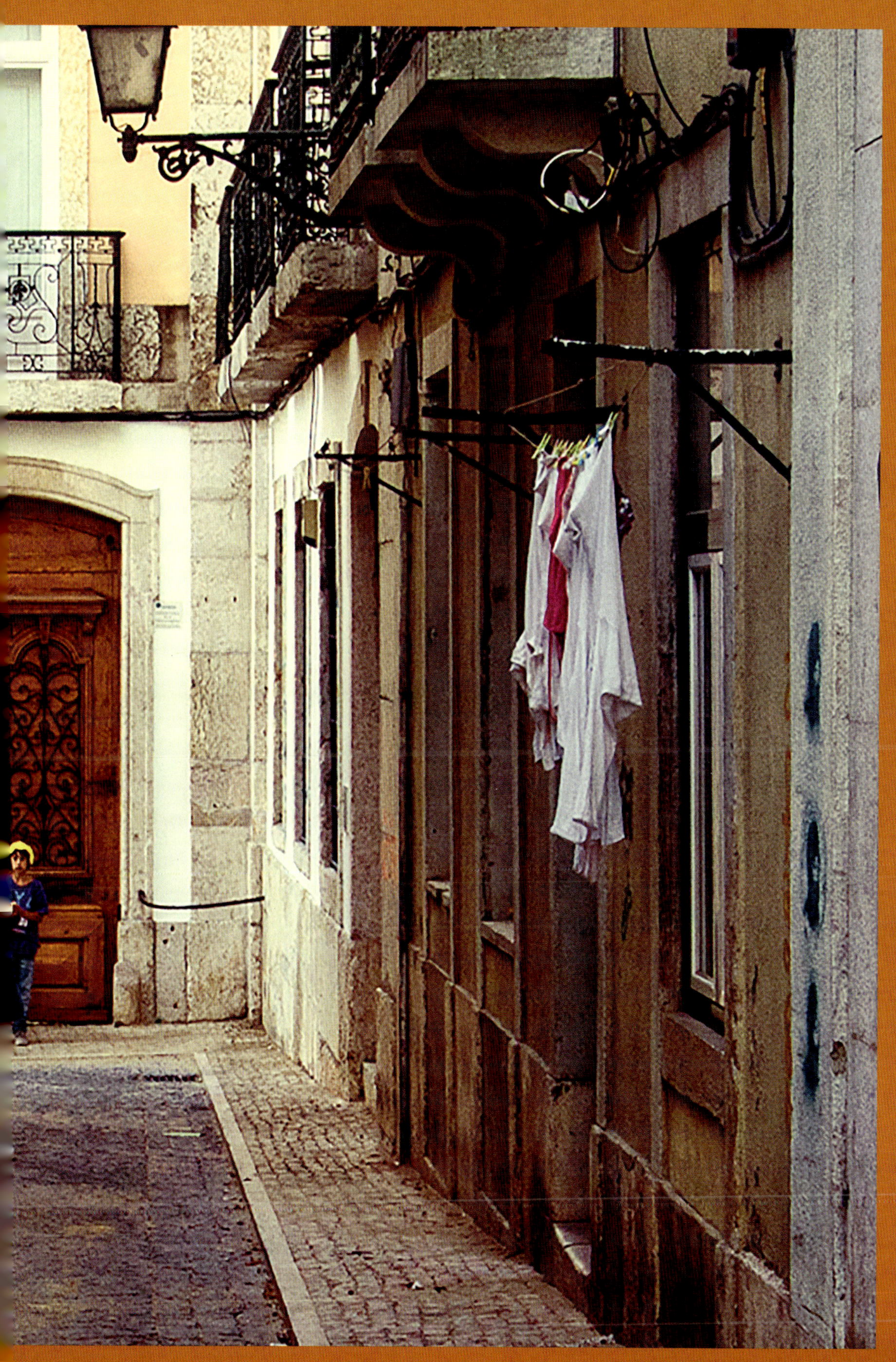

A form of social capital Modern sport forms part of people's body style practices and cultural choices. It has been used as a social glue, a factor in nation-building, a projection of soft power and a form of cultural diplomacy. It can cross borders and forms a global idiom in which intercultural relations are enhanced. Yet sport can also act as a social toxic, prompting outbursts of nationalism, cheating, state-sponsored doping, corruption and the exploitation of people from emerging nations. *By Joseph Maguire*

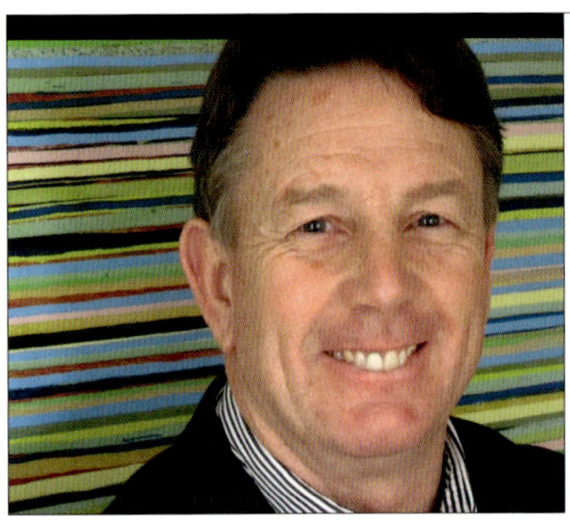

tury these seemingly paradoxical features – nationalism and universalism – characterised global sport. At various times, nation-states have implicitly or explicitly been faced with and have taken advantage of a range of foreign policy concerns and opportunities via sport. Sport has been used variously as a social glue, a factor in nation-building, a projection of soft power and a form of cultural diplomacy – especially in the Cold War period. Less well-known is the use that global sport has been put to in spying and intelligence gathering.

Modern sport emerged out of its European homeland in the mid-to-late nineteenth century. Diffusing along the lines of Empire, sport spread to all parts of the globe. Bound up in a resurgence of nationalism and nation-state rivalries, international sport competition was marked from this beginning with complex foreign policy implications and concerns.

With the rebirth of the Olympic Games in 1896, a range of 'patriot games' were evident. In contrast to this explicit connection between sport and nationalism, the Olympic movement claimed an ability to fulfil a broader role of enhancing intercultural communication and fostering goodwill across nations – in part, by drawing inspiration from Hellenism and aspects of the British public school ethos.

During the course of the twentieth cen-

Transnational problems

In the early 21st century, in the enlarged EU, across Europe as a whole, or in the wider world, nation-states now grapple with problems that go beyond the traditional boundaries of the nation and have become transnational in nature and global in range. With the realignment of the nation-state, through which sovereignty is sometimes shared, diluted and pooled, and more porous boundaries, foreign policy practitioners are now required to be more sensitive to, and adept at handling, these concerns that surface across a range of cultural and social flows – including global sport.

Yet, several concerns characterise the structure and practice of global sport. These include: questions of governance, democracy

and transparency; the bidding for, hosting of, and claims made regarding the legacy flowing from the staging of mega-events and nation-building; processes of migration, identity politics, and the movement of both highly-skilled and vulnerable bodies (e.g. elite athletes and child trafficking); and sport, development strategies, conflict resolution, peacebuilding and global health concerns and UN Millennium goals.

In each of these areas, complex questions of policy arise concerning the formulation and projection of soft power, the image of the nation and the interplay between sporting politics, and politics and sport. Fundamentally, consideration of the relationship between foreign policy and global sport has to wrestle with the broader question of how the nation-state formulates its approach based on a more realpolitik or 'ethically based' approach to the problems outlined.

Links between sport, leisure and culture

Several key issues can thus be identified that highlight the interconnections between sport, foreign policy and cultural diplomacy.

Let us first consider the links between sport, leisure and culture. For better, and worse, modern sport is part of the cultural fabric of advanced industrial societies. Irrespective of questions of high or popular culture, modern sport is part of the body style practices and cultural choices of people in civic society. These practices are, nevertheless, contoured and shaped by gender, class, ethnic and other fault lines of societies. They are also patterned by the actions of nation-states, by both the domestic and the foreign policy objectives pursued and the cultural strategies adopted. The bidding for and claims legacy of hosting mega-events is a case in point.

Secondly, this state of affairs is nothing new. Two interconnected processes, as noted above, underpinned the emergence and global diffusion of sport in the late nineteenth century: nationalism and internationalism. The anthem, the emblem and the flag were as much part of cultural ceremonies of global sport as were the claims made for the power of the modern Olympics to spread a message of internationalism.

Then, as now, new nations would seek to join the IOC and FIFA as well as the League of Nations or the United Nations. In the context of multi-sport events such as the Olympic Games inter-state relations were being exercised – albeit in a less sophisticated way than now. A prime example of how sport, cultural diplomacy and foreign policy intertwined was in the context of the formation of the British Empire Games (BEG). Held, for the first time, in Hamilton, Canada, in 1930, the British Empire Games sought to tie the economic, political and cultural ties of the Empire together.

By way of illustration, consider the involvement of Irish athletes in these inaugural games. Their participation evoked issues of national and cultural identity and were interwoven with questions concerning the organisation of sport on a pan-Ireland basis

> **The anthem, the emblem and the flag were as much part of cultural ceremonies of global sport as were the claims made for the power of the modern Olympics to spread a message of internationalism.**

and the allegiance of teams in international competition. The Irish Free State (IFS) had been established in 1922, though six counties of Ireland had remained part of the United Kingdom (UK). This territory was to become known as Northern Ireland. In the following period, culminating in the establishment of the Irish/Eire Constitution (1937), several amendments were made to IFS laws that removed reference to an oath of allegiance to the British crown and severed links to UK jurisdiction, but crucially maintained that 'the whole island of Ireland its islands and the territorial seas' formed a single 'national territory'.

Soft and hard power interwoven

Despite this context, and the related tension that emerged around 'Irish' involvement in the Olympic Games at that time, 'Ireland' participated both in the inaugural BEG in 1930 and also in 1934, but by 1938 only Northern Ireland was involved. Significantly, the BEG were replete with the pageantry of the Empire and with athletes swearing allegiance to the crown. Participation in the BEG highlights the role of sport in constructing different ideas of what it means to be Irish during a period that was characterised by palpable resistance to participation in English or British sports teams and political separation. The Games of the 1930s also reflected much of the politics of the then waning Empire – soft and hard power aspects of foreign policy were interwoven.

Yet, over time, as that Empire faded away, the Games have remained, though its title has changed, currently called the Commonwealth Games. While former colonies are now independent states and the economic links between Commonwealth nations and the 'Mother Country' have lessened, the cultural links have remained and are viewed as part of the social cement that ties this disparate group of people together. In this sense, these sportive ties are yet another example of soft power.

In light of this example a third point can be made. That is, sport, both within society and in inter-state/cross cultural/civilisational relations, can take two broad overlapping forms. Sport has not some trans-historical essence. Rather, it is a form of social capital – that has both dark and light forms. Sport acts as a 'social glue' – bringing people of a society or across societies together. Sport then, can act as a 'global village'. This can be done by the actions of athletes such as Muhammad Ali or by the collective sense of loss and grief prompted by the death of the Australian cricketer Phillip Hughes in late 2014. In this sense sport can cross borders and forms a global idiom in which intercultural relations are enhanced. Yet, sport can also act as a social toxic – prompting outbursts of nationalism, cheating, state-sponsored doping, corruption and the exploitation of people from emerging nations – as athletes and workers – and the exploitation of the environment – on sea, land and air. Sport then, acts as a form of 'global pillage'.

Global pillage

A final point can be made that relates to this issue of forms of social capital, of global village and global pillage. Here, consideration can be given to elite sport labour migration and mega-event bidding and how those involved in the formulation and implementation of foreign policy, can adopt a stance that ranges from a classical realpolitik to a more 'ethically based' approach. As part of the sports medical industrial complex (SMIC), states increasingly utilise all relevant national resources in order to guarantee success in international competition.

International sporting success thus involves a contest between systems involving the availability and identification of human resources; methods of coaching and training; the efficiency of particular sports organisations and the depth of knowledge of sports medicine and sports sciences. The development of a sport within a particular society also depends on the status of that society in the international rank order of specific sports. Less developed African nations, for example, tend to under-utilise their talent and performers and/or lose them to more powerful nations.

Given that nation-state prestige is at stake in global sport competitions it is no surprise that an international rank order has developed. This ranking of nation-states is reinforced by the status accorded to specific sports, leagues and clubs and, in many instances, are combined with the mutually reinforcing process whereby a (re)branding and marketing of the city, region and nation in which the club is located, occurs. Activities of this nature also find expression in the investment in mega-events, such as world cup competitions.

The reality is that nation-state prestige leads not only to such processes but also investment in specific sports, medals, sport stars and migrants. Consider the investment of the New Zealand Rugby Union in the grounds of its major clubs, the development of the Tri-Nations competition and the Super 12, the re-branding of host cities as tourist destinations and the identification and recruitment of not only 'local boys' but also Pacific Islanders – the latter policy arguably denuding those countries of their indigenous talent.

Such processes are readily understandable if a realpolitik approach to sport and foreign policy is adopted. The projection of soft power allows the nation to remain competitive in the international rank order of nations and sports medical industrial complex and has the added advantage of sport acting as a social glue that keeps the nation-state 'together'. Wrapping the people and the nation in the flag becomes the unstated norm of state policy.

Are there or should there be limits to such an approach? A different approach to foreign policy and the use and projection of soft power would be to adopt a more 'ethically based stance'. Here, a contribution to UN Millennium Goals and 'development through sport' is relevant.

A tool for social development

The British Foreign and Commonwealth Office (FCO) have long recognised the role that the British Council and the BBC play in this regard. UK Sport, an arm of the British state, has also noted that developing sport across the Commonwealth and beyond not only provides access to overseas facilities but also helps promote British sport and influence overseas. Thus, 'these development programmes promote expertise in sport and demonstrate the importance of sport as a tool for social development, as well as creating signifi-

> **As part of the sports medical industrial complex (SMIC), states increasingly utilise all relevant national resources in order to guarantee success in international competition.**

cant goodwill that extends influence abroad'.

Invariably, nation-states veer between these polar extremes, often exercising both – with different sectors of the state apparatus competing for predominance regarding the ethically based or realpolitik stance they adopt.

The importance of the topic at hand should not be underestimated and relegated to secondary consideration when formulating and enacting cultural policy in general and foreign policy in particular. In global sport more generally what is at stake is perhaps the most fundamental question facing us as we address globalisation processes – that is, whether globalisation is leading to a more cosmopolitan embrace and emotional identification between people, societies and civilisations or if it has unleashed a new wave of ethnic defensiveness, nationalism and a rejection of other cultures and civilisations.

This issue of hostility or friendship, of social capital, of a glue or toxin, of a realpolitik or ethically based approach, should also help frame how we make sense of a nation-state's foreign policy stance to sport more generally. And, given the ongoing peace process in Ireland, is it possible that athletes from the Irish Republic would once again compete in the Commonwealth Games?

Joseph Maguire is a professor at the School of Sport, Exercise and Health Sciences, Department of Exercise and Sport Sciences at Loughborough University (UK), and the University of Copenhagen.

A love affair with dictators Corruption, greed, political tactics, and human rights violations are casting clouds over recent and future mega sporting events. Looking ahead at the next locations to host such events, it is clear that there is a trend towards autocratically ruled countries. Indeed, recent examples from Switzerland, Norway, and Germany confirm that a functioning civil society and democratic structures with potential for referendums are a hindrance to being awarded such events. *By Marianne Meier*

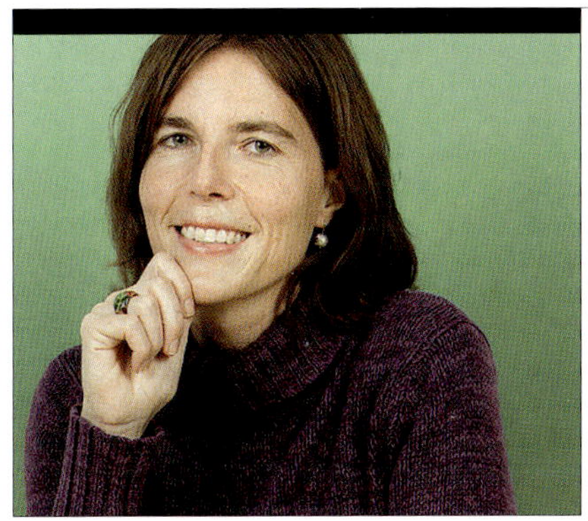

The Olympic Games, the FIFA World Cup and other mega sporting events are some of the world's great unifying moments. They bring people together in an international celebration of outstanding performance, intercultural spirit, peace, and human solidarity. Children and adults alike look forward to these events and the many benefits they have to offer.

However, these benefits are not universally shared. Corruption, greed, political tactics, and human rights violations are casting clouds over recent and future mega sporting events. They may directly and indirectly affect human and children's rights, or aggravate those already existing in the country. Of course it is undeniable that mega sporting events provide many social opportunities and reasons for public pride. But on the other hand it is equally undeniable that they are not positive for everyone.

Most major sports governing bodies boast about the formal ethical constituencies that they have given themselves. But in many cases these exemplary objectives remain empty phrases. The Olympic Charter proclaims: 'The goal of Olympism is to place sport at the service of the harmonious development of humankind with a view to promoting a peaceful society concerned with the preservation of human dignity'. However, forced evictions and increased policing are illustrations of the consequences of mega sporting events for the local population, which contradict these fundamental principles of the Olympic movement.

The FIFA Statutes 2015 contain similar inconsistencies between theory and reality. The FIFA General Provisions foresee, for instance, an article on non-discrimination 'of any kind against a country, private person or group of people on account of race, skin colour, ethnic, national or social origin, gender, language, religion, political opinion or any other opinion, wealth, birth or any other status, sexual orientation or any other reason is strictly prohibited and punishable by suspension or expulsion'. With regard to the FIFA Statutes and the publicly displayed homophobia linked to the Winter Olympics in Sochi 2014, how is it possible that the next FIFA World Cup will again take place in Russia? And what about the FIFA World Cup 2022 in Qatar? This future Arab host country also criminalises homosexuality.

What is the value of charters?

What is the value of charters, statutes and principles, if they are not or insufficiently respected and implemented? Looking ahead at the next locations to host mega sporting events, it is clear that there is a trend towards autocratically ruled countries. This tendency has also been noted by the Danish magazine Sport Executive, coining the title 'When sport falls in love with dictatorship'.

This tendency seems so obvious that even Jérôme Valcke, former FIFA Secretary General, publicly stated in April 2013 that democracy can be inhibiting for a World Cup: 'When you have a very strong head of state who can decide, as maybe Putin can do in 2018... that is easier for us organisers than a country such as Germany, where you have to negotiate at different levels'. Indeed, recent examples from Switzerland, Norway, and Germany confirm that a functioning civil society and democratic structures with potential for referendums are in fact a hindrance to being awarded such events.

Ongoing reports focusing on the negative effects of mega sporting events on workers and the local population, along with referendums that have decided against hosting the Olympic Games, have resulted in a paradigm shift from within the system.

The National Olympic Committees (NOCs) of Switzerland, Austria, Sweden, and Germany have presented recommendations to the IOC with regard to their negative experiences in applying for the Olympic Games. These four NOCs mainly asked for more dialogue and support for host cities and a stronger focus on sustainability. They also suggested more flexibility and solidarity in terms of the costs and risks linked to a bid. Many of their reform propositions were introduced in the Olympic Agenda 2020 that was presented by the IOC in December 2014.

Earlier in the same year – under pressure from sponsors, media and civil society – former FIFA President Blatter also made statements on the bidding mechanisms for future FIFA tournaments: 'The Congress will be called in to award the World Cup in the future and I will make sure that the Congress can also look at the social, cultural, let's say the human rights situation'.

In terms of constituencies, a milestone was set in the course of the extraordinary FIFA Congress in February 2016. In the shadow of the presidential election, 'human rights' entered the FIFA Statutes. Up to this point, FIFA officials had always rejected any links between human rights violations and their major tournaments. Their strategy was mainly to draw the attention to their 'sport for development' projects run by the FIFA CSR department to make up for the negative effects of mega sporting events on local populations. The amended FIFA Statutes now foresee that 'FIFA is committed to respecting all internationally recognised human rights and shall strive to promote the protection of these rights.' This paragraph is a first step, but FIFA and its new president will have to walk the talk.

Mega sporting events are driven by various stakeholders and staged in a very complex environment. It is not only sports governing bodies such as FIFA and the IOC that are involved, but also public authorities, organising committees, and sponsors. The complexity is also nurtured by the variety of affected sectors representing civil society which involve human rights, labour, housing, LGBT, anti-corruption, and so on.

The responsibility for ensuring that local populations are protected from the risks created by mega sporting events delivery processes does not fall solely to the sports governing body that owns them. National and local governments, organising entities and sponsors are all protagonists within the hosting process and therefore also obliged to ensure human rights are upheld in every domain, including delivery, event-related labour practices, infrastructure development, security, etc. These stakeholders also have to recognise the vulnerabilities of different social groups.

And these vulnerabilities exist throughout all phases of the event life-cycle, from the bid phase to the 'legacy' period. The UN Guiding Principles on Business and Human Rights state that business enterprises have the responsibility to respect human rights, wherever they operate, independent of a state's ability or willingness to fulfil its own human rights obligations, even though it does not diminish those obligations.

All stakeholders involved in bidding for and hosting mega sporting events must acknowledge and meet their responsibilities to minimise risks and stop any human rights violations related to such an event. But with a 'just do no harm' approach, the potential in, through and around sport and mega sporting events is not tapped. There is also a stakeholder responsibility to ensure that positive effects and opportunities are created by and for the local population, especially children, throughout the life-cycle of the event.

However, such positive changes will not happen by coincidence. They need thoughtful planning, explicit commitment and strong leadership from the very top; especially by the event owners. But any effect will only be promising and sustainable if the local population is consulted and actively involved from beginning to end.

Human rights must be a core requirement of the entire bid and hosting process, and overseen by an effective framework for implementation that includes access to remedy, human rights due diligence and risk assessment. Event owners must also recognise that not all host countries or cities will have equal capacity to achieve the expected human rights standards. In such cases, decisions

Ongoing reports focusing on the negative effects of mega sporting events on workers and the local population, along with referendums that have decided against hosting the Olympic Games, have resulted in a paradigm shift from within the system.

must be taken carefully and support given to improve local capacities. A host community that suffers in the name of sport must be avoided at all costs.

Instead of assuming responsibility, senior officials of sports governing bodies still keep repeating in public that they are 'not the United Nations'. Their rhetoric concentrates on the fine line between the indirect and direct influence of mega sporting events, often hiding behind legal formalities. Should it not be a core interest of any serious sport entity and its values that nobody's rights are violated as a result of mega sporting events? A global sports tournament can only be truly successful if it does not harm the local population. Although host states bear the main responsibility for human rights abuses that occur in their countries, sports governing bodies also have a responsibility to respect and use all their influence in assuring human rights and the true values of sport.

The case of Brazil

The need to both mitigate negative effects and maximise the positive opportunities before, during and after mega sporting events has been identified. For this purpose, a strong interdisciplinary alignment and coordination of research evidence is needed, together with a cross-sectoral approach.

In terms of academic work, Celia Brackenridge's report on 'Child Exploitation and the FIFA World Cup: A Review of Risks and Protective Interventions' (Brunel University, London, 2013) was a milestone.

Due to the fact that Brazil was assigned to host the two most prestigious mega sporting events within two years – 2014 and 2016 – there is a growing body of research available for this country.

Related to the 2014 FIFA World Cup, research was conducted by the Dundee University which identified four key violations to children's rights in Brazil related to hosting mega sporting events. These violations were police and army violence, displacement, sexual exploitation, and child labour. This research also highlighted an increased vulnerability of specific children regarding rights violations. This most vulnerable group consisted of children in street situations and residents of favelas. The available evidence also draws attention to the fact that children do not live in isolation and are also vulnerable to the rights violations experienced by their families and communities.

A UNICEF (2014) study, based on data from 190 countries, highlighted that globally in 2012 Brazil had the second highest rate of child homicide, especially among young males aged 10-19. Yet, statistical data from the National Dial 100 hotline suggests that the number of reported violations against children increased by 17% in the twelve host cities during the month of the 2014 FIFA World Cup compared to the same month in 2013 (National Secretariat for Human Rights of the Federal Government, 2014).

According to the Dossier on Mega Sporting Events and Human Rights Violations in Rio de Janeiro (2015), many disadvantaged communities in Brazil have been forcibly removed to clear space for big infrastructure projects connected to mega sporting events. In Rio, at least 4,120 families have already been evicted from their homes and 2,486 are still threatened with forced removals to make way for projects directly or indirectly associated with the 2016 Olympic and Paralympic Games. Due to these evictions many children are no longer able to go to school. They lose access to education, health and other vital social services.

In preparation for the 2016 Olympics, the community of Vila Autódromo is facing extreme pressure from Rio's City Hall. The residents were asked to leave their homes to make way for Olympic infrastructure, often going without electricity and facing difficult living conditions. The formerly thriving community with shops, a community association and attractive streets, now resembles a war zone. For those families who remain, life is a constant battle to anticipate the next move by the authorities. The residents have to show a pass to access their own houses through the main Olympic Park site. And they are only allowed to receive visitors to their homes with an authorisation.

The 2014 FIFA World Cup and the 2016 Olympic Games have both greatly aggravated

The 2014 FIFA World Cup and the 2016 Olympic Games have both greatly aggravated the level of police and army violence in Rio de Janeiro. Violence against homeless children and adolescents, during protests and evictions, and in favelas has been reported.

the level of police and army violence in Rio de Janeiro. Violence against homeless children and adolescents, during protests and evictions, and in favelas – particularly by the UPPs (Brazil's Military Police Force) – has been reported. These 'security measures', especially in the so-called 'pacification operations' have caused many casualties and human rights violations. Many children and adolescents have shown signs of psychological and emotional damage due to these traumatic experiences.

Despite the growing number of substantial evaluations and studies linked to mega sporting events and human rights, there is still a lack of long-term research. Moreover, the trend of staging future mega sporting events in autocratically ruled countries also increases risks for researchers and investigative journalists in terms of safety and security. Critical questions and investigations regarding mega sporting events and human rights are not welcomed in Russia, Qatar or Beijing.

With regard to the complexity of mega sporting events, a broader human rights framework is needed to advocate for labour rights, LGBT rights, children's rights, environmental and anti-corruption requirements. Besides this cross-sectoral approach, strong coalitions are necessary if they are to be heard within major sports governing bodies. For this purpose, a united effort has been made to form the Sport and Rights Alliance (SRA), a coalition of leading NGOs and trade unions engaged in addressing the decision-makers of international sports governing bodies. Real change is based on a dialogue on values and evidence around needed reforms on the bidding process for future mega sporting events.

Next to alliances and pressure exerted by civil society, the aforementioned UN Principles of Human Rights and Business provide solid guidelines for concrete measures at a policy level. Currently, civil society networks are asking the major sports governing bodies to issue a public human rights commitment and policy; to put in place a human rights capacity; to ensure access to remedy; to undertake human rights due diligence; to conduct monitoring of all stages of the mega sporting events; and to enable external independent monitoring.

Within the framework of the UEFA EURO 2008 in Austria and Switzerland, the UEFA officials described their strategy to the host cities as: 'You bring the house, and we bring the party.' But in a respectful and decent society, people help to clean the house and share costs after a common event. The house owner will be taking the main decisions. That is why consultation with and the participation of civil society and local groups are necessary at every phase in the event's life-cycle.

Ethical principles are set out in the Olympic Charter and the FIFA Statutes. But a lot of work still needs to be done in terms of implementation, since these key principles are non-negotiable. The complex challenges of mega sporting events require reliable cooperation between all stakeholders and a sustainable approach for the sake of humankind.

Marianne Meier is a historian and expert in sports pedagogy. She is a lecturer and heads up the Children Win project at the Terre des Hommes International Federation.

'The Enterprise' The US Department of Justice have a name for FIFA: 'The Enterprise', as if it were an organised crime syndicate. Wherever there is big money in sport, there seems to be corruption. Raising awareness of bribery in sports is a cornerstone in the fight against sports corruption. Can we clean up corruption in major sports around the world? *By Frank Vogl*

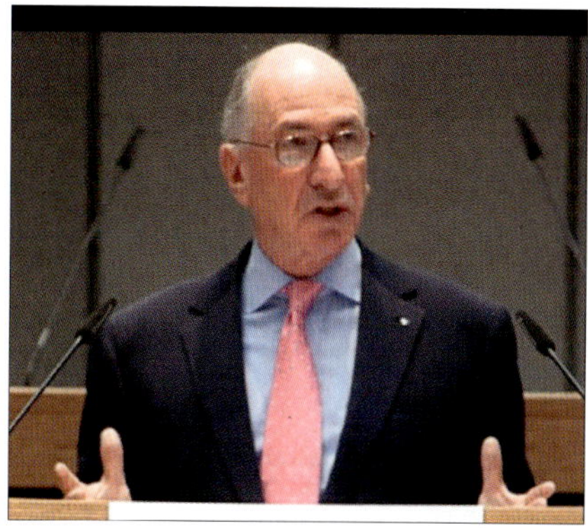

World soccer may have a new boss, but it will take long-term sustained efforts by FIFA to convince fans across the globe that the organisation has really changed and is serving their interests, rather than its own.

After all, many mega-sporting events around the world today, including those arranged by FIFA of course, suffer from a severe deficiency: money drives them to the point where what happens on the playing field is almost incidental.

Just consider the number of arrest warrants, investigations and criminal allegations that are issued against the men (almost exclusively) who are running so many of the international sporting associations.

In just the latest incident, the UK House of Commons' Committee on Media, Culture and Sport called top international tennis executives to testify this week over alleged match-fixing.

This action follows recent joint reports by Buzzfeed and the BBC on the results of an investigation into large-scale gambling on fixed matches.

Noting that, 'More than 40 top-flight tennis matches were identified by bookies as "suspicious" in a three-month period in 2015, international gambling outfits have a "blacklist" of more than 350 professional tennis players who are considered too risky for bookmakers to offer odds on.'

Wherever there is big money in sport, there seems to be corruption. And the cash involved is huge: according to estimates by auditors PriceWaterhouse Coopers, the total of 2015 global sporting revenues exceeded $145 billion.

Now, in a 360-page report on bribery and match-fixing in sports, anti-corruption organisation Transparency International stresses, 'The primary responsibility for reform lies with sports organisations.' It further adds, 'This needs to be matched by sustained engagement with intergovernmental organisations, governments, athletes, sponsors, supporters and civil society.'

But the report makes it very clear that forging such a coalition is extremely difficult. That reality must provide comfort to many of the leaders of world sport. They must fervently hope to be able to continue enjoying lavish lifestyles, unpublished salaries and operating with seeming impunity.

Despite the complaints about big-time sports and their powerful leaders, from American football and US university sports to global soccer, from the Olympic Games (from bribery to doping) to Formula 1 car racing, they all constantly appear to put their self-interest well above the interests of the billions of global sports fans.

Transparency International's Managing Director Cobus deSwardt is right in asserting in the preface to the 'Global Corruption Report: Sport' that 'Sport is a symbol of fair play around the world.' But leaders of many major sports have brazenly shown a total disregard for fairness.

'In the last five years, over 1,000 sports events – from top-level soccer games to Olympic badminton matches to international cricket competitions – have been fixed', writes Canadian academic and author Declan Hill in the new report.

The report's compelling conclusion is that dramatic reforms are absolutely vital. One can only hope that the unprecedented assault on the big mess that is the Fédération Internationale de Football (FIFA) might open the door to extensive change that has positive spillover effects onto other sports.

One of the first things to understand is that some global sporting associations operate like the Mafia. FIFA has at times been compared to the Cosa Nostra, while the image it seeks to project of itself is that of the Red Cross.

'The Global Corruption Report: Sport' highlights a 2002 U.S. ESPN soccer story that tracks the increasing collusion between corporate marketing outfits and FIFA from 1974 onwards as João Havelange from Brazil and then his chosen successor, Sepp Blatter from Switzerland, ran FIFA. Leaders of global sports associations across the world have an arrogance that suggests they believe they are both untouchable — and that cash is always king.

Powerful German corruption case

For example, German prosecutors built a powerful corruption case against the long-time boss of Formula 1, Bernie Ecclestone. When he saw which way the wind was blowing in the trial, he did what he always does and offered cash. The trial was terminated, Ecclestone went free and the court pocketed $100 million of his money.

Or take the example of Sepp Blatter who blames politics for all his troubles. He is in complete denial about the corruption in his domain. He told the Financial Times last October that he would still be running world soccer and would not have been indicted by the U.S. Justice Department if he had ensured that the 2022 World Cup had been awarded to the United States instead of to Qatar. Talk about a man living in a parallel universe of made-up 'reality'.

The troubles at FIFA have shocked the sporting world and shone a powerful media spotlight on the universe of sports racketeering. The U.S. Department of Justice has called FIFA 'The Enterprise', as if it were an organised crime syndicate. It also issued 47 indictments against 25 conspirators. Under pressure from U.S. authorities, Swiss officials raided FIFA's Zurich offices and started their own investigations.

The Americans pounced because many of FIFA's alleged crooked deals involve major international marketing contracts with U.S. companies. But why are the Americans going after FIFA? The U.S. action has led to investigations of soccer corruption in Trinidad, Brazil and other countries.

As the U.S. Justice Department pointed out, according to FIFA, 70% of its $5.7 billion in total revenues between 2011 and 2014 was attributable to the sale of TV and marketing rights to the 2014 World Cup. Indeed, the scale of cash in major sporting events has now reached vast proportions, from the estimated $50 billion spent by the Russians on the Sochi 2014 Olympic Winter Games to the countless billions that Brazil will spend on this year's Summer Olympics.

In addition to the arrogance of their leaders, many international sporting associations — despite the vast revenues they receive from business deals — enjoy not-for-profit legal status without mandated public reporting requirements. In many cases, they are also headquartered in countries that do not have a governmental tradition of looking at the ethics of such organisations.

A further critical obstacle to reform concerns the types of people who run major sporting associations. The new TI report's editor, Gareth Sweeney, notes: 'The administration of sport is often overseen by ex-athletes with little prior experience in management, ope-

The administration of sport is often overseen by ex-athletes with little prior experience in management, operating through very linear hierarchical organisational models. To make things worse, fans who support various sports with their money have no power.

rating through very linear hierarchical organisational models. While these models may have worked in the past, many international sports organisations (ISOs), regional confederations and national sports organisations (NSOs) have simply not kept pace with the huge commercial growth of the sector, and have even chosen not to adapt in order to protect certain self-interests, including high salaries, bonuses and virtually limitless tenures.'

To make things worse, fans who support various sports with their money have no power. They may detest the match-fixing and riots in the streets, as they have done in some Asian countries over cricket corruption, however they show no signs of abandoning their favoured sports as a substantial protest. That fact is cynically exploited by the 'managers' of international sports.

Corporate double standards

The corporations that pay huge amounts to advertise big sports ($10 million per minute at the recent U.S. Super Bowl of American football) have a long tradition of befriending leaders of international sports. They must have known about the corrupt practices, but closed their eyes so as not to disrupt their business plans. It was only after the U.S. Justice Department acted against FIFA and media focus on corruption kept rising that multinational corporations long involved in soccer indicated they would back away from FIFA unless meaningful reforms were undertaken.

Former German Olympic athlete Sylvia Schenk has been active and effective in recent years in leading TI-Germany's campaigns to strengthen transparency and accountability in professional sports in Germany.

Schenk argues in the concluding essay of the new TI report that there has been progress over the last eight years, from getting the German football association to address match fixing, to improving governance in sports associations.

She concludes that raising public awareness of bribery in sports is hard work, it pays off only gradually, but it can be effective 'and may prove to be a cornerstone in the fight for a world free of (sports) corruption.'

Frank Vogl is co-founder of Transparency International (TI) and has been engaged with global economics, banking, governance and anti-corruption for more than 40 years, as a World Bank senior official, as an anti-corruption civil society leader, and as a top-level advisor to financial institutions. Founded in 1993, today TI is the world's largest anti-corruption organisation, operating in more than 100 countries. Frank Vogl has written and lectured extensively about corruption across the globe. For more than 15 years, Frank Vogl has been associated with the New Israel Fund – the leading civil rights and social justice foundation supporting organisations across Israel in support of democracy and human rights. Frank Vogl is an advisory council member of the United Nations Association of the Greater Washington Metropolitan Area; he is a former Board member of the Ethics Resource Centre; and he is a member of the Wisemen public relations association.

An arena for nationalist sentiments

An arena for nationalist sentiments Sport is a culture, a language that helps nations, cities, communities and individuals to communicate. Sport events are inherently political, particularly when associated with national teams and international competitions. They can fulfil diplomatic functions and provide spaces for peaceful conflict resolution, but at the same time they allow the rallying of nationalistic sentiments. *By Bernd Reiter*

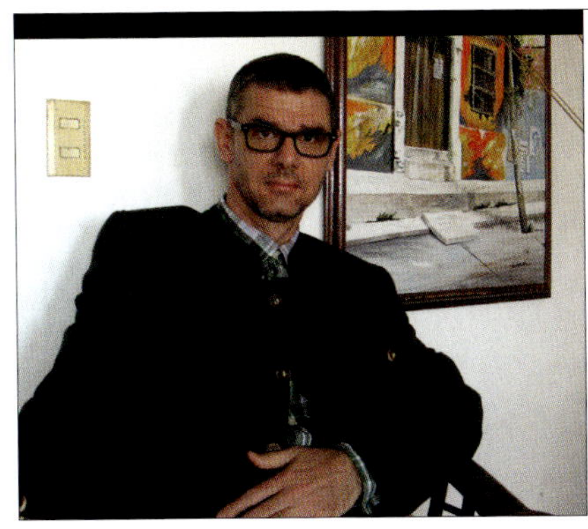

Sports events, particularly when linked to international competitions, are political spaces par excellence in that they allow for the rallying of nationalist sentiments in an environment that is perceived as safe and non-violent. International sports events are able to bring the people of a country together by overcoming internal divisions, if only temporarily. They can even make it possible to address and resolve international resentments. International sporting events can also provide a space for cooperation and hence the first steps towards rapprochement between otherwise divided nations.

Soccer and cricket are perhaps the best examples of this. The Indian and Pakistani national cricket teams are able to play against and with each other – even when their countries' official diplomatic relationship is tense.

In 1998, Iran and the USA played each other at soccer without any major incidents. The political dimensions of such encounters are quite obvious and often manifest themselves in a strong societal and political reaction in the immediate aftermath of such games.

In short, sports events are inherently political, particularly when associated with national teams and international competitions. As such, they are core elements of nationalism and the international order. In his book 'Nations and Nationalism Since 1780', Eric Hobsbawm has demonstrated that nationalism is an invented tradition. First of all it has to be proposed, or invented, and then instilled in people's minds through the use of symbols, emblems, and similar appeals to a people's emotions. The media is a necessary ingredient in the dissemination of nationalist ideas and proposals as nationalism cannot survive without broad dissemination. Of course, international sports events provide all the necessary ingredients for instilling nationalist sentiments among the people of a participating country. Athletes wear national symbols; national hymns and anthems are played and sung; media coverage is extensive. As such, international sporting competitions provide a safe outlet for international tensions and a way to rally the people of a country behind a common banner – whether it is invented or not.

Seen from this angle, international sports events are genuinely positive, helpful, and desirable events that have an important role to play in conflict avoidance and the channelling of nationalist emotions into a safe and controlled arena. Sports events can fulfil diplomatic functions and provide spaces for peaceful conflict resolution. Why would anybody criticise this very accepted practice?

It's not that I dislike physical activity – I'm an avid practitioner of a number of sports. I not only love sport, but I believe everyone should get physically active for the sake of their health and as a way of engaging in a fun, communal activity. But I do have problems with certain elements in professional, and particularly international, sports competitions.

Avenues for international sports events

Firstly, while international sports events may serve as avenues for international diplomacy and even lead to overcoming national animosities, sport is also one of the core elements used to rally nationalist sentiment. In other words, if, like me, you perceive nationalism as a problem, then sport is not the way to overcome it – precisely because it is the use of symbols and emblems in sport that creates nationalistic sentiments. Sport serves nationalist purposes by providing a way of 'imagining the nation'.

Even if the resulting nationalism is of the more benign kind – as is the case with Brazilians, who tend to see themselves as a nation of soccer players and samba dancers – sports events still provide the means to foster and forge nationalist sentiments. The content may vary, but the difference between people who see themselves as dancers and those who see themselves as soldiers is quantitative not qualitative.

Sporting competitions, particularly those that are organised internationally and promoted as huge media events, provide the means to forge and disseminate nationalist sentiments. They are not the best way of combating such sentiments. Put simply: if we want to dilute the power of nationalism, we need fewer, not more, international sports competitions.

Secondly, it seems that capitalism and market competition have totally changed what sport used to be and can be, and there are two trends at the heart of this change. On the one hand, there is the undue influence of (big) money on sports. With some athletes earning millions of dollars or euros, some professional sports have become extremely inflationary, elevating some athletes to the status of multi-millionaires and transforming some clubs and associations into corrupt money pits. FIFA is just one of many examples of how money distorts and detracts from the essence and core of sporting activity. On the other hand, it appears that sport has become so embedded in capitalism that winning at any price has become the single focus and goal of athletes and teams. Just as capitalist markets are driven by competition, capitalist sports leave no room for cooperation and community building.

As a result, when operating under a capitalist logic, sporting activity loses its ability to bring people together and forge bonds between individuals, groups, countries, and nations. Instead of providing a space for peaceful interaction and conflict resolution, some international sports events become battlegrounds in their own right, where animosity is promoted rather than reduced.

The negative influence of money and capitalism in this transformation can easily be gauged by comparing high-money sports events with those that are less monetised. Today, it seems to me that women's soccer is outdoing the men's game in terms of sportsmanship and attitude. The Olympics provide a telling counterpoint to most World Cups – precisely because the influence of money on the Olympics is kept at bay.

Thirdly, instead of providing a controlled and safe environment for individuals and groups to channel their emotions and even frustrations into a sports event, we are increasingly witnessing how the organisers of sports events are neglecting this role and instead providing safe havens for those who use crowds to voice their anger and hate. We now routinely read about Spanish soccer fans who abuse black players in extremely discriminatory and racist ways – without triggering decisive action from their teams or the associations to which they belong.

While some actions are taken only reluctantly, decisive action against racism and discrimination would require much more severe sanctions to be imposed on the teams and fans who allow this kind of discrimination to thrive. A team that harbours racism should be banned from playing for a whole season – and if it continues to offend it should be disbanded altogether.

Capitalism and market competition have totally changed what sport used to be and can be.

Neo-Nazis and soccer

In Germany, neo-Nazis have a long history of gathering at soccer events and using the crowd to spread their nasty blend of violence and hatred. However, instead of addressing this issue directly by targeting the neo-Nazis and the teams who shelter them, the German police is called upon to protect ordinary citizens and their property from the violent excesses of neo-Nazis and their hate-inspired followers. Racism and violent extremism have found refuge in sport associations and clubs to such extent that these clubs must be forced to take much more decisive action against racism and hatred. They can no longer provide a platform for hatred and racism – and if they do, they should be dissolved.

Neo-Nazis and hooligans are, however, only the tip of the proverbial iceberg in this discussion, as 'ordinary' citizens can all too quickly turn into violent monsters when faced with the fans of an opposing sports team.

The kind of violence and destruction of property that routinely occurs during major sports events has become so disproportionate that it calls the whole activity into question. Hundreds of police officers are deployed whenever major sports events are held, and have to keep the opposing fans apart as if they were lions in a zoo. These fans also routinely march through cities and damage and destroy whatever they find in their way – be it cars, windows, storefronts, or public property.

I see no good reason why ordinary citizens should allow their tax dollars to be spent on hosting events where fan violence costs thousands of public dollars or euros, while the participating teams earn millions but re-

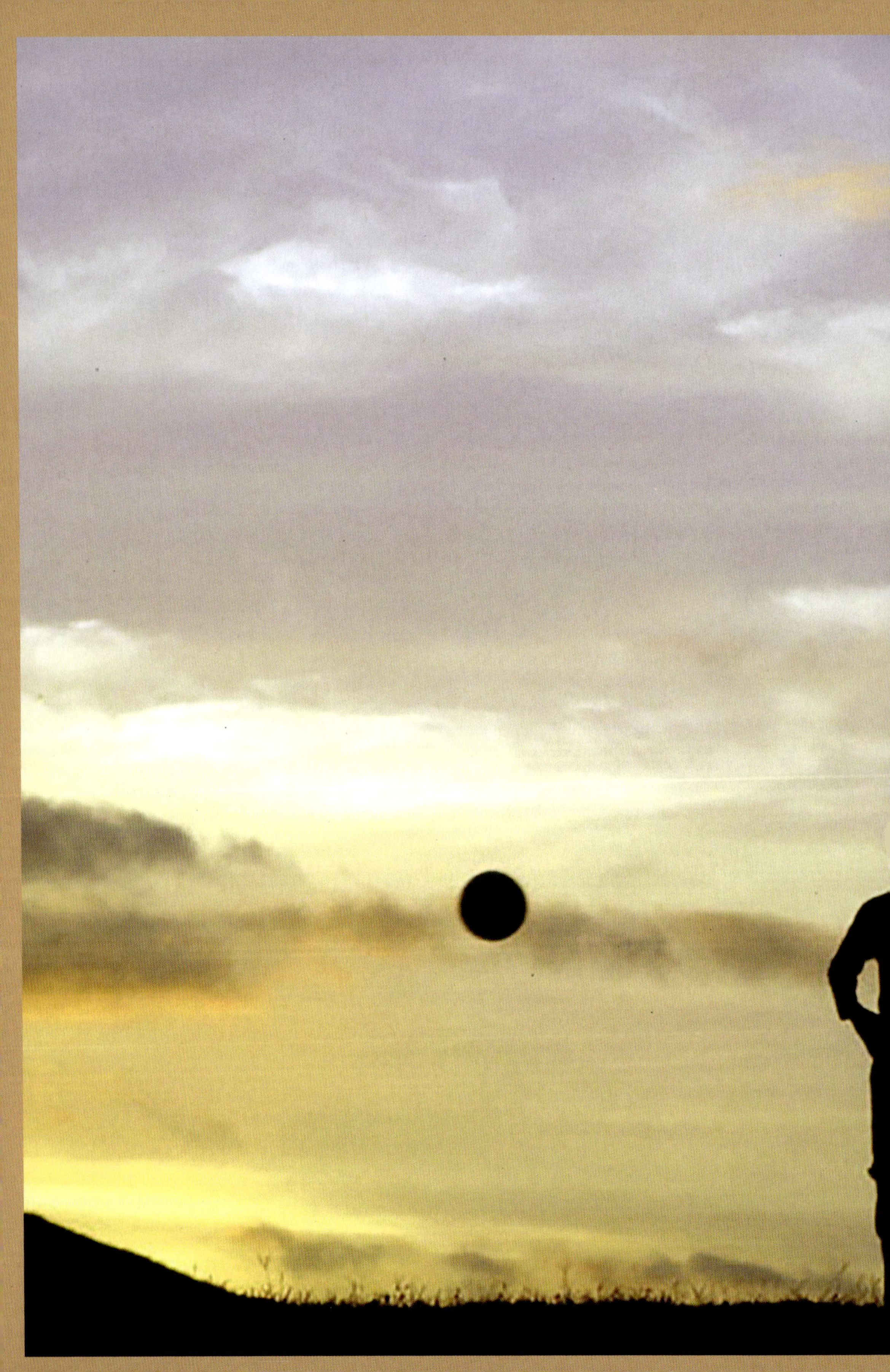

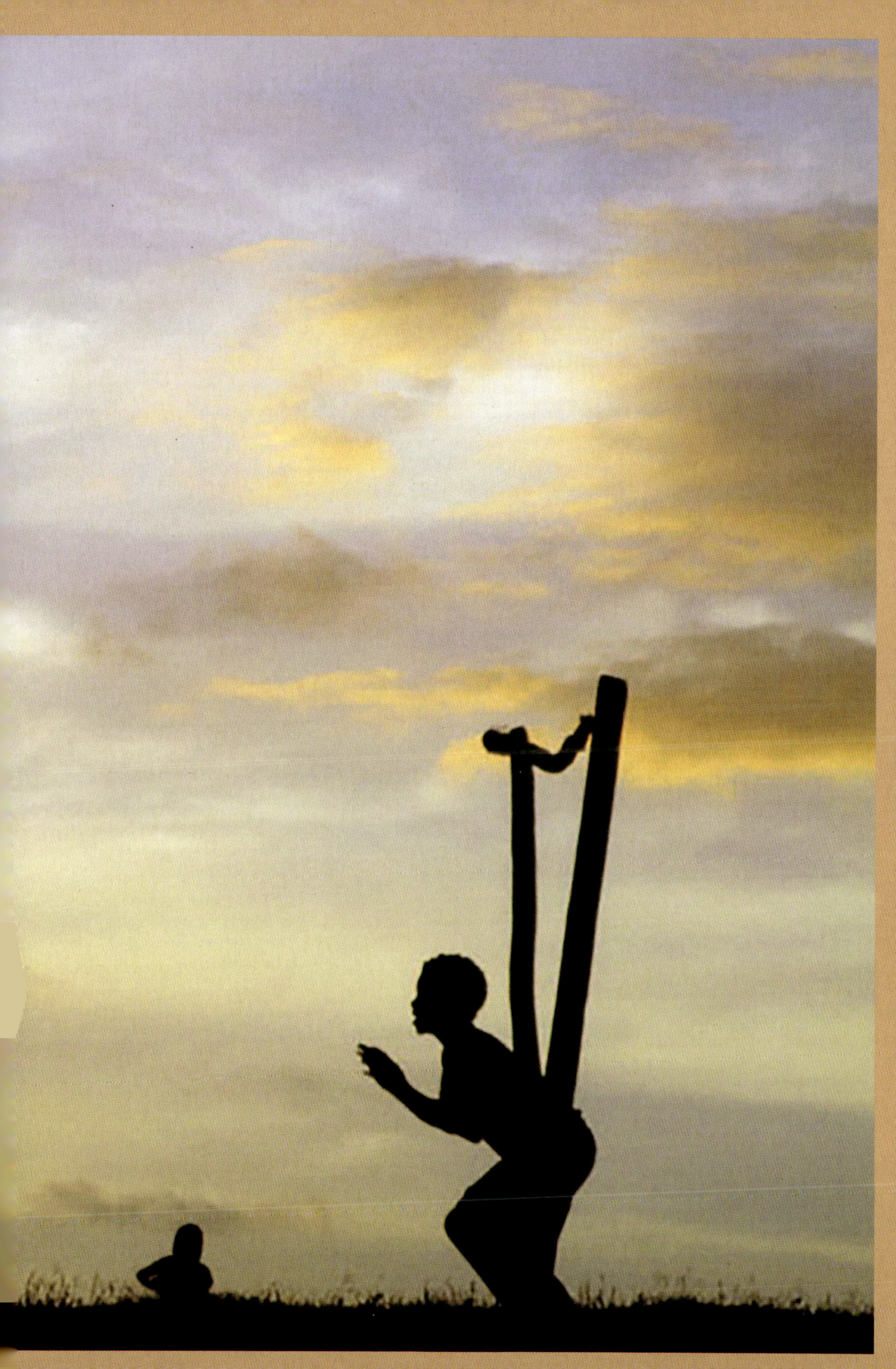

fuse to take an active role in preventing this violence and havoc.

Fourthly, while sports may provide an avenue for the prevention of violence and even a platform for international diplomacy, most sports are still heavily male-dominated and the associations that organise national and international competitions still constitute a playground for the 'good old boys'.

FIFA may be an extreme example, but it is certainly not the only association that is dominated by elderly men and has a colonial bias. When money runs the show, it also comes as no surprise that the world's rich countries and regions control the game. Under such conditions, instead of creating a better and fairer world, sport contributes to upholding male dominance and colonial power.

Finally, sport has an eerie connection to militarism and totalitarianism – or at least it has the potential to do so. Anyone who has watched Leni Riefenstahl's 'Triumph of the Will' has seen how this potential was thoroughly milked by the Nazis in Germany. As Riefenstahl demonstrates, sport can be used to forge unity and an organic oneness with a group, and as such it has the potential to switch off individualism and critical opinions. Soldiers can be forged through sport, as was the case in Nazi Germany.

When this kind of group pressure and conformity reaches its highest level, the result can be that non-conformist individuals are at risk of being singled out, mistreated, and shunned.

A form of torture

I suspect we can all tell stories of our school days, when the kids who were unwilling or unable to take part in sport sometimes suffered severe physical and emotional consequences. Some of my classmates found PE classes were quite simply a form of torture spearheaded by conformity-minded quasi-fascists who were authorised to serve as physical education teachers.

Sport is a beautiful and healthy thing. At its best, it can build a sense of community and bring people together. It can prolong the lives of those who are physical active on a regular basis. But if sport becomes too money-driven and capitalist; if sports teams shelter racists and provide them with a platform to spread their venom; and if sports fans abuse the publically funded arenas that they occupy on their way to a game and if their teams shy away from their responsibility of providing a safe, controlled environment, then I believe sports event can no longer be justified and should no longer be held.

Sport and physical activity can also easily become a way of marginalising and stigmatising those who are perceived as 'less able'. Sports events then become a place where

There should always be space for non-conformity, and group pressure should always be held at bay so that it does not develop into totalitarianism and fascism.

discrimination and hatred are fostered and allowed to spread. Whenever this happens, sport loses its justification.

This does not mean that organised physical activity and sports events are inherently bad. Rather, it means that their organisers are called upon to provide an environment and an incentive structure that is safe and conducive to cooperation and community building. When sport becomes a harbinger of racism and an excuse for viciously shunning and mistreating those who are perceived as less able or different, then such sport events should be stopped.

There should always be space for non-conformity, and group pressure should always be held at bay so that it does not develop into totalitarianism and fascism. And finally, male bias should be actively combated by actively recruiting and promoting women – not just among athletes, but particularly in the ranks of the organisers of sports events and competitions.

Finally, taking money out of sports would serve the sport, the players, and the countries and communities involved in this activity. It would also have the potential to restore what I believe was the original premise of physical activity and sporting competition: building bridges, bringing people together, teaching kids how to follow rules, and investing in one's health and wellbeing.

Bernd Reiter is Professor of Political Science and Latin American Studies at the University of South Florida in Tampa. His research interests include democracy, civil rights, participation, civil society and education.

Ping-pong and cricket diplomacy The 1971 table tennis world championships triggered a friendship between US player Glenn Cowan and Zhunag Zedong of China. This led to the US team being invited to visit China. They were the first sports team, and indeed the first American group of any kind, to travel to China since 1949. Mao remarked: 'This Zhuang is not only a good table tennis player, he's also a good diplomat.' An insider's view of how sport can help to build ties between nations.
By Karl-Heinz Schneider

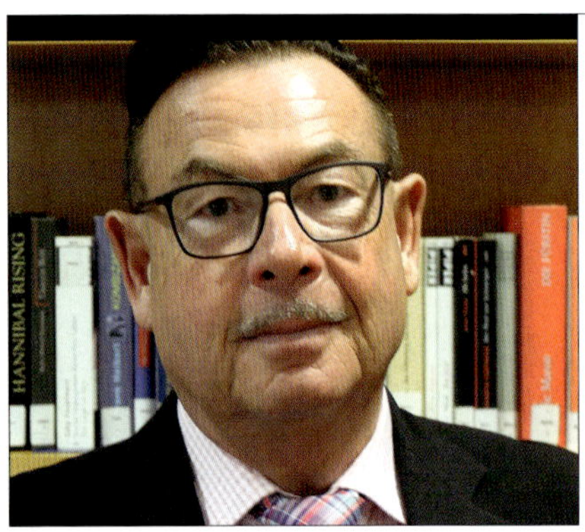

A Chinese teacher taught me an old Chinese saying: 'A journey of a thousand miles begins with a single step'. For Germany and China, one such step was taken in April 2008 when Germany's Federal Ministry of the Interior and the General Administration of Sport of China signed a General Memorandum of Understanding on Sports Cooperation. There is no doubt that sport and sports policy can break down barriers between nations and contribute to detente and peace. But despite this, in 2007 the Beijing Olympics attracted a huge amount of criticism at home and abroad. Some European cities, including in France, displayed banners and posters that were critical of China. This culminated in critical statements and demands being made by politicians, such as the former President of the European Parliament Hans Gert Pöttering, who threatened a European boycott of the Olympics in China and called on the Chinese government to hold talks with the Dalai Lama.

Germany's minister of the interior at that time, Wolfgang Schäuble, was not impressed by this scenario and insisted that bridges could be built through a targeted, bilateral cooperation on sport, which would serve mutual understanding much better than calls for boycotts. He held an official meeting with China's sports minister, Liu Peng, during the latter's visit to Germany in 2007, and I had an opportunity to spend a few days with the Chinese delegation. Liu Peng immediately agreed to my proposal regarding drawing up a joint agreement, and the text was ready shortly afterwards.

A window of opportunity

Interior minister Schäuble and a delegation travelled to Beijing before the Olympic Games to hold discussions on sports policy. It was important for him to visit before the Games opened in order to benefit from the momentum of this visit. The agreement that he signed with China on that occasion is still the only one ever made between a German interior minister and a foreign country in the realm of sport.

Emphasis on exchange and cooperation

Like other agreements made between the German interior ministry and other countries, this agreement has the legal status of a memorandum of understanding. In it, both parties emphasise exchange and cooperation in the area of sport based on mutual respect, equality and mutual benefit, while respecting human rights and building the Olympic spirit.

The signing of this Memorandum of Understanding triggered a series of congresses, symposiums and workshops in 2009, 2010, 2011 and 2013, jointly funded by Germany and China.

The first such event took place in November 2009 at Bejing Sport University under the banner of Sport Brings Our Nations Together. In his welcome address, Wolfgang Schäuble noted that this symposium was laying the foundation for a totally new chapter of sporting collaboration between Germany and China.

Another milestone in China and Germany's bilateral efforts to promote peace and rapprochement was the first Sino-German Sports Law Conference, held in Bonn in October 2010. It was a great success for international sports cooperation, attracting delegates from China, Germany, Belgium, Switzerland, and even the USA, along with representatives of the EU Commission.

It is not uncommon for these kinds of joint projects to gradually fizzle out, but this was not the case with China. Many more sports policy symposiums were held over the years that followed. This collaboration is significant because sport and sports policy are closely linked to many areas of society. Particular interdependencies exist with politics, the economy, media and the education system. And yes, sport has an ambivalent relationship with peace and violence. As history has shown, sport has often been used as a way of promoting particular ideologies.

Sporting arms race

During the Cold War, class warfare was brought into the stadium by the military and a 'sporting arms race' began. The battle over political differences was continued using other means and on other stages.

However, the idea of sport, as it is also formulated for the Olympic Games, remains one of peace. The emphasis is on sharing and getting to know different cultures, and in this way building ties between people across national borders. In this sense, sport can even be at the cutting edge of diplomacy, as shown by the 'ping-pong diplomacy' that took place between the US and China during the Nixon era. In 1971 political relations between China and the USA were at a low ebb. The two countries had troops supporting opposing sides in the Vietnam War, and the Korean War was still far from forgotten.

As history has shown, sport has often been used as a way of promoting particular ideologies.

The 1971 table tennis world championships held in Japan triggered a friendship between US player Glenn Cowan and Zhunag Zedong of China. The friendship that grew between the two athletes led to the Chinese leadership inviting American players to come to China to play some friendly matches (and allegedly allowed them to win).

This American table tennis team was the first group of any kind from the US to visit China since 1949. When Mao Zedong learned of these activities he supposedly said: 'This Zhuang is not only a good table tennis player (he was world champion three times), but also a good diplomat.' Despite many misgivings, particularly on the part of the US, the American players travelled to China.

High-level meetings

A Chinese sports delegation was subsequently invited to the USA. There are reports that a baseball game took place, and surprisingly the Chinese won. Shortly afterwards a high-level meeting was held between politicians on both sides. And finally in 1972 US President Richard Nixon travelled to China. Since then, political relations between the two countries have steadily improved, with diplomatic relations being officially opened in 1978. Richard Nixon commented on his visit to China: 'This was the week that changed the world, as what we have said in that Communique is not nearly as important as what we will do in the years ahead to build a bridge across 16,000 miles and 22 years of hostilities which have divided us in the past'.

In 1979 China became a member of the IOC and took part in the Olympics for the first time in 1984 in Los Angeles. In 2008

The established sports system within a country reflects its orientation and interest in culture, politics, social ideology and business.

it hosted the Games for the first time, and we now know that they will be held again in China. There is still a hope that politicians on both sides will use the Olympic spirit for the benefit of humankind.

The established sports system within a country – and I think this also applies to Germany – reflects its orientation and interest in culture, politics, social ideology and business.

At this point it would seem appropriate to examine particular occurrences, such as buying the right to host World Cups and corruption within the DFB, FIFA and IOC, but that would be a step too far. However, one thing is clear: a country's established sports system is a kind of 'miniature' of that country's overall system. If we use its system and phenomenology for political ends, then sporting relations can be used to achieve closer relations between countries.

The role of sport in peacekeeping

So far, it seems that studies have not been able to prove beyond doubt that sport is able to secure peace. But it is safe to say that sport has a role to play in terms of socialisation and integration. In international relations, the way that institutions present sport also has a great deal of symbolic significance. It can allow key conditions to be set that are necessary for creating international relations in a peaceful way.

Alongside the aforementioned ping-pong diplomacy, history also provides us with other examples of how sport has a role in peacekeeping. We will take a look at the role of sport in South Africa under Nelson Mandela; the 'cricket diplomacy' between India and Pakistan in 2004; and finally attempts to use sport and sports policy to help resolve the Middle East conflict between Israel and Palestine.

South Africa began enforcing its apartheid structures after the end of the Second World War. Sport was used as a political instrument. It was run by a post-colonial elite and was primarily aimed at whites. As a result, an international lobbying initiative led to calls for a sports boycott. In 2007, Nelson Mandela recognised the power of sport and its particular potential when he said: 'Sport has the power to unite people in a way little else can. Sport awakes hope where there was previously only despair. It breaks down racial barriers. It laughs in the face of discrimination. Sport speaks to people in a language they can understand.' The decades of sporting discrimination in South Africa were certainly part of the momentum that led to the fall of the apartheid regime. When Mandela took over as president, he tried to harness the power of sport by energetically working to promote the nation's sporting development.

There are reports that a baseball game took place, and surprisingly the Chinese won. Shortly afterwards a high-level meeting was held between politicians on both sides. And finally in 1972 US president Richard Nixon travelled to China.

Sport also had a positive effect on the conflict between India and Pakistan. Echoing the ping-pong diplomacy of 1971, the matches played between India and Pakistan in 2004 were referred to as 'cricket diplomacy'. The Indian team went to Pakistan to play a series of friendly matches, with a view to creating closer ties through sport. This was the first time a cricket series had been played between the two countries since 1989, and it led to people rethinking their view of the other side as 'the enemy'.

Football for Peace

The Football for Peace initiative launched in 2000 also had the objective of using sport and wide-ranging sports projects to help resolve the conflict between Israel and Palestine. With the support of the UK and a number of Jewish and Arab communities, it was possible to build excellent social contacts between children.

There had already been successful collaborations in many areas of sport at non-governmental level involving NGOs, sports associations, universities and other institutions. But now the idea was to intensify sports cooperation between Germany's ministry of the interior, which is responsible for sport in Germany, the Israeli sports ministry and the body responsible for sport in Palestine. The aim was to organise a conference or symposium, perhaps initiated by Germany, and involving Israeli and Palestinian sports experts.

Bringing the two sides to the table

The aim was to get the two sides round the table. An initial meeting was held between a delegation from the German interior ministry and the Israeli sports ministry in 2009 to discuss the main points to be included in a joint agreement. I signed the first General Memorandum of Understanding between the two ministries in Bonn in October 2010, along with the director of sport from the Israeli ministry of sport.

The agreement made a commitment to sport policy cooperation between the two ministries and included the joint organisation of events. In light of the political situation, the idea soon emerged to organise a larger international conference that would highlight the role of sport as a mediator between nations.

In September 2011, under the patronage of UNESCO, the first joint international conference organised by the German interior ministry and the Israeli sports ministry was held at the Wingate Institute in Netanya, Israel, titled 'Sport, A Mediator Between Cultures'. 350 experts from across the Mediterranean region attended the conference, which was opened by Israeli sports minister Limor Livnat and Christoph Bergner, secretary of state responsible for sport in Germany's ministry of the interior. Unfortunately no sports experts from Palestine managed to attend, an absence that the Israeli side explained was due to security reasons.

As the conference was organised under the auspices of UNESCO, it was also attended by Willi Lemke, Special Adviser to the UN Secretary-General on Sport for Development and Peace. With his assistance, we and a German delegation spontaneously drove in a UN convoy to visit General Rajoub at his home in Ramallah.

This visit to Jibril Rajoub, Head of the Palestinian Supreme Council for Sport and Youth Affairs, in Ramallah laid the foundations for the agreement that was signed on 18 June 2012 in Bonn.

Sharing knowledge and experience

Of course this Memorandum of Understanding on Sports Cooperation also highlighted the importance of sharing knowledge and experience, supporting training camps and, above all, being willing to take part in projects that promote peace and coexistence in the Middle East. On the occasion of the signing of the memorandum in Bonn, I took the opportunity to accompany General Rajoub and Salah Abdel, the Palestinian ambassador to Germany, on a visit to the home of Konrad Adenauer in Rhöndorf. While strolling through Adenauer's rose garden, it

Even sports policy has its limits. But it can still be an important instrument for peace policy in the Middle East that should not be underestimated.

became clear that there was a strong desire to take the collaboration forward in the planned form, and today I can still be an important instrument for peace policy in the Middle East that should not be underestimated. UNESCO, the EU Council and the European Union need to intensify their commitment to this process. I can still hear Rajoub's deep voice in my ear. The plan was to hold a joint congress in Amman with delegates from Germany, Israel, Palestine and Jordan. I subsequently tried to get Jordan on board, but my last conversation with the Jordanian ambassador in Berlin in 2013 revealed that this was not possible due to the state of political relations between the countries involved.

Once again it became clear that even sports policy has its limits. But it can still be an important instrument for peace policy in the Middle East that should not be underestimated. UNESCO, the EU Council and the European Union need to intensify their commitment to this process.

Karl-Heinz Schneider was head of European and international sports policy at the German Ministry of the Interior for 15 years. He organised the UNESCO World Sport Ministers Conference (MINEPS) in Berlin in 2013. He is currently a group head at the German Federal Academy of Public Administration in Brühl, part of the Federal Ministry of the Interior.

Strong girls – strong communities

Strong girls – strong communities Sport for development projects don't just aim to achieve the specific development goals laid out in their conception and planning – they also call into existence, nurture and network important civil society eco-systems, which increase the resilience of communities in some of the most deprived, war-torn and under-developed communities on earth.
By Heather Cameron

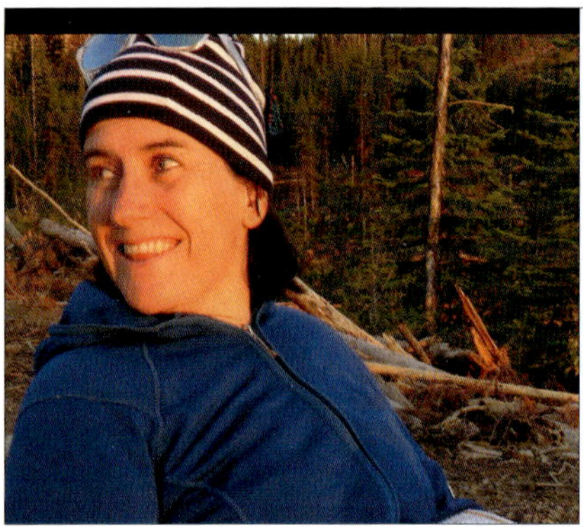

Sports clubs are the engines of social engagement and integration for migrants. In Germany, for example, more than 1 in 3 migrants is a member of a sports club, in contrast to only 15 percent who engage in cultural, music or other leisure time clubs. And membership potentials are not exhausted yet, because the participation rates of migrants are still visibly below the rates of people without a migration background. This is only one small example of how sport can be a driver for social change, in particular the increasing participation of marginalised groups in civil society organisations. This challenge is being taken up by sports for development projects in a wide range of countries and at a number of institutional levels.

And yes, sport has a potential impact on development projects that aim to build ci-vil society, particularly in foreign policy. The United Nations characterise sport for development projects as 'the intentional use of sport, physical activity and play to attain specific development and peace objectives, including, most notably, the Sustainable Development Goals (SDGs).'

While many of the sustainable development goals can certainly be reached through civil society sporting organisations, I will discuss in more detail the goals of quality education (goal no. 4), gender equality (no. 5) and reduced inequalities (no. 10) as well as health (no. 3) and peace (no. 16) as globally accepted goals.

According to the World Bank, civil society refers to 'the wide array of non-governmental and not-for-profit organisations that have a presence in public life, expressing the interests and values of their members or others, based on ethical, cultural, political, scientific, religious or philanthropic considerations.' Non-governmental and non-profit organisations work to grow and strengthen civil society at different levels. First of all, they work at the grassroots level, which happens in the form of local activism and programmes that directly support the individual.

The second level is the foreign policy level of states such as Germany, including its federal level institutions such as the German Ministry of Economic Cooperation and Development (BMZ) or the German Corporation for International Cooperation (GIZ). Gerd Müller, German Federal Minister for Economic Cooperation and Development, argues: 'I see sport as a priority of development cooperation – one which we seek to develop in collaboration with our partners in sport, civil society, business and academia, and with ordinary committed people.'

The third level includes global United Nations programmes such as the UN Office for Sport for Development and Peace.

I'd like to discuss the contribution of sport to civil society through the perspective of sport for development programmes that I have built over the past twenty years or worked on as a consultant.

A GIZ paper states that it aims to 'use sport as an innovative instrument to support the achievement of development objectives: we do not promote sport in order to train better and more successful athletes, rather we use sport as a transmitter for reaching development policy objectives.'

The decisive difference between sports development and sport for development is the expected outcome. Sport for development

While boxing has been a focus of the organisation, the curriculum has always included elements of democratic education, leadership development as well as instruction on health and personal safety topics.

projects use sport as a means to reach development goals like the Sustainable Development Goals. Sports development, on the other hand, means the development of sport infrastructure, organisations and the achievement of national or regional sporting success.

We will apply the term development goals to the context of Germany, even though Germany itself is not the focus of 'development programmes' in the traditional sense. Sport for development projects are used in Germany to improve social cohesion and integration, recently and importantly within the context of the so-called 'refugee crisis'.

My experience of using sport to achieve social or political development began at a grassroots level with my development of boxing training for women in the Berlin neighbourhood of Kreuzberg in 2001, together with the local sports club Seitenwechsel e.V. Our cooperation later grew into Boxgirls Berlin e.V. It was the first boxing club of its kind, with a female board, trainers and athletes and is to date the largest women's boxing club in Europe.

While boxing has been a focus of the organisation, the curriculum has always included elements of democratic education, leadership development as well as instruction on health and personal safety topics. For its vigorous advocacy regarding women's leadership and organisational capacity building, Boxgirls e.V. was awarded the title 'Model Project of the UN Year of Physical Activity and Sport' in the category of social integration and urban peacemaking in Germany. With its boxing and leadership programmes, Boxgirls Berlin e.V. attracted not only white, German-speaking women, but also girls and women from ethnic minorities and migrant communities in Berlin, groups that are otherwise severely under-represented in civil society organisations.

Boxgirls is thus a civil society organisation that provides many people with their first opportunities for leadership. In Boxgirls' case, these people are likely to never have been considered as candidates for leadership in their lives.

Boxgirls South Africa NPC works on a similar model to its sister project in Berlin. BGSA is a civil society organisation that strengthens girls' agency in the township Khayelitsha in a sport and leadership programme. It started off as a local grassroots organisation and was able to secure funding from a Swiss foundation in 2015 to train girls at 20 schools. In the Boxgirls After-School Club, participants not only learn self-defence and presentation skills, but also improve their academic skills and build their social capital. Ndvile, a 15-year-old alumna of the Boxgirls programme, describes the personal effects of the programme she has experienced: 'Boxgirls has helped me to be more focused on my school work and know the importance of education… [Boxgirls] teaches you to have self-respect and responsibility.'

On a collective level, Boxgirls contributes to social change by engaging in debates about public space and public goods or bringing topics like gender-based violence onto the national agenda. Public events, such as the celebration of International Women's Day on 8 March, not only engage the participants' families and the wider community in a fun and interactive way, but also create a space to discuss women's rights and peace-building. Another prominent issue in the communities in which we work is the health of mothers and babies, which is also an integral part of the sustainable development goals.

Creating spaces for public discussion

As a grassroots civil society organisation, the BGSA staff and peer-educators are members of the very communities they serve. This builds social capital and stronger networks of practice in these impoverished areas.

We used our knowledge of youth engagement and development gained from sport clubs, to create programmes for the German school setting. Overcoming social inequalities in the German educational system by targeting school children and educators has been a focal area of the activities of the CamP Group social enterprise. Our program RespAct uses sport to raise children's awareness of neighbourhood challenges and violence prevention in Berlin's most impoverished and densely populated areas. Our participants gain knowledge about democratic processes at the local level through a range of different formats and attain the skills required to become active members of civil society.

Here, sport functions as a tool for team-building and increasing the self-confidence of children who are otherwise severely marginalised because of their socio-economic status and cultural backgrounds. In school development programmes and workshops we also train teachers and youth workers in child-centred and participative sports games to improve the classroom learning environments. We measure the social impact of our work rigorously through participant surveys, qualitative interviews and focus groups in order to continuously improve our pedagogical methods, and support our advocacy on the communal level.

CamP Group's newest initiative involves 'welcome classes' ('Willkommensklassen') where young migrants, including many refugees, learn about German language and culture before entering the regular educational system. Our sport programmes JumpIn and RespAct for welcome classes foster integration and exchange between language learners and other children at school to overcome language and cultural barriers. Sport for development methods prove critical here where there is no shared language or culture; sport and movement provide a way to create better social cohesion and improved learning outcomes for the most challenged and challenging young people in the school system.

In comparison with a grassroots organisation like Boxgirls, which develops emerging youth leaders, Camp Group gGmbH provides training and leadership development for people who are already professionals and working inside educational and other institutions.

Sharing strategies for social change

The German Ministry for Economic Cooperation and Development created the Sport for Development sector programme in 2013 to develop innovative approaches using sport for development in order to contribute to the achievement of global goals in education,

Sport and movement provide a way to create better social cohesion and improved learning outcomes for the most challenged and challenging young people in the school system.

health and HIV prevention, gender equality, violence prevention and conflict solution, good governance, inclusion and environment.

I worked as a consultant for the Sport for Development sector programme in Afghanistan with staff from the Afghan Ministry of Education to develop a culturally appropriate, child-centred sports curriculum for girls at school, which demonstrates the principles applied for successful sport for development projects.

The school environment, a closed gymnasium, is often the only place girls have to play, run or do sports due to the cultural context of modesty, and pubic space as a male realm. By supporting the Ministry of Education in Afghanistan to develop further teaching tools for this marginalised target group, the BMZ is furthering goals towards the wider inclusion of girls and women in society, their right to education and to physical and mental health, which we know are developed through school sport programmes.

Other GIZ Sport for Development sector programmes use sport to improve themes as diverse as vocational training, HIV prevention and violence prevention. Future programmes will support programmes for refugees abroad. The German BMZ and GIZ Sport for Development sector programme works with government partners to provide funding and technical support for civil society or government institutions to achieve development goals through sport. So it is not aimed at creating leaders like Boxgirls, or training existing leaders like Camp Group, but funding and providing technical expertise for fellow governments to further grow the capacity of their own civil society organisations to solve development challenges.

For the United Nations, building civil society through sports for development projects has been a priority for almost fifteen years, since resolution 58/5 of the United Nations was adopted in 2003. It underscores the importance of 'sport as a means to promote education, health, development and peace'. As a political entity at the highest, global level, the United Nations Office for Sport, Development and Peace (UNOSDP) runs different activities including the UNOSDP Youth Leadership Camps on all continents to enhance social awareness and civil society engagement.

A UN paper states that 'Most of these youth have only very basic education levels, limited resources with which to carry out their projects and do not have a proper forum where they can learn best practices or develop their leadership skills.' So the idea of a Youth Leadership Programme was conceived in order to support such young people by giving them access to the theoretical and practical training they need to improve their projects and their own professional progress, and to support them once they go back to their communities.

Leveraging the power of sport

The UNOSDP convene youth leadership camps to achieve this mission, bringing civil society leaders together (volunteers, leaders of sports clubs, coaches and directors) in a donor country to help develop and accelerate their programmes.

The current United Nations Secretary-General's Special Adviser on Sport for De-

velopment and Peace, Wilfried Lemke, also has a long history in sport and politics. Before he was appointed to his current position at the UNOSDP, he was Senator for the Interior and Sport and the Senator for Education and Science in the German State of Bremen and the manager of German second division football club Werder Bremen for almost two decades. Due to his career as a German policy-maker, Lemke is familiar with Germany's foreign policy goals and its rights-based framework.

It is not just the UNOSDP that is leveraging the power of sport for development to work towards the Sustainable Development Goals. Others in the UN system are also using sport: UNESCO, UNAIDS, and UN Women to name but a few.

Sport falls under the remit of UNESCO within the organisational structure of the United Nations. Furthermore, on matters concerning development through sport, the agency responsible is the United Nations Office on Sport for Development and Peace (UNOSDP). 'UNOSDP acts as a mediator between the United Nations, its member states, individual (sports) organisations, civil society, the private sector, academia and the media', states a BMZ paper.

It becomes clear that Sustainable Development Goals can be successfully and efficiently pursued through sport for development projects aimed at the individual and communal

The school environment, a closed gymnasium, is often the only place girls have to play, run or do sports due to the cultural context of modesty, and pubic space as a male realm.

(grassroots organisations), international (programmes by BMZ and GIZ) and the supranational global level (UNOSDP), and should thus play a vital role in national foreign and development policy.

Sport for development projects do not only aim to achieve the specific development goals laid out in their conception and planning, but they also call into existence, nurture and network important civil society eco-systems which increase the resilience of communities in some of the most deprived, war-torn and under-developed communities on earth. Now we need to increase the visibility of these projects and the impact that they have, in order to create stronger networks and share best practices, scaling their successes quickly and efficiently in communities internationally in order to achieve the SDGs.

This has already begun, with the GIZ in partnership with the UNOSDP taking a leading role in finding and sharing best practices in sport for development in Germany at an international level. In order to support the achievement of the SDGs this process must continue and expand throughout countries in Europe and internationally.

Heather Cameron is Professor of Integration and Educational Science at the Freie Universität Berlin and Professor Extraordinarius at the University of the Western Cape, South Africa. She is the founder of Boxgirls International, an organisation that has received many awards, including the Sonderpreis der Bundeskanzlerin as part of the startsocial competition. In 2010 the German Association of University Professors and Lecturers named her University Lecturer of the Year for her 'professional and extra-curricular engagement', and its exceptional impact on increasing public awareness and appreciation of her profession.

Can gold medals increase a country's prestige? Due to a lack of commercial interest, many Olympic sports can only be successfully and professionally run with the help of state funding. But what benefits do medals and victories actually bring to the nations involved? Does success in Olympic sports actually have a positive impact on people's perceptions of a country? And does elite sport actually promote mass sport? *By Jan Haut*

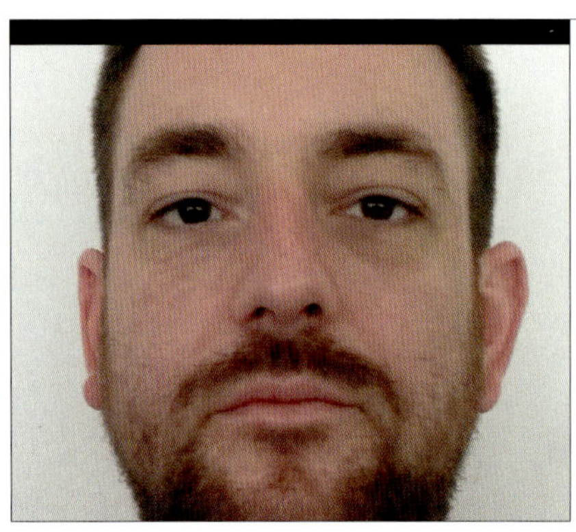

As we know, the GDR was particularly involved in developing a state sports system that had a major impact on the nature and direction of Olympic sport, all in an effort to gain international recognition and demonstrate its superiority over the West. This system included well thought-out and highly organised doping practices, along with legal measures to identify and train talented children and young athletes. State funding was funnelled into those sports that offered the best chances of winning medals. The GDR and the Cold War may be long gone, but many of their strategies have been adopted by other countries around the world – not just China and North Korea, but also many 'Western' nations.

Britain is now viewed as a key example in this respect. After many years of poor perfor-mances, it is once again an Olympic superpower, thanks to a 'no compromise' strategy that involves pouring money into sports that offer a good chance of victory, while totally with-drawing support from other less successful sports. According to the German Minister of the Interior, Germany will also undertake a programme of far-reaching reforms after the Rio Olympics, and it is likely to focus more strongly on sports that offer the best chance of winning medals.

Leaving the moral aspects aside for a moment, let us look at the actual effectiveness of this kind of sports policy strategy. Does success in Olympic sports actually have the same positive impact on people's perceptions of a country, as is the case with football? The initial answer is: it depends. Winter sports naturally involve a much smaller circle of nations who can participate in competitions. But the different sporting disciplines at the summer Olympic games are also followed with varying degrees of interest around the world. Surveys suggest that many Germans still view win-ning medals in athletics and swimming as far more important than success in other sports – and these two disciplines are generally the ones that attract the largest viewing figures.

Globally, the 100-metre sprint (especially the men's) is considered to be much more prestigious than, say, the light welterweight boxing competition.

Then again, you wonder whether Germany's strong medal tally in canoeing has much influence on the global perception of the country, particularly as interest in this sport mainly comes from Eastern Europe and other nations that pursue a wide range of sports (though not the USA). In short, apart from a few globally popular competitions, international audiences are very much focused on specific sports and can vary significantly in size. This means that the potential for attracting international attention and improving a country's image through sporting success also varies widely from sport to sport.

Germany's sports policy is generally not interested in such subtle distinctions, as the government does not support individual sports, but leaves the distribution of funding to the German Olympic Sports Confederation (DSOB). Success is generally measured in terms of the overall medal haul and the country's position on the medal table. Igno-

Britain is now viewed as a key example in this respect. After many years of poor performances, it is once again an Olympic superpower, thanks to a 'no compromise' strategy that involves pouring money into sports that offer a good chance of victory, while totally withdrawing support from other less successful sports.

ring the fact that this is not considered an official ranking by the IOC – Rule 57 of the Olympic Charter prohibits the drawing up of any global ranking by country in order to avoid international disputes and sporting arms races – the medal table still provides an abstract form of ranking that offers other, more limited, benefits in terms of prestige.

Unknown Chinese athletes

As our Dutch colleagues have remarked: medal tables don't tell any stories! That is left to the individual competitions, and to the competitors and teams involved. Chinese athletes continue to be unknown, despite the fact that they won 100 medals in front of their home crowd (including 51 gold medals), with China topping the medal table. However, one story that many people remember is one of failure, namely that of the hurdler Liu Xiang, who as defending champion was forced to drop out of the competition at the last minute due to injury.

It is 'Olympic moments' like these that stir up our emotions and remain in our memories for years to come – no matter where we live. They cannot be planned, whatever a country's sports policy, nor can they be identified from a scan through the medal table.

People were asked to think back to the last Olympics and say whether individual sportsmen and women, or even countries as a whole, evoked negative memories. China, the most successful nation in 2008, was the country most often cited by a long, long way, not only because of suspicions of doping, but also because respondents felt that China's young sportsmen and women were being instrumentalised and drilled too hard.

Obeying the rules

So turning sporting success into international prestige must begin by obeying the rules. Whether that is actually the case on the field of play is now a lot easier for the viewer to determine thanks to today's sophisticated technology. But whether everything is done properly off the field of play, that is to say during preparation and training, can only be determined to a limited extent because of the lack of an effective global monitoring system.

The question international sports fans have to ask themselves is whether they trust a particular athlete, country and sports system. This question of confidence when it comes to sporting success has been highlighted in certain remarks about Jamaican sprinter Usain Bolt. In the survey mentioned above, Bolt was the international athlete who was most often mentioned for evoking positive memories. But he was also came second when it came to evoking negative memories because many people found it hard to believe that he could turn in such performances and still be 'clean'.

However, in sport, especially Olympic sport, being 'clean' is generally a necessary, but not always sufficient, prerequisite for success to be recognised. When it comes to abiding by the rules, many people in many countries (precise data on this issue is lacking) also expect adherence to the informal principles of fair play. The word 'Olympic' stands for the promise of respectful, peaceful, 'humane' competition, in which success should not be achieved at the expense of all other values.

At least this is what it once claimed to stand for (similar to the Fairtrade label on food).

Of course, these expectations do not only extend to the behaviour of individual sportsmen and women in specific competitive situations, but also to the more abstract competition that takes place amongst nations, and not least to the way countries' sports systems and officials deal with their own athletes. As a result, the sporting success that emanates from the hosting of major sports events by countries with dubious regimes is not necessarily met with blanket international enthusiasm, especially if it is perceived that certain standards have not been maintained.

Conversely, democratic states that also push the boundaries of these standards in an attempt to maximise success and improve their self-image also run the risk of alienating their own sporting population. The reason so many cities in Western democracies are increasingly reluctant to host the Olympics is not because the people of Hamburg, Oslo or Boston have lost interest in sport per se – the people of these cities are actually significant-

The reason so many cities in Western democracies are increasingly reluctant to host the Olympics is not because the people of Hamburg, Oslo or Boston have lost interest in sport per se – the people of these cities are actually significantly more active than ever before – but because they are evidently not interested in the kind of sport that the IOC stands for.

ly more active than ever before – but because they are evidently not interested in the kind of sport that the IOC stands for.

Striving for legitimacy

The same applies to the other promises that are made to justify funding and support for elite sport. For example, there is no empirical evidence to support the idea that sporting success leads to a lasting sense of patriotism or national pride. Football is somewhat less vulnerable to outside influence by the state due to its commercial success and can therefore project a more realistic image of human endeavour ('first food, then morals'), whereas Olympic sport (or many of the sports represented at the Olympics at least) relies much more heavily on public funding and therefore tries much harder to prove its legitimacy through its apparent or actual social achievements.

It also cannot be proved that success in elite sport leads to more people taking up sport. If sport is a public affair (and if it is funded by the state, then it definitely is), then it is important to ask what sport we really want. What role should the chances of success really play and what emphasis should be placed on other considerations? Of course foreign policy issues should be included in any such debate. And we can certainly discount the idea that 'the more we win, the more people will love us'.

Jan Haut is a lecturer and researcher at the Institute of Sports Sciences at the Goethe University of Frankfurt in Germany. His main areas of study include the societal role of competitive sports, the social theory and social history of sport, social inequalities in sport, and sport and culture.

The rules of the global game When sport has been reduced to watching great guys doing great things on TV while we munch some goodies and have a beer, it is not only sport, but culture in its wider sense that has become a producer and consumer affair, rather than something that create ourselves. Meanwhile, the Olympics and MSN (Messi, Suarez, Neymar for the illiterate) will keep us busy on our couches. *By Ladislau Dowbor*

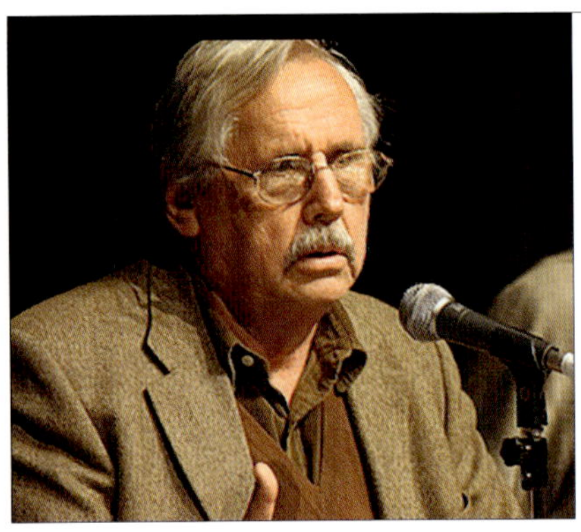

It is hard to refrain from thinking that we are living in a giant circus. As we sit on a couch after a bizarre day of working and hours of commuting, the surreal soap operas on TV bring us an overview of the global game: so many bombs over Syria, more refugees at the borders, the troubles with big finance, the latest goals from Lewandowski, the discussion over whether Russia should participate in the Olympics in Brazil, or whether Rio de Janeiro will get everything ready in time. Oh yes, and who, after Hungary, Greece, Poland and the UK is threatening to leave the EU, in the name of superior national ideals.

It sure is some game. Reports by Crédit Suisse and Oxfam show us the huge divide between the owners of the game and the spectators: 62 billionaires own more wealth than the poorest 50 percent of the world's population. Did they produce all this? Evidently, it all depends on what part you play in the game. In São Paulo the very rich who crowd into the Alphaville condominium are fenced and guarded, while the poor residents of the neighbourhood call themselves Alphavella. Someone has to cut the grass and deliver the groceries.

According to the WWF's global report on wildlife destruction, 52% disappeared during the 40 years from 1970 to 2010. Many water sources are contaminated or are drying up. The oceans are crying for help, air-conditioning is booming. Forests are being cut down in Indonesia, which has taken over from the Amazon region as the world's number one region for deforestation. Europe has to have renewable energy, cheap meat and beautiful mahogany.

The Tax Justice Network has shown that some \$30 trillion are held in tax havens, compared to a global GDP of \$73 trillion in 2012. The Bank for International Settlements in Basel shows us that outstanding derivatives, the speculation system on basic commodities, reached \$630 trillion, generating the yo-yo effect in the prices of basic economic staples. The biggest game on the planet involves grain, ferrous and non-ferrous minerals, and energy. These commodities are basically in the hands of 16 corporations, most of whom are formally headquartered in Geneva, as revealed by Jean Ziegler in 'La Suisse Lave Plus Blanc'. There is no referee in this game, we are in a guarded environment. The French have an excellent description of our times: on vit une époque formidable!

We did a thorough job in 2015: a global assessment on how to finance development in Addis Ababa, the sustainable development goals for 2030 in New York, and the compact on climate change in Paris. The challenges, solutions and costs have been clearly set out. Our global equation is simple enough to formulate: the trillions in financial speculation have to be redirected to fund social inclusion, and to promote the technological paradigm change that will allow us to save the planet. And ourselves, of course.

But to stimulate the players, it is the wolves of Wall Street who have drawn up the moral code for this sport: Greed is Good!

Drowning in statistics

We are drowning in statistics. The World Bank suggests we should do something about the next four billion, meaning the number of human beings who have 'no access to the

Money at the top generates fabulously rich degenerates who will buy football clubs, before finally thinking about the future in their old age and creating an NGO. Just in case.

benefits of globalisation', a quite tactful reference to the poor. We also have the billions who live on less than two dollars a day, and even the billion living on less than $1.25 a day. FAO shows us in great detail where the world's 800 million hungry people are located, Unicef counts the roughly 5 million children who die each year because of insufficient access to food or clean water. That's about four New York towers a day, but they die in silence in poor places, and their parents are helpless.

Things are improving, certainly, but the trouble is we have 80 million more people every year – roughly the population of Egypt – and growing. A reminder will help, for no one really grasps what a billion is: when my father was born, in 1900, we were 1.5 billion, now we are 7.2 billion. I am not speaking of ancient history, this is my father. And since it is not in our everyday experience to grasp what a billionaire is, here's another image: if you invest a billion dollars in some fund that pays a paltry 5 percent interest, you earn $137,000 dollars a day. There is no way you can spend that, so you feed more financial circuits, getting more fabulously rich and feeding more financial operators.

Investing in financial products pays more than investing in the production of goods and services – like the good old useful capitalists did – so there is no way that access to money will stabilise, much less trickle down. Money has a natural attraction to where it will best multiply, it is part of its nature, and of bankers' natures. Money in the hands of the bottom of the pyramid generates consumption, productive investment, products and jobs.

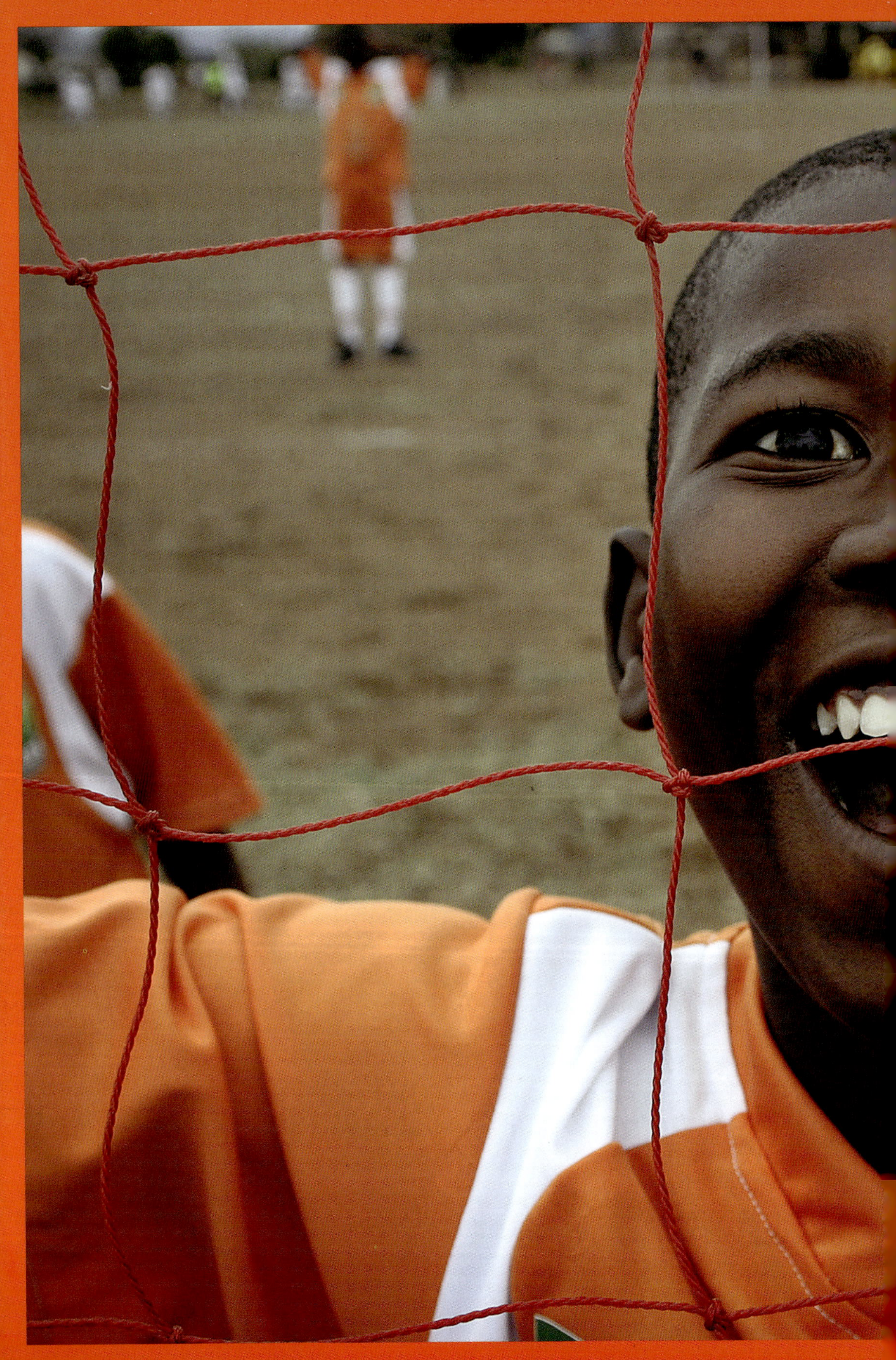

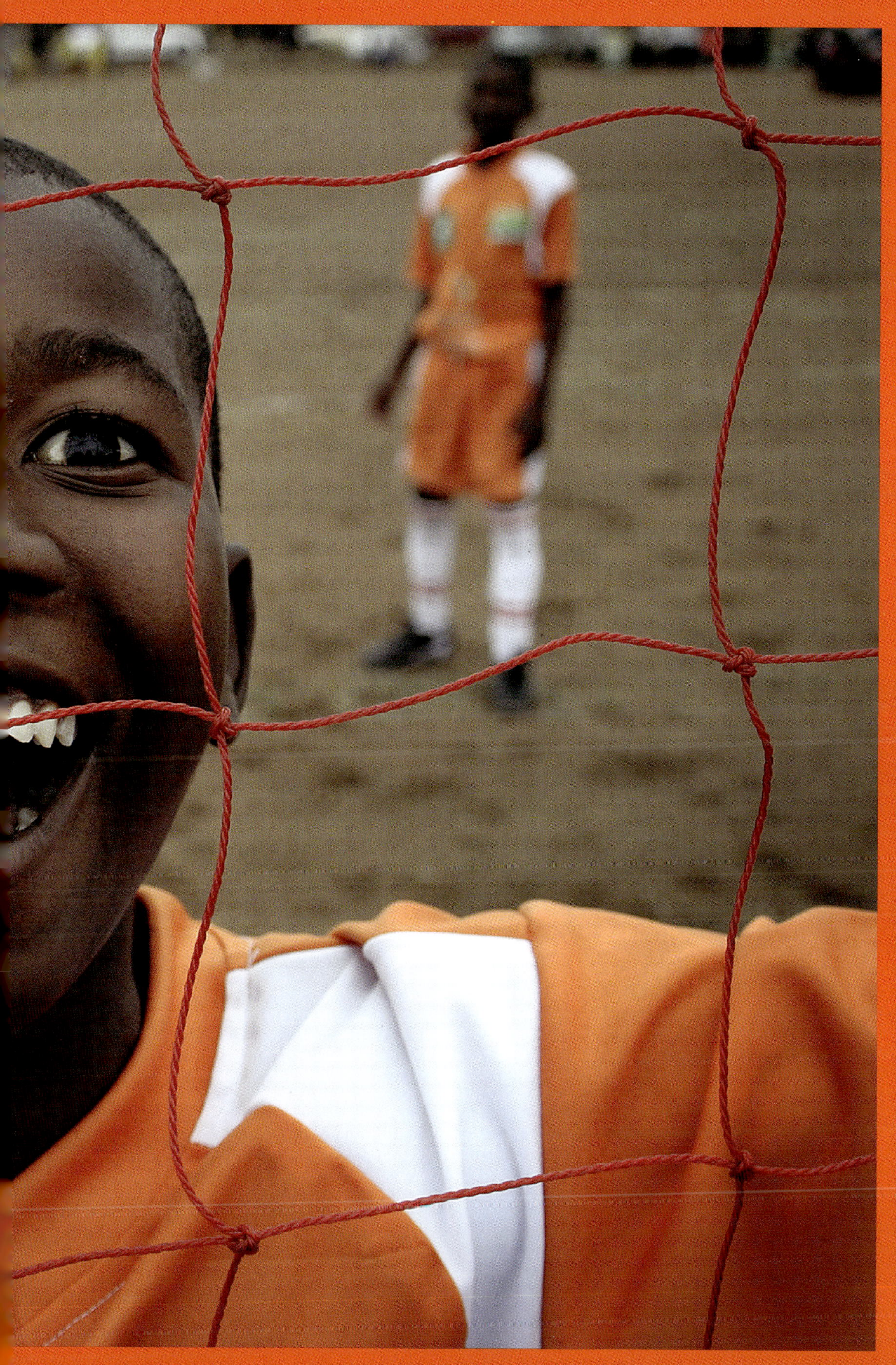

Money at the top generates fabulously rich degenerates who will buy football clubs, before finally thinking about the future in their old age and creating an NGO. Just in case.

A global fix

Many people understand that the rules of the game are rigged. It is time for a global fix when these same fabulously rich people donate to politicians and promote legislation to suit their growing needs, making speculation, tax evasion and overall instability a structural and legal process. Lester Brown did his environmental sums and wrote 'Plan B', clearly showing that our present Plan A is dead. Gus Speth, Gar Alperovitz, Jeffrey Sachs and many others are working on 'The Next System', implying and showing the present system has gone beyond its own limits.

Joseph Stiglitz and a score of economists launched 'An Agenda for Shared Prosperity', rejecting 'the old economic models': according to their view, 'equality and economic performance constitute in reality complementary and not opposing forces'. France created its Alternatives Economiques movement; we have the New Economics Foundation in the UK; and students of traditional economics are boycotting their studies at Harvard and other top universities. Mehr licht!

And the poor, very clearly, are fed up with this game. There remain very few isolated and ignorant peasants ready to be satisfied with their lot, whatever that may be. Poor people around the world are increasingly aware that they could have a good school for their kids,

How can we expect to have peace across the lake we call the Mediterranean if 70% of the jobs are informal, and youth unemployment is over 40%? And on TV they are watching the leisure and prosperity just across the sea in Nice?

and a decent hospital for them to be born in. And besides, they see this can work on TV: in Brazil 97% of households have TV sets, even if they have no decent sanitation.

How can we expect to have peace across the lake we call the Mediterranean if 70% of the jobs are informal, and youth unemployment is over 40%? And on TV they are watching the leisure and prosperity just across the sea in Nice? We bombard them with ways of life that are out of their economic reach. None of this makes sense, and on a shrinking planet, it is explosive. We are condemned to live together, the world is flat, the challenges are for all of us, and the initiative must come from the better off. And, fortunately enough, the poor are not what they were any more.

Culture and conviviality

I have always taken a much wider view of culture than the 'Ach! said Bach!' tradition. I think it includes having fun with others, whether building or writing something, or just fooling around. Conviviality. I recently spent some time in Warsaw. Summer weekends, the parks and squares full of people, and cultural activities everywhere. In the open air, with lots of people sitting on the ground or on simple plastic chairs, a theatre troupe was playing a parody of the way we treat old people. Little money, lots of fun. Just a little further on, in different parts of the Lazienki park, numerous groups were playing jazz or classical music, people were sitting on the grass or on improvised seats, and kids were running around.

In Brazil, with Gilberto Gil at the ministry of culture, a new Pontos de Cultura policy was created. This meant that any group of youngsters who wanted to form a band could ask for support, be given musical instruments or whatever they needed, and organise shows or produce online. Thousands of groups sprang up – stimulating creativity only requires a little scratch, it seem s that the young have it under their skin.

The policy was strongly attacked by the music industry, saying we were taking the bread out of the mouths of professional artists. They don't want culture, they want an entertainment industry, and business. Fortunately, this is breaking down. Or at least, cultural life is springing back. Business has an impressive capacity for being a killjoy.

The carnival in São Paulo, in 2016, was incredible. Coming full circle, street carnival and improvised, unleashed creativity is now back on the streets, after having been

The entertainment carnival is there, of course, and tourists pay to sit and watch the dazzling and rich show, but the real fun is elsewhere, where the right for everyone to dance and sing has been taken back.

tamed and transformed into disciplined and expensive showbusiness by the Rede Globo communication mogul. People were out improvising hundreds of events throughout the city, once again it was a popular chaos, as it had never ceased to be in Salvador, Recife and other poorer regions of the country. The entertainment carnival is there, of course, and tourists pay to sit and watch the dazzling and rich show, but the real fun is elsewhere, where the right for everyone to dance and sing has been taken back.

A consumer affair

I used to play football pretty well, and I would go with my father to watch Corinthians play in the traditional Pacaembu stadium in São Paulo. Magic moments, life-long memories. But mostly we played among ourselves, wherever and whenever we could, with real or improvised balls. This is not nostalgia for the good old days, rather a confused feeling that when sport has been reduced to watching great guys doing great things on TV, while we munch some goodies and have a beer, it is not only sport, but culture in its wider sense that has become a producer and consumer affair, not something we create ourselves.

In Toronto, I was amazed to see lots of people playing in so many places, kids and old folks, because open public spaces can be found everywhere. Apparently, in sports anyway, they are surviving through having fun together. But this obviously is not the mainstream. The entertainment industry has penetrated every home in the world, every computer, every cell phone, waiting rooms, buses. We are a terminal, a node in the extension of a kind of giant and strange global chatter. This global chatter, with evident exceptions, is funded by advertising.

The huge advertising industry is funded basically by a handful of corporate giants whose survival and expansion strategy is based on people becoming essentially consumers. The system works because we dutifully adopt obsessive consumer behaviours instead of playing music, painting a landscape, singing with a bunch of friends, playing football, or swimming in a public pool with our kids.

A bunch of consumer suckers

What a bunch of consumer suckers we are, with our two-or-three room apartment, sofa, TV, computer and cell phone, watching what other people do.

Who needs a family? In Brazil marriage lasts 14 years and going down, our average is 3.1 persons per household. Europe is ahead of us, 2.4 per household. In the US only 25% of households are made up of a couple with kids. Same in Sweden. Obesity is booming, thanks to the sofa, the fridge, the TV set and the goodies. Also booming is child obesity surgery, a tribute to consumerism. And you can buy a wrist-watch that will tell you how fast your heart is beating after you have walked two blocks. And a message has already been sent to your doctor.

What is this all about? I see culture as the way we organise our lives. Family, work, sports, music, dancing, everything that tells me whether my life is worth living. I read books, and have a siesta after lunch as any civilised human being should. All mammals sleep after eating, we are the only ridiculous biped who rushes off to work. Well, of course, there is this bloody GDP business. All the really pleasant things I mentioned do not raise GDP, much less my siesta hammock. They only raise our quality of life. And GDP is so important that the UK has included estimates of prostitution and drug sales so as to improve the rate of growth figures. Considering the kind of life we are building, maybe they are right.

We need a reality check. The wretched of the earth will not disappear, building walls and fences will not solve anything, the climate disaster will not go away unless we face our technological and energy mix, money will not flow where it should unless we regulate, people will not create a political

The system works because we dutifully adopt obsessive consumer behaviours instead of playing music, painting a landscape, singing with a bunch of friends, playing football, or swimming in a public pool with our kids.

force strong enough to support the necessary changes unless they are effectively informed on our structural challenges. Meanwhile, the Olympics and MSN (Messi, Suarez, Neymar for the illiterate) will keep us busy on our couches. As it will, quite frankly, the author of these lines. Sursum corda.

Ladislau Dowbor is an economist. He teaches at the Catholic University of São Paulo, works with numerous government and non-profit institutions, and with different agencies of the United Nations. He is the author of more than 40 books and of a number of technical studies in the area of development planning. His publications are posted in full on the http://dowbor.org website, free for non-commercial use (Creative Commons). For those with a sense of humour, an updated and revised edition of the Ten Commandments can be read at http://dowbor.org/2010/04/the-ten-commandments-apr.html/

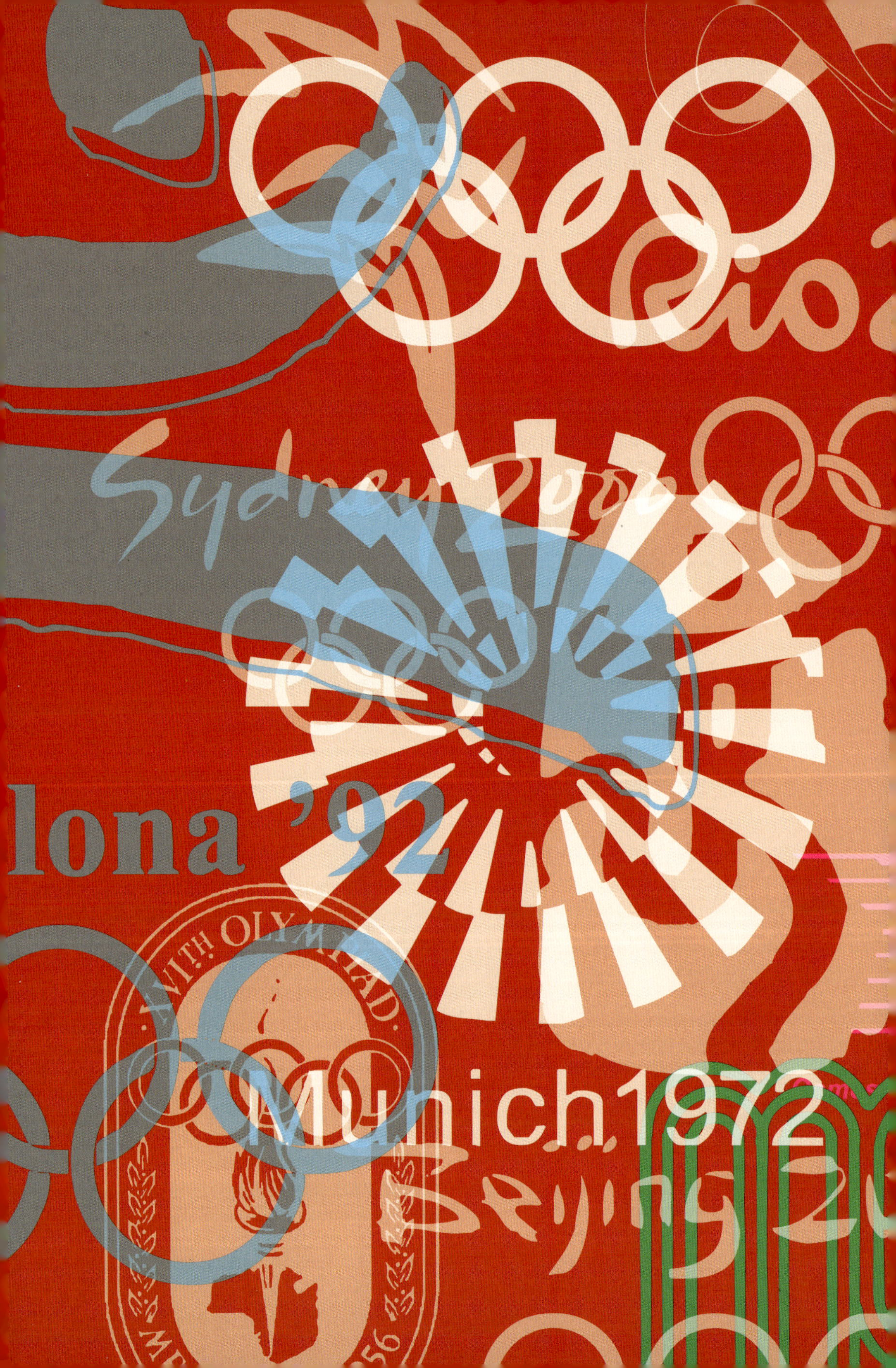

Sydney 2000
lona '92
Munich 1972
XVITH OLYMPIAD

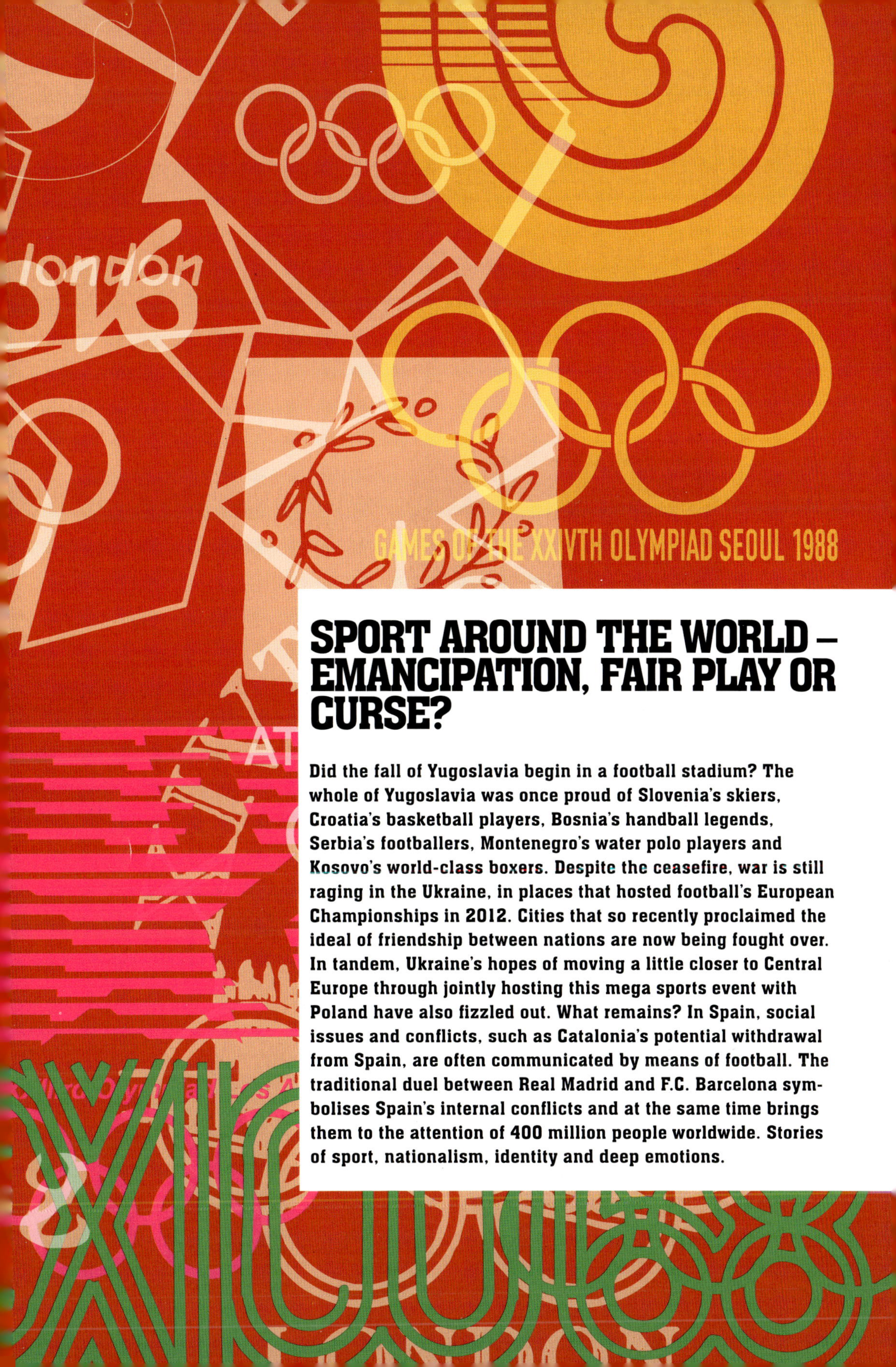

SPORT AROUND THE WORLD – EMANCIPATION, FAIR PLAY OR CURSE?

Did the fall of Yugoslavia begin in a football stadium? The whole of Yugoslavia was once proud of Slovenia's skiers, Croatia's basketball players, Bosnia's handball legends, Serbia's footballers, Montenegro's water polo players and Kosovo's world-class boxers. Despite the ceasefire, war is still raging in the Ukraine, in places that hosted football's European Championships in 2012. Cities that so recently proclaimed the ideal of friendship between nations are now being fought over. In tandem, Ukraine's hopes of moving a little closer to Central Europe through jointly hosting this mega sports event with Poland have also fizzled out. What remains? In Spain, social issues and conflicts, such as Catalonia's potential withdrawal from Spain, are often communicated by means of football. The traditional duel between Real Madrid and F.C. Barcelona symbolises Spain's internal conflicts and at the same time brings them to the attention of 400 million people worldwide. Stories of sport, nationalism, identity and deep emotions.

Sport is also war The whole of Yugoslavia was once proud of Slovenia's skiers, Croatia's basketball players, Bosnia's handball legends, Serbia's footballers, Montenegro's water polo players and Kosovo's world-class boxers. In sports halls and football stadiums, for many years sport provided a gauge for measuring of the mood of the nation. But in the 1990s this was suddenly a thing of the past. The gauge was broken. *By Beqë Cufaj*

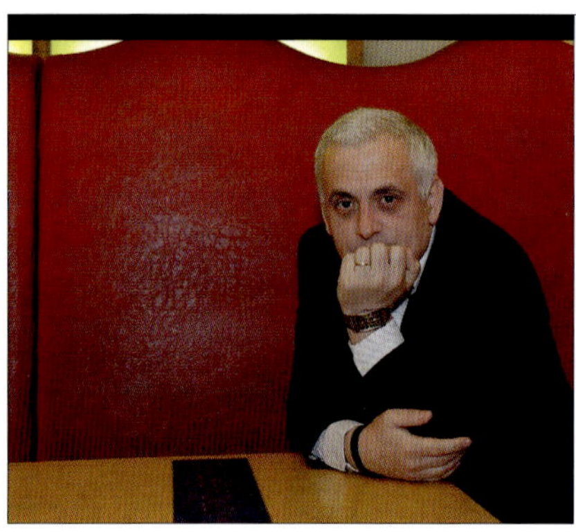

26 years on, I don't remember exactly where I was on 13 May 1990. What I do know is that I was a student during that spring and I was feeling very excited about starting a new chapter of my life in a new world that was filled with joy, but also with sadness, and the fear that the political situation in Kosovo and Yugoslavia as a whole had fundamentally and ominously changed.

By the end of the Second World War, Kosovo had not only suffered the worst destruction but was also the least developed region in the new state of Yugoslavia. The latter was made up of six republics: Serbia, Montenegro, Croatia, Bosnia, Macedonia and Slovenia, and the two autonomous provinces of Kosovo and Vojvodina. It was home to 22 million people, with Albanians being the largest minority. Numbering around 3

million, they lived in Kosovo in southern Serbia and also in parts of Macedonia and Montenegro.

The Albanians differed from their neighbours and fellow citizens in that they did not speak a Slavic language. So whereas Slovenians had few problems understanding Macedonians, and the difference between the Croat and Serb languages is similar to the difference between the German spoken by Bavarians and Berliners, the Albanians in the socialist state of Yugoslavia did not feel that they were automatically integrated into the new multi-ethnic state. Quite the opposite, in fact. The Albanians had the country's highest illiteracy rate – 97% of this mostly rural population could neither read nor write – and had a fundamentally hostile attitude towards the Slavs, a feeling that was reciprocated. Many Albanians had converted to Islam during the centuries of Ottoman rule in order to preserve their national identity and language. This all meant that the circumstances were hardly ideal for a peaceful coexistence with the Slavs.

On top of this, almost half of all Albanians were living outside Albania. The king collaborated with Mussolini's fascists and the German forces during the Second World

War. When the war ended, he was forced out and the country joined the ranks of communist states.

A history of separation

The history of separation began, and its effects were felt not only by Albanians and their neighbours, but by the whole of Europe eight years ago, when the world's newest state, Kosovo, announced its independence.

The Albanians in former Yugoslavia were largely uneducated and lived in a very patriarchal society. Some were Muslims, some were Catholics, and their rituals were very different from those of their Slavic, Orthodox neighbours. Yugoslavia's communists, with Marshal Tito at their head, diagnosed their malaise as illiteracy, a problem that had to be tackled with the utmost urgency. A campaign was launched to 'educate the Albanians', motivated by communist ideologies and a dangerous upsurge of nationalism and separatism. Hundreds and then thousands of Albanians were admitted to colleges and universities in the former Yugoslavia. From Ljubljana to Zagreb, Sarajevo and particu-

From Ljubljana to Zagreb, Sarajevo and particularly Belgrade, skilled workers were trained with a view to returning them to the Kosovan capital of Pristina once they had qualified as teachers, doctors, army officers, writers, or sports trainers, so that they could pass on their education to the masses.

larly Belgrade, skilled workers were trained with a view to returning them to the Kosovan capital of Pristina once they had qualified as teachers, doctors, army officers, writers, or sports trainers, so that they could pass on their education to the masses. This was a sign of their strong interest in accepting coexistence with the Slavs as long as they were accorded certain rights. They were awaited by a communist government that was aiming to build a country and integrate them into its multi-ethnic body.

Educating ethnic Albanians at top universities led to something that few people ever expected in the wake of the Second World War. In the early 1970s a university was established in Pristina, which offered a range of basic subjects and opened its doors to thousands of Albanian students. Now they no longer had to travel to other parts of the country in order to get an education. But this all came to an end when Slobodan Milosevic withdrew the province's autonomy.

After my military service in the Yugoslavian army – at the time the fourth largest in Europe – I returned to Kosovo and my hometown of Pristina, where suddenly everything had changed. The new Serbian president Slobodan Milosevic had revoked Kosovo's autonomy. Other republics such as Slovenia, Croatia, Bosnia and Herzegovina, Montenegro and Macedonia had introduced new multi-party systems without any undue upheaval. In each federal state, communists turned into socialists or social democrats, and the remaining parties consisted of groups with strong nationalistic tendencies who added the suffix 'democratic'. In other words, they were preparing for the dissolution of Yugoslavia and the independence of the republics. It all began with the expansionism of Belgrade and the leader of the Serbian communists, Slobodan Milosevic. Unlike the others, they had discovered a simple formula with a terrible resonance – the combination of nationalism and socialism.

Traumatised and shocked, Albanians soon found themselves being barred from state institutions, universities, bureaucracy, the health system, schools and sports arenas. Huge battles broke out about the 'national' and 'ethnic' supremacy of the three largest groups, the Serbs, Croats and Slovenians. Multi-ethnic Yugoslavia was made up of eight federal republics that were presented to the world as one nation in every area, from sport to foreign policy.

Libertarian autocracy

The fact that this succeeded was down to the libertarian autocrat Josip Broz Tito. He held together this model of socialism for 40 years, albeit with an iron fist, and at the same time achieved the impressive feat of keeping his distance from the Soviets and the Chinese. He invented the concept of communal and industrial 'self-management', which combined an external touch of socialism with an internal hint of capitalism and provided the formula for the 'third way'. In this way it drew certain elements from America and others from the Soviet Union. Until the 1980s this policy meant that Yugoslavia had a stronger economy than countries like Greece and Portugal.

But by 1990 the country had left behind the paradise of the Tito era, the Cold War was over, and the strong economic ties that Yugoslavia had built with competitors in both East and West were now crumbling.

Economic difficulties led to competition for resources, and to envy and petty jealousies between the main groups. The tremors could now be felt throughout the multi-ethnic state. Socialists were transformed into 'Serbs' with a dash of 'socialist' and a big dose of 'national'.

The Croats and Slovenians experienced similar changes. In Serbia the communist apparatchik Milosevic gained broad support. He was seen as the right man to lead the whole nation in the name of Serbia. With terrible speed he used his powers to instigate something that no one believed possible: new wars. Fratricidal, civil wars in their own country.

After the fall of the Iron Curtain, this happened in many other countries of former Eastern Europe. In Washington, London, Paris and Bonn it was assumed that non-aligned Yugoslavia would find the transition much easier than other countries in Eastern Europe. This proved to be a bitter mistake, and a naive one.

What was known as the great Yugoslavian nation began to devour itself from the inside. And this was clearly reflected in and around sport. The whole of Yugoslavia was once proud of Slovenia's skiers, Croatia's basketball players, Bosnia's handball legends, Serbia's footballers, Montenegro's water polo players and Kosovo's world-class boxers. But now it was clear that Slovenians played for Slovenia, and Serbs played football for Serbia – not for Yugoslavia. Until the end of the 1980s, sporting champions all proudly and visibly bore the flag of Yugoslavia. They were hailed as heroes in their own republics and were respected athletes throughout the country. But all this gradually stopped when nationalism began to spread its tentacles.

A mini global power

From 1945 to 1990 Yugoslavia's athletes were world-famous, a kind of mini global power at international sporting competitions. Sport was an intrinsic element of the lives of all young people. In the country's interior, it was an essential part of everyday life, and weekends were all about football. There had long been a National Football League that included teams from different parts of the country – but now old rivalries and enmities were once again rearing their ugly heads. Sport made it very obvious that old animosities between Croats and Serbs or Albanians and Serbs were intensifying.

These enmities were leftovers from the First and Second World Wars. Tito's regime swept unresolved conflicts and unsolved crimes under the carpet for the sake of maintaining social harmony, but after his death they returned to the people of former Yugoslavia, and now they were no longer shrouded in the ideology of fraternity and unity (Bratsvo i Jedinstvo). In sports halls and football stadiums, for many years sport had provided a gauge for measuring the mood of the nation. But now this was a thing of the past. The gauge was broken.

Sport was an intrinsic element of the lives of all young people. In the country's interior, it was an essential part of everyday life, and weekends were all about football.

While Poles, Czechs, Slovaks, Bulgarians, Romanians and other nations were finding ways of setting up multi-party systems in a relatively peaceful manner, a new wind was sweeping through Yugoslavia's new parties – and it was to turn into a hurricane. This was becoming clearer with every day that passed. We could read it in the political reports in the newspapers, and in the evenings we watched it on TV in our living rooms – the emotional and national fracturing of the Yugoslavian state had become normalised madness. Sports arenas became the place to unleash political frustrations and ambitions, and the former communist cadres took full advantage of this. Just like in the Cold War, these dramatic conflicts began with signs and moods – until the point where everything got out of hand and the real battle, the hot war, began.

It all started in a stadium

Unbelievably, the battle began on 13 May 1990 in a football stadium. But first let's remember the events of exactly 10 years earlier. On 4 May 1980, just after 3pm, it was announced that Josip Broz Tito had passed away. In the Croatian coastal town of Split, the 22 footballers of opposing teams hugged each other, sat on the pitch and cried. The match was between Croatia's famous Hajduk team and Serbia's historic Crvena Zvezda club, Red Star Belgrade.

Ten years later, on 13 May 1990, a match was being played in Zagreb, the Croatian capital, between two great rivals: Serbia's Red

Star and Croatia's Dinamo Zagreb. The game escalated and went down in history as one of the events that marked and symbolised the beginning of the end for Tito's Yugoslavia. Serbian and Croatian fans went on a rampage, leaving 79 police officers and 59 spectators injured. It was a miracle that no one died among the dozens of people who were injured, some critically.

The game was supposed to be played in the Maksimir stadium on that Sunday afternoon. But it never happened. Before the match started the BBB (Bad Blue Boys) fans of Dinamo and the Delije (Heroes) fans of Zvezda began fighting. The police were outnumbered and totally unprepared. They intervened but either could not (the Serbian version) or did not want (the Croatian version) to separate the fans. Instead they were drawn into the fighting. As the police officers were mainly Serbs, Croatian politicians used the events surrounding this match as an excuse for carrying out ethnic 'cleansings' within the police force.

The situation escalated 40 minutes before the game, when the players were warming up on the pitch. Thousands of right-wing BBB fans stormed the pitch and ran towards the south stand, which was already full of Delije fans and adorned with Serbian symbols. The Red Star players, led by captain Dragan 'Piksi' Stojkovic, fled back to their changing room. A few Dinamo players stayed on the pitch. Zvonimir Boban, a Croatian player, became something of a hero when he kung-fu kicked a policeman and then made himself scarce. The crowd roared 'Boban-e, Boban-e!' – the 'e' at the end of his name is the vocative case in Serbo-Croat. For Croatian nationalists this kick became a symbol of their resistance to the hated Belgrade regime. A little irony of history is that the police officer attacked by Boban was a Croat.

For many footballers and citizens, the 13th of May was the spark that lit the flame. For days afterwards, the events in the Maksimir stadium dominated the conversation in newspapers, pubs, offices and factories. Opinions were starkly divided – the Croats laid all the blame on the Serbian fans, while the Serbs claimed the Bad Blue Boys were solely responsible. And above all they saw the events of 13 May 1990 not only as the harbinger of what was to follow, but actually as the start of the war.

This view was echoed by Croatian author Hrvoje Prnjak, also an active member of the BBB, when he wrote: '13 May 1990 stays in our memories as the culmination of many years of tension, which just one year later triggered the real war.' In the real, hot war that followed, football fans could be found on the front line. They were some of the first volunteers who signed up to 'defend' their country and their people. And they often headed for the front armed with the flags and symbols of their clubs.

Along with the BBB fan group and Torcida from Hajduk Split on the Croatian side, they were predominantly from Delije on the Serbian side. The leader of the Delije fans was Zeljko Raznatovic, who later became the irregular soldier and notorious Mafia boss known as Arkan. He gathered Red Star's various fan groups into one unit. When war broke out, many of the Delije fans joined 'Arkan's Tigers', who spread fear during the Yugoslavian civil war of 1991-1995. Arkan, a pastry chef turned career criminal and murderer, was assassinated at a luxury hotel in Belgrade in January 2000. His assassins were sentenced to a total of 120 years in prison, but the background to this killing has never been fully explained.

Despite the furore unleashed by the events of 13 May 1990, they were not really a surprise. In Yugoslavia, it was clear that football fans were not just interested in the game when they flocked to the stadiums. In the late 1980s, when political and ethnic animosities were escalating, the behaviour of many dyed-in-the-wool fans became increasingly nationalistic and whole groups of fans turned into ethnic nationalist movements. The stadiums became their political stage, a place for proclaiming their political and nationalistic propaganda.

Everything that was taboo and forbidden in other areas of society, such as singing national anthems and wearing nationalist symbols, was openly flaunted by fans in the sports arenas. This symbolic communication was characterised by a deep hatred. Sporting rivals were now considered to be members of a hostile political, national and religious group.

In the late 1980s, when political and ethnic animosities were escalating, the behaviour of many dyed-in-the-wool fans became increasingly nationalistic and whole groups of fans turned into ethnic nationalist movements. The stadiums became their political stage, a place for proclaiming their political and nationalistic propaganda.

In Belgrade, Croatian athletes were mocked with crude banners calling them 'Ustashas', Croatian fascist collaborators during the Second World War; and in Zagreb and Split Serbian fans were bombarded with insults such as 'Cigani!' (gypsies) or 'Ubij Srbina!' (Kill the Serbs). And today, little has changed.

In the wake of the mass riots of May 1990 football clubs from Croatia, Slovenia and Kosovo immediately withdrew from the national leagues. They said this was in protest against 'Serbian rule'. 'Yugoslavia' with Serbia at its head was no longer a country. The capitulation of the multi-ethnic state in the Zagreb football stadium marked the beginning of the end for Yugoslavia. The whole world knows what happened next. This huge European drama in the midst of the euphoria triggered by the fall of the Berlin Wall had many acts and many ups and downs.

The dramatic collapse of Yugoslavia was accompanied by a sense of optimism as people looked forward to a bright and peaceful future. And the images of war that shocked Europe were accompanied by dancing Eastern Europeans as they celebrated their liberation from the Soviet Union. In Europe people thought that the horrors of 1941 and 1945 could never be repeated. This meant that they were totally unprepared for the smaller-scale but comparable horrors that dominated the 1990s in Slovenia, Croatia, Bosnia and Herzegovina and Kosovo, involving mass graves, the murder of children and old people, the genocide at Srebrenica, hordes of refugees and aeroplanes bombing bridges and houses.

The destruction of a multi-ethnic state in Europe happened in plain sight – in a country that triggered happy memories for many people in Germany, France, Britain, the USA and Austria. They had visited its beautiful coast as tourists, admired Yugoslavia's top athletes, and heads of government had welcomed the country's autocratic father, Josip Broz Tito. 10 years of brutal war destroyed a country that Europeans felt they knew.

After the end of the war in Kosovo in 1999, new nations emerged as components detached from the former whole. They were societies that had been through terrible suffering, that were inwardly traumatised and now facing an uncertain future.

And now, after all this, the fans in the stadiums no longer have to draw on resentments from the Second World War when they want to insult their neighbours. Now they can look to more recent conflicts. The end of the wars that broke up the country marked the end of direct violence, but also marked the beginning of a deep-rooted social transition with a very nationalistic flavour.

'Knife, Wire, Srebrenica'

On 12 October 2005 the teams from Serbia-Montenegro and Bosnia-Herzegovina met at the Red Star stadium in Belgrade to contest a key qualifying match for the World Cup in Germany. The war in Bosnia-Herzegovina had been over for 10 years. But Serbian hooligans replayed it in the stadium and on the streets of Belgrade in a mini war against the Bosnian fans. 11 people were injured. With gestures and words they threatened the victims of the Bosnian war with a continuation of the brutality. It culminated with Serbian hooligans rolling out a huge banner with the words 'Knife, Wire, Srebrenica', a deliberate insult to the victims of the worst massacre of the Yugoslavian war in 1995.

As if using data from a seismograph, the events in football allow the last 25 years of the former Yugoslavia's history to be reconstructed, including the collapse of its government and society.

The same applies to the events of 10 October 2014 in Belgrade. During a qualifier for the European Championships in Belgrade, Serbian and Albanian players began brawling. The British referee abandoned the game just before half-time. In the 42nd minute a drone flew over the stadium carrying a flag depicting the outline of a – fictitious – Greater Albania. According to the Serbian media, the man behind it was the brother of Albanian Prime Minister Edi Rama, who himself is in favour of reconciliation. His brother set off the drone from the VIP box.

Serbian player Stefan Mitrovic, who plays for the German team SC Freiburg, ripped the flag from the drone as Albanian players piled into him. Angry Serbian fans stormed the pitch and attacked the Albanian players, who tried to flee to the changing room. After an hour's break the Serbian footballers returned to the pitch to say goodbye to their fans. Reports in the Serbian media claimed that the Albanian players had refused to continue with the match. Their condition was that all the – mainly Belgrade – fans should leave the stadium.

According to the Albanian Football Association, UEFA had recommended that no Albanian fans should travel to the game. In return, the following year no Serbian fans were to travel to the game in Tirana. Apparently the national associations had agreed to this.

Relations between the two nations are still strained. With its large Albanian population, Kosovo was part of the former Yugoslavia for many years. It then became part of Serbia, before the final war in 1999 later led to the territory declaring its independence. The riots in the Belgrade stadium in October 2014 initially threatened the planned visit of Albanian Prime Minister Edi Rama to Serbia. On 22 October 2014, he was to be the first Albanian head of government to travel to Belgrade. The visit would have fallen through if it had not been for the calls made by Angela Merkel to Edi Rama in Tirana and Prime Minister Aleksandar Vucic in Serbia.

Now that we are in 2016, have we learned anything? I'm not sure. History repeats itself, and this is also reflected in sport. The fact that the sparks flew in a stadium in the former Yugoslavia and ignited a war perhaps means we are now better able to identify the sports arenas, football grounds and training camps where trouble could be brewing today.

Perhaps we now pay a little more attention to sportsmen and women who are a little too passionate? Venice Flying Services – Huffman Aviation was the name of the flying school attended by Mohammed Atta (33) and Marwan Al-Shehhi (23), who were 'average pilots' according to their instructor. Here they practised their attacks for 'sporting' purposes and later became notorious on 9/11 when they attacked Western lifestyles, security and freedoms. It was a declaration of war that has since escalated to bring us the consequences we see today.

No, it would not be right or fair to brand sport – and certainly not my favourite sport, football – as a troublemaker. Team spirit, fairness, the joy of movement – sport has so many benefits, including fair competition. But it also acts as a seismograph for society. It uncovers and can even promote ambition, rivalry, deceit, hatred, nationalism, fanaticism and megalomania.

It is striking how nowadays people brand athletes as their countries' 'heroes' or as 'losers'. Just like in the Cold War, they seem to be used as a measure of a country's standing. In parallel with this phenomenon, we observe the growth of irrational and dangerous nationalist tendencies and religious fanaticism. We see floods of refugees trailing across fields, at borders, on railway lines and streets, all as a result of this painful trend.

Whenever I think about refugees it reminds me of my schoolfriend in Kosovo, Ismet. Ismet and I were always playing football. We called him 'Žungul' because he was the spitting image of the Yugoslavian legend from Hadjuk in the late 1970s. Nowadays it would be like having a friend who looked like Cristiano Ronaldo. Ismet was a huge

It would not be right to brand sport as a troublemaker. Team spirit, fairness, the joy of movement – sport has so many benefits, including fair competition. But it can also uncover and can even promote ambition, rivalry, deceit, hatred, nationalism, fanaticism and megalomania.

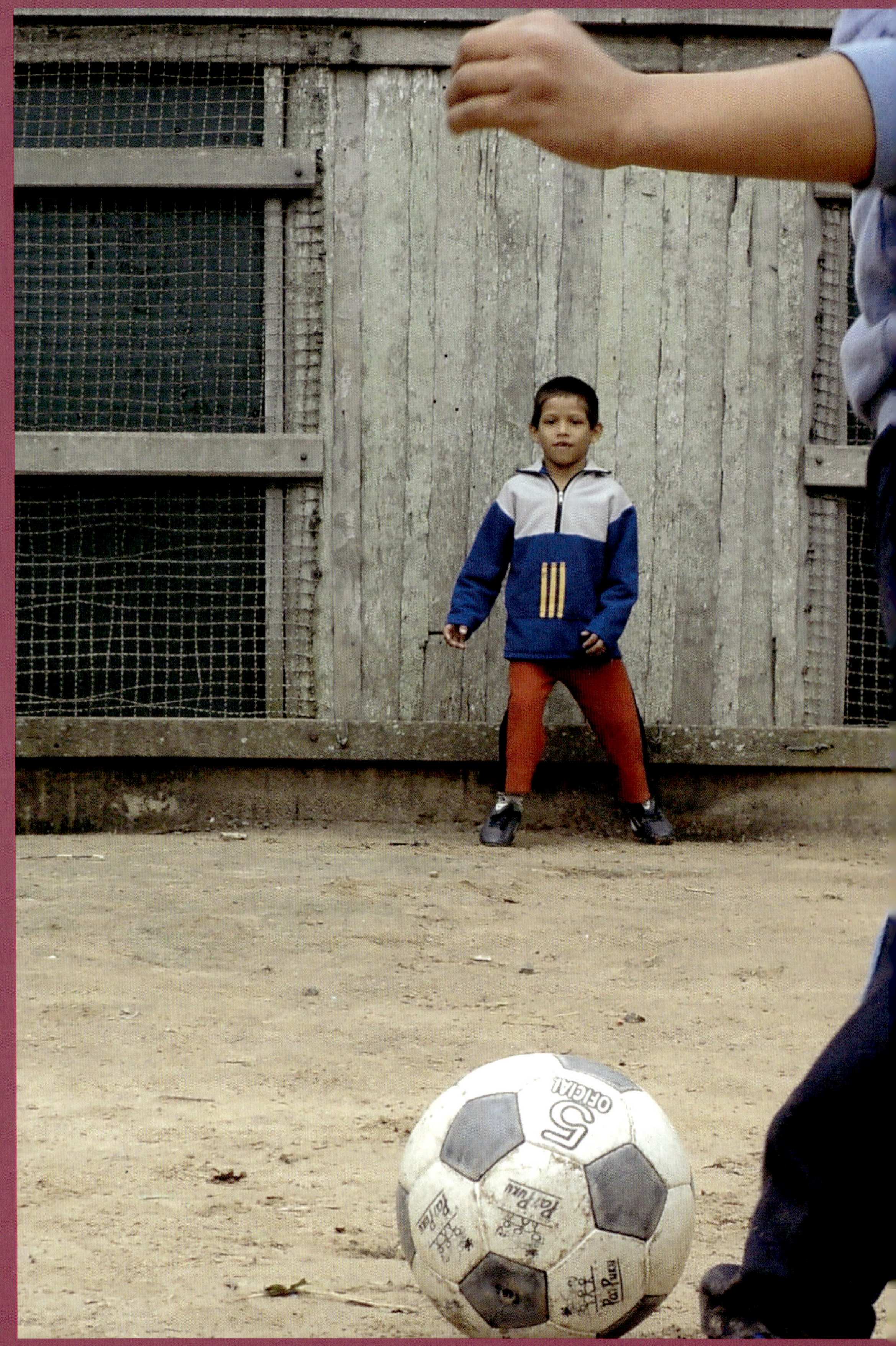

OFICIAL
5
Pai Puku
Pai Puku
Pai Puku

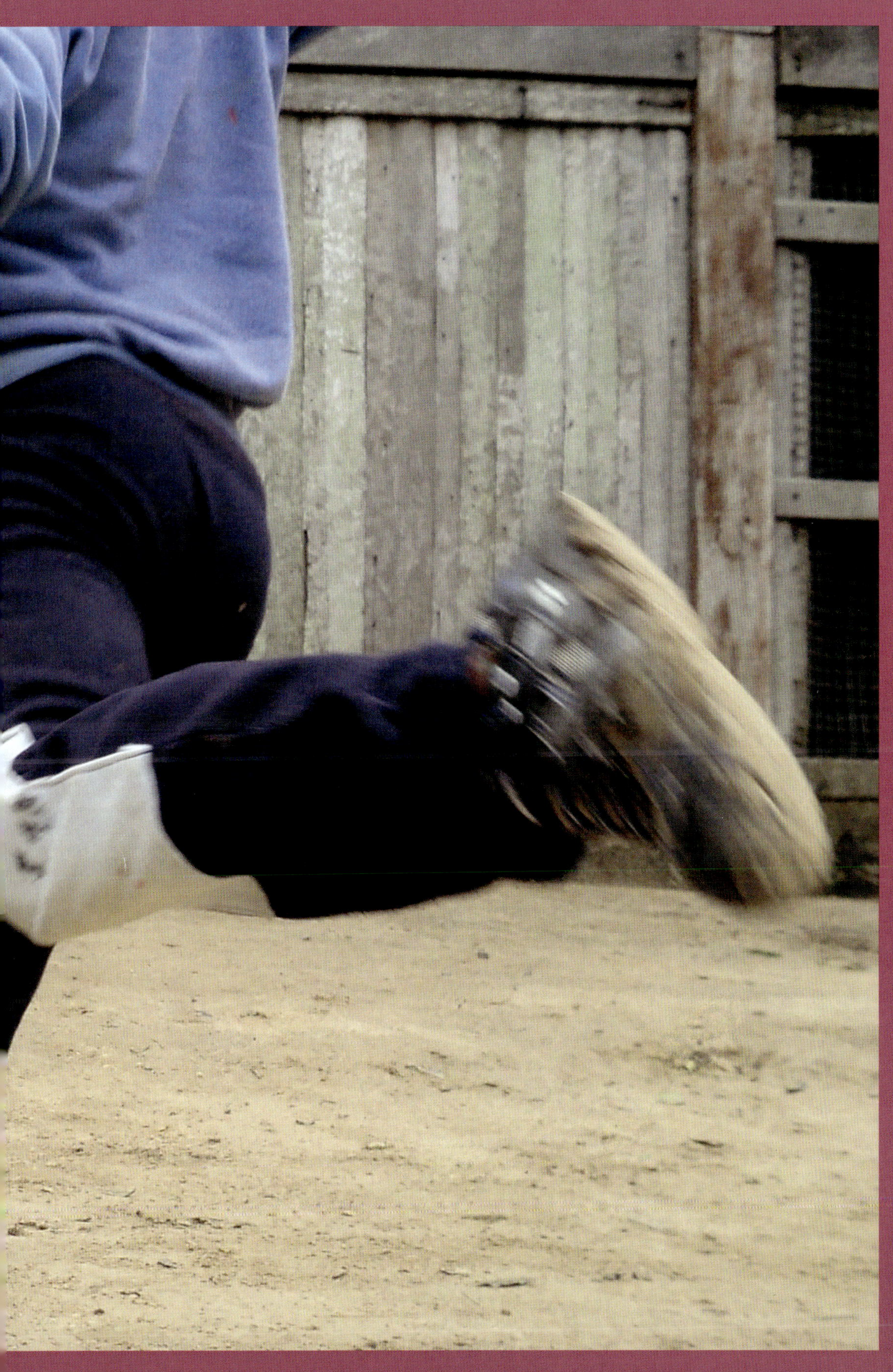

sporting talent, but his problem was that he was born in the wrong place at the wrong time. Born in 1970, he could have been one of the greats of our generation if world events had not so destructively thrown our lives into disarray.

I'll never forget the first time I was reunited with Ismet in Germany. It was in 1996, when my daily life revolved around my student residence in Stuttgart and whether I should become an academic or a writer. One day I suddenly saw Ismet walking down Königstraße. He was working as a florist! This huge talent from our childhood was now a florist in Stuttgart, in Germany. I was utterly astonished. We were no longer concerned with football and our youthful dreams. There were refugees everywhere in the Balkans and all over Europe. We no longer had to risk life and limb, and Ismet had had a stroke of luck by finding himself a job as a refugee. When I asked him whether he had tried to introduce himself to a club such as VFB Stuttgart, he responded in a flash: 'It's too late for all that' – despite the fact that he was only 26 years old. Today, 20 years later, I regret asking that question.

For a few months I saw Ismet selling his flowers, then he disappeared. He probably became a father, found another job and brought up his children – perhaps they are now playing football somewhere. Thousands of former refugees from the former Yugoslavia who scattered across Europe turned to professional sport, from Scandinavia to Germany, Austria to Switzerland, and now they are in their second and soon third generation. Children whose parents came from Serbia, Croatia, Slovenia and Albania are now playing football for Germany and France. Some of those whose parents live in the West have returned to play in their former homes, where they now have to learn about the country and its language.

It may sound crazy, but many Albanians were proud to share the Brazilian World Cup glory of Shkodran Mustafi when he played in defence for the German team in 2014. When he visited Kosovo he was welcomed by the president, prime minister, minister for sport and thousands of fans. In Switzerland half of the national team is made up of Albanians from Kosovo and Macedonia. At the European Championships in France the Albanian team will be playing against Albanians – some of whom are now Swiss. The father of two players from Kosovo, Taulant and Granit Xhaka, was pressured by the Swiss and Albanian public to decide which team his sons should play for. So now Granit

Thousands of former refugees from the former Yugoslavia spread across Europe and turned to professional sport, from Scandinavia to Germany, Austria to Switzerland, and now they are in their second and soon third generation.

will be playing for Switzerland and Taulant for Albania. May the best man win! Fairness and talent should be the victors.

Perhaps the biggest irony in this story of how sport has been abused and misused by nationalists is how sport once again finds itself in exile. In the diaspora, a new mixture of emotions can arise thanks to the experiences of flight. We are happy to be with others but also happy to be ourselves, we can be with others yet also be on our own. This would make a good platform for the future of sport.

Beqë Cufaj, born 1970, is a Kosovo Albanian writer who lives with his family in Stuttgart. He studied languages and literature in Pristina and today writes for a number of newspapers in the Balkans and Western Europe, including the *Frankfurter Allgemeine Zeitung*, the *Neue Zürcher Zeitung* and *Courrier International*. He has published several volumes of essays and prose. In 2000 he published *Kosova - Rückkehr in ein verwüstetes Land* (pub. Zsolnay). This was followed in 2005 by his novel *Der Glanz der Fremde*. His most recent novel entitled *projekt@party* is published by Secession Verlag.

Ukraine goes into extra time

Ukraine goes into extra time The cities that hosted Euro 2012 are currently at war, despite the ceasefire. There is now fighting in places where the ideals of friendship between peoples were once celebrated. Hopes that Ukraine could move a step closer to central Europe by hosting this mega sports event in conjunction with Poland have been shattered. What remains? Writer and football fan Serhij Zhadan reports from a war-weary country on the outer edges of Europe. *By Serhij Zhadan*

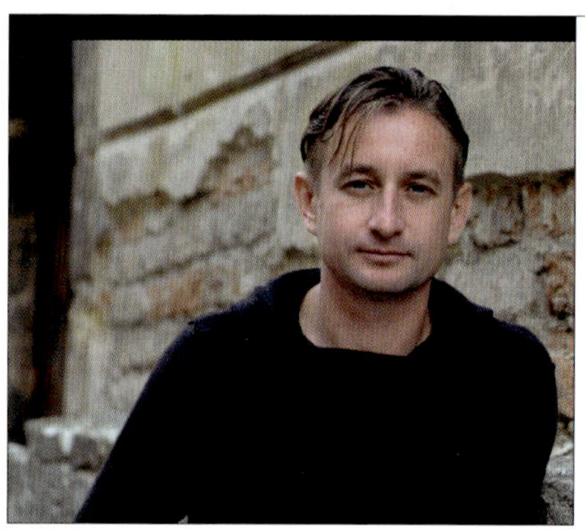

It's strange to talk about Ukraine 'before the war'. This expression suggests a certain catastrophism. What is clear is that after the war some things will never be the same again. It is also clear that war is the starkest and most significant designation that can ever be devised for us all. War changes everything – people, country, circumstances.

Even after the end of the war – a state that currently seems very uncertain and indistinct – it won't be possible to simply carry on as if nothing has happened. Perhaps this is why we've started using the expression 'before the war' more and more often. People want to remember the time before all the deaths, before all the bloodshed, before the arrival of armed strangers in our country. What was life like three, four years ago? What remains?

Four years ago, Ukraine lived for football. This might sound a little crazy, but it's true. Four years ago there were serious discussions in Ukraine about how football was the only national idea that could really unite the diverse and disparate Ukrainian people. Four years ago Ukraine was getting ready for the European Football Championships. Simply being given the opportunity to host these championships was seen as proof enough that Ukraine was now considered an established and forward-looking country.

Of course there were also a number of other factors at play that painted an altogether less rosy picture, and even back then there were several incidents that could have cast a shadow over the festivities and which are worth looking at in more detail.

Firstly, it should be remembered that at the time when it was preparing for the European Championships, the country was being run by President Viktor Yanukovich, a politician whose popularity among the people was already rapidly declining and whose reputation around the world was the subject of some debate.

I can still remember the countless discussions that took place among EU Europeans about the approach they should adopt towards the championships. On the one hand, it was a great opportunity to support the country in its efforts to encourage people to go down the European route. But at the same time, Ukraine was being ruled by a regime that was not particularly compatible with the idea of democracy and European integration.

Europe's leading politicians who wanted to grace the sporting festival with their presence would have to shake Yanukovich's hand at a time when the President had just imprisoned his main political opponent, Julia Tymoshenko. In the eyes of many Europeans – and, in all honesty, in the eyes of many Ukrainians – it was becoming more and more difficult to associate the president with the idea of civilised and equitable partnerships and relations. This mean that the 'festival of sport' was doomed to being politicised from the very beginning.

Ukraine was not, of course, unique in this respect, as sport has always to a greater or lesser extent been subjected to the influence of big money, and hence of politics. Broadly speaking, the European Championships

were meant to be seen as an ambitious major project that would help to improve the country's image and, more importantly, that of its president. This was a highly significant moment in the history of an independent Ukraine.

It should be said that as a result of this excessive politicising of Euro 2012, even the Ukrainians themselves were divided in their attitude towards the event. Some of them were more or less determined to boycott the championships, or at least ignore them. Their argument was that the championships were simply part of the state's attempts to improve its standing, to confer some legitimacy on itself and to clean up its corrupt image, all at the expense of football.

The preparations for the European Championships therefore raised a whole series of questions in people's minds, particularly with respect to the transparency and efficiency with which the allotted money was being spent. Many saw Euro 2012 as little more than an expensive toy that required huge subsidies.

A reflection of society

And when significant amounts of money are involved, people's greed tends to grow. The reality in Ukraine was that some people were determined to use football to line their own pockets. This had the effect of dampening people's trust and enthusiasm. It turns out that the whole idea of hosting the European Championships was fraught with awkward questions.

> **Four years ago, Ukraine lived for football. This might sound a little crazy, but it's true. Four years ago there were serious discussions in Ukraine about how football was the only national idea that could really unite the diverse and disparate Ukrainian people.**

Hardly surprising, as sport acts as a reflection of society and can often paint a more accurate and objective picture of it than its culture. And this was particularly true of Ukraine in this instance. Of course football could not escape the traditional components of political and social life in Ukraine – the populism of the ruling regime, the corruptibility of public officials, the oligarchy that existed within the business world. And this is precisely what happened as Ukraine prepared for the most important event in its history. At this point, it is worth putting politics to one side for a moment and addressing the topic of football itself.

When I describe the European Championships as the most important event in the history of independent Ukraine, I am, of course, exaggerating. But only a little. Football was alway more than just a sport in Ukraine.

And it's easy to explain why. Like every society that has achieved independence and is looking to establish its own identity, Ukrainian society was quickly and nervously trying to build the foundations that would provide it with stability and harmony following the collapse of the Soviet Union.

The legacy of the country's links to the Soviet Union included not only a huge amount of resources and the economic prospects associated with this kind of wealth, but also a whole range of significant and serious problems related to the particular nature of the country's historical development and the differences in ideological and political priorities at various levels of society.

Ukraine had in fact never been a monolithic country that was united in its needs and in its search for its own way forward. Ukrainian society was strangely united by an unusual mixture of genuine nostalgia for the Soviet Union, pro-Russian sympathies and pro-European intentions. It seems to me that these internal contradictions and conflicts suited the politicians. It is always possible to win more votes when there is an atmosphere of confrontation and division, and Ukrainian politicians have taken advantage of this fact for years, irrespective of their political orientation.

However, society itself was never going to benefit from a permanent state of confrontation. Particularly during Yanukovich's time in office, the country was like a boat whose passengers could never agree what direction to sail in. The passage of time has shown that while the passengers were arguing, the boat was slowly and inexorably being driven onto dangerous rocks – rocks that the passengers never knew existed.

But what has all this got to do with football? During the years between the country's declaration of independence and the Maidan revolution in Kiev in 2014, the Ukrainian people had few uniting elements. This is hardly surprising. What could unite the Russian-speaking people of the Crimea with the inhabitants of Galicia or Transcarpathia? Their history? No, this was more likely to divide them. Their language? Also a no. The church? No, not this either.

For a series of objective and subjective reasons, the culture of an independent Ukraine was never going to provide the link that would contribute to unity and understanding. Each Ukrainian region voted for its own politicians and led its own life. Every effort by the state to create a unified political, cultural and informational entity failed in most cases due to propaganda – either domestic or Russian.

The idea of consensus

And yet the idea of creating social consensus never really went away. People were always interested in any idea that might unite the Ukrainian-speaking, Greek Catholic inhabitants of Western Ukraine and the Russian-speaking mountain people of the Donbass region. The need for such an idea was ever-present and from time to time found its expression in the everyday lives of the average Ukrainian. The country had consistently demonstrated that it was capable of finding a solution to every situation by finding areas of common interest.

The Ukrainians have always been keen to find their own place in their own country, to discover their true identities, and this quest has often been quite successful. One of these elements in developing a new Ukrainian identity was sport. Because unlike language and religion, sport offers space for compromise and a sense of belonging, without the need to sacrifice personal principles and convictions. It is possible to be a fan of the national team without having to switch from the Russian camp to the Ukrainian camp. It is possible to cheer on the Klitschko brothers without being in favour of European integration.

One of these elements in developing a new Ukrainian identity was sport. Because unlike language and religion, sport offers space for compromise and a sense of belonging, without the need to sacrifice personal principles and convictions.

Indeed, it is victories by Ukrainian sportsmen and women that have, in many cases, brought about changes in the country. Posters of Andriy Shevchenko or the Klitschko brothers have adorned many Ukrainian children's bedrooms – in the east of the country just as much as in the west. Politics had nothing to do with it. I have vivid memories of the 2006 World Cup in Germany, the first and, as it happens, last time that the Ukrainian team played in the World Cup. I remember how after each victory by the Ukrainian team, people in the Russian-speaking and apparently 'un-Ukrainian' city of Kharkiv thronged the streets, proudly waving Ukrainian flags.

The new generation of Ukrainians was formed not in schools and libraries but in stadiums and at rock concerts. While the state had no real national idea, football and rock stars did: that it was 'cool' to be Ukrainian, that Ukrainians could be successful and prosperous, that they could win, that they could be interesting. A simple idea, maybe, but a sincere one. The idols of the young Ukrainians were not politicians or civil society actors, but football strikers and rock singers. Politicians drew the short straw in this respect.

I remember how Ukrainian presidents officially opened the stadiums in the run-up to the European Championships. I know what it was like in Kharkiv when Viktor Yushchenko arrived to open a stadium that had recently been refurbished by local oligarch Oleksandr Yarolslavsky. Nobody in Kharkiv had voted for Yushchenko and the president was in his last year of office. Even those who had stood and cheered on the Maidan in 2004 were disappointed in him.

It is easy to imagine what sort of reaction the president received when he entered the stadium. Every word of Yushchenko's speech was met with a denigrating roar from the stands. It was no different for Yuchchenko's successor, Viktor Yanukovich, when he opened the stadium in the Western Ukrainian city of Lviv – he chose to give his speech via video link but was still greeted with a deafening roar. This city has never liked politicians. The fans rightly viewed these presidential appearances as having less to do with a love of the game of the masses than with a desire to court cheap publicity.

Football itself, however, really did unite the people. The national team played in cities across Ukraine and attracted general support. Having said that, it is understandable that not everyone in the stadiums in Donetsk or Kharkiv was prepared to sing the national anthem. But the national team still played for everybody, irrespective of whether they knew the words or didn't want to know them as a matter of principle. The majority of fans in the Ukrainian stadiums welcomed the European Championships as being a huge privilege and a source of great joy, irrespective of which Ukrainian club they supported.

Active growth of the Ultras

But there is one more important point. A couple of years before Euro 2012, the so-called Ultra movement began an phase of active growth in Ukraine. Ukrainian clubs had always had their superfans, but organised and structured fan communities with all their various attributes and rituals, such as banners, songs, flash mobs and ideologies were a relatively new phenomenon. It is in-

teresting to analyse all this in the context of the last two years – from the revolution in Kiev to the Russian intervention in Crimea and the Donbass region. These are events that were directly influenced by the Ultras from the Ukrainian clubs.

This does not only relate to the fans of Dynamo Kiev and Karpaty Lviv who supported the Ukrainian revolution from the very beginning, but also to the Ultras from other Ukrainian teams, from cities such as Kharkiv, Dnipropetrovsk, Odessa and Donetsk in Eastern Ukraine, who went out on the streets and played a key role in the events of the winter and spring of 2014.

It is important to understand that many of the groups involved – activists and volunteers – were to some extent formed on the terraces of the football stadiums. This means that football actually played an ideological role in the conflict too, however strange this may sound.

When we talk about fan movements, it is important to understand that in Ukraine they differ little from those in other European countries. They have the same unconditional love for their own club and an equally passionate hatred of the opposition; the same categorical rhetoric, radical messages and strict codes of conduct. And the same fan wars – though these wars never affected the national team. In principle it is normal to support the national team, and we have to remember this when talking about the 2012 European Championships. Because – at the risk of repeating myself – the European Championships represented a significant moment in the development of the national identity of millions of Ukrainians.

I will not go into detail about all the scandals and disputes that surrounded Euro 2012. It is more interesting to talk about the atmosphere that prevailed during the tournament. For the first time, the whole of Europe was focused on Ukraine – not because of some new revolution or corruption scandal, but for positive reasons. Huge numbers of tourists made their way to Ukraine. The Ukrainians wanted to project a positive image of themselves and their country. Quite simply, they wanted people to like them. And they generally succeeded.

Those of us living in Kharkiv will never forget the huge numbers of Dutch people who turned up in the city. The Dutch fans were officially due to be accommodated on an island on the edge of the city, but in reality they occupied the whole city, organised marches and, on occasion, filled every bar and restaurant. it was really lively and bright – quite literally, as their orange shirts shone out in every park and on every beach. But more important than the shirts was the festive atmosphere. Despite all this, there was still the occasional unnecessary, but fortunately not too obvious, political gaffe. Before the game between Portugal and the Nether-

People generally understood that this celebration of football would cost the country a great deal of money. But once the celebrations were over and the fans had all gone home, we were left with new stadiums and the same old oligarchs. Only two years were to pass before the war started.

lands, Cristiano Ronaldo led out a young boy in a football shirt. It later emerged that the boy was the son of the local governor. A total coincidence, nothing personal. Then there was the somewhat uninspiring performance by the Ukrainian team, which failed to make it out of the group stage. People generally understood that this celebration of football would cost the country a great deal of money. But once the celebrations were over and the fans had all gone home, we were left with new stadiums and the same old oligarchs. Only two years were to pass before the war started.

Political caprice and social apathy

And what came after the European Championships? Political caprice and social apathy, a strengthening of the Yanukovich regime and the feeling that nothing was going to change – the power of the Party of Regions appeared to be strong and stable. Nobody felt safe. Even the above-mentioned Kharkiv oligarch Yarolslavsky found himself being forced to sell his football club to Yanukovich's men. The party was over, it was back to reality. Hosting the championships had provided us with new stadiums and airports, but these useful but only local changes were all we had to show for it.

Ukraine dropped off the radar again – and the country's rulers showed no signs that they wanted to get back on it. There were also no signals from Ukrainian society. People continued to go to football matches and the fans carried on supporting their teams as they had before. The national team got on with trying to qualify for the World Cup. In the autumn of 2013 the Ukraine team made it to the play-offs and were due to play France.

The first match was played in Ukraine and the national team pulled off a sensational 2:0 win. President Yanukovich was at the game, and was so happy when Ukraine scored that he stayed firmly in his seat – unleashing a wave of irony and sarcasm, but that was as far as it went. In the return match, France won 3:0 and so qualified for the World Cup. And the revolution began in Ukraine.

A one-off event

Today, the events of two years ago seem somewhat strange and impetuous. Who cares about corruption scandals and the arrogance of the Ukrainian oligarchs when people are dying on a daily basis? Who cares about football when we are being subjected to artillery fire and land mines? The problems we had back then now seem laughable and naive. But what conclusions can we draw when we try to analyse and evaluate what happened? Could the European Championships have changed the country? Of course not. Football, especially Ukrainian football, is part and parcel of the economic and social life of the country, just like any other business.

A country that is totally under the influence of oligarchs and corruption was never really going to be changed by a football tournament, especially when the competition itself was financed by the same oligarchs. Talking to people from the Schengen Area were hardly going to change the basic attitudes of the Ukrainian people. The 2012 European Championships were simply a one-off event that hardly anyone thinks about now they

are faced with the stark reality of war. Honestly, we have much bigger concerns these days than football.

What is modern football anyway? An expensive toy bought by rich people on a whim. The rich are prepared to finance things that generate no real profit just for the sake of fun and status. In today's Ukraine, the situation of football reflects the situation of the country as a whole: Shakhtar Donetsk, the club owned by oligarch Rinat Akhmetov, abandoned the occupied city and the players now train in Lviv. The Donbass Arena, the pride of Akhmetov and the whole region, now stands empty. Occasionally photos turn up on the internet showing armed separatists posing for photos against the background of the deserted stadium.

But the stadium remains untouched – just like most of Akhmetov's operations – and there are still a great many questions about the role played by Ukraine's most powerful oligarch in this war.

The president of FC Metalist Kharkiv, the Yanukovich man who forced Kharkiv oligarch Yarolslavsky to sell the club, fled Ukraine along with Yanukovich. Proper financing of the Kharkiv club stopped immediately, the top foreign players left, and the club ended up languishing in the lower reaches of the league table.

The situation in the Ukrainian league was also difficult – the teams from the Donbass region (of which there are several) had to leave the occupied zone. The total number of teams in the league has dwindled, but this has attracted little attention, despite the fact that the Ukrainian team has qualified for the European Championships to be held in France this summer. Many Ultras got involved in the war. Many footballers are helping the military. Individual positions have to be judged first and foremost in the context of the war and the battle of ideologies.

The national team's striker Yevhen Seleznyov, for example, who recently moved from Dnipro to a Russian club, was immediately declared to be a traitor. Meanwhile, the national team's goalkeeper, Denys Boyko, who when speaking regularly switches from Russian into Ukrainian, became an instant hero. Regardless of who you are – professional footballer or football fan – war dictates its own rules and codes of conduct. It can't be any other way. It will be different after the war.

But what should we expect 'after the war', in the more or less distant future? Ukrainian football is hardly going to blossom; the country's economy is in a terrible state; and, judging by the policies of the Ukrainian government, we should not expect to see many changes. What we can assume is that football will do what it can to survive.

It seems unlikely that football will have the same effect on people that it had before the war. Many Ukrainians now see things very differently as a result of the war. This is particularly the case with patriotism. In the past, singing the national anthem in a

Such understanding will be born of a very bloody and brutal confrontation, as a consequence of a battle against a perfidious enemy, for whom fair play simply doesn't exist.

stadium made a statement (or was simply posturing), it was a provocation, a declaration. For many citizens today, the words of the national anthem have become much more than just the lyrics of a song.

As for the Ukrainian national flag, this will no longer be seen as the sole preserve of football fans, especially after it was ripped down from government buildings and peppered with gunfire at the front. Now we view many things differently – perhaps we see them in a more serious and responsible light. Football as a national idea, as a basis for creating mutual understanding, has become superfluous. Such understanding will be born of a very bloody and brutal confrontation, as a consequence of a battle against a perfidious enemy, for whom fair play simply doesn't exist.

Today we can simply say that of course Ukraine was not ready for war. It had not prepared for it. It did not need it. And yet when we look back at the development of the country over the last 25 years, we can see that the Ukraine that was built during this period by Ukrainian politicians was wrong for everyone. It was wrong for those who were nostalgic for the Soviet Union, and also for those who saw Europe as the only hope for the country's future.

I think I am right in saying that the decaying and corruption-ridden political and economic system of post-Soviet Ukraine was actually to nobody's liking. This was the basic reason behind the revolution. It is ridiculous to assume that people would allow themselves to be beaten with police batons simply because they wanted to support the

EU Association Agreement. People went to the Maidan because they no longer wanted to live in what was then 'pre-war' Ukraine, because they wanted change. And while there have been few changes in the last two years, we can assume that there is still a long way to go, that Ukraine's future has not yet been decided and that it is therefore too soon for us all to start relaxing. Whatever happens, we must not stand still.

In this respect, Euro 2012 feels like an after-image of the past, an emblem of a country that no longer exists. A country with all its strengths and weaknesses. We can look back to the past and only see the strengths. Or we can keep these strengths in mind but also try to analyse the weaknesses in order to find ways of overcoming them. It is clear that the country will never be the same again. What it will be like, is down to us. And of course football will be different too. We can only hope that it will be fair. Like everything else in our country.

Serhij Zhadan was born in 1974 in Starobilsk in the province of Luhansk Oblast (Ukraine) and is the most popular Ukrainian poet and author of his generation. He graduated with a dissertation on Ukrainian Futurism and is one of the main proponents of the alternative cultural scene in Kharkiv. He has published numerous volumes of poetry since 1995, and has also been writing prose since 2003. In spring 2012 an anthology compiled by Zha dan entitled *Totalniy Futbol. Eine polnisch-ukrainische Fußballreise* [Total Football. A Polish-Ukrainian Journey] was published by Suhrkamp Verlag. This English article is based on a German translation of the original Russian text by Pavel Lokshin, n-ost.

Sport for communists At about age 10 something happens to the children of the United States. Soccer is dropped, quickly and unceremoniously, by approximately 88 percent of all young people. The kids move on to baseball, football, basketball, hockey, field hockey, and, sadly, golf. Shortly thereafter, they stop playing these sports, too, and begin watching them on television, including, sadly, golf. What is happening across the Atlantic? The writer Dave Eggers tells the true story of American soccer. *By Dave Eggers*

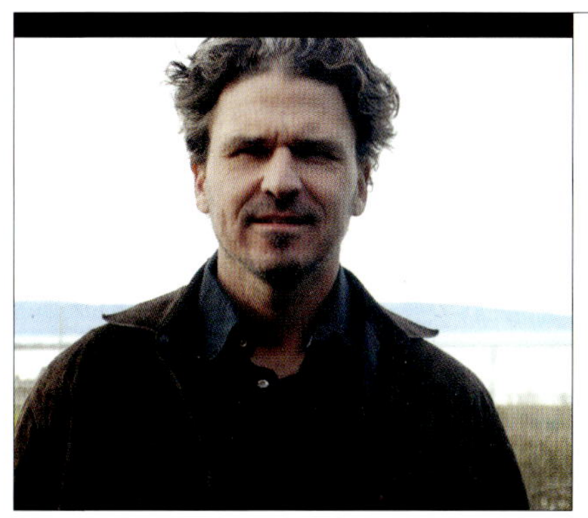

When children in the United States are very young, they believe that soccer is the most popular sport in the world. They believe this because every single child in America plays soccer. It is a rule that they play, a rule set forth in the same hoary document, displayed in every state capital, that insists that 6-year-olds also pledge allegiance to the flag – a practice which is terrifying to watch, by the way, good lord – and that once a year, they dress as tiny pilgrims with beards fashioned from cotton.

On Saturdays, every flat green space in the continental United States is covered with tiny people in shiny uniforms, chasing the patchwork ball up and down the field, to the delight and consternation of their parents, most of whom have no idea what is happening. The primary force behind all of this is the American Youth Soccer Organisation, or AYSO. In the 1970s, AYSO was formed to popularise soccer among the youth of America, and they did this with startling efficiency. Within a few years, soccer was the sport of choice for parents everywhere, particularly those who harboured suspicions that their children had no athletic ability whatsoever.

The beauty of soccer for very young people is that, to create a simulacrum of the game, it requires very little skill. There is no other sport that can bear such incompetence. With soccer, 22 kids can be running around, most of them aimlessly, or picking weeds by the sidelines, or crying for no apparent reason, and yet the game can have the general appearance of an actual soccer match. If there are three or four coordinated kids among the 22 flailing bodies, there will actually be dribbling, a few legal throw-ins, and a couple of times when the ball stretches the back of the net. It will be soccer, more or less.

Because they all play, most of America's children assume that soccer will always be a part of their lives. When I was 8, playing centre midfielder for the undefeated Strikers (coached by the unparalleled Mr. Cooper), I harboured no life expectations other than that I would continue playing centre midfielder until such time as I died. It never occurred to me that any of this would change.

But at about age 10, something happens to the children of the United States. Soccer is dropped, quickly and unceremoniously, by approximately 88 percent of all young people. The same kids who played at 5, 6, 7, move on to baseball, football, basketball, hockey, field hockey, and, sadly, golf. Shortly thereafter, they stop playing these sports, too, and begin watching these sports on television, including, sadly, golf.

The chosen sport of communists

The abandonment of soccer is attributable, in part, to the fact that people of influence in America long believed that soccer was the chosen sport of communists. When I was 13 – this was 1983, long before glasnost, let alone the fall of the wall – I had a gym teacher, who for now we'll call Moron McCheeby, who made a very compelling link between soccer and the architects of the Iron Curtain. I remember once asking him why there were no days of soccer in his gym units. His face darkened. He took me aside. He explained with quivering, barely mastered rage, that he preferred decent, honest American sports where you used your hands. Sports where one's hands were not used, he said, were commie sports played by Russians, Poles, Germans, and other commies. To use one's hands in sports was American, to use one's feet was the purview of the followers of Marx and Lenin. I believe McCheeby went on to lecture widely on the subject.

It was, by most accounts, 1986 when the residents of the United States became aware of the thing called the World Cup. Isolated reports came from foreign correspondents, and we were frightened by these reports, worried about domino effects, and wondered aloud if the trend was something we could stop by placing a certain number of military advisers in Cologne or Marseilles. Then, in 1990, we realised that the World Cup might happen every four years, with or without us.

At the same time, high-school soccer was booming in the suburbs of Chicago, due in large part to an influx of foreign exchange students.

My own high-school team was ridiculously good by the standards of the day, stacked as it was with extraordinary players from other places. I can still remember the name of the forward who came from, I think, Rome: Alessandro Dazza. He was the best on the team, just ahead of Carlos Gutierrez (not his real name), who hailed from Spain and played midfield. Our best defender was a Vietnamese-American student named Tuan, and there was also Paul Beaupre, who was actually from our own WASP-filled town, but whose name sounded French. We were expected to win State, but we did not come very close. Homewood-Flossmoor, we heard, had a pair of twins from Brazil.

A short time later, after the growth of professional indoor soccer and then some vague stabs at outdoor leagues, we proved to the world that the United States was serious, or relatively serious, about soccer, and the World Cup came to America in 1994. At least 4 to 5 percent of the country heard about this, and some commensurate percentage of them went to the games. This was enough to fill stadiums, and the experiment was considered a success.

In the wake of the Cup in America, other outdoor leagues have struggled to gain footing, and the current league seems more or less viable, though newspaper coverage of the games usually is found in the nether regions of the sports section, near the car ads and the biathlon roundups.

Our continued indifference to the sport worshipped around the world can be easily explained in two parts. First, as a nation of loony but determined inventors, we prefer things we thought of ourselves. The most popular sports in America are those we conceived and developed on our own: football, baseball, basketball. If we can claim at least part of the credit for something, as with tennis or the radio, we are willing to be passively interested. But we did not invent soccer, and so we are suspicious of it.

The second and greatest, by far, obstacle to the popularity of the World Cup, and of professional soccer in general, is the element of flopping. Americans may generally be arrogant, but there is one stance I ... stand behind, and that is the intense loathing of penalty-fakers. There are few examples of American sports where flopping is part of the game, much less accepted as such. Things are too complicated and dangerous in football to do much faking. Baseball? It's not possible, really – you can't fake getting hit by a baseball, and it's impossible to fake catching one. The only one of the big three sports that has a flop

With soccer, 22 kids can be running around, most of them aimlessly, or picking weeds by the sidelines, or crying for no apparent reason, and yet the game can have the general appearance of an actual soccer match.

factor is basketball, where players can and do occasionally exaggerate a foul against them, but get this: the biggest flopper in the NBA is not an American at all. He's Argentinian! (Manu Ginobili, a phony to end all phonies, but otherwise a very good player.)

Built upon transparency

But flopping in soccer is a problem. Flopping is essentially a combination of acting, lying, begging, and cheating, and these four behaviours make for an unappealing mix. The sheer theatricality of flopping is distasteful, as is the slow-motion way the chicanery unfolds. First there will be some incidental contact, and then there will be a long moment – enough to allow you to go and wash the car and return – after the contact and before the flopper decides to flop. When you've returned from washing the car and around the time you're making yourself a mini-bagel grilled cheese, the flopper will be leaping forward, his mouth Munch-wide and oval, bracing himself for contact with the earth beneath him. But this is just the beginning. Go and do the grocery shopping and perhaps open a new money-market account at the bank, and when you return, our flopper will still be on the ground, holding his shin, his head thrown back in mock-agony. It's disgusting, all of it, particularly because, just as all of this fakery takes a good deal of time and melodrama to put over, the next step is so fast that special cameras are needed to capture it. Once the referees have decided either to issue a penalty or not to our Fakey McChumpland, he will jump up, suddenly and spectacularly uninjured – excelsior! – and will kick the ball over to his teammate and move on.

American sports are, for better or worse, built upon transparency, or the appearance of transparency, and on the grind-it-out work ethic. This is why the most popular soccer player in American history is Sylvester Stallone. In fact, the two greatest moments in American soccer both involved Sylvester Stallone. The first came with 'Victory', the classic film about Allied soccer-playing POWs, and the all-star game they play against the Nazis. In that film, Stallone plays an American soldier who must, for some reason – no-one can be expected to remember these things – replace the goalie on the POW team. Of course, Stallone knows nothing about soccer, so he must learn to play goalie (somewhere, Moron McCheeby grins triumphantly). Stallone does this admirably, the Allies win (I think), and as the crowd surrounds them, they are hidden under coats and fans and sneak away to freedom.

The second most significant moment came when the World Cup came to the United States, in 1994. It is reported that Stallone attended one of the games and seemed to enjoy it.

It's inevitable, given the way the U.S. teams are improving every year, that eventually we will make it to the semi-finals of the World Cup, and it's likely, one would think, that the United States will win it all in the near future. This is a country of limitless wealth and 300 million people, after all, and when we dedicate the proper resources to a project, we get the job done (see Vietnam, Lebanon, Iraq). But until we do win the Cup, soccer will receive only the grudging acknowledgement of the general populace.

Dave Eggers is the author of ten books, including most recently *Your Fathers, Where Are They? And the Prophets, Do They Live Forever?*, *The Circle*, and *A Hologram for the King*, which was a finalist for the 2012 National Book Award. He is the founder of McSweeney's, an independent publishing company based in San Francisco that produces books, a quarterly journal of new writing (McSweeney's Quarterly Concern), and a monthly magazine (*The Believer*). McSweeney's also publishes *Voice of Witness*, a non-profit book series that uses oral history to illuminate human rights crises around the world. Eggers is the co-founder of 826 National, a network of seven tutoring centres around the country and Scholar-Match, a non-profit organisation designed to connect students with resources, schools and donors to make college possible. He lives in Northern California with his family.

The taxpayers' burden and dribbling prejudices Football in Brazil gained in popularity for many years, and was increasingly regarded as a space where people from different social classes and with different skin colours could come together. Brazilian football was perceived as a symbol of democracy, of Brazilian culture and identity. But in the run-up to the 2014 men's football World Cup, Brazil's cities were overtaken by a process of public politicisation and protest. What were the reasons for this? And what is the role of women's football in Brazil? *By Julia Haß*

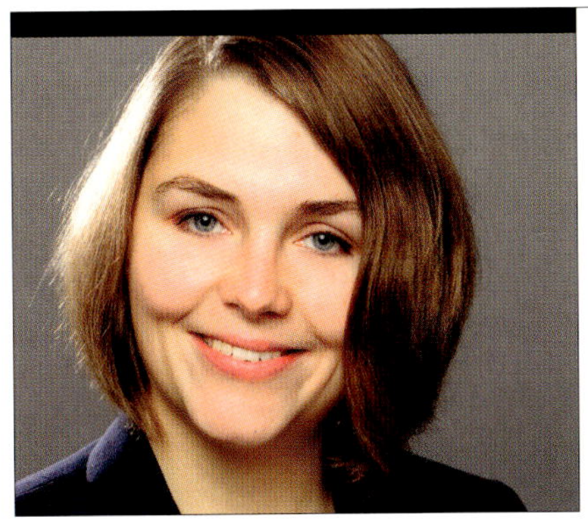

At the time of the 2013 Confederations Cup, initial demonstrations had already been triggered by price increases in public transport in São Paulo and other Brazilian cities. Social media was used to spread information and organise nationwide protests. Protesters criticised the high expenditure of taxpayers' money on the men's football World Cup, in particular because there was a lack of state investment in public health and public education. Not all investments, for instance in some of the new football stadiums, seemed reasonable in the eyes of Brazilians.

Furthermore, poor neighbourhoods in Rio de Janeiro and São Paulo were displaced from the urban centres to the peripheries. These urban changes were justified by the construction of infrastructures for sport events. It is not surprising that the slogans 'World Cup for the rich' and 'There won't be a World Cup' were prevalent during the demonstrations. The fact that only a small well-to-do section of the Brazilian population could afford local ticket prices and watch the games at newly built or renovated football stadiums seemed to confirm the critical slogans.

Individuals and groups who had condemned the corruption and violence of Brazil's police force before 2013 felt their criticisms were confirmed by state policies during the World Cup. Some of them felt that the public attention attracted by the mega-events, particularly in the international media, was advantageous for demanding political and social change. Others were sceptical about the positive impact of international events on the political situation in their country. Another group disagreed with the criticisms or even felt disturbed by the protesters. As the opening ceremony drew nearer, the protests in Brazil's cities began to drop off, but social discontent and political tensions did not disappear.

The 2014 World Cup 2014 – in economic terms the world's biggest sporting event –

symbolically manifested another area of social conflict: the deep gender inequalities in Brazil's national sport. Since the beginning of the 20th century, women have represented a minority in Brazilian football. Female players did not receive social support. From 1941 to 1979, a law even prohibited Brazilian women from playing football.

Nowadays, despite positive changes, a lack of knowledge about women's football and prejudices about female players are still prevalent in Brazilian society. As is the case in many other countries, media reports on international women's football tournaments, such as the women's football World Cup, is still rare in Brazil. Despite football's huge popularity, professional female players receive little public attention. Women's football is frequently represented as less attractive and inferior to the men's game. However, in 2014 and in 2016, representatives of women's football clubs and civil society tried to benefit from the publicity attracted by the male-dominated mega sports events in their country. In the following passages, I will analyse these strategies and show how mega sports events have an impact on women's football in Brazil. To begin, I will explain the history and current situation of women's football in Brazil.

An unequal story

A few words on the history of Brazilian women's football: at the end of 19th century, football was introduced in South America and Brazil by English traders. In the early years, the game was played solely by white Brazilian middle and upper classes. In the decades that followed, primarily in the 1920s, football clubs increasingly opened up to members of lower social classes and

people of Afro-Brazilian origin. This was remarkable in view of the yawning chasm between different social classes at that time. Only a few decades before, through the abolition of slavery in 1888, Afro-Brazilian people had become Brazilian citizens. In the 1920s, Afro-Brazilians were still not fully integrated and suffered discrimination in Brazilian society. However, from the 1930s and 1940s onwards, football gained in popularity and was increasingly regarded as a space where people from different social classes and with different skin colours could come together. Brazilian football was perceived as a symbol of democracy, of Brazilian culture and identity.

Nevertheless, almost since football was first introduced to Brazil, women were excluded. Yet, there were women who played football at the beginning of the 20th century. Newspapers in São Paulo reported for the first time in 1913 about football matches between female teams, but women represented a minority and were not supported by society. When the media reported on female football matches, as was the case in the 1940s in Rio de Janeiro, journalists employed mockery and double entendre in their reports. Women's football was not taken seriously.

At the same time, women's position in society and their participation in sport was being discussed in the Brazilian public sphere as well as in other countries worldwide. The majority had a patriarchal mindset, deeming women to be physically weak and generally inferior to men. The practice of physically demanding sports, such as football or boxing was perceived as incompatible with the 'female nature'. In 1941, the National Brazilian Sport Council prohibited women from playing football by law.

The law remained in force for almost 40 years and caused a stigmatisation of female football in Brazilian society. Even after the law was abolished in 1979, women's football was still strongly criticised. In the 1980s and 1990s, narratives on players' physical appearance were prevalent in media reports on matches between female teams. On the one hand, journalists presented sportswomen as sexual objects, but at the same time female football players were described as 'male' and speculations were voiced about their sexuality. Their sporting performances received little attention.

Nevertheless, from the 1980s onwards, female amateur football teams and tournaments were founded in many Brazilian cities. In a few places, such as São Paulo and Rio de Janeiro, even professional or semi-professional women's teams were founded. In the 1990s and 2000s, Brazilian national women's football team participated successfully in international competitions, such as the 2004 Olympic Games. The Brazilian Marta Vieira da Silva won World Player of the Year five times. Nowadays, despite the very positive results in international competitions, representatives of Brazilian women's football associations still criticise skill levels in women's football. The prevalence of prejudices against women's football and the dominance of male representatives are obstacles to the further development of women's football in Brazil.

In the context of the men's 2014 World Cup and the 2016 Olympic Games, media attention has been drawn to Brazilian sportswomen. In Rio de Janeiro, the NGO Rede de Desenvolvimento Humano (REDEH) and the social football club Estrela Nova organised an exhibition and youth sports activities in June and July 2014. REDEH was founded in 1990 and advocates environmental policies and women's rights. In the 2000s, the NGO started to work on sports issues. REDEH identified football as a space in Brazilian society that is still characterised by gender hierarchies; so the men's World Cup seemed a favourable moment to discuss these inequalities publicly. Since its foundation in 2009, Estrela Nova has been fighting for the strengthening of women's football in Rio de Janeiro. The football club offers practice sessions for boys and girls from poorer neighbourhoods.

Engaging in poor neighbourhoods

In their exhibition 'Mulheres no campo: driblando o preconceito' ('Women on the football pitch: dribbling prejudices') at the Museu da República in the centre of Rio de Janeiro, REDEH and Estrela Nova recalled the history of Brazilian women's football.

In 1941, the National Brazilian Sport Council prohibited women from playing football by law. The law remained in force for almost 40 years and caused a stigmatisation of female football in Brazilian society.

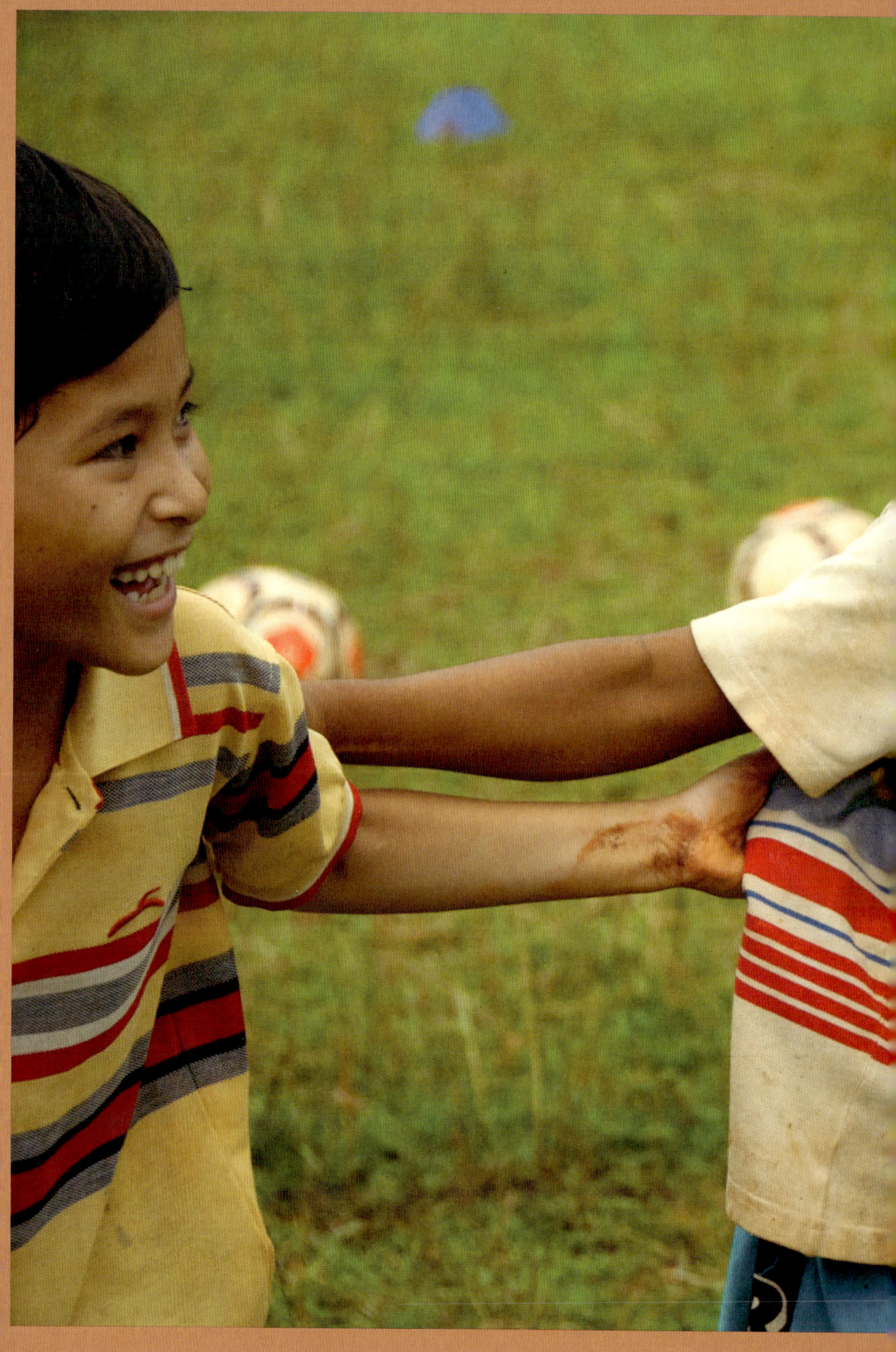

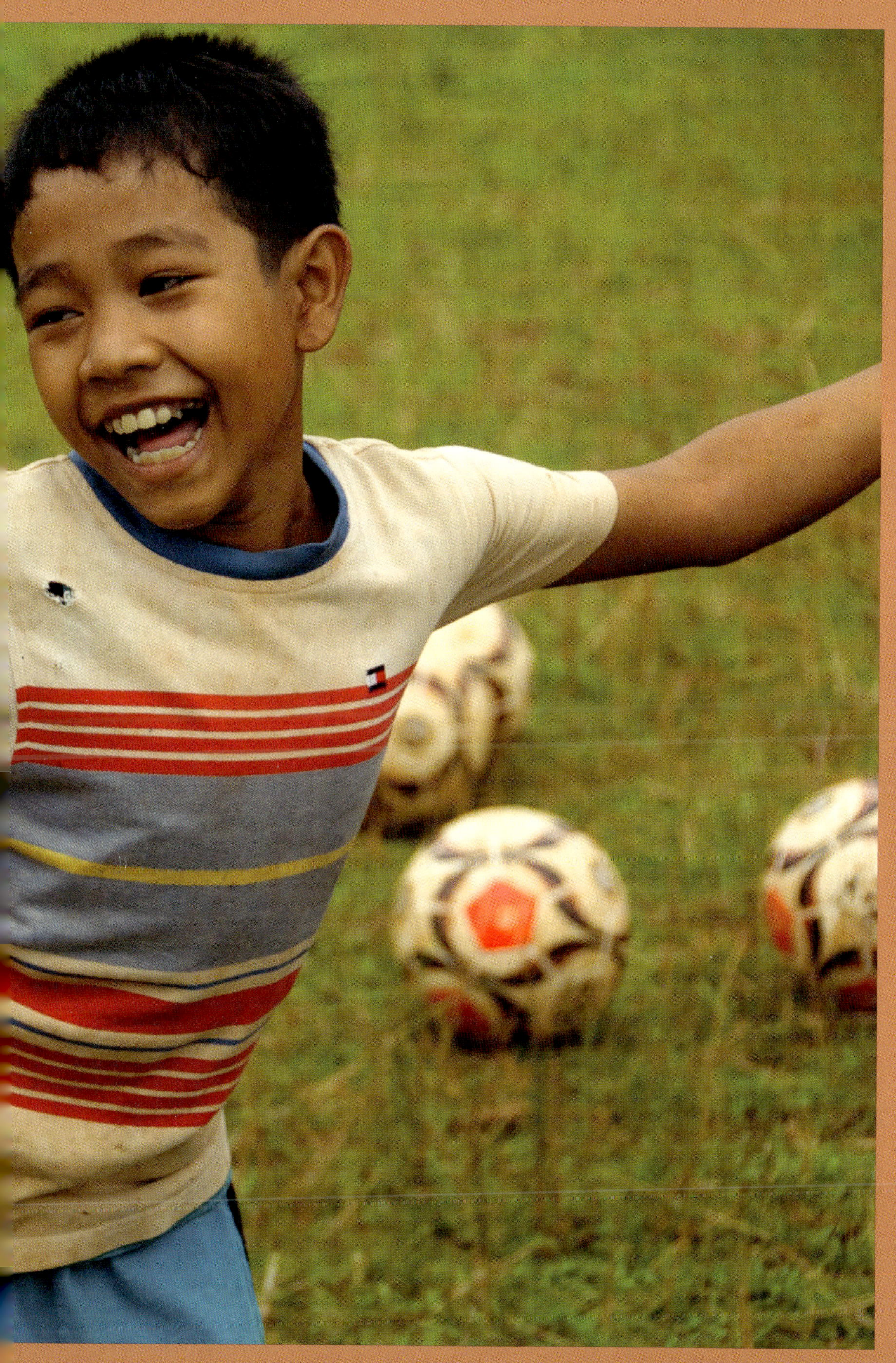

For instance, the female team Esporte Clube Radar was the first female team in Brazil to participate successfully in international football competitions in the 1980s. However, the team from Rio de Janeiro went unmentioned for a long time in historical narratives about Brazilian football, in monographs and in the national football museum. The exhibition's organisers tried to make the accomplishments of female teams more visible.

REDEH and Estrela Nova also organised tournaments for boys and girls. During these football matches, the usual gender separation in football was suspended. By letting boys and girls play together, the NGOs tried to dissolve prejudices on the football field. The boys should see the girls as equal players. As it took place in Rio de Janeiro, the site of several World Cup matches, the exhibition and sports activities attracted the attention of local and international journalists.

Other NGOs and public institutions have also benefited from the mega sports events held in Brazil. In May 2015, the national football museum in São Paulo, Museu do Futebol, opened a new exhibition area displaying the history of women in Brazilian football. Until that point, the museum, which had been founded in 2008, had almost exclusively presented men's football and male Brazilian players. Now, new exhibits present the history of women's teams and female athletes. Newspaper articles illustrate the years when male journalists and doctors pleaded for the exclusion of women from Brazilian football and when women were banned from playing in the 1940s. In a similar way to the exhibition curators in Rio de Janeiro, the academics at the museum in São Paulo took advantage of the recent mega sports events in their country to gain public attention.

In the run-up to the Olympic Games 2016, REDEH is pursuing a similar gender-political strategy to that followed during the World Cup. Brazilian women have been discriminated against in many Olympic disciplines in the past. Nowadays, female athletes are still a minority in many sports – in Brazil and many other countries worldwide. In the context of the Olympic Games in August 2016 the NGO is planning to turn the spotlight on female potential in sports through an educational programme.

Not only Brazilian activists, but also international civil society organisations are also using the mega sports events in Brazil to discuss social and gender inequalities in football and society. The German NGO Discover Football, for instance, organised an exhibition and a training camp for girls from socially marginalised neighbourhoods in Rio de Janeiro during the men's World Cup in 2014. Afterwards, Discover Football published information on these events on their website. The NGO is continuing its international struggle for women's football and women's rights in Brazil. Hence, Brazil and Rio de Janeiro in particular have become stages for national and international gender policy commitment.

Brazilian women's football not only benefits from the mega sports events through the added media and political attention, but also on a material level. The international football federation FIFA provided Brazil with additional funds for hosting the men's football tournament, but a part of the funds had to be used for to develop gender-specific sports programmes, including women's football.

Along with organising tournaments for up-and-coming women players, the Brazilian Football Federation promoted football projects for girls, such as Estrela Nova, with in-kind donations. From the perspective of Estrela Nova, the donations also had an important immaterial value and a motivational impact. For the first time, the NGO gained public recognition for its social commitment from a Brazilian football institution. But the gender-specific promotion through FIFA is only envisaged for a limited period. As similar funding from the Brazilian Football Federation is rare, it is likely that support for women's football organisations will decline once again. In this case, the 2014 World Cup will have had only a limited positive effect.

Nevertheless, the Olympic Games in 2016 also have a positive effect on Brazilian women's football and in particular on the national women's team. Since its creation at the end of the 1980s, the Brazilian national women's team has received little support from Brazilian football institutions, making it difficult for them to participate in international competitions such as the Olympic Games.

Discontinuities in the Brazilian professional women's football league and the dissolution of women's teams due to lack of funding in women's football were behind the lack of practice and tournament experience. Despite

Brazilian activists and international civil society organisations use mega sports events in Brazil to discuss social and gender inequalities in football and in society.

the existence of talented female athletes in the Brazilian team, it was difficult to compete against countries with highly competitive national leagues, such as the USA or Sweden.

However, today the Brazilian female team is undergoing much more intense preparation than in previous competitions. The chance of putting in a convincing performance at the Olympic Games in Brazil has encouraged funding for the women's national football team. Yet, it is unlikely that women's football will continue to be funded and sustain positive effects after the international competitions are over. Besides, women's local amateur football will probably not benefit from these incentives.

To sum up: in 2013 and 2014, in the run-up to the World Cup and Olympic Games in their country, Brazilians protested against social inequalities. Gender inequalities strongly affect different spaces in Brazilian society. These inequalities were voiced by a smaller group of protesters. Women's football clubs, local and international NGOs and academics created political programmes on gender issues and benefited from national and international media attention during the men's World Cup and before the Olympic Games. They have managed to raise public awareness about gender inequalities in Brazilian sports, and especially in football, and to discuss women's rights. Women's football has also benefited from Brazil being the host country for international mega sports events, as some groups and organisations have received additional funding. However, despite the positive effects thesse events, it is probable that the promotion of women's football is not long term. And anyway, investment in women's football remains insignificant in Brazil compared to investment in men's football. In light of previous mass political protests, many social and political issues seem to have been left unresolved in the run-up to the Rio Olympics. It is still unclear how the political and social dynamics will develop by August 2016. In the case of new protest movements, mega sports events might again play a significant role.

Julia Haß is a cultural anthropologist specialising in Latin America. She is writing her doctoral thesis on gender relations in women's amateur football in Brazil and is an associated PhD student at the international graduate school 'Between Spaces' at the Institute of Latin America Studies at the Freie Universität Berlin. She is currently working on a research project on football, gender and transculturalism in Brazil.

A healthy old age

China is an old country. Its ancient culture, philosophy and 5,000-year-old history harbour many ways of staying healthy: harmony of body and soul, yin and yang, the balance between movement and stillness. Today, more and more old people are taking advantage of these traditions to stay fit and healthy.

By Yongxian Li

As Chinese society ages, sport is becoming an important tool for improving people's quality of life, and not only that of the elderly. The Chinese government and society as a whole are now increasingly turning to sport as a way of improving the nation's health. China has its own traditional culture of exercise, and this is becoming increasingly popular with its older population. According to international standards, a population is classified as 'ageing' when the over-60s represent more than 10 percent of the total population. At the end the 2005 the number of over-60s in China hit the 144 million mark, which is 11 percent of the total population.
By 2020, it is estimated that the number of over-60s will reach 248 million, or 17.2 percent of the total population. Chinese experts estimate that a high point of 437 million, or some 30 percent of the total population, will be reached in 2051.
Low birth rates and growing life expectancy are the main reasons for the ageing of the Chinese population. In the 1970s, the People's Republic attempted to reduce the number of children in the country, issuing a decree in 1980 limiting the number of children a family could have to one – a

decree that only began to be phased out in 2013. This has led to China's current demographic problem.

An ageing society

In an attempt to prevent the further ageing of its population, China announced the official ending of its one-child policy in 2015. In future, couples will be allowed to have two children. However, many parents simply can't afford a second child due to the rising costs of housing and education. This won't change with the end of the one-child policy.

Since the economic reforms began, the country's restrictive household registration system (Hukou) has been gradually relaxed, resulting in more than 80 million migrant workers, predominantly young men, moving into the cities to earn more money. The result of this migration is the 'empty nest' villages populated only by older people. In rural areas, 60 percent of the population are over the age of 60. Official forecasts suggest that this number will grow by around 850,000 every year, reaching 120 million in the next 20 years.

The policy that was introduced in the 1970s of restricting couples to one child in urban areas and to two or three in the countryside certainly had the effect of slowing down China's population growth, but it also turned the country's age pyramid on its head. These days, older people can expect to enjoy a life expectancy and modest level of prosperity that previous generations never had the chance to experience, but it is not something they are necessarily celebrating. Only a few people are guaranteed an adequate pension.

According to Chinese law, the official retirement age is 60 for men and 55 for women (50 for some). China has a population of more than 1.33 billion, but only around 30 percent of people are entitled to a state pension. In many cases, the country's welfare system still requires families to provide for their older family members because it makes little provision for old-age pensions. Most older people continue to be supported by their families and by agriculture.

But the country's modernisation means that lifestyles are changing. Society has become much more mobile. Parents and their grown-up children no longer live in the same place and today's young adults no longer necessarily want to live with their parents. Older people are increasingly moving into old people's homes.

There are currently more than 50 million old people in China who do some form of sport or exercise. This represents 36.5 percent of the country's total elderly population. Around one third of them live in cities, meaning there are 17 million seniors in urban areas who are doing sport. It is clear that as regional economies and cultures develop, more and more people are taking up sport.

Recent studies suggest that older Chinese who exercise tend to spend a relatively long time on each session, with around 80 percent of them spending longer than an hour each time. On average this amounts to 300 hours a year.

Studies show the following:
- Better-educated people tend to do sport more often.
- Their sports are generally privately funded and self-organised.
- The more educated they are, the more older people are likely to exercise within the framework of a sports club/community or business/company or to take advantage of opportunities provided by commercial operators or school and university sports.
- Parks, streets, back yards and public spaces are the places most often used for doing exercise.
- Regular training, long sessions and endurance tend to be the order of the day.
- Opportunities for sport should be free or cost very little.

Older people generally prefer traditional sports and those that have developed out of the Chinese exercise culture. Walking, jogging, table tennis, badminton, qigong, tai chi, aerobics and dancing are the most popular forms of sport and exercise. Chess, Yangge, tai chi and qigong are all considered part of traditional Chinese exercise culture. Cycling, badminton and table tennis also have a long tradition in the country. Aerobics, dancing, jogging, fishing and swimming have also become fashionable amongst older people.

In recent times, local governments have reacted to the rapidly ageing population by setting up sports clubs for seniors in the cities and provinces. With the exception of Tibet, where the concept of the sports club is still in its infancy, the other 30 provinces, the autonomous regions, the direct-controlled municipalities, the Xinjiang Task Force and other entitities such as the railway, forestry, electronics and oil industries have all started setting up sports clubs for people over the age of 60.

Urban areas and regions with strong economies tend to have high participation rates, a good sports infrastructure and plenty of sports facilities compared to rural areas and regions with weaker economies.

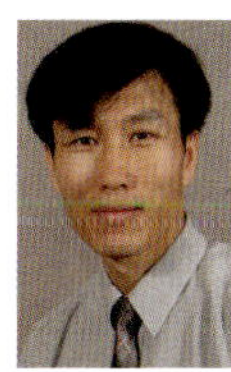

Yongxian Li, born 1971, is a visiting lecturer at the German Sport University Cologne. He specialises in sports policy and the exercise culture in China.

A symbol of Spain's internal battles Spain must be one of the most football-crazy countries in Europe. Social issues and conflicts, such as Catalonia's potential secession from the Spanish state, are often mirrored on the football pitch. The traditional El Clásico duel between the capital's most famous club, Real Madrid, and the Catalan team FC Barcelona has become a symbol of Spain's internal battles over issues of nationality, as well as being a magnet for 400 million fans worldwide. *By Julian Rieck*

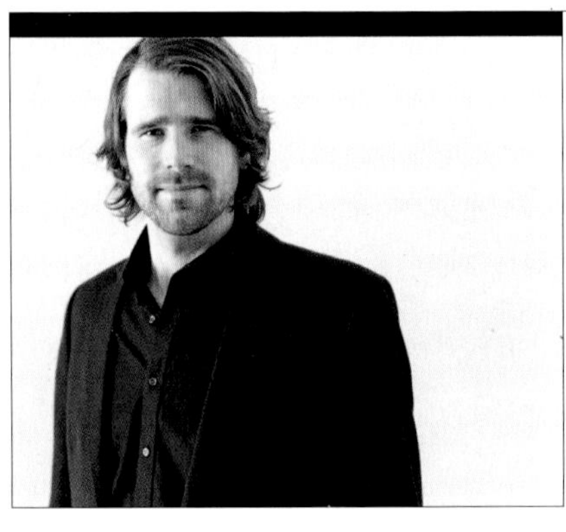

Interest in La Liga, the Spanish equivalent of the German Bundesliga or the English Premier League, is as strong as ever, despite the clubs' dubious machinations, multimillion-euro debts, and financial and fiscal scandals, not to mention the often violent encounters between their die-hard fans. 'Marca', Madrid's football daily, has the highest circulation of any newspaper in the country apart from 'El País', reaching an estimated readership of 2.5 million via bars and cafés. In the era of smartphones and social media, it seems likely the real figure is even higher.

The traditional El Clásico duel between the capital's most famous club, Real Madrid, and the Catalan team FC Barcelona has become a symbol of Spain's internal battles over issues of nationality, as well as being a magnet for 400 million fans worldwide. It is unclear whether the millions of international fans who tune into the game really understand the politically charged nature of this match. If we want a better understanding of how football has become such a mass phenomenon in Spain, we need to go back in time and examine the role played by three clubs in particular: FC Barcelona, Real Madrid and Athletic Bilbao. If football has become politically and symbolically charged in Spain, then it is these three clubs that are at the epicentre. They also happen to be the only clubs that – coincidentally? – have never been relegated from the Spanish Liga.

The importance of football in Spain is closely tied in with the socio-economic changes that affected the country during the 20th century. As in many other countries, football was imported into Spain from England and to some extent from Switzerland. The first reference to football dates back to 1870 in Jerez. British miners working in the Rio Tinto copper mine used to play cricket and football in their spare time, as reported by the local daily newspaper 'El Progreso'. The new sport took off and was soon played in many parts of the country, particularly in coastal regions. From its beginnings as a minority sport, by the 1950s it had ousted bullfighting as the country's biggest spectator sport.

The first official football club, the Recreation Club, was founded in 1889 in the small western Andalusian town of Huelva. Another region that was central to the development of football on the Iberian Peninsula was the Basque Country. This area was also strongly influenced by the English, who came as students or on business, and this was also reflected in the playing style of the Basque teams. No clubs of any note were established in Madrid and Barcelona until the turn of the century. Atlético Madrid, who won the Spanish league in 2014, started out as an offshoot of Athletic Bilbao in 1903. Meanwhile, it was a Swiss immigrant, Hans Gamper, who was behind the founding of F.C. Barcelona in 1899.

In 1898 Spain lost Cuba and the Philippines, the last major colonies of an empire that had once spanned the globe. This loss was viewed as a source of national shame and, as in many other European countries, it led to football becoming an important symbol of national strength.

Initially, football in Spain was organised along regional lines. From the 1920s the game became more professional, including the establishment of a national league, the Primera División, and the first professional footballers. Spectator numbers and revenues started to grow, while games against non-regional opponents became easier and more practical as transportation became better and faster. As a result, regional rivalries also became more pronounced. In these early days, there were also the first signs of the friend-foe atmosphere that would later prevail between Madrid at the centre and the 'peripheral nationalism' of the Basque Country, Catalonia and Galicia. In spite of this initial politicisation of football and the natural crossover into state and economic institutions, this proved to be merely a foretaste of the social divisions and conflicts that were to develop during the 20th century and which would be mirrored on the football pitch.

Spread of Catalan nationalism

From 1923, Spain was ruled by a military dictatorship under Miguel Primo de Rivera, backed by King Alfonso XIII. As part of the process of centralisation, many of Catalonia's historic rights were curtailed in order to halt the spread of Catalan nationalism, which had been growing since the 19th century. During a friendly match between FC Barcelona and another Catalan team, CD Jupiter, in 1925, an English marine band played the Spanish national anthem Marcha Real but also the British God Save the King. While the Catalan fans in the Les Corts stadium – the forerunner of the current Camp Nou – booed and whistled the Spanish anthem, they loudly and enthusiastically applauded the English one. FC Barcelona was banned from all activities for six months. As a result, the club's Swiss president and founder Hans Gamper decided to return to his home country.

The introduction of a national league at the time when peripheral nationalism was being suppressed – not only in Catalonia, but also in the Basque Country and Galicia – led to these regions developing a stronger sense of regional and nationalist identity. As a result, Real Madrid was increasingly viewed throughout the country as a club with an all-Spanish identity. Santiago Bernabéu, who was president of the club for 35 years and who is seen by many as the very incarnation of Real, is said to have celebrated every one of his team's goals during his active career with a cry of 'Viva España!'

Republic without Real

When the country became a republic in 1931, the designation Real was initially dropped from the names of clubs and associations. Real Madrid reverted to being Madrid Football Club, its original name when it was founded in 1902. However, sport in general was treated fairly liberally under the Republic. Sports associations were given a substantial degree of autonomy and were not subordinated to state institutions. All this was to change with Franco's coup in the summer of 1936. However, the advance of Franco's troops was successfully halted at the gates of Madrid in November 1936, and the capital remained in Republican hands throughout the country's three-year civil war. The revolutionary forces of the anti-Fascist parties seized control of the city, as they had in Barcelona. For sport, this meant integration into the Federación Cultural Deportiva Obrera (Cultural Federation of Workers' Sports). The result was that the clubs, stadiums and the whole infrastructure of the sport effectively came under the control of the trade unions.

Even the former royal club in Madrid became de facto a 'proletarian' club. Meanwhile, the two most important individuals in the club's recent history – Bernabéu, who has already been mentioned, and Ricardo Zamora, who was widely recognised as the best goalkeeper in the world in the 1920s – both openly supported the Franco camp, with Bernabéu even serving as a volunteer on the front in Catalonia.

When the Republican government fled from Madrid to Valencia, the headquarters of the Spanish Football Association was relocated to Barcelona. Other cities with first division football clubs such as Seville and Oviedo ended up in the rebels' zone of influence. With the outbreak of civil war, it was no longer possible to run football in a regulated way, so the Campeonato de Catalunya was set up in October 1936 to help clubs continue to generate income. An attempt by Madrid Football Club to join the competition was vetoed by FC Barcelona, who felt their participation would destroy the regional character of the tournament, and who perhaps also wanted to exclude additional rivals.

In 2009, FC Barcelona called for the title they had won in 1937 as champions of the Mediterranean League to be recognised as an official Spanish title (the clubs from Madrid and the Basque Country had declined to play in the competition). So far they have been unsuccessful. FC Sevilla, on the other hand, were allowed to claim the official Spanish title for 1939, even though the competition they won was only played in the Francoist zone. So, in spite of the war going on, football continued to be played by both sides and was effectively pressed into service by the warring parties. An Euskadi team from the Basque Country set off around the world to canvass support for the resistance against the national forces and for the Basque regional government.

Two days after the team set off in 1937, the Basque holy city of Guernica was destroyed by the German Condor Legion. That same summer, Francoist troops took Bilbao. The team travelled through several Latin American countries, taking part in and even winning the Mexican league. Very few of the delegates returned to Spain in the end, with most of the players staying in Mexico and signing for local teams. FC Barcelona also travelled to North America to raise money in the summer of 1937. Only 8 of the original 20-man delegation eventually returned to Spain.

In 1937 a new football association was also set up in the 'Nationalist Zone' as an alternative to the existing Republican organisation, in an attempt to create a sense of normality. The successful tours undertaken by the Catalans and Basques and the positive response they received around the world motivated the insurgents to also use football for propaganda purposes, though only in their fascist 'brother nations' of Portugal, Italy and Germany. As FIFA still only recognised one association per nation state, neither Republican nor Francoist teams were accepted by the organisation. However, once it became clear that the advance of Franco's troops would not be halted, the 'Nationalist' football association was soon recognised as Spain's official organisation.

The national team's colours were also changed from the former classic red, symbol of both the Republic and the hated communism, to a Francoist blue. The choice of colour was an allusion to the uniform shirts worn by the fascist Falange, whose militias had supported the military coup from the very beginning, and which was officially recognised as the ruling party in 1937. The fact that the Selección went back

to playing in classic red after 1947 can be seen as part of the Franco dictatorship's attempts to cover up its fascist origins after the Second World War and present itself as a Catholic, authoritarian and anti-communist regime.

When the Spanish Civil War ended in 1939 with the victory of the Francoists, efforts were made to create a major team in the capital under the name Aviación Nacional. It was to be a symbol of centralism and act as a counterweight to the successful regional teams. The idea was to merge Real Madrid, who regained their name in 1941, and local rivals Atlético Madrid. At that time, Atlético were playing under the name of Atlético de Aviación and were sponsored by Franco's airforce. The latter were extremely unpopular in Madrid, as the fact that they had bombed the capital – and particularly the workers' neighbourhood – was still fresh in everyone's memory. Real were able to resist this takeover attempt thanks to the power struggles between different factions within the regime, and the club's good relations with the leaders of the 'New State'.

Franco's regime was, of course, extremely hostile towards Republican institutions, including the football clubs from the former Republican Zone. In the first edition of 'Marca' in October 1938, the sports journalist and Basque Falangist Jacinto Miquelarena described the football during the time of the Second Spanish Republic as a 'red orgy of the lowest and vilest regional passions [...]. Almost all of them acted in a separatist and rude way when Spanish championship games were being played.'

The country's new rulers decided to restructure sport along Italian and German lines to reflect a fascist ideology. Sport was seen as a

An Euskadi team from the Basque Country set off around the world to canvass support for resistance against the national forces and for the Basque regional government.

way of strengthening the nation and preparing it for potential wars. Julián Troncoso, the new president of the Spanish Football Association and a lieutenant-colonel in the army, referred to the role of sport in restoring the country's greatness when he stated in 1939: 'We must all get used to the idea that in future sport will no longer be a leisure activity, but an essential tool for making the men of this country stronger and preparing them for particular types of actions and acitivities, whenever they may be called upon to carry them out.' To this end, sport was put under the direct control of the Falange, the fascist ruling party. The Delegación Nacional de Deportes, a national sports authority similar to the NS League of the Reich for Physical Exercise, was set up under the control of General José Moscardó, who was venerated as a war hero.

'Hispanicisation'

This institutional restructuring was accompanied by the 'Hispanicisation' of Spanish football – by assimilating peripheral nationalism into the central state. Fútbol Club Barcelona had to change its name to Club de Fútbol Barcelona, while Sporting Gijón Deportivo became known as Gijón. Madrid Football Club had to change its name too and was initially know as Madrid Club de Fútbol. The Falange sought to exert its influence on practically all aspects of public life, including sport. The new regime secured the necessary control over football by insisting that the board of directors of every club include a minimum of two Falange members.

After the Civil War, Real Madrid was initially anything but successful, although they did manage on a couple of occasions to win the Copa del Generalísimo, as the Spanish cup competition was then known. Indeed, in 1943

and 1948 they only just managed to avoid being relegated to the second division. During this period, other teams were much more successful than the Madrid club that would go on to win so many titles.

The current polarisation between Real Madrid and FC Barcelona can probably be traced back to this time, and many observers believe it was particularly triggered by the cup match in 1943. Barça had won the first leg at home 3:0, but Real beat their Catalan opponents 11:1 in the return leg in Madrid. It is said that police officials went into the Barcelona changing room before the match and pressurised the players. The bad blood between the two teams was subsequently made worse by some controversial refereeing decisions and the transfer of Alfredo di Stéfano to Real after he had already signed a contract with Barça.

The demeanour of Santiago Bernabéu was also a source of major irritation for many Barça fans, who considered him to be persona non grata following his wartime activities on the Catalonian front. After Real lost to Barça in the 1968 cup final, Bernabéu is reported to have said: 'I admire Vila Reyes [President of Espanyol Barcelona]; if only for the fact that he is president of a club in Catalonia that has the word Espanyol in its name. And anybody who suggests that I don't like Catalonia is wrong. I love and admire it, despite the Catalans.' This kind of statement was, of course, just what many of the supporters of FC Barcelona liked to hear, as it was only when Madrid saw them as the enemy that they could raise their profile – in their own eyes at least – not only as a Catalan club, but as a club of opposition, including during the years of the dictatorship.

However, we should not overstate this view of themselves as being anti-Francoist. For example, Miró-Sans, who was president of FC Barcelona for many years, was not antipathetic to the Franco regime and had also enjoyed good relations with Real Madrid's board members.

After their 11:1 victory in 1943 Bernabéu's Real Madrid was regularly portrayed as 'Franco's club'. And it is true that there were close links between the club and certain representatives of the regime. But this was true of other clubs too. However, it was Real Madrid that carried out certain official tasks that the state was not able to do itself, especially from the mid-1950s onwards. After 1945, Spain was classified as a fascist country by the United Nations and excluded from all UN organisations. It only had diplomatic relations with a handful of countries at that time and was starkly divided into winners and losers of the Civil War.

At a time of hunger and deprivation, football became a welcome distraction from the hardships of everyday life. Ticket sales and tours abroad made it possible to pay for expensive stars such as Alfredo Di Stéfano in 1953 and Ferenc Puskas in 1956. Another potential source of income was soon to open up when, in 1955, Real Madrid was actively involved in setting up the European Cup, now known as the Champions League. Real went on to win the first five of these championships.

Politically, the 1940s and 1950s represented a period of nationalisation in Spain and the victorious Francoist regime also tried to use sport as a political lever in the movement towards centralised national integration and political

Sport was seen as a way of strengthening the nation and preparing it for potential wars.

socialisation, especially where the younger generation were concerned. The aim was to crush separatist aspirations once and for all. Catalonia and the Basque country were accused of being loyal to the Republic and were punished by being deprived of some of their special, historic rights. Ultimately, however, subordination to the central state was not brought about by destroying regional identities but by manipulating them. This meant they lost their historic, official special status, while being allowed to maintain regional traditions in order to underline the diversity of Spain – meaning Castilian Spain – as a whole.

This type of policy was also mirrored in the regime's approach to sport. On 16 March 1941, the Spanish Football Association organised two matches on the same day: in one match a team of Castilian footballers played against a team of Catalan players in Madrid, while in the other, the national team played against the Portuguese national team in Bilbao. The intention was clearly to highlight the fact that regional traditions were not so much being wiped out as subordinated to the idea of a greater Spain.

During the 1950s Real Madrid was increasingly viewed as 'the' Spanish team and, as such, the symbol of Spanish identity as a whole. As Real enjoyed more and more international success, their domestic rivals became increasingly convinced that they not only had to compete with Real on the pitch, but that Real were backed by the official might of the state.

The growing perception of Real as being Spain's (football) ambassadors in the world resulted from the fact that, after qualifying for the World Cup in 1950, the national team failed to qualify again until 1962. The European Championship was first held in 1960. The Spanish national team also played very few friendlies during the years of international isolation. Football was also seen as a way of channelling the nationalist sentiments of the Basques, Catalans, Galicians and Valencians – a kind of safety valve for social tensions. During the early days of the dictatorship, the football stadium was one of the few public places where people were still allowed to speak regional languages that were prohibited elsewhere. There was a gradual relaxation of this language policy in the early 1960s, and in 1960 Barça's club newspaper even published its New Year greetings in Catalan.

Football was also meant to help dissuade the Spanish people from becoming politically active. For example, matches were played on 30 April and 1 May in order to avoid potential worker protests. Vicente Calderón, then President of Atlético de Madrid, described this attempt to give football a depoliticising role during a TV interview in 1969: 'It is hoped that football dulls people's brains and that they (the people) spend the three days before and after the game thinking about football. Then they they won't be thinking about dangerous things.' It is hard to say whether this policy of national integration and the attempt to dumb down the people through football actually worked. It seems unlikely that football matches could stem or even halt dissident activities. Of course the regime had plenty of opponents who had no interest in football or sport in general, so they would not have been affected by such measures, and some will have deliberately avoided sporting events for precisely this reason.

It is worth mentioning that while Real Madrid was increasingly associated with national identity, foreign players such as the Argentinian Alfredo Di Stéfano, the Hungarian Ferenc Puskas and the Brazilian Didi, and even footballers from other regions of Spain such as the Basque goalkeeper Ariquistáin, were also generally accepted when they committed themselves to Madridismo. In 1966 Puskas even stated on TV that he was going to vote 'yes' in the referendum on the final Francoist constitution, the 'ley orgánica'. The regime presented the vote as a plebiscite on Franco and the dictatorship, and it amounted to a definitive institutional legitimisation of the regime. To the outside world, Real's foreign players made the club seem almost cosmopolitan and created the impression that Spain was actually a free and open country.

For many supporters of the Francoist state, Athletic de Bilbao was the true Spanish team because of its rule of only employing Basque players. Franco himself is said to have admired the Basque club for 'maintaining the purity of its blood', even if Basque separatism made it impossible for him to say such a thing in public. Following FC Barcelona's cup win against Athletic de Bilbao in Madrid in 1953, the Spanish-Filipino journalist Eduardo Teus mused all the more openly about the cultural, religious and linguistic construct of the concept of 'Hispanidad': 'In footballing terms, the raza española can be compared to the crusaders from Athletic de Bilbao, the very essence of a Spanish club, without foreign influence... FC Barcelona did not want to be associated with Spanishness, so it decided to create an international team, a concept that calls to mind so many degenerate ideas'. By 'degenerate ideas' he meant the political theories of liberalism and communism, which were considered very un-Spanish in Francoist ideology and could only have been introduced from abroad. The Civil War – which had been given the status of a 'crusade' – was meant to allow the Nationalists to drive these kinds of ideas out of Spain.

Despite having one or two players of non-Spanish origin, the image of Real Madrid was very important to the regime, particularly on its travels abroad. This was not because Franco had pressured officials at the club or was pursuing a grand scheme relating to the sport, but more that the regime took advantage of Real's participation and success to project an image of Spain. Looking back at the role of Real during the dictatorship, the Spanish journalist Alex Botines wrote in 1975: 'For years Real Madrid was the team that was the bedrock of support for the Franco regime. The club demonstrated to the whole of Europe that Spain was still an important country, despite the fact that it was a late developer – both out of necessity and through its own choices. Real Madrid was regarded as the exception to this underdevelopment and allowed us to hold our heads high on the international stage.'

Here, Botines was expressing the concerns felt by many Spaniards during the 1950s and 1960s: the economic backwardness of the country; the worry of not being thought of as a real member of 'modern' Europe because of the Fascist dictatorship; and – after the Civil War and years of international condemnation – a desire to feel they could finally lift their heads a little higher. The Francoist ruling elite was well aware of the fact that Real Madrid was playing an ambassadorial role for Spain.

In 1948 the Spanish Minister of Foreign Affairs had banned the Selección from "playing matches against non-friendly states in which there was a calculable risk of defeat."

In 1959, the Secretary General of the Falange, José Solíus Ruiz, went as far as to say: 'You've achieved far more than the many embassies that God's own people have around the world. People who once hated us, now understand us thanks to you, because you've torn down so many walls. [...] Your victories fill all Spaniards with genuine pride, in Spain and beyond the borders of our motherland. And when you return to the changing room after a game, you know that all of Spain is with you and by your side, full of pride because of your victory, which allows the Spanish flag to fly so high'.

Recording of the national anthem

Every time the influential Real Madrid official Raimundo Saporta travelled abroad, he made sure he had a recording of the Spanish national anthem and a Spanish flag in his luggage, in order to avoid any diplomatic faux pas. An example of such a blunder happened on 12 May 1955 at a friendly match between the Galician team Celta de Vigo and FC Toulouse. Thousands of exiled Spaniards lived in Toulouse and the city was even host to party congresses organised by left-wing groups such as the Social Democrats, who were banned in Spain.

Before the game, spectators apparently played the Republican national anthem and waved Republican flags, without the club making any kind of protest. Saporta wanted to prepared for this kind of eventuality. And in 1963 he was also given the tricky task of ensuring that the two matches between the basketball teams belonging to Real and ZSKA

Moscow went smoothly, particularly as this was to be the first official contact between the two countries since the Civil War. Only three years earlier, in 1960, the Spanish Minister of the Interior had prevented the Spanish national football team from travelling to Moscow for the first ever European Championship, and this political interference in the affairs of sport had provoked international outrage.

Real Madrid was a popular choice of opponent for international friendlies, and there were two main reasons why the team was important to the foreign policy interests of the Franco regime. Firstly, there was a lot of money to be made, and secondly, club officials would report back to the Spanish Ministry of Foreign Affairs on the situation in the countries visited after every international trip. The matches played in the Soviet Union and Yugoslavia even served to establish the first informal contacts with two countries with whom Spain had no formal diplomatic relations.

Members of the opposition were able to draw a clear distinction between their passion for football and the obvious attempts by the regime to instrumentalise the sport. Occasionally the regime's attempts to carefully manage its international image backfired when Real Madrid games abroad were used as an opportunity to stage protests against the Franco regime. As Real was not able to maintain its run of international success during the 1960s, and international relations started to normalise due to a general policy of détente, the regime no longer needed to rely on alternative, unoffi-cial representatives to pursue its foreign policy objectives as it now had access to traditional diplomatic channels.

Even though Santiago Bernabéu was always at pains to stress that he and 'his' club served the people and Spain rather than the regime, Real naturally profited in many different ways from its close ties to the dictatorship. The club was accorded a range of political favours, including speeding up the bureaucratic process for granting naturalisation to foreign players, and conspicuous access to luxury goods. During the later stages of the dictatorship in the early 1970s, clubs like FC Barcelona and Athletic Bilbao started to use the 'football stage' to position themselves politically. The Catalan flag was officially flown at games played at the Campo Nou even before Franco's death in 1975, and the team's captain wore the Catalan colours as an armband. Barça's 5:0 victory over Real in 1974, which helped the Catalan club to win the league for the first time since 1960, was seen as a political symbol, and for many it signalled the end of the dictatorship.

In October 1975, just a few weeks before Franco died, Athletic Bilbao players wore black armbands during a league game. They claimed they were wearing the armbands to commemorate the death of a member of the club. But it was quite clear that this was a silent protest against the death sentences passed by the already ailing regime, which had attracted international condemnation. At the Basque derby game between San Sebastián and Bilbao in December 1976, the two captains held aloft the Ikurriña, the Basque flag that was still banned, as an open demonstration of support for the special rights of the Basque people that had been denied under the dictatorship.

The public perception of the clubs from Madrid, Barcelona and Bilbao during the Franco dictatorship still plays an important role today when it comes to both their support and their political significance. Athletic Bilbao has always had a policy of only playing native-born Basque players. Their squad currently includes Iñaki Williams, who has African parents but was born in Bilbao. This represents a certain softening of their policy as the club adapts to the realities of globalisation.

In October 2012, Barça fans demonstrated in favour of independence from the Spanish state after precisely 17.14 minutes of the Clásico against Real Madrid. This was a clear reference to the end of the War of the Spanish Succession in 1714, in which the Kingdom of Aragón, to which the County of Barcelona then belonged, lost its special rights.

This particular demonstration in favour of an autonomous Catalonia resulted in un-

Football was also seen as a way of channelling the nationalist sentiments of the Basques, Catalans, Galicians and Valencians – a kind of safety valve for social tensions. During the early days of the dictatorship, the football stadium was one of the few public places where people were still allowed to speak regional languages that were prohibited elsewhere.

precedented media coverage of the separatist cause. Barça defender Gerard Piqué celebrated not his club's victories, but and the Spanish team's World Cup and European Championship success by waving the Catalan flag, which guaranteed him a hostile reception in many Spanish stadiums.

Meanwhile, striker David Villa was celebrating the World Cup win with the Asturian flag. This provoked no such hostile reaction from football fans, but was actually seen as being very Spanish. Pep Guardiola stood as a candidate for the separatist alliance Junts pel Si (Together for Yes) in the Catalan regional elections in September 2015. In early 2016, a regional government was put in place that, for the first time since the end of the dictatorship, was in a position to draw up a concrete plan for independence. It remains unclear what this could mean in terms of a newly independent Catalonia becoming a member of the EU, or indeed FC Barcelona remaining in the Spanish league.

At European level, Madrid is threatening to block any attempt by Catalonia to join the EU. Perhaps Barça, like AS Monaco, could play in the French Ligue 1 as a non-French club. However, from a sporting and emotional perspective, this would not be a good option for the attractiveness of the Spanish Liga or for F.C. Barcelona itself.

Julian Rieck is a historian, and is currently studying for a doctorate at the Humboldt University of Berlin.

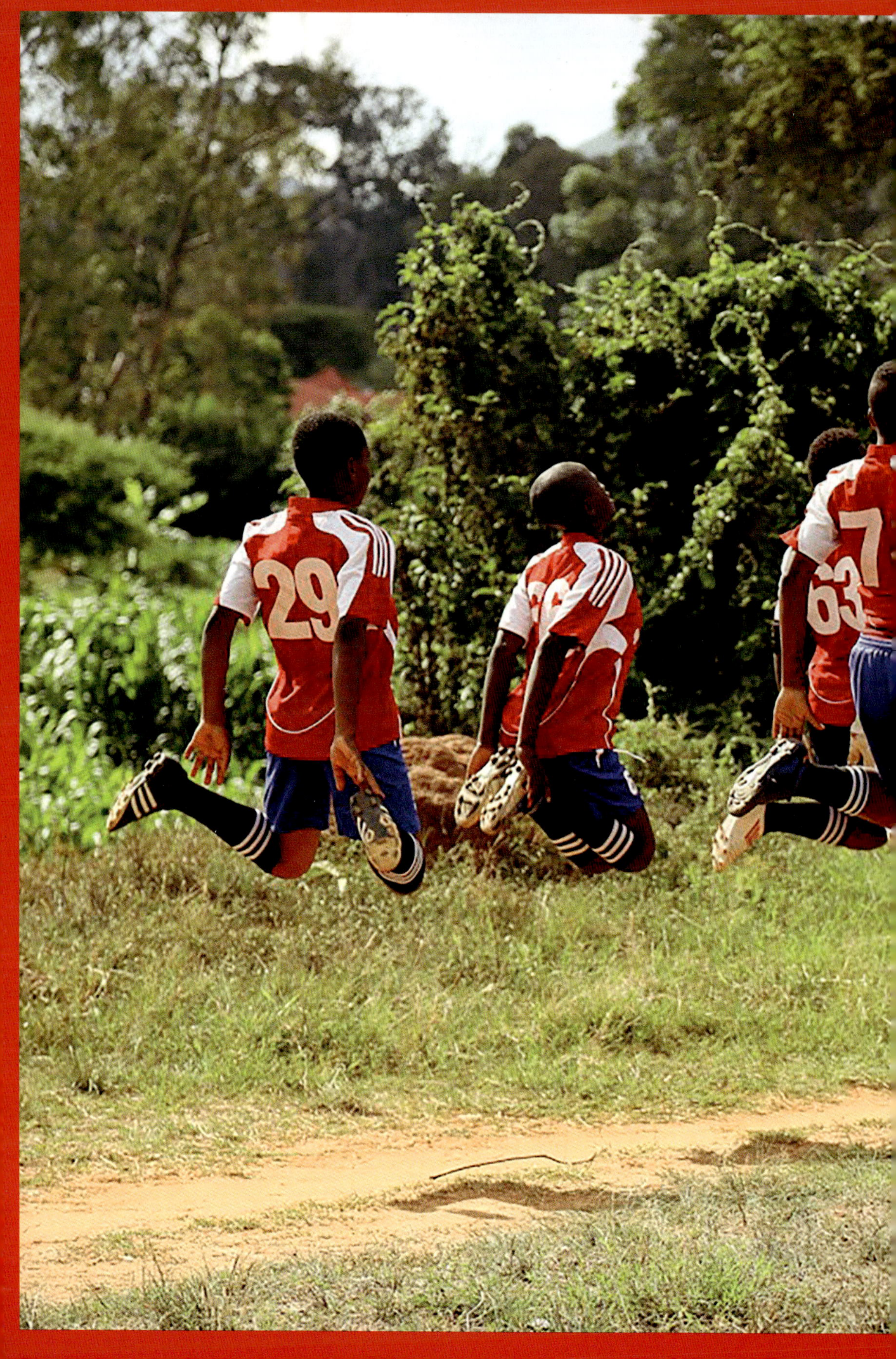

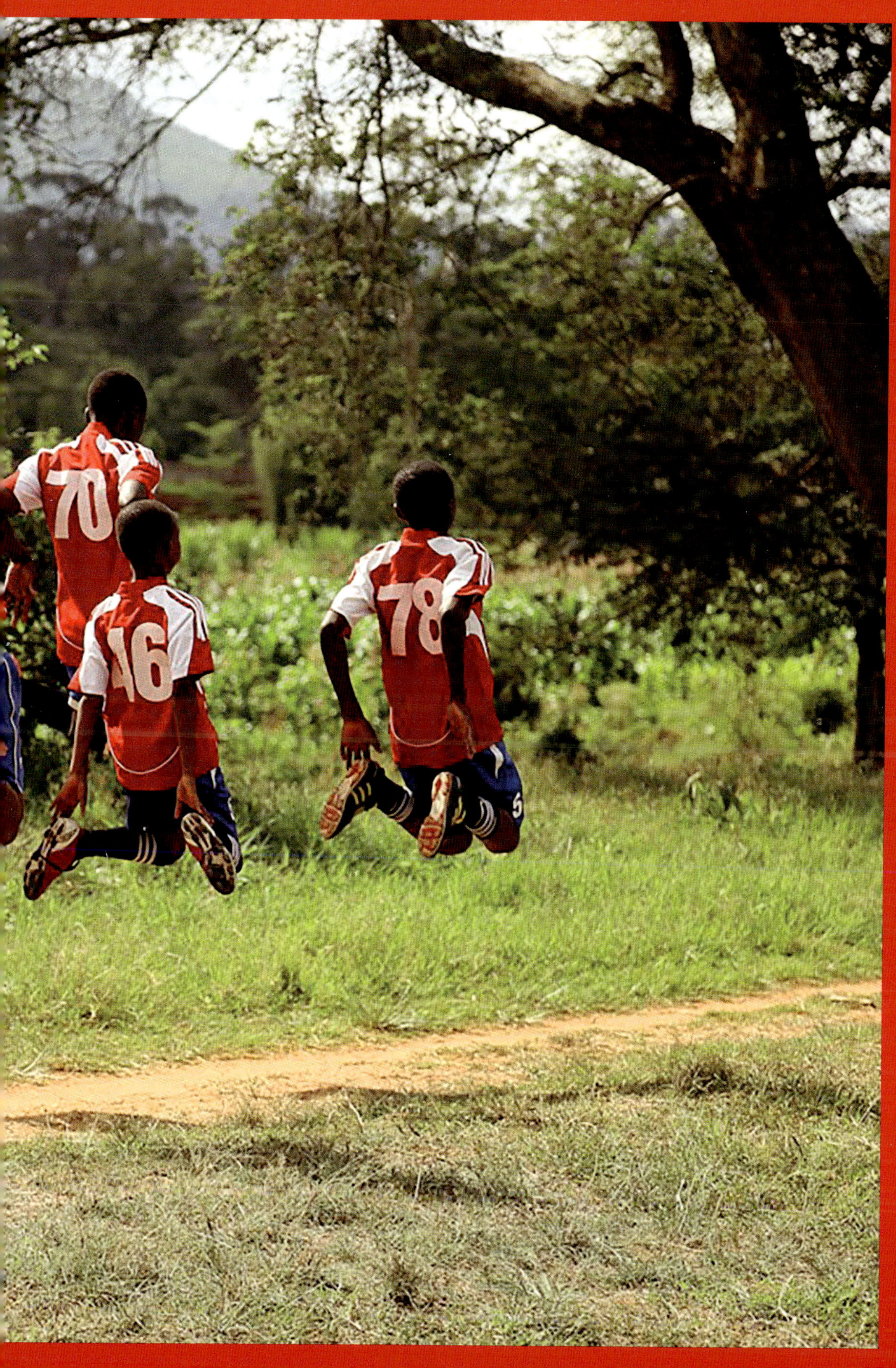

Building a nation, destroying a nation? Much of the literature dealing with sport and nationalism has been centred on the role of sport in nation-building processes, but far less attention has been devoted to its more destructive side as a factor in the disintegration process of a state. Yugoslavia's disintegration began in a football stadium. It turned into a social arena where politically loaded slogans and other forms of nationalist paraphernalia became increasingly prevalent at football games. *By Dario Brentin*

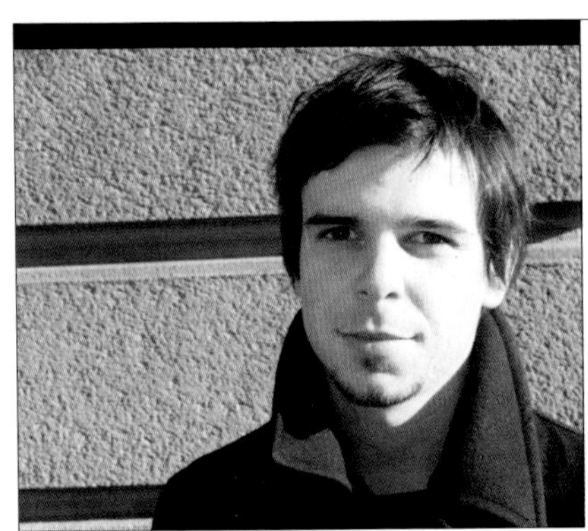

There is a widely accepted idea in both academic and popular understanding that sport represents a major ritual of popular culture that perpetuates the concept of the nation as an 'imagined community', a term coined by the American political scientist Benedict Anderson. It is a social field encompassing social axioms, values and norms, thereby (re-)producing them. Particularly when it comes to national imagination, sport functions as a symbolic (and actual) field in which all complexities of the 'nation' can be reduced to more tangible and digestible entities. Most famously, the historian Eric Hobsbawm once noted that the imagined community is so much more 'real' when it is represented through eleven named players who symbolically embody the nation in their performance.

With regard to modern nationalism, the term 'sportive nationalism' refers to the argument that sport draws its strongest ideological momentum from the fact that it ostensibly represents a 'true' and 'genuine' expression of patriotism and passionate nationalism. It stipulates that this genuine support for the nation is not related to official forms of government-sanctioned expressions of national belonging. This ambiguity is epitomised in the capacity of sport to oscillate between being a legitimator and contestant of political authority and the political representatives of the 'nation'. It is precisely this area of ideological ambiguity that is worth focusing on. While a great deal of the academic literature dealing with sport and nationalism has been centred on the role of sport in nation-building processes, far less attention has been devoted to its more destructive side as a significant social factor in the disintegration process of a state.

National(ist) motor

The history of sport in the later years of socialist Yugoslavia makes for an intriguing case study that exhibits both the both integrating and disintegrating potential of sport, and particularly football. During the late 1980s, and more particularly in the very early 1990s, it was Yugoslav football that prominently highlighted the structural crisis in which the country found itself. Apart from severe economic problems, hyperinflation and a drastic rise in unemployment, the inability of the Yugoslav political elites to resolve what was initially an economic crisis gradually aggravated social problems. These were accompanied by the rise of nationalist politics and demands for stronger autonomy in some republics of the socialist federation. This increased politicisation of everyday life 'from above' was mirrored in the field of sport through the politicisation of spectators 'from below'.

A space for political radicalisation

At the time, Yugoslav football had deteriorated into an increasingly contested space, with supporters demonstrating open allegiances with particular Yugoslav nationalities and promoting violence against other ethnic groups; a taboo within the socialist federation, where the ideology of Brotherhood and Unity still represented a fundamental pillar of political self-understanding. The stadium was turning into a social arena in which politically loaded slogans and other forms of nationalist paraphernalia were becoming the dominant sight at football games across the federation. The anonymity of the stadium made

Emulating and exacerbating the radicalised political discourse against each other, the reoccurring symbolic and literal violence emblematised the increasingly fragile condition of the Yugoslav federation at that time.

it difficult to prosecute people for displaying illegal national flags, political messages, songs and banners, with stadia thus representing a de facto space for political radicalisation that was outside the law.

Nevertheless, this phenomenon remained predominantly visible within a fairly marginalised social group: football fans. Or, to use the sociologist Srdjan Vrcan's terminology, Yugoslav 'football fan tribes'. Emulating and exacerbating the radicalised political discourse against each other, the reoccurring symbolic and literal violence emblematised the increasingly fragile condition of the Yugoslav federation at that time. Within a very short period of time, football became one of the major mobilising tools for nationalist ideology and an intriguing social field in the process of Yugoslav disintegration.

One intriguing incident stands out when talking about Yugoslav sport history and has provoking continuous popular and academic interest for more than twenty five years: the Maksimir riots of 13 May 1990. It was the day when the 'eternal rivals' in the Yugoslav football league, Red Star Belgrade and Dinamo Zagreb, clashed at Zagreb's Maksimir stadium. Instead of a spectacle of sporting rivalries, the game turned into chaos and had to be suspended due to violent clashes between the two opposing sets of fans. Even today, the incident is commonly referred to in the post-Yugoslav space as the symbolic day socialist Yugoslavia's dissolution began, or 'the day the war started'.

CNN summarised the global fascination with the Maksimir riots – which is manifested in the countless academic and popular publications that are usually triggered by anniversaries – when in 2011 it suggested that due to its magnitude and historic significance, it should be listed as one of only five football games that 'changed the world'.

The timing of the game was indeed historic. It took place only two weeks after the first democratic election in the still socialist republic of Croatia, which saw the pro-independence nationalist forces around Franjo Tudjman and his Croatian Democratic Union (HDZ) win the elections. The political landscape of Yugoslavia was rapidly transforming, accelerated by global developments and the ongoing domestic political crisis, with pro-independence and nationalist political forces all over the federation increasingly gaining momentum and institutionalising their political power.

The tensely awaited game escalated into wild stadium and street fights and violent clashes between supporters – the Delije of Red Star Belgrade and Dinamo Zagreb's Bad Blue Boys. Interestingly the Delije were headed by the future Serbian war criminal and paramilitary leader Željko Ražnatović, nicknamed 'Arkan'. Although there had been several smaller incidents on Zagreb's city streets during the afternoon, the rival 'fan tribes' were nonetheless allowed to enter the stadium, which was described by Yugoslav media commentators as looking more like a gladiatorial arena than a football stadium. As soon as the stands were occupied and the groups had taken their positions, they started exchanging highly charged political, ethnic and religious insults in the form of banners, flags and chants.

Shortly afterwards, the Delije started tearing down parts of the stadium; a fairly regular practice in the repertoire of football fan tribes in their attempts to humiliate the opposing fans by destroying their most sacred space of identification. Their action resulted in immediate but minor physical altercations with Dinamo supporters in the southern stands of the stadium. The confrontation, however, soon escalated when other Bad Blue Boys decided to join in with their fellow supporters. What followed was an hour- long chaos with the Bad Blue Boys breaking through the fences and engaging in a massive brawl with the Delije as well as police forces on the pitch. The totally outnumbered and poorly organised federal police could not prevent what would turn out to be the worst riot in Yugoslav sporting history, and it was transmitted live on television to the entire federation.

Croatian pantheon of national heroes

Even within these exceptional circumstances, there was still one moment that stood out. At one point, with the chaos still raging, the 19-year-old Dinamo Zagreb captain, Zvonimir Boban ran onto the pitch, trying to help a Dinamo supporter who was being beaten by the police. He used a – now legendary – kung-fu kick against a Yugoslav police officer. In this way, Boban, who later reached global fame with AC Milan, strikingly captured the antagonisms of the Yugoslav crisis.

The magnitude of his kick, however mythologised it may have become in the contemporary context, lay in its symbolic message. Boban did not strike down one single police officer, but rather a representative who stood symbolically for the Yugoslav state. His act ultimately earned him a place in the Croatian pantheon of national heroes.

The Maksimir riots, while symbolically significant, should nonetheless be understood as a condensed symptom of the ongoing political crisis in socialist Yugoslavia, most strongly manifested in the rise of Serbian and Croatian nationalism. The riots were rather a social mechanism that publically and forcefully expressed social tensions and the public frustration with a political system that was still in denial over the severity of the crisis in which it found itself. Without diminishing the symbolic significance of the Maksimir riots, they have to be included in a series of football-related incidents that happened in close proximity in order to fully grasp the mobilising power of football for nationalist ideology at that time.

What can be established is that the Yugoslav 'war(s)' definitely did not start at Maksimir on 13 May 1990. Rather, the incident set in motion a process in which football would grow into representing a social field in which physical and symbolic violence became a general and almost legitimate form of conflict 'resolution'. Football games began mirroring the weakness of the Yugoslav state, the symbolic transformation of spectators into soldiers, the mobilisation of nationalist agendas and ultimately the country's dissolution.

Less than a month after the Maksimir riots, the Yugoslav national football team was scheduled to play a friendly match against the Netherlands at the very same stadium. It was the last preparatory match for Yugoslavia's top footballers before heading to the 1990 FIFA World Cup in Italy. The team mainly consisted of players who had won the FIFA U-20 World Cup in Chile three years earlier, with the team being

> **Rather, the incident set in motion a process in which football would grow into representing a social field in which physical and symbolic violence became a general and almost legitimate form of conflict 'resolution'.**

eager to have a significant impact at senior level, too. The team itself was headed by the 'last Yugoslav', Ivica Osim, who is still widely considered to have been the mastermind behind the successful 'golden generation' of Yugoslav football.

With the political climate still tense from what had happened a few weeks earlier, the game was labelled by many media commentators as an indicator of whether the riots had been a genuine and popular expression of Croatian nationalism and opposition towards Yugoslavia or whether they were just a one-off incident that got out of hand.

Shortly after the two teams came on the pitch it became evident that Maksimir stadium would once again be at the centre of a Yugoslav-wide debate about fan behaviour as manifestations of political ruptures in the country. Supporters in the roughly half-full stadium greeted the Yugoslav team with boos and jeering and verbally attacked the players and head coach Osim. Not only did the spectators drown out the Yugoslav anthem 'Hej Slaveni' but they sang the unofficial (now official) Croatian anthem 'Lijepa naša'. The act was a clear message from the 20,000 spectators that they no longer accepted Yugoslav state symbols as their own, particularly if they were superior to Croatian symbols.

The game itself became utterly secondary, with Yugoslavia losing to the Netherlands 0:2. Many commentators were left perplexed because most games involving the Yugoslav national team had until then been largely spared any chauvinist incidents, and the national team was widely perceived as being a strong (popular) cultural force of integration. That summer the Yugoslav national football team played an inspired World Cup in Italy, only to lose on penalties in the quarter final against Argentina. It was doomed to be the last major football tournament for a unified Yugoslav team.

By August 1990 the Yugoslav state crises had deepened alarmingly with the jibes and rhetoric of the preceding months and the inability to resolve the constitutional crisis, leading to the so-called 'log revolution'. It saw the Serbian minority in the Croatian hinterland of Krajina revolting against the newly elected Croatian governance by sealing off the region around the city of Knin, bringing the country to the brink of war. This crisis was highly anticipated in the heavily politicised field of Yugoslav football fan tribes.

Fans set flag on fire

On 26 September 1990 another game in the Yugoslav football league escalated into a Yugoslav-wide debate about football, hooliganism and nationalism. Less than 100 kilometres from the uprising's epicentre in Knin, the game between Hajduk Split and Partizan Belgrade at Split's Poljud stadium once more epitomised the volatile situation the federation was in. During the game a large group of the organised section of the Hajduk Split fans, the Torcida, decided to explicitly express their opposition towards Yugoslavia. Their initial pitch invasion turned into a far-reaching political statement after it was followed by another even more symbolic act. The supporters targeted the highest point of the stadium where several flags were hoisted, took down the Yugoslav flag, set it on fire and hoisted the burning flag back up the pole. This all happened against the background of constant 'Croatia – independent state' and 'Burn the flag' chants coming from the stands.

The outstanding aspect of their actions was, as noted by the sociologist Dražen Lalić, the fact that the aggression was not directed at a direct rival, as there were no Partizan supporters present at the stadium. The Torcida had directed their

anger at one of the most meaningful national symbols of Yugoslavia – its flag. The symbolic burning of the flag powerfully symbolised the erosion and utter lack of state legitimacy.

This period of highly politicised football games in the Yugoslav federation was concluded one month later on 17 October. It was the day when a selection of Croatian players, under the label of the Croatian national team, played an international friendly against the USA's national team in Zagreb. In order to make this possible, the Croatian football association, which was still part of the Yugoslav association, cleverly used a legal loophole in the statutes that allowed 'national selections' to play international friendlies too. The fact that the game actually took place can be identified as a significant diplomatic success, with the entire occasion included in a set of national(ist) celebrations that took place during those days.

Just one day earlier, the city had celebrated the re-installation of the Ban Josip Jelačić sculpture in Zagreb's main square. As a symbol of Croatian resistance against the Ottoman Empire, the sculpture had been removed during communist rule. The game was considered to be an integral part of these celebrations. National imagery and symbols were meticulously designed with the Croatian chequered patterns and the Ban Jelačić monument juxtaposed with the Stars and Stripes and the Statue of Liberty. The newly elected Croatian government thus purposefully utilised the game to signal to the United States of America and the international community, that it was ready to stand on its own feet as an independent nation-state.

To date, popular discourse both in the region and beyond has been widely uncritical in adopting the mythologised construct of the

Maksimir riots as an initiator of the Yugoslav break-up. Often arbitrarily used as an example characterising a 'prelude to war', the riots cannot be singled out if our aim is to grasp the extent to which football played a role in the country's disintegration.

To counter the standard argument, we only have to look at sport events that took place just a few months later; for example the fact that Dinamo Zagreb played against Red Star Belgrade almost a year after 'the war started' on 18 May 1991 at Maksimir stadium, only this time without any incident. Furthermore, the story of the great Croatian national hero Zvonimir Boban, is rather flimsy if we add that after his suspension from Yugoslav football ended, he played for Yugoslavia on several occasions. The last time was in Belgrade against the Faroe Islands on 16 May 1991, when the political conflict in Yugoslavia had actually already turned into war.

But today, 25 years later, the Maksimir riots are remembered in a number of ways in the post-Yugoslav space. Research by the anthropologist Ivan Djordjevic has shown that in Serbia, media and popular narratives about the riots are mostly characterised by 'silence'. Furthermore, there is no mythologisation of the riots by Delije. This is quite understandable, since they were ultimately the symbolic losers of the riots, particularly

Just one day earlier, the city had celebrated the re-installation of the Ban Josip Jelačić sculpture in Zagreb's main square. As a symbol of Croatian resistance against the Ottoman Empire, the sculpture had been removed during communist rule.

if we interpret them as 'the day the war started'.

In addition, Serbian public discourse is still very strongly defined by a lack of consensus in dealing with the Yugoslav wars of the 1990s and the question of Serbian responsibility. With regard to football 'fan tribes', who were among the first to volunteer for and operate in paramilitary combat, this means having to construct a sense of pride for having given their lives in a war in which Serbia officially never took part.

From spectators to soldiers

In Croatia on the other hand, the Maksimir riots have to be identified as a contemporary national myth. Its main mythologising function is to support the dominant national narrative on Croatia's formative years: namely the inevitability of the Yugoslav dissolution and the formation of a Croatian nation state as a conditio sine qua non. The politicising and subsequent ideological exploitation under the Tudjman regime produced a mythologised narrative, identifying the riots as a symbolic initiation of the so-called Homeland War.

This particular interpretation of the incident is not without reason. It allowed the Tudjman regime to include the riots into their narrative of Croatian statehood and how it was established. It perpetuated the narrative of an overwhelming popular support for Franjo Tudjman and his Croatian Democratic Union (HDZ) from the moment of their electoral victory; something that does not hold up under the spotlight of social research. The final year of socialist Yugoslavia was much more a contested political struggle than a 'manifestation of people's will'. The notion of the ideological homogeneity of

Croatian society was thus constructed in order to exclude political alternatives and competing narratives and function as a mechanism for securing legitimacy.

While it is difficult to argue that sport, and in particular football, did not play a significant role in late socialist Yugoslavia's history as a social field of nationalist mobilisation, the games discussed here nonetheless have to be understood in the context of political cleavages and radicalised tensions within the federation. However, the broadly established popular narrative that the 'war started at Maksimir' on 13 May 1990, even if only symbolically, is rather problematic. The riots were neither the start of the conflict nor its initiation, but rather a powerful manifestation of the rise (or decline) of football to being a significant nationalising and homogenising social field in all the Yugoslav republics, but most openly in Croatia and Serbia. The gradual transformation of football spectators into soldiers and the rising level of physical violence as a 'legitimate' form of conflict-solving furthermore blatantly mirrored Yugoslavia's weakness to deal with a crisis that would ultimately lead to its dissolution.

Dario Brentin, born 1984 in Zagreb, is a University Assistant at the Centre for Southeast European Studies (CSEES) at the University of Graz, Austria. Currently he is also completing a PhD candidate in Social Sciences at the School of Slavonic and Eastern European Studies (SSEES) at University College London (UCL), focusing on sport and identity in post-socialist Croatia.

Swede of the year The story of footballer Zlatan Ibrahimović is that of the son of immigrants who made it out of the ghetto, excelled in the world's football stadiums, married a blond Swedish girl and was successfully integrated into Swedish society. It is a story of an outsider who was so assimilated into Swedishness that he came to symbolise something very Swedish.

By Anders Ravn Sørensen

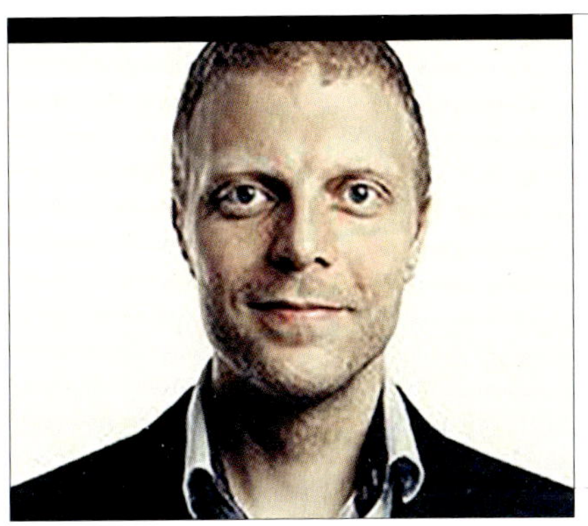

It was absolutely incredible. On that dark and cold Stockholm evening in November 2012 Sweden beat England 4-2 in an international soccer friendly. Trouncing a star-littered English team was a remarkable accomplishment in itself. But it was more than the result. In what the sports press described as a 'magical' performance, Swedish team Captain Zlatan Ibrahimović had completely taken over the stage, scoring all four of Sweden's goals – each one more beautiful than the next. The fourth goal in particular was a definite candidate for one of the best in the history of the sport. With a wondrous bicycle kick 30 yards out, from a preposterously high angle, Ibrahimović hit a volley that arched over the stranded goalkeeper Joe Hart and dropped into the goal. Swedish fans were ecstatic. Even the visiting English fans were compelled to applaud. Zlatan Ibrahimović is worthy of attention for more than just his accomplishments on the football field. He is also a potential subject for scholarly analysis because of his status as a vehicle of Swedish nationalism that, paradoxically, espouses a certain 'otherness' that stems from his immigrant background.

The nationwide celebration of Ibrahimović raises interesting questions on the significance of celebrated sports superstar with immigrant roots, and the roles that these athletes play in the continuous construction and potential reconstruction of nations. Is Ibrahimović capable of pushing and redefining the boundaries of the Swedish nation? I would argue that Ibrahimović has become a potent symbol of Swedishness that both reproduces existing narratives about the Swedish nation and at the same time potentially redefines the boundaries of that nation. By introducing the concept of nation work in the context of sports celebrities, I argue that such celebrities can both reinforce and potentially alter what it means to belong to a national community.

That evening in November 2012 Ibrahimović was a national hero. He was widely embraced and celebrated by pundits, mainstream politicians and the media. In December following the game against England, the Swedish Language Council even included a new verb, 'at zlatanera' (to Zlatanate) into its list of new words in 2012. The word meant to do something audacious or immensely impressive. For sure, Zlatan Ibrahimović had transcended the sphere of sports to become more than a brilliant footballer. He was a Swedish cultural phenomenon – with his own word in the national dictionary.

An ambiguous national symbol

Yet, even though Ibrahimović was celebrated as a national hero with his word in the dictionary, and even though he in 2015 was voted Swede of the Year by a major Swedish newspaper he remained a somewhat ambiguous national symbol. Not everybody agreed on his symbolic meaning. He was Swede of the year, yes. Captain of the national soccer team, yes – but there was also something inherently foreign and slightly exotic about him. Prominent members of the right-wing Swedish Democrats (a party that is strongly sceptical about immigration and that has been gaining popular support) often highlighted his 'otherness' and stated that they did not consider him to be really Swedish. In a radio broadcast on national radio, Swedish Democrat board member Mattias Karlsson explained that he did not regard Ibrahimović as 'Swedish in the way he thinks, acts and talks. He displays an attitude that in many ways does not feel typically Swedish... He displays a body language and a language in general that I do not really comprehend as Swedish.'

But how can Ibrahimović be considered both Swedish and non-Swedish at the same time, and what is it about him that has made him a Swedish symbol yet at the same time somewhat different? The answer has to do with his immigrant background, and existing ideas about the Swedish nation.

Ibrahimović grew up in Rosengård a neighbourhood of concrete apartment buildings in the suburbs of Sweden's second-largest city, Malmö. With more than 80 percent of the population being of non-ethnic Swedish decent, Rosengård is certainly vying for the label of ghetto with its comparatively high crime rate and host of social problems.

In this environment Ibrahimović, son of a Croat and a Bosnian Muslim, scored his first goals on the local asphalt pitches. Having toured with a couple of the local teams, from which he was often banned due to his short temper and lack of discipline, young Ibrahimović eventually made it to the first team of Malmö FF. From here his career was propelled into the hemisphere of European club football when he signed for clubs such as Ajax Amsterdam, Juventus, Inter, Barcelona and Paris Saint-Germain.

The story of Zlatan Ibrahimović, as it is often told in Swedish media, is a story of the son of immigrants who made it out of the ghetto, excelled in the world's football stadiums, married a blond Swedish girl, Helena Seger, whom he met when he was only nineteen, and was successfully integrated into Swedish society.

It is a story of an outsider who was so assimilated into Swedishness that he came to symbolise something very Swedish. This narrative was authoritatively disseminated by Ibrahimović himself and his biographer David Largercranz in the widely published and acclaimed autobiography 'I am Zlatan

Ibrahimović' from 2012. With the aid of Lagercranz's forceful prose the book perpetuated the narrative of Zlatan's personal success, and his success as a different yet fully accepted Swede.

The myth of Zlatan

In a recent article on media discourses about Zlatan Ibrahimović and the story of Ibrahimović's road to inclusion, literary scholar Christine Sarrimo (2015) described how an 'immigrant's path from provincial otherness to a Western literary space' has gradually developed into a mediatised myth. This myth not only walks hand-in-hand with the commercialisation of Ibrahimović as a brand, but at the same time it serves an ideological purpose.

This ideology, Sarrimo writes, 'fulfils the political vision of the immigrant being assimilated and integrated into Swedishness'. The myth not only fuelled the brand that was Ibrahimović, but the myth was also very much in consonance with prevailing political ideas about Sweden as an open and culturally diverse society, (although the recent refugee crisis in Europe challenges Sweden's historical commitment to be a safe haven for refugees and immigrants).

The Swedish Language Council even included a new verb, 'at zlatanera' (to Zlatanate) into its list of new words in 2012. The word meant to do something audacious or immensely impressive.

After the 4-2 victory over England another Swedish national player, Kim Källström, praised Ibrahimović and emphatically reiterated the narrative of Zlatan as a unifying figure who incarnates a new and inclusive Swedish identity. 'With foreign-born parents and certain problems in society' Källström explained, 'he can hopefully unify the country in a good way. Football builds bridges. He's a modern Swede who stands for the new Sweden'.

As such, through Kim Källström, the mythical narratives of Ibrahimović become performative in the sense that they themselves contribute to a collective understanding of Swedishness that is reified through a range of different media: newspapers, books and not least commercials.

The myth of Zlatan was not only reproduced by the sports press. The narrative of Ibrahimović as a 'modern Swede' who 'stood for the new Sweden' was skilfully exploited when in 2015 Swedish carmakers Volvo launched a campaign to promote the new Volvo XC70. Central to the campaign was a two-minute film in which we see Ibrahimović hunting a stag in the snow-covered landscape of Northern Sweden. He goes swimming in an icy lake and drives his Volvo XC70 through blizzard-stricken roads. In between these images of classic Swedish scenes, we see short glimpses of Ibrahimović's wife Helena Seger and his children.

In the background Zlatan himself, with a distinct accent, slowly recites a slightly modified version of the Swedish national anthem. The film ends with Ibrahimović stating that he 'will live and die in Sweden' while a text explains that the new Volvo model (and implicitly Ibrahimović as well) are 'Made by Sweden'. The film was a success and it boosted Volvo's sales. The car company managed to appropriate Ibrahimović's national ambiguity in the context of the Volvo brand – which itself was facing a potential challenge under the influence of globalisation as the company had recently been bought by new Chinese owners.

But the film remained more than a commercial success. With its impressive images and its narrative of Ibrahimović as a new modern Swede, the commercial also spurred strong positive emotional responses. In one of the country's largest newspapers, cultural editor Rakel Chukri, admitted that she was brought to tears by the commercial when Zlatan uttered the last sentence about living and dying in Sweden. 'Despite my obvious reservations about Volvo's owners being Chinese, and despite the stereotypical display of masculinity' Chukri wrote, 'I could not help but interpret the film as revenge on all dyspeptic critics who have refused to accept that Zlatan is in fact Swedish'.

The above descriptions of the Zlatan myth and its potential performativity invites questions about the role of famous sports figures in redefining and pushing the boundaries of nations. Are athletes such as Zlatan Ibrahimović capable of influencing the way that national communities perceive themselves and reproduce national identities? In the case of Zlatan Ibrahimović, it seems plausible that his mythical character and image as a new, modern and multicultural Swede contributes to an incremental redefinition of Swedishness.

Nation work

Within the literature on nationalism and national identity, the concept of nation work has gained prominence in recent years. The nation work approach builds on the recent 'cognitive shift' within nationalism studies that emphasises categorisation and classification over traits and substance.

Nation work entails the habitual and everyday maintenance and redefinition of nations at the margins. Nation work involves a process of categorisation that helps to distinguish different nations from each other, it involves a specification of members of national communities that is mediated trough other identity categories such as race, gender or ethnicity, and it acknowledges, in the words of sociologist Kristin Surak, that 'who we are may be established not only vis-a-vis them, but also other members of us. A person may be a particularly good or bad

He goes swimming in an icy lake and drives his Volvo XC70 through blizzard-stricken roads. In between these images of classic Swedish scenes we see short glimpses of Ibrahimović's wife and his children. He slowly recites a slightly modified version of the Swedish national anthem.

member, a typical or strange member, an exemplary or phony member, of the national community. Here contrast is made against neither an external other, nor even an internal other'.

The idea of nation work seems a promising analytical avenue when it comes to understanding what an individual such as Ibrahimović is doing to the Swedish nation. My suggestion is that he is 'working' it. What the mediatised myth of Zlatan does is to offer new categories of identification within the framework of the Swedish nation. Zlatan Ibrahimović (or more precisely, the narratives about him) helps distinguish the Swedish nation from other nations. But his Swedishness is configured by his immigrant background. This makes him a different kind of member of the Swedish community; one that other members are able to mirror themselves in and use as a marker of identity. In short, the myth of Ibrahimović potentially pushes the boundaries of the Swedish nation, as it offers a new category of identification as a 'modern' Swede that arguably is a little different, but still as Swedish as they come.

Anders Ravn Sørensen is Assistant Professor at Copenhagen Business School in the Department of Management, Politics and Philosophy. His main areas of research are nationalism studies, cultural history and organisation studies. He has published articles on the uses of history in organisations and the appropriation of national history for identity and brand purposes.

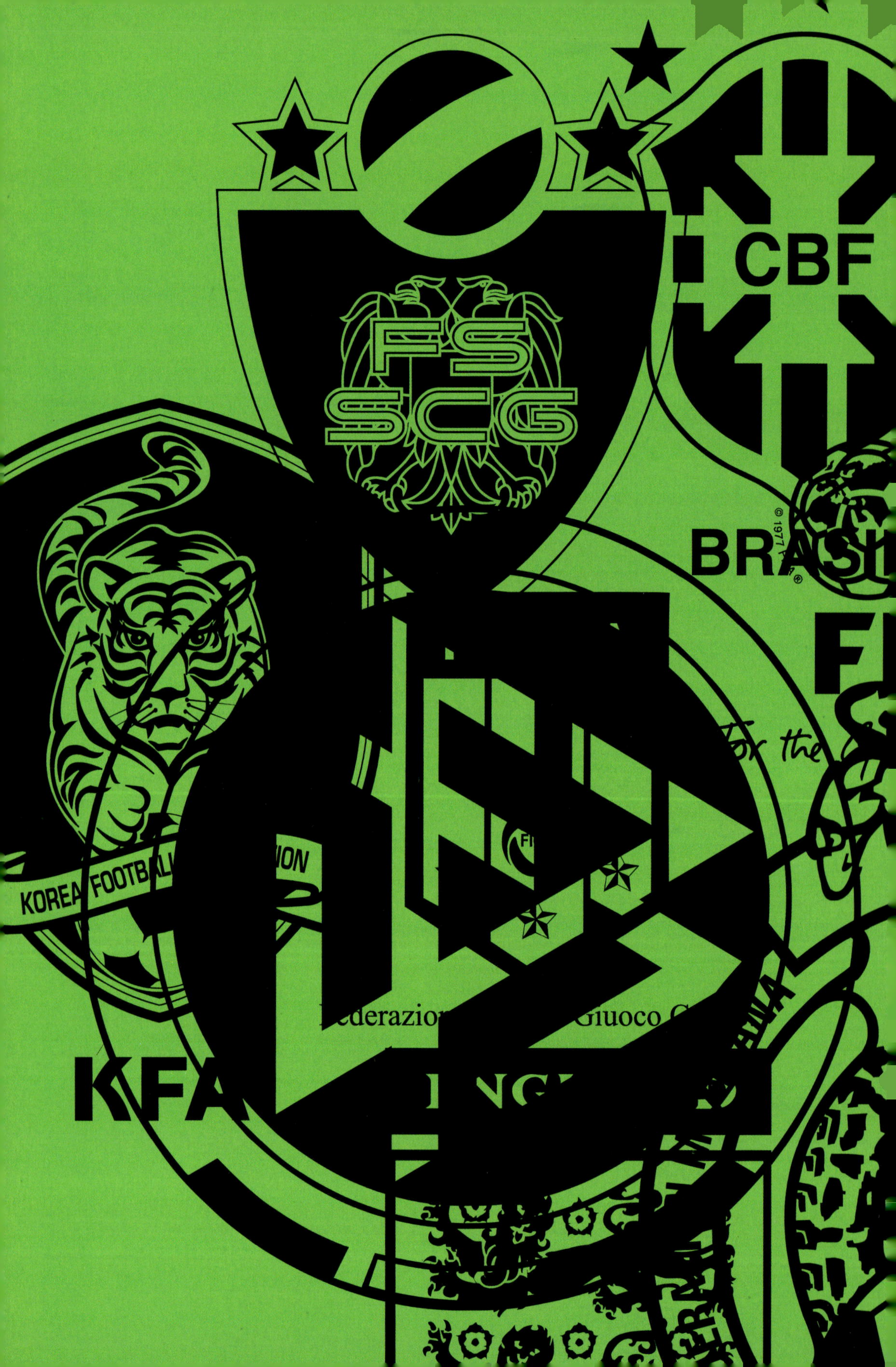

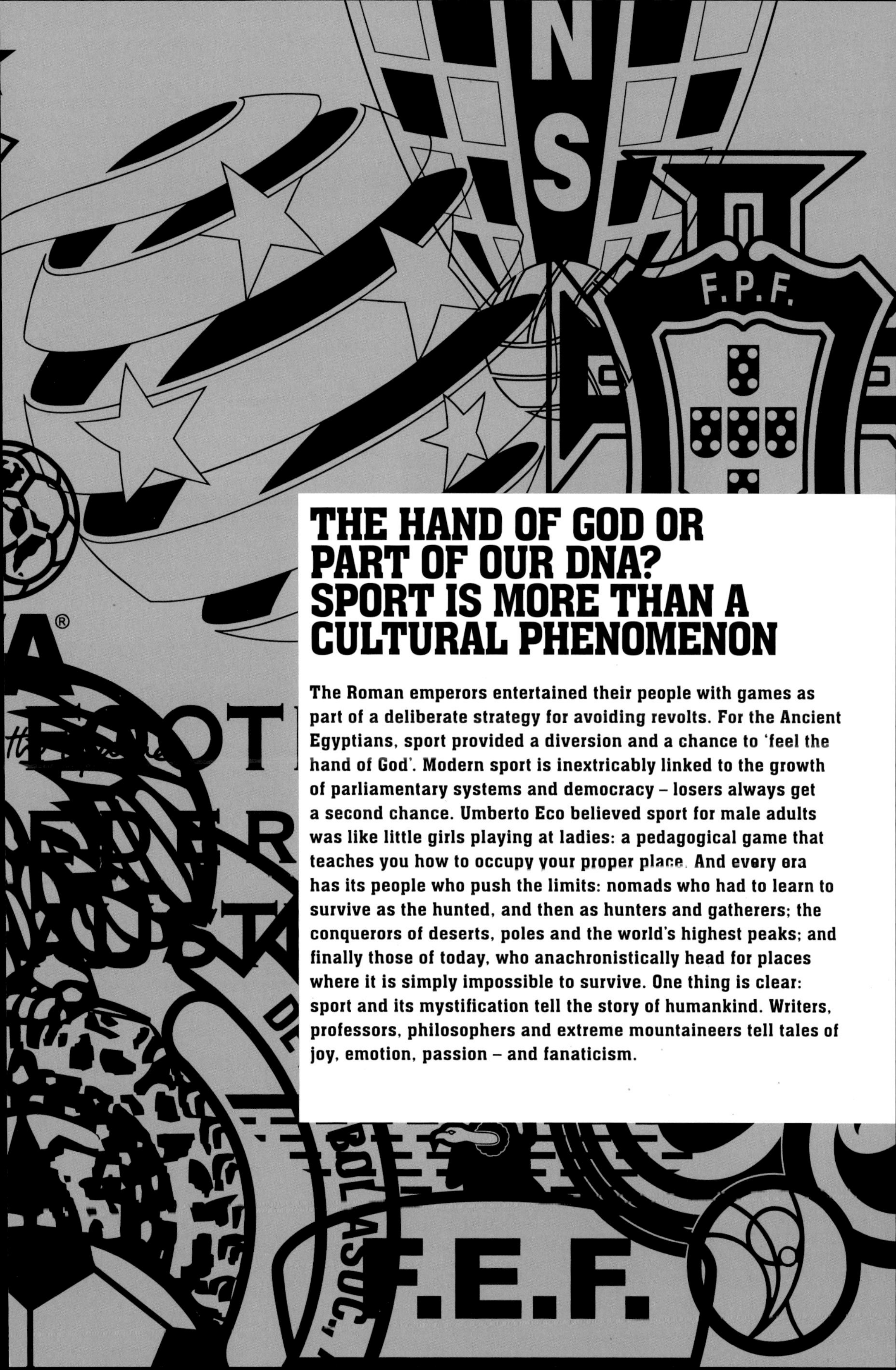

THE HAND OF GOD OR PART OF OUR DNA? SPORT IS MORE THAN A CULTURAL PHENOMENON

The Roman emperors entertained their people with games as part of a deliberate strategy for avoiding revolts. For the Ancient Egyptians, sport provided a diversion and a chance to 'feel the hand of God'. Modern sport is inextricably linked to the growth of parliamentary systems and democracy – losers always get a second chance. Umberto Eco believed sport for male adults was like little girls playing at ladies: a pedagogical game that teaches you how to occupy your proper place. And every era has its people who push the limits: nomads who had to learn to survive as the hunted, and then as hunters and gatherers; the conquerors of deserts, poles and the world's highest peaks; and finally those of today, who anachronistically head for places where it is simply impossible to survive. One thing is clear: sport and its mystification tell the story of humankind. Writers, professors, philosophers and extreme mountaineers tell tales of joy, emotion, passion – and fanaticism.

A force for emancipation and discrimination

A force for emancipation and discrimination The development of modern sport is inextricably linked to parliamentarism, industrialisation and the advancement of the principle of competition in business and society. Losers always get a second chance, an opportunity to recover and make a comeback. While the logic of winning is by definition undemocratic, and indeed inherently elitist, the long process of becoming a winner has the effect of encouraging and fostering democracy.

By Andrei S. Markovits

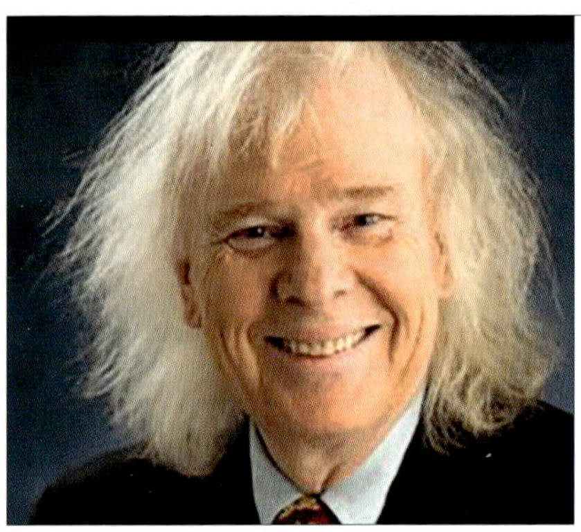

The word 'sport' comes from the Middle English 'disport' or 'desport', which can best be defined as 'to amuse oneself', 'frolic' and also 'divert oneself'. So sport involves amusement, diversion and games. Here the English language with its words 'game' and 'play', along with 'match', with its four meanings of ignite/light, harmonise/correspond, contest/compete but also deceive/defraud, is much more nuanced than the German 'Spiel' and the French 'jeu'.

And indeed modern sport is a gift to the world from the two English-speaking democracies – chiefly Britain, but also the USA. Of course just about every culture has always played 'games', an essential constitutive element of modern sport. As the great Dutch cultural historian Johan Huizinga wrote long ago in his classic book 'Homo Ludens', it seems to be in people's genes, or at least in their social DNA, to play – somehow and somewhere.

Play is a ubiquitous human activity. And like play, physical activity, another key constituent of sport, is also ubiquitous in the world. The Romans played harpastum, an ancient kind of football; the Chinese also enjoyed ball games, as did the Egyptians, Incas and of course many Native American peoples. In Europe, France was a particular hotbed of ball games, and the mediaeval football games of Italy and England live on in 'calcio fiorentino', which is played all summer long in the Piazza Santa Croce in Florence, to the delight of locals and tourists alike, and in the Royal Shrovetide football match that takes place every Shrove Tuesday and Ash Wednesday in the Derbyshire town of Ashbourne, the most famous of the many folk football games that are still played in Britain.

It is no coincidence that folk football is also known as mob football, as these matches are contested by large and above all unknown numbers of players in two 'teams'. Rules are few and at times there is a touch of violence, or at least rowdiness. The vague rules have changed over time and never been institutionalised in the modern sense, so these games remain incomprehensible to outsiders. This means they have never lost their provincial, local character, which is part of their often well-marketed charm in our highly mobile and globalised world.

In Shrovetide football, the Up'Ards, people who live north of the river, face the Down'Ards from south of the river in a game that lasts for hours and roams around the whole town and its surrounding area. Its key legacy lies in the word 'derby', a football match between traditional local rivals, which is referred to as a classico in Romance languages and as rivalry games in North American English.

It seems that all cultures have always recognised and played these kinds of games. A few years ago a Romanian colleague assured me that baseball is a Romanian invention, because in Romania and elsewhere there are a great many games of the bat-and-ball variety. These are the predecessors to modern variants such as tennis, cricket, baseball and other sports involving hitting a ball with a bat or racket.

Development of modern sport

But what is particularly interesting is the fundamental change from occasional and of course local pastimes to the development of modern sport. This required the setting of some not strictly adequate, but absolutely necessary conditions, which were welcomed primarily by Britain and then by the USA.

I would like to briefly outline the work of Berlin historian Christiane Eisenberg (and

It seems to be in people's genes, or at least in their social DNA, to play – somehow and somewhere. It is a ubiquitous human activity.

particularly her book 'English Sports und Deutsche Bürger') and the work of the legendary Harvard scholar Barrington Moore Jr. ('Social Origins of Dictatorship and Democracy') in this area in order to highlight the key factors that led to the development of modern sport in England and how this contrasts with its absence in Germany, Austria, France and other countries of continental Europe.

1. The permeability of the aristocracy and middle classes. The German aristocracy was much more exclusive than the British, and paradoxically it was also more numerous and impoverished. While the British nobility was thoroughly commercialised, their German counterparts remained largely untouched by this development. The main reason for this was the principle of primogeniture in the British aristocracy. The oldest son automatically inherited the title while the rest of the family had to earn their living outside the household. This led to the British aristocracy entering professional and commercial life, so in a way they became middle-class.

2. The powers of the British monarchy were curtailed early on.

3. The emergence of parliamentarism.

4. The early onset of the commercialisation of business and society, even before the Industrial Revolution.

5. The promotion of the principle of competition in business and society.

6. By the late 18th century, the idea of gambling – that unequal lottery that is based on pure luck and organised by the state – had led to the development of information science, expertise, training and regulated ways of thinking and acting in boxing, horseracing, golf and cricket, and this was crucial to their success.

In his ground-breaking studies on the connection between skill and luck, particularly in the areas of investment, inventions in various fields, and sport, Scott Page of the University of Michigan demonstrates how the culture of gambling and socially constructed actions – such as sport – promote the components of skill, so expertise, knowledge and data gathering, in contrast to 'pure' games of luck in which few cognitive abilities are invested, practised and learned.

The English sports economist Stefan Szymanski compares early developments in sport in the UK and USA with those of France and Germany, and shows that the main difference between them was the strength of the middle classes in the former and the strength of state authority in the latter. In the 17th century the people of the British Isles (particularly England and Scotland) were developing what Szymanski calls 'associativity' with others, so a tendency towards creating social groups in voluntary organisations that were not subject to any kind of state intervention. Clubs were perhaps the most important of these.

Such clubs were created for the strangest of reasons, often quite at random or because of personal preferences for pastimes that brought together its founders and members. They included totally frivolous games that

Socially constructed actions – such as sport – promote the components of skill, so expertise, knowledge and data gathering, in contrast to 'pure' games of luck in which few cognitive abilities are invested, practised and learned.

were quite pointless in and of themselves. Szymanski pithily describes this as 'flagrant pointlessness'.

There is certainly no real point or problem-solving purpose to hitting a small ball towards a little hole 100 yards away using strange-looking clubs, but in Scotland this came to be known as 'golf'. At first, strange games such as golf and cricket had little sense in and of themselves. But over time they developed into complex and modern networks of competing clubs, which soon created a set of rules. In this way they constructed and promoted the languages of golf and cricket with all their grammar, rules and exceptions.

To begin with, these ball games were quite pointless. They had no military purpose and did not train the body in ways that might be of service to the state, as was very often the case in Germany and France. It was only later, in the post-Napoleonic and particularly the Victorian era in Britain, that these games were used for purposes such as 'muscular Christianity' and other ideological purposes in terms of upbringing, education and physical training – of course for young men only – and legitimised and justified in this way. In contrast to Britain, this way of dressing sport in ideological garments in order to legitimise the system and serve the state (particularly in team sports) only occurred later in the USA.

There is no doubt that baseball successfully ousted cricket in US sports culture in the 19th century because it was seen a way of asserting American identity over British identity. In the 18th century we see how this new domain that would come to be known as sport began to promote the idea of performance as the most important element.

In the end it was the Sephardic Jew Daniel Mendoza (1764–1836), who was not only the first true sports star in Britain – and hence the world – but who is still referred to and recognised as the 'father of scientific boxing', the first person to successfully integrate and apply modern methods in this sport.

Gentlemen and players

Incidentally, it is said that Mendoza was the first Jew to speak to King George III. En route to the team sport of cricket that was codified in 1787, the meritocracy of the sport also meant that at the Marylebone Cricket Club (MCC), where Thomas Lord opened a

A few years ago a Romanian colleague assured me that baseball is a Romanian invention, because in Romania and elsewhere there are a great many games of the bat-and-ball variety, the predecessors to modern variants such as tennis, cricket, baseball and other sports involving hitting a ball with a bat or racket.

playing field in 1786 that came to be known as Lord's, the North London mecca of cricket, 'gentlemen' could join 'players' on the same pitch and play with and against each other in total equality, although the changing rooms of gentlemen and players remained segregated until the 1960s, and team captains had to come from the ranks of the gentlemen.

It is important to note that – in contrast to the etatist developments in German states and France at that time – the prominence of the MCC as the ultimate decision-maker on all things relating to cricket did not emerge through state intervention or through the club's own efforts, but through a process of a gradual levelling of all institutions that were relevant to the game and embedded in England's middle class society, a result of the 'associativity' as defined by Szymanski.

Even then we observed the parallel action of the two dimensions that are inherent to sport and still exist and define it today: the meritocratic performance and results-related dimension on the field, in the arena and on the part of the players themselves, which works in a binding and integrative way; and the off-field dimension that is group-affirming and emphasises differences, which in contrast leads to division and separation.

Nowhere are these two competing characteristics of modern sport that prima facie exclude each other while still being symbiotic better described than in what I believe is the best book on sport ever written: 'Beyond A Boundary' by C.L.R. James. This book provides an excellent overview of the colonially oppressive yet at the same time meritocratically freeing power of cricket.

Norbert Elias was right when he linked

the development of modern sport in Britain and particularly England – above all as the origin of many team sports using a ball-shaped object – to a particular phase in the development of civilisation and middle class society. In terms of timing and structure, these coincided with the founding of the Bank of England, the abolition of state censorship and the beginnings of an executive branch run by a cabinet, which Jürgen Habermas believes were central to Britain's democratic development and the emergence of its middle class.

Systematising competition

As betrayed by the terms 'fair play' and 'amateur', or the wonderful English expression 'to be a good sport', these structures harbour a certain tolerance of losing. Only the political systems of parliamentary organisations, liberal democracies even – where a certain tolerance of even the harshest opposition and antinomy is the norm that preserves their existence – could systematise competitions in which there are always winners and losers, but whose attraction lies precisely in this dichotomy. Losers always get a second chance, an opportunity to recover and make a comeback. While the logic of winning is by definition undemocratic, indeed inherently elitist because there can only be one winner, the long process of becoming a winner has the effect of encouraging and fostering democracy.

It was not such a long journey from the amateur games in public schools and the Oxbridge cosmos to the dictum of Vince Lombardi, the almost mythical ex-coach of the Green Bay Packers, whose name today ad-

It is not by chance that modern sport reflects the essence of its creator, that is to say the liberal democracies. At the beginning, at least nominally, everyone has the same access and starting conditions, all take part under equal terms and follow rules that have been understood and approved by everyone involved, but in the end there can only be relatively few winners.

orns the championship trophies of American football and who summed up the essence of modern sport when he said: 'Winning is not everything, it's the only thing'. And the words of Bill Shankly, the no less legendary former manager of Liverpool FC, when he suggested that football is not a matter of life and death, but much, much more than that.

If we substitute football with North America's Big Four (baseball, basketball, American football and ice hockey); with cricket in Pakistan, India, Australia and New Zealand; and with certain other team-based ball games in other countries, then we have the essence of this structure, which I call 'hegemonic sports cultures'.

It is not by chance that modern sport reflects the essence of its creator, that is to say the liberal democracies. To begin with, at least nominally, everyone has the same access and starting conditions, all take part under equal terms and follow rules that are understood and approved by everyone involved, but in the end there can only be relatively few winners.

The uncertainty of every result, perhaps the key difference between sport and all other areas of entertainment and the arts, also represents a democratising moment – because for every undertaking that on paper seems hopeless, there is always the chance of an upset, the implicit possibility that David could beat Goliath. But paper is one thing, the playing field is another. Without this uncertainty, sport just turns into a show like 'entertainment wrestling' where the roles of winner and loser are staged.

I will now take a brief look at the emancipatory and cosmopolitan dimensions of sport. More specifically, I would like to do this via the three axes of class, race and gender – the holy trinity of social sciences in today's America.

Let's begin with class. Broadly speaking, the predecessors of sport until the post-Napoleonic era were spontaneous, non-organised, often crazy, violent and almost exclusively local folk events for the lowest social classes. This then changed drastically with the wide-ranging reforms and reconceptualisation of sport as part of the mens sana in corpore sana ideology at the public schools and universities such as Oxford and Cambridge.

Sport became the domain of gentlemen, a pastime for the elite, for whom taking part is

In the USA, in the first half of the 20th century the urban sports of boxing and basketball were disproportionately popular with Jews, and this urban character led to their growing popularity with Afro-Americans in the second half of the century.

much more important than winning, which is frowned upon. And, for God's sake, sport is no longer allowed to have anything to do with money – sportspeople can never be paid! Amateurism and ambitious dilettantism were declared as the ideal that everyone had to follow. The background to this is clear: amateurism, which was deliberately falsely and misleadingly linked to the Ancient Greeks in order to legitimise class exclusivity and give it a cultural gloss, was invented and propagated by the elite of Oxbridge and the public schools in order to make it difficult, if not impossible, for people of lower social classes to take part.

Upholding the idea of amateurism

Let's just think about why tennis and cricket players always have to wear white. It means that dirt quickly shows up, so that clothing has to be constantly washed, something that presented a real obstacle to poorer people at that time. And why were cricket matches always played during the week and over several days? Until the late 20th century, the ethics and metrics of upholding the idea of amateurism quite simply gave legitimacy to such important sporting entities as the Rugby Union and, above all, the Olympic Games.

The elite culture of Oxbridge students in the 1860s and 1870s still remains the all-encompassing ideology of American college sport, which is run by so-called student athletes. For most participants this flies in the face of reality (almost all the over 430,000 current student athletes receive no payment, go on to pursue other careers and practice their sport during the four years of their university undergraduate courses simply for enjoyment), but in the culturally significant sports of college basketball and college football it leads to significant contradictions, conflicts and transgressions.

Class exclusivity begins to change

This class exclusivity began to change around 1869, when the Cincinnati Redstockings baseball team turned into the world's first fully professional sports team, meaning that for the first time 25 individuals received a set salary for playing a children's game in front of an audience. And it should be noted that most of the Redstockings players came from humble backgrounds, and there was only one player who came from Cincinnati. So from then on the logic of winning turned into the logic of the best player, regardless of geographical origin, particularistic obstacles and characteristics considered to be restrictive. At heart, this is the logic behind globalisation, a social driver that is inclusive and hence cosmopolitan because of its absolute focus on winning.

This democratisation of baseball continued with the founding of the first professional sports league in the world, the National League of Professional Baseball Clubs, in 1876. In the 1870s and 1880s, similar developments were playing out in parallel on the other side of the Atlantic, where association football was becoming increasingly commercialised, and therefore more professional and socially inclusive.

The English professional football league was founded in 1888, turning the game into the country's most democratic sport.

While rugby explicitly turned away from these democratic and commercial developments and swore quasi-eternal loyalty to its elite amateur status, the clubs in the Rugby Football Association that were mainly based in the working-class areas of the Midlands split away and set up the Rugby League, a separate institution based on professional players. It also developed its own code, which was different from the classic Union game, and therefore a new sports language.

In contrast, the Union game only turned professional in summer 1995, so exactly 100 years after it had frowned upon the working-class Rugby League with professional players. The tension and divisions around professionalisation, class origins and the milieu of association football and rugby union is best described in the following words, attributed to either Oscar Wilde or Rudyard Kipling (the origin of this saying is still not quite clear): 'Rugby is a game for barbarians played by gentlemen; football is a game for gentlemen played by barbarians.'

Let us now turn to race, and I would like to include religion in this category, as I find it makes little sense to worry about whether being a Jew is a religious or ethnic category. In ethnically pluralist countries, all types of sport are affected by ethnic codes and concerns.

For example, in South Africa rugby is still largely the preserve of whites – despite the film 'Invictus' and the World Cup victory in 1995 – or more precisely the preserve of Afrikaaners; while association football continues to be almost exclusively the sports culture of the country's black citizens.

In the USA, in the first half of the 20th century the urban sports of boxing and basketball were disproportionately popular with Jews, and this urban character led to their growing popularity with Afro-Americans in the second half of the century.

Racial integration of baseball

Racial integration, particularly in baseball with Jackie Robinson in 1947, marked the start of a series of key years for racial equality in the USA: 1954 (Brown vs. Board of Education); 1964 (Civil Rights Act); 1965 (Voting Rights Act); 1967 (Loving vs.Virginia) and 1972 (Title IX of the Education Amendments of the Civil Rights Act); a trend that was continued with the election of black mayors, members of Congress, senators, university presidents and, finally, the country's president. Jackie Robinson, Willie Mays and Henry Aaron in baseball; Jim Brown, O.J. Simpson, Walter Payton and Doug Williams (the first black quarterback to win the Superbowl) in football; Bill Russell, Wilt Chamberlain, Kareem Abdul-Jabbar, Earvin 'Magic' Johnson and Michael Jordan in basketball were and remain key figures in the long and ongoing emancipation of Afro-Americans in the USA; their outstanding sporting achievements have made them important agents of this social change.

As my co-author and University of Michigan colleague Lars Rensmann points out about his hometown of Dortmund and his favourite club Borussia, black Brazilian players Dedê and Julio Cesar have exercised an enlightening and extremely cosmopolitan influence on the town's culture and its people thanks to their excellent performances on the pitch.

Of course there have been and remain diehard racists and counter-cosmopolitan fans and citizens who will always remain immune to such developments, indeed who are even spurred on by the resentment they arouse. Yet there is no doubt that the performances on the field of representatives of ethnic minorities (who are almost always discriminated against and often even hated and spurned) have an emancipatory character, for two reasons.

Firstly, even the biggest racist learns to respect and appreciate an outstanding performance in a game that he loves for the team that he adores; indeed, he is almost obliged to accept this milieu. And secondly, the top performances of representatives of such ethnic minorities embody an incredibly important moment of affirmation, giving them confidence and advancing their participation in society as a whole and improving their potential for acceptance.

Zinedine Zidane symbolised a key moment of integration for many French citizens with Maghreb origins; Joe Louis was a key figure in the growing self-assurance of America's black citizens; and it is impossible to fully understand the integration of American Jews into the country's cultural mainstream without 'Hammerin' Hank' Greenberg and Sandy Koufax. Racism still exists in the stadiums of the English Premier League, but it has declined in direct proportion to

Among sportsmen, there is no equivalent of former tennis player Anna Kournikova: someone who becomes a global star based on their sex appeal rather than on the basis of consistent sporting success.

the growing numbers of black players on the pitch.

In short, the sporting performances and successes of the representatives of discriminated ethnic minorities smooth the way to their acceptance and integration into society. The more of such ethnic outsiders who emerge as successful figures in hegemonic sports cultures, the more accepted their ethnic groups will be by society. As ever, in this case quantity also possesses qualitative characteristics. For a long time, being accepted and noticed has not meant being respected, let alone loved. As we know from pertinent studies from the USA, people draw a distinction between black stars in sport, films, TV and music and 'normal' black people. Michael Jordan, Tiger Woods, Will Smith and Oprah Winfrey (far and away the richest woman in the USA) are not really seen by the public as being black; their fame has transformed them into transcendent stars whose ethnic background is irrelevant and not consciously perceived.

And now we come to the third factor, that of gender. With the exception of a few religions, in today's liberal democratic industrialised countries I am not aware of any public institutions or structures that exercise such an impenetrable, consistent, strict and a priori totally self-evident and fully legitimised gender segregation as sport – not in politics, business, academia, education or the arts. 'Sexual apartheid', as it was so appositely described by Paul Hoch a few years ago, although I prefer to call it 'gender apartheid', in order to highlight the social concept of gender rather than the physical determination, solely and exclusively defines the essence of sport.

Of course in all the other social spheres

The sporting performances and successes of the representatives of discriminated ethnic minorities smooth the way to their acceptance and integration into society.

mentioned above men still dominate. Patriarchy is still thriving – it's still a man's world. But at least over the last 30 or 40 years women have clearly challenged the Victorian middle-class hegemony and gained a strong foothold in some institutions that were formerly totally dominated by men.

But with very few exceptions this is not the case in sport. Of course there are some sports that are fully integrated right up to Olympic level and where women and men compete against each other, such as dressage and the Finn, 49 and Tornado sailing classes. And of course there have always been women who have managed to break through the iron cage of men's sport and directly challenge the opposite sex.

In 1973 Billie Jean King beat her male counterpart Bobby Riggs in the ultimate, very symbolic Battle of the Sexes tennis match. Swedish golfer Annika Sörenstam and her American colleague Michelle Wie have at times tried their luck on the men's tour; and the US racing driver Danica Patrick has now been successful for some time in the male domain of motorsport, and in 2008 she was even the first woman ever to win a race in the popular IndyCar series.

However, it is clear that such phenomena are very much one-offs and clear exceptions to the rule. But there is one immanent question: why, particularly in team sports, does it seem exotic and absurd to even occasionally consider the possibility of wide-ranging gender integration?

Why couldn't football teams play with five women and six men or vice versa? Apart from the Dutch sport of korfball, there are no mixed teams at the highest level in any sport, with the two sexes playing side-by-side in the same team. Why is this? Why do women only play against women and men only against men? Of course men can usually run faster, jump higher and are stronger than women. But isn't it possible to interpret citius, altius, fortius in a way that integrates gender? Why do we totally accept and more or less approve this gender apartheid, this clear discrimination in the area of physical activity, when we reject it totally in intellectual areas?

Gender apartheid

Despite the gender apartheid that exists in sport, over the last four decades women have broken into and conquered new worlds that were previously quite unthinkable, as I demonstrate with Lars Rensmann in our book 'Gaming The World: How Sports Are Reshaping Global Politics And Culture'. We only have to think of the incredible progress of women's sport in male-dominated team sports that have ruled the hegemonic sports cultures of Western countries for more than a century.

Zinedine Zidane symbolised a key moment of integration for many French citizens with Maghreb origins; Joe Louis was a key figure in the growing self-assurance of America's black citizens.

Until the 1970s in Germany, female football players played with smaller, lighter balls. They had no studs on their boots, played only for 60 minutes, were subjected to regular gynaecological examinations and had to submit to other similarly discriminatory and humiliating conditions. In the USA, up to the 1970s women's basketball teams were made up of 6 to 9 players (instead of the normal 5 in men's teams) and were only allowed to dribble once – later twice and in the 1970s even three times – before they had to pass the ball to another player.

It was 1982 before the National Collegiate Athletic Association opened its doors to the first women's basketball team. Since then, players at top teams such as Connecticut, Tennessee, Maryland, Stamford, Texas and Notre Dame have become real stars, with their matches regularly attracting up to 20,000 spectators and respectable TV viewing figures among the US sporting public.

Among sportsmen, there is no equivalent of former tennis player Anna Kournikova: someone who becomes a global star based on their sex appeal rather than on the basis of consistent sporting success.

With the help of in-depth interviews, I have been working with PhD student Jennifer California from the University of California in Berkeley to examine how the constructs and debates on sexuality and gender are different for sportswomen than for their male colleagues. We have shown how the rare violent acts committed by women in the heat of battle – such as in college basketball and college football – are immediately sensationalised and evaluated by the public according to quite different criteria than similar events

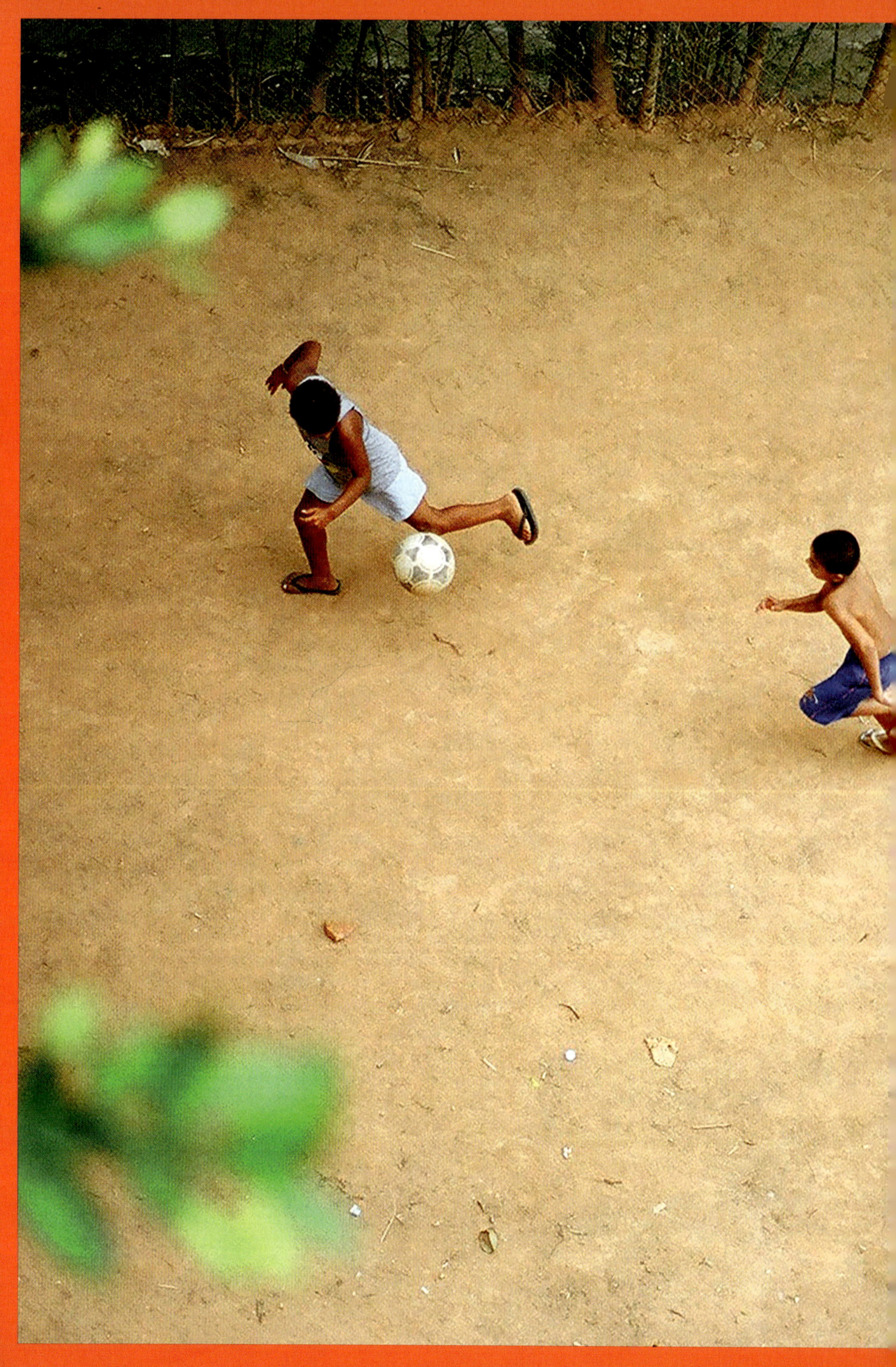

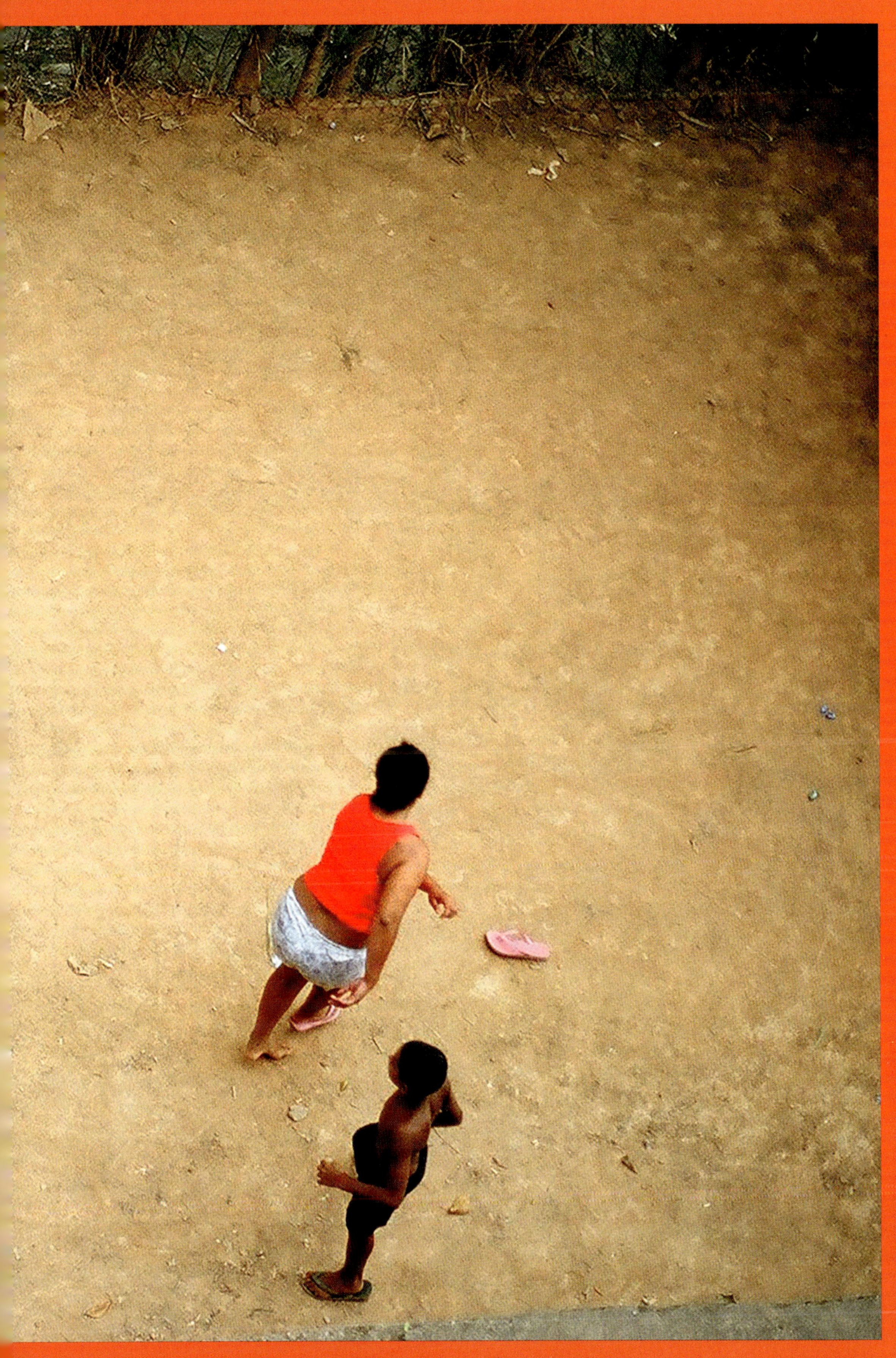

in men's sport, which are more or less everyday occurrences.

When women demonstrate expertise, knowledge and enthusiasm for sport, men tend to tolerate them rather than viewing them as equal partners.

It is interesting that this fear of intruding into a new milieu where they are not welcome only manifests itself in young female college students when it comes to sport. It is not prevalent in the discourse on politics, economy, culture and society, nor in study subjects, even in areas that still have a male connotation, such as physics and mathematics.

There are no examples of this in the world of sports language and sports cultures, which are still so male dominated. To some extent, acceptance has to come from the participants themselves, and we know that such informal legitimisation and 'naturalisations' are often more difficult than those that come from above or from outside.

All's fair in love and war

It is clear that from the moment that winning and victory became the be-all- and-end-all of sport – and not only simply taking part, as the media would still lead us to believe at the Olympic Games and many other tournaments – sporting activity has been accompanied by hostile, intimidating and discriminatory moments and activities between the players themselves, and particularly between their fans. In any competition, winning is linked to passion, so every time and in every constellation it will produce modes that at least tolerate behaviour that potentially breaks the

When women demonstrate expertise, knowledge and enthusiasm for sport, men tend to tolerate them rather than viewing them as equal partners.

rules, and may even promote such behaviour in order to gain victory.

When I hear the English phrase 'all's fair in love and war', I always add 'and in sport'. The boundary between fair fan behaviour and excited, but acceptable, support for your team on the one hand and unfair behaviour on the other is extremely fluid. It changes diachronically and synchronically and varies from sport to sport. In golf it is totally unacceptable to even cough, let alone shout, fidget or disturb the players' concentration in any way, whereas in basketball it is de rigueur during a free throw.

Changes in fan behaviour

The democratisation of tennis has also led to a change in the fans' behaviour. Over the last 20 years is has become normal to loudly cheer on one's favourite player until just before the serve, in this way spoiling their opponent's concentration. Interestingly, in tennis and golf acceptable forms of fan support have changed massively in team events such as the Davis Cup, Ryder Cup and President's Cup. Now cheering on the home team and taunting and opposing the visiting team is not only deemed totally acceptable, but even encouraged and required.

When these tournaments were played almost exclusively by American, Australian and British gentlemen, it was normal to politely applaud the opponents and be respectful when they were playing. People were among 'their own', part of an almost hermetically sealed group of insiders in terms of gender, class and race.

But when the sport became increasingly open to everyone, and when that most poisonous of all passions – nationalism – became involved, it became normal to deride, taunt, and spit at opposing teams and players, and even to throw beer, batteries and coins at them – actions that would give the home team a home advantage using every possible means and ignoring all social rules and conventions.

In this way, the boundaries between devoted fans and hooligans have become increasingly amorphous and unclear, because it is part of the competition to upset and unsettle the opponent, to shake their confidence so that they lose the game. What is allowed and not allowed? Should it be allowed to derive enjoyment from wading knee-high in the blood of dead Catholics, as the supporters of Glasgow Rangers do at least three times a year when they play against local rivals Celtic in the notorious Old Firm derby? ('Up to our knees in Fenian blood' is a line from the loyalist song 'The Billy Boys'.)

Should it be allowed to mention Auschwitz, Hitler, killing Jews and plays on words about Hamas and gas, as the away fans of Ferencváros, Feyenoord and Chelsea do regularly in different variations when their teams play the 'Jewish teams' MTK, Ajax Amsterdam or Tottenham Hotspur? Does it go beyond the acceptable when, in the decisive seventh game of the NBA final, the visiting team, the Los Angeles Lakers, have to endure a changing room in Boston Garden on a scorching hot day where there is no air-conditioning but the heating is blasting out – and surprise, surprise! – there's not a plumber in sight who can fix this 'problem'. Or if the fire alarm suddenly goes off at four in the morning in the visiting team's hotel and mysteriously it can't be switched off for an hour?

Clearly, it is considered to be a totally legitimate element of every sport to get into the opponents' heads and play with their minds. As part of my research into this topic in collaboration with a social psychologist and biologist, I would like to show that the main element of the huge home advantage is not the strange place, the unfamiliar playing location, the hotel, the different food or the long journey.

The home advantage

It is not specifically about logistics and organisational issues, but actually about the twelfth man in football, the seventh in ice hockey, the sixth in basketball, and so on – in short, it is the crowd, the fans and the atmosphere that they create that helps the home team and makes it difficult for the visiting team. We know that refereeing decisions in the North American Big Four demonstrate a

The boundaries between devoted fans and hooligans have become increasingly amorphous and unclear, because it is part of the competition to upset and unsettle the opponent, to shake their confidence so that they lose the game.

clear bias towards the home team, and this has also been examined in similar studies on the German Bundesliga and other European football leagues. There is a statistically significant variance that favours the home team. At the same time, studies from Italy show that the home advantage totally disappears if a team is forced to play their home games in an empty stadium.

The referees also lose at least a shred of their professionally imposed impartiality in the heat of battle and favour the home team, certainly for reasons of self-preservation and probably also because it is much more pleasant for people to be met with praise and love rather than threats, humiliation and hatred.

In this respect it is interesting to note that in the USA, a society that most statistics and indicators clearly show is more violent than Europe, violence, hatred, discrimination and exclusion are less prevalent in popular sports, and particularly in the dominant team sports of baseball, football, basketball and hockey than is the case in European football, which is the equivalent of the US Big Four in every respect. This applies to both quantity and quality. A few brief reasons for this are as follows:

1. The much higher numbers of women and families who attend Big Four games in the USA compared to football in Europe.
2. The Big Four teams have fewer political, religious, ethnic and other ties that create identity and hence fanaticism than is the case in European football.
3. Distances are much greater, meaning that it is much less usual for away fans to travel with their team than is the case in European football.
4. It is unusual for there to be two or more rival teams in the same area. In Europe this is still the case in most cities, and it was even more prevalent until relatively recently. Apart from Los Angeles, New York and Chicago, no cities in North America have more than one team in a league and sport; and where there are two teams they play in leagues that rarely meet, such as the American and the National League in baseball, so there is not such a strong history of bitter defeats and the associated need for revenge as is the case in European football.
5. Finally, and most importantly, in the USA there was an active and substantial civil rights movement that of course has not achieved all its aims, but it has outlawed explicit and publicly expressed racism, as unfortunately is still the case in the stadiums and arenas of Europe.

Without wishing to delve too deeply into theoretical issues at this point, I would like to refer to the American social scientist Robert D. Putnam. More than most other structures, sport has a high degree of 'bridging capital' and 'bonding capital' as Putnam describes them so aptly in his classic book 'Bowling Alone'. And if the 'bonding' capital hugely and consistently overwhelms the 'bridging' capital, the danger of a counter-cosmopolitan attitude, its mobilisation and finally manifestation in the form of unruly behaviour or even violence is very high.

Do you speak sport?

A final point: for me, sport is the structural equivalent of language. You 'speak' football, baseball, basketball and cricket. Just like real languages, you learn these sporting languages better and more easily if you learn them at a young age. As with all languages, the meta level is crucial and leads to the decisive mechanisms of inclusion or exclusion. Of course this does not mean that it is not possible to learn languages – including sporting languages – perfectly at a later stage in life, but it is very likely that you will still speak this language with an accent if you have not learned it before the age of around 12 to 14. This has been clearly shown by linguistic experts such as James Flege. Of course having an accent has nothing to do with one's ability in the language, both spoken and written. Joseph Conrad, who was born Józef Teodor Konrad Korzeniowski, only learned to speak fluent English when he was in his twenties, and he spoke with a very strong Polish accent throughout his life. Despite this, he became one of the English-speaking world's most significant authors of all time.

For me, learning the language of sports and real languages is clear and axiomatic proof of having an international, cosmopolitan mindset. This is why I am always so happy when some of my American students turn out to be experts or at least have an interest in football; and when my European students in turn have a corresponding interest in the North American sports languages of the Big Four, baseball, basketball, football and ice-hockey, and are motivated to learn more about them. Because in both cases they are actively appropriating a new culture. They are showing interest and involvement in something strange that they then appropriate through active intellectual and emotional engagement. Just as learning languages broadens people's horizons and gives them the means to access cultures that were previously foreign, the same applies to the polyglot world of sport. Surely there can be no better reason for being a true sports fan, expert and enthusiast?

Andrei S. Markovits teaches Political Science, Sociology and German Studies at the University of Michigan in Ann Arbor. He was born in Timişoara in Romania in 1948, the son of Hungarian-speaking Jewish parents, and emigrated with his father to Vienna when he was nine years old. In 1967 Markovits moved to the United States, where he acquired five degrees at Columbia University in New York. He has lectured at numerous top American universities and been a guest professor at many universities in Germany, Switzerland, Israel and Austria. Markovits has been awarded a number of research grants, including by the Institute for Advanced Study Berlin (Wissenschaftskolleg zu Berlin) and the Center for Advanced Study in the Behavioral Sciences at Stanford University. This article is based on a lecture given as part of the *Wiener Vorlesungen* lecture series in Vienna, published by Picus Verlag.

Sport is man, sport is society

Sport is man, sport is society Talk about soccer requires a more than vague expertise, but, all in all, it is well-focused. It doesn't oblige you to intervene personally, because you are talking about something played beyond the area of the speaker's power. For the male adult it's like little girls playing ladies: a pedagogical game, which teaches you how to occupy your proper place. *By Umberto Eco*

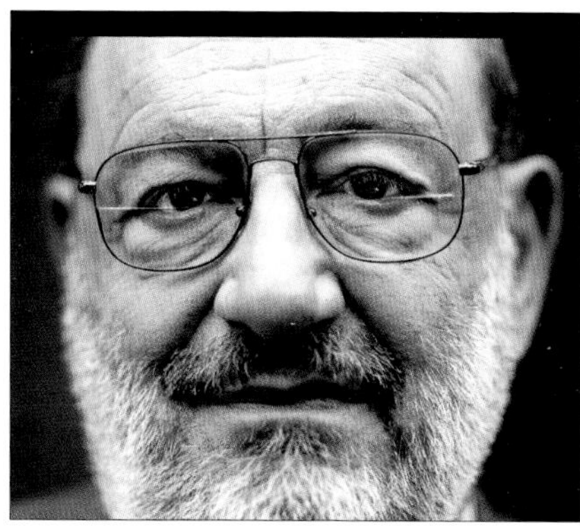

There is one thing that – even if it were considered essential – no student movement or urban revolt or global protest or what have you would ever be able to do. And that is to occupy the football field on a Sunday. The very idea sounds ironic and absurd; try saying it in public and people will laugh in your face. Propose it seriously and you will be shunned as a provocateur.

Not for the obvious reason, which is that while a horde of students can fling Molotov cocktails at the jeeps of any police force, and that at most (because of the laws, the necessity of national unity, the prestige of the state), no more than 40 students will be killed; an attack on a sports stadium (such as the recently thwarted attack in Paris) would surely cause the massacre of the attackers, indiscriminate, total slaughter carried out by self-respecting citizens aghast at the outrage.

You can occupy a cathedral, and you'll have a bishop who protests, some upset Catholics, a fringe of approving dissidents, an indulgent left-wing, the traditional secular parties (secretly) happy.

And you can occupy a party's headquarters, and the other parties, with or without a show of solidarity, will think it serves them right. But if a stadium is occupied, apart from the immediate reactions, the disclaiming of responsibility would be total: Church, Left, Right, State, Judiciary, Chinese, League for Divorce, anarchist unions, all would send the criminals to the pillory.

So there is a deep area of the collective sensibility that no one, whether through conviction or demagogical calculation, will allow to be touched. And there is a profound structure of the Social whose Maximum Cement, if broken up, would cause a crisis in every possible associative principle, including the presence of man on earth, at least as he has been present in the last tens of thousands of years.

Sport as a calculated waste

Sport is Man. Sport is Society. But if an overall revision of our human relationships is in process, let it also touch Sport. At this ultimate root it will discover the inconsistencies of Man as a social animal. Here what is not human in the relationship of sociality will emerge. Here the deceptive nature of the Classical Humanism will become dear, founded on Greek anthropolalia, founded in turn not only on contemplation, the notion of the city or the primacy of Doing, but on sport as a calculated waste, as a masking of the problem, 'chatter' raised to the rank of tumour. In short – and this will be explained below – sport is the maximum aberration of 'phatic' speech and therefore, finally, the negation of all speech, and hence the beginning of the dehumanization of man or the 'humanistic' invention of an idea of Man that is deceptive at the outset.

Sports activity is dominated by the idea of 'waste'. In principle, every sports act is a waste of energy: if I fling a stone for the sheer pleasure of flinging it – not for any utilitarian end – I have wasted calories accumulated through the swallowing of food, earned by work. Now this waste – I must make myself clear – is profoundly healthy. It is the way that it is proper to play. And man, like every animal, has a physical and psychic need for play. So there is a recreational waste that we cannot renounce: It means being free, freeing ourselves from the tyranny of indispensable work.

If, as I fling my stone, another man beside me aims to fling one still farther, the recreation takes on the form of 'contest', also a waste, of physical energy and of intelligence, which provides the rules of the game. But this recreational waste proves a gain. Races improve the race, contests develop and control the competitive spirit, they reduce innate aggressiveness to a system, brute force to intelligence.

But in these definitions lurks the worm that undermines the action at the roots: contest disciplines and neutralises the aggressive charge, individual and collective. It reduces excess action, but it is really a mechanism to neutralise action.

From this nucleus of ambiguous healthiness (a healthiness that is 'healthy' up to the point where a boundary is crossed – as you can die of an excess of that indispensable liberating exercise that is laughter, and Margutte explodes from exaggerated health) leads to the first degenerations of the contest: the raising of human beings dedicated to competition. The athlete is already a being who has hypertrophised one organ, who turns his body into the seat and exclusive source of a continuous play. The athlete is a monster, he is the Man Who Laughs, the geisha with the compressed and atrophied foot, dedicated to total instrumentalisation.

The athlete as monster

But the athlete as monster comes into existence at the moment when sport is squared, when sport, that is, from a game played in the first person, becomes a kind of disquisition on play, or rather play as spectacle for others, and hence game as played by others and seen by me. Sport squared equals sports performance.

If sport (practised) is health, like eating food, sport seen is a defrauding of health. When I see others play, I am doing nothing healthy, and I am only vaguely enjoying the health of others (which in itself would be a sordid exercise of voyeurism, like watching others make love), because in fact what I enjoy most are the accidents that will befall those who are healthily exercising, the illness that undermines this exercised health (like someone who watches not two human beings but two bees making love, while waiting to witness the death of the drone).

To be sure, someone who watches sport performed by others becomes excited as he watches; he yells and gesticulates, and so he is performing physical and psychic exercise, and reducing aggressiveness, and disciplining his competitivity. But this reduction is not compensated, as when one exercises sport, by an increase of energy or by an acquired control and self-mastery. On the contrary, for the athletes are competing in play, but the voyeurs compete seriously (and, in fact, they beat up one another or die of heart failure in the grandstands).

As for disciplining competitivity, which in exercised sport has the two aspects of increasing and losing one's own humanity, in

But if an overall revision of our human relationships is in process, let it also touch Sport. At this ultimate root it will discover the inconsistencies of Man as a social animal.

athletic voyeurism it has only one aspect, the negative. Sport is presented then, as it has been over the centuries, as instrumentum regni. These things are obvious: the circenses restrain the uncontrollable energies of the crowd.

But this sport squared (which involves speculation and barter, selling and enforced consumption) generates a sport cubed, the discussion of sport as something seen. This discussion is in the first place that of the sports press, and therefore sport raised to the nth power. The discussion on the sports press is discourse on a discourse about watching others' sport as discourse.

Present-day sports, then, is essentially a discussion of the sports press. At several removes there remains the actual sport, which might as well not even exist. If through some diabolical machination of the Mexican government and chairman Avery Brundage, in agreement with all the TV networks in the world, the Olympics were not to take place, but were narrated daily and hourly through fictitious images, nothing in the international sports system would change, nor would the sports discutants feel cheated.

So sport as practice, as activity, no longer exists, or exists for economic reasons (for it is easier to make an athlete run than to invent a film with actors who pretend to run); and there exists only chatter about chatter about sport. The chatter about chatter of the sports press constitutes a game with its full set of rules: you have only to listen to those Sunday morning radio broadcasts where they pretend (raising support to the nth power) that some citizens gathered in the barber shop are discussing sport.

Or else you can go and listen to such talk where it occurs. It will be seen, as for that matter everyone knows already, that evaluations, judgements, arguments, polemical remarks, denigrations, and paeans follow a verbal ritual, very complex but with simple and precise rules. In this ritual, intellectual energies are exercised and neutralised; physical energies are no longer in play, so the competition shifts to a purely 'political' level. In fact, the chatter about sports chatter has all the characteristics of a political debate. They say what the leaders should have done, what they did do, what we would have liked them to do, what happened, and what will happen. Only the object is not the city (or the corridors of the state house) but the stadium, with its locker rooms.

Such chatter seems therefore the parody of political talk; but since in this parody the strength that the citizen had at his disposal for political debate is vitiated and disciplined, this chatter is the ersatz of political speech, but to such a heightened degree that it becomes itself political speech.

Afterwards, there's no more room – because the person who chatters about sport, if he didn't do this, would at least realise he has possibilities of judgement, verbal aggressiveness, to employ somehow. But sports chatter convinces him that this energy is expended to conclude something. Having allayed his doubt, sport fulfils its role of fake conscience. And since chatter about sport gives the illusion of interest in sport, the notion of practising sport beco-

> **The chatter about sports chatter has all the characteristics of a political debate. They say what the leaders should have done, what they did do, what we would have liked them to do, what happened, and what will happen. Only the object is not the city (or the corridors of the state house) but the stadium, with its locker rooms.**

mes confused with that of talking sport; the chatterer thinks himself an athlete and is no longer aware that he doesn't engage in sport. And similarly he isn't aware that he could no longer engage in it, because the work he does, when he isn't chattering, tires him and uses up both the physical energy and the time required for sports activities.

Idle talk

This chatter is the sort of thing whose function Heidegger examined in 'Being and Time' under the heading of 'idle talk': 'Idle talk is the possibility of understanding everything without previously making the thing one's own. If this were done, idle talk would founder; and it already guards against such a danger. Idle talk is something which anyone can make up; it not only releases one from the task of genuinely understanding but develops an undifferentiated kind of intelligibility for which nothing is closed off any longer.... Idle talk does not aim to deceive. Idle talk does not have the kind of Being which belongs to consciously passing off something as something else.... Thus, by its very nature, idle talk is a closing-off, since to go back to the ground of what is talked about is something which it leaves undone.'

Certainly Heidegger wasn't thinking of idle talk or chatter as totally negative: chatter is the everyday manner in which we are spoken by pre-existent language rather than our bending language to ends of comprehension and discovery. And it is a normal attitude. For it, however, 'what matters is that there is talk'. And here we come to that function of language that for Jakobson is the phatic function, that of contact. On the telephone (replying 'Yes, no, of course, fine...') and in the street (asking 'How are you?' of someone whose health doesn't interest us, and he knows it, and in fact he plays along, in answering 'Fine, thanks'), we conduct phatic discourse indispensable to maintaining constant connection among speakers; but phatic speech is indispensable precisely because it keeps the possibility of communication in working order, for the purpose of other and more substantial communications.

If this function atrophies, we have constant contact without any message. Like a radio that is turned on but not tuned, so a background noise and some static inform us that we are, indeed, in a kind of communication with something, but the radio doesn't allow us to know anything.

Chatter then will be phatic discourse that has become an end in itself, but sports chatter is something more, a continuous phatic discourse that deceitfully passes itself off as talk of the City And Its Ends.

Born as the raising to the nth power of that initial (and rational) waste that is sports recreation, sports chatter is the glorification of Waste, and therefore the maximum point of Consumption. On it and in it the consumer civilisation man actually consumes himself (and every possibility of thematising and judging the enforced consumption to which he is invited and subjected).

A place of total ignorance, it shapes the ideal citizen so profoundly that, in extreme cases (and they are many), he refuses to discuss this daily availability has for empty discussion. And so no political summons could affect a practice that is total falsification of every political attitude. Thus no revolutionary would have the courage to revolutionise the availability for sports chatter; the citizen would take over the protest, or suddenly rejecting, and with desperate distrust, the intrusion of reason in his reasonable exercise of highly rational verbal rules.

Thus the students in Mexico City died for nothing when they protested against the Olympic Games. It seemed reasonable for an Italian athlete to say nobly: 'If they kill any more, I refuse to jump'. But it

Born as the raising to the nth power of that initial (and rational) waste that is sports recreation, sports chatter is the glorification of Waste, and therefore the maximum point of Consumption.

was not established how many they would have to kill for him not to jump. And if he then didn't jump, would be enough, for the others, to talk about what would have happened if he had jumped.

Many malignant readers, seeing how I discuss here the noble sport of soccer with detachment, irritation, and (oh, all right) malevolence, will harbour the vulgar suspicion that I don't love soccer because soccer has never loved me, for from my earliest childhood I belonged to that category of infants or adolescents who, the moment they kick the ball – assuming that they manage to kick it – promptly send it into their own goal or, at best, pass it to the opponent, unless with stubborn tenacity they send it off the field, beyond hedges and fences, to become lost in a basement or a stream or to plunge among the flavours of the ice cream cart. And so his playmates reject him and banish him from the happiest of competitive events. And no suspicion will ever be more patently true.

Everyday unreality

I will say more. In an attempt to feel like the others (just as a terrified young homosexual may obstinately repeat to himself that he 'has' to like girls), I often begged my father, a sober but loyal fan, to take me with him to the game. And one day, as I was observing with detachment the senseless movements down there on the field, I felt how the high noonday sun seemed to enfold men and things in a chilling light, and how

As far back as I can remember, soccer for me has been linked with the absence of purpose and the vanity of all things... and perhaps for this reason I (alone, I think, among all living creatures) have always associated the game of soccer with negative philosophies.

before my eyes a cosmic, meaningless performance was proceeding. Later, on reading Ottiero Ottieri, I would discover that this is the sense of the 'everyday unreality', but at that time I was thirteen and I translated the experience in my own way; for the first time I doubted the existence of God and decided that the world was a pointless fiction.

Frightened, as soon as I had left the stadium, I went to confession to a wise Capuchin who told me that I certainly had an odd idea, because reliable people like Dante, Newton, Manzoni, Gioberti and Fantappié had believed in God without the slightest difficulty. Bewildered by the consensus, I postponed my religious crisis for about another decade – but I have been telling all this to indicate how, as far back as I can remember, soccer for me has been linked with the absence of purpose and the vanity of all things, and with the fact that the Supreme Being may be (or may not be) simply a hole. And perhaps for this reason I (alone, I think, among living creatures) have always associated the game of soccer with negative philosophies.

The passion of soccer

Now, however, I must say that I am not against the passion of soccer. On the contrary, I approve of it and consider it providential. Those crowds of fans, cut down by heart attacks in the grandstands, those referees who pay for a Sunday of fame by personal exposure to grievous bodily harm, those excursionists who climb, bloodstained, from the buses, wounded by shattered glass from windows smashed by stones, those celebrating young men who speed drunkenly through the streets in the evening, their banner poking from the overloaded Fiat Cinquecento, until they crash into a juggernaut truck, those athletes physically ruined by piercing sexual abstinences, those families financially destroyed after succumbing to insane scalpers, those enthusiasts whose cannon-crackers explode and blind them: They fill my heart with joy. I am in favour of soccer passion as I am in favour of drag racing, of competition between motorcycles on the edge of a cliff, and of wild parachute jumping, mystical mountain climbing, crossing oceans in rubber dinghies, Russian roulette, and the use of

I am in favour of soccer passion as I am in favour of drag racing, of competition between motorcycles on the edge of a cliff, and of wild parachute jumping, mystical mountain climbing, crossing oceans in rubber dinghies, Russian roulette, and the use of narcotics.

narcotics. Races improve the race, and all these games lead fortunately to the death of the best, allowing mankind to continue its existence serenely with normal protagonists, of average achievement. In a certain sense I could agree with the Futurists that war is the only hygiene of the world, except for one little correction: It would be, if only volunteers were allowed to wage it. Unfortunately war also involves the reluctant, and therefore it is morally inferior to spectator sports.

For I am speaking of spectator sports, mind you, not of sport. Sport, in the sense of a situation in which one person, with no financial incentive, and employing his own body directly, performs physical exercises in which he exerts his muscles, causes his blood to circulate and his lungs to work to their fullest capacity: sport, as I was saying, is something very beautiful, at least as beautiful as sex, philosophical reflection, and pitching pennies.

But soccer has nothing to do with sport in this sense. Not for the players, who are professionals subjected to tensions not unlike those of an assembly-line worker (except for questionable differences in pay), not for the spectators – the majority, that is – who, in fact, behave like hordes of sex maniacs regularly going to see (not once in their lifetime in Amsterdam but every Sunday, and instead of) couples making love, or pretending to (something like the very poor children of my childhood, who were promised they would be taken to watch the rich eating ice cream).

Now that I have posited these premises, it is clear why I feel so relaxed during football World Cups. Rendered neurotic, like everyone else, by tragic world events when we have to devour newspapers and stay glued to the TV awaiting the latest escalation in terror, in the weeks that are dominated by football I can happily skip reading the papers, avoid TV, at most have a quick scan of the news. For the rest, the papers and the TV talk about things I want to hear nothing about.

The devotion of the mass media

There's no need to ask ourselves why the World Cup has so morbidly polarised the attention of the public and the devotion of the mass media: From the famous story of how comedy by Terence played to an empty house because there was a trained bear show elsewhere, and the acute observation of Roman emperors about the usefulness of circenses, to the shrewd use that dictatorships (including the Argentinian) have always made of great competitive events, it is so clear, so evident that the majority prefers soccer or bicycle racing to abortion, that it isn't even worth reflecting about. But since external pressure impels me to reflect I might as well say that public opinion, especially in

Italy, has never needed a nice international championship more than it does now.

In fact, sports debate (I mean the sports shows, talk about it, the talk about the journalists who talk about it) is the easiest substitute for political debate. Instead of judging the job done by the minister of finance, you ask whether the final or decisive game will be decided by chance, by athletic prowess or by diplomatic alchemy.

Little girls playing ladies

Talk about soccer requires, to be sure, a more than vague expertise, but, all in all, it is limited, well-focused; it allows you to take positions, express opinions, suggest solutions, without exposing yourself to arrest, to loyalty oaths, or, in any case, to suspicion. It doesn't oblige you to intervene personally, because you are talking about something played beyond the area of the speaker's power. In short, it allows you to play at the direction of the government without all the sufferings, the duties, the imponderables of political debate. For the male adult it's like little girls playing ladies: a pedagogical game, which teaches you how to occupy your proper place.

At moments like this, when preoccupa-

> **In the weeks that are dominated by football I can happily skip reading the papers, avoid TV, at most have a quick scan of the news. For the rest, the papers and the TV talk about things I want to hear nothing about.**

tion with the causa publica (the real one) is so traumatic, do we look at ourselves, as critical Italians and Europeans? For us, the World Cup is like the parmesan on our macaroni. Finally, some news that isn't about terrorism! Perhaps it would be best to engage in fewer political discussions and in more circenses sociology. Also because there are circenses that do not appear to be such at first glance, such as certain conflicts between police and 'extremists', that only take place on Saturdays, between 5pm and 7pm.

Umberto Eco, born in 1932, was a novelist, columnist, philosopher and media scholar. His works include *History of Beauty* and the novel *The Name of the Rose*, which brought him international fame. The above article is based on his book *Faith in Fakes: Travels in Hyperreality*, published in English by Vintage and translated from the Italian by William Weaver. Umberto Eco died in February 2016.

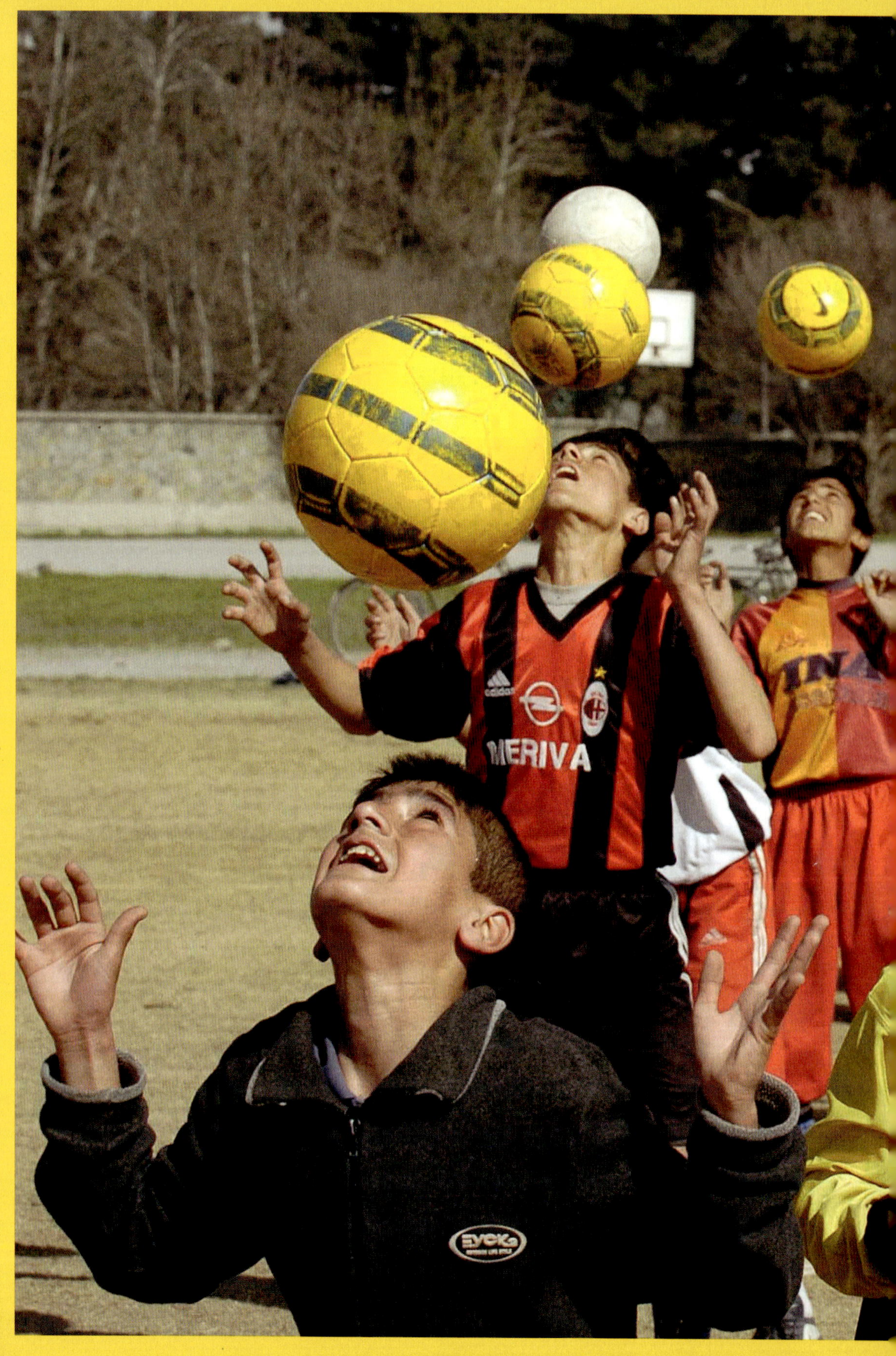

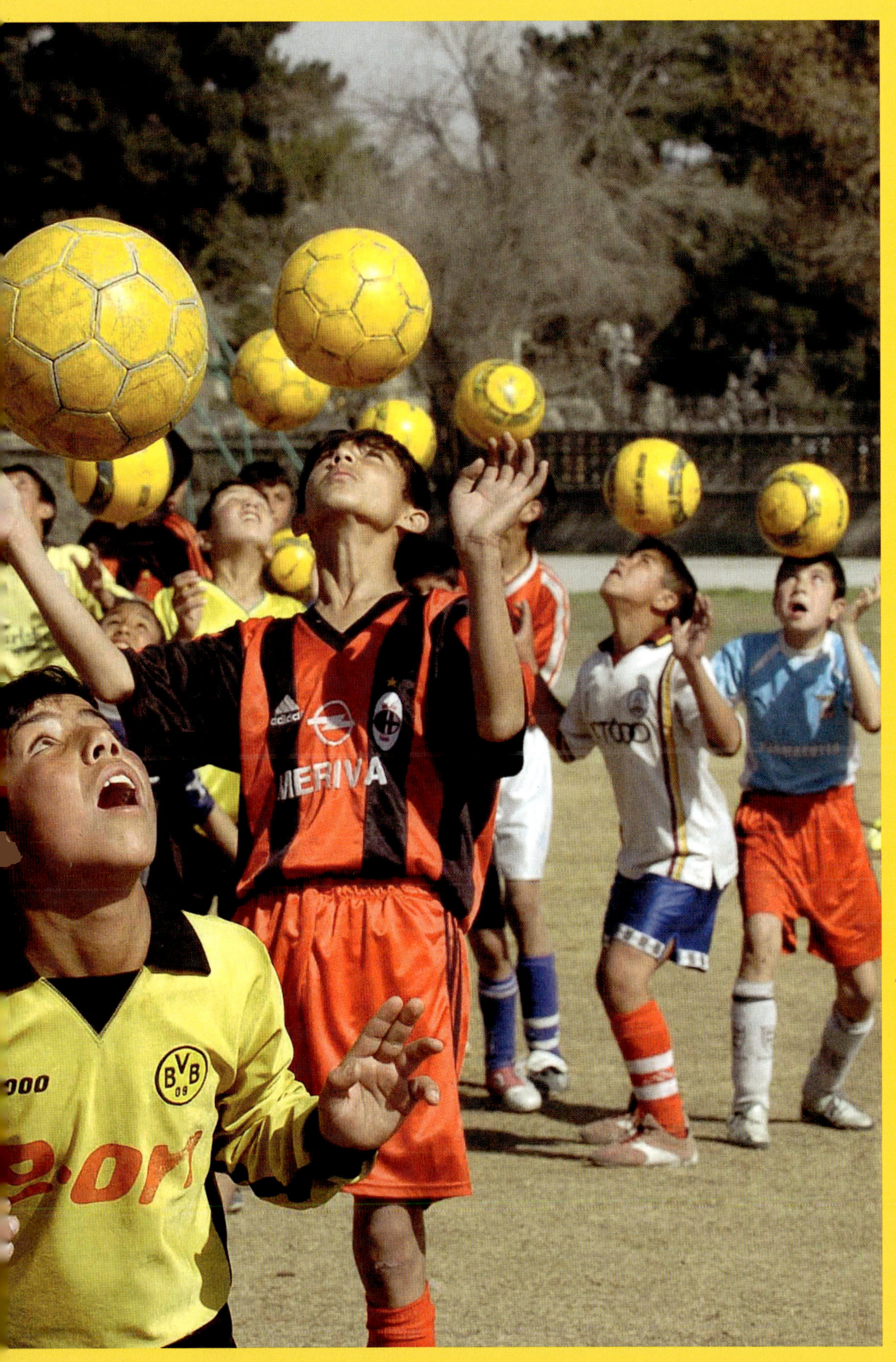

A stage for protests

A stage for protests Mexico City 1968: with their Black Power salute, Afro-American athletes Tommie Smith and John Carlos protested against racial discrimination at the Olympic medal ceremony. Sport will always have a political dimension and will always provide a stage for protests. *By Jürgen Mittag*

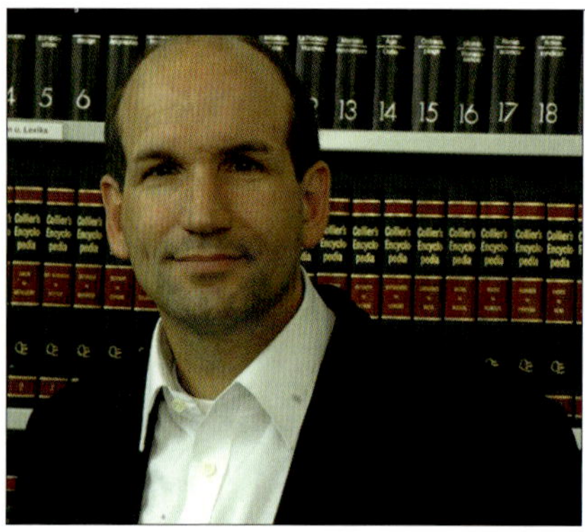

Friday, 29 January 2016 – the referee blows his whistle to start a match between AE Larissa and AO Acharnaikos in the second division of the Greek football league. But, to the amazement of fans and media alike, the players from the two clubs don't actually touch the ball. Instead they sit down on the pitch in silence for two minutes in order to demonstrate against European refugee policy and draw attention to the plight of thousands of people fleeing from Turkey to Greece by boat in often highly dangerous circumstances.

Tuesday, 9 February 2016 – a German cup match kicks off between Stuttgart and Dortmund. There are no Dortmund fans cheering on their team and the away team section of the stadium is empty. It is 18 minutes before the BVB fans start to troop into the stadium, in what is a protest against ticket prices of up to 70 euros. To further underline their message, the Dortmund fans throw tennis balls onto the pitch at the start of the second half and complain that football is in danger of losing its character as the people's sport.

These two examples from the world of European professional football serve to highlight how important sport has become as a platform for political protest. They also demonstrate the different ways in which such protests can be made, and the wide range of issues that underlie such protests. Sport – and especially professional football – is a global mass phenomenon that has become an essential element in many people's everyday lives.

And, as such, sport isn't just about individual physical fitness or some kind of collective trial of strength, but represents an important part of social communication due to its considerable potential for mobilising public opinion. It is hardly surprising, therefore, that sport is often seen as the ideal medium for reflecting the widest possible range of political, social, cultural and economic issues.

The result is that the stage provided by sport is regularly sought out and exploited by various actors with a particular point to make. And, indeed, the point they want to make might well relate to a problem with a particular sport itself, as was the case in the second of the football matches mentioned above. Or it could be – as with the first example – that the issue has nothing to do with a particular sports event per se, but the sport in question provides a useful external framework for highlighting that issue. In both cases, it is clear that this kind of sports-related protest often attracts a significant amount of media coverage because of the popularity of the sport. However, interest in the subject can also tail off just as quickly.

The issue of sports-related protest has, until now, attracted only limited interest from academics. Although there have been many instances of this kind of protest, so far no-one has carried out a systematic analysis that goes beyond an initial examination. A good example of the poor state of research in this area is the eight-volume 'International Encyclopedia of Revolution and Protest, 1500 to the Present', which includes no mention of sport at all in its 250-page index.

In light of this situation, I would like to look at some excellent examples, both past and present, of how sport has successfully been used as a vehicle for protest. In doing so, I would like to focus on the variety of forms of expression used and the different types of action taken, rather than on the actual issues

Sport is often seen as the ideal medium for reflecting the widest possible range of political, social, cultural and economic issues.

themselves. By adopting this approach, it should be possible to create a bridge between sports-related and protest-related research, as the American historian and sociologist Charles Tilly has done in the international field and the sociologist Dieter Rucht has done in the German-speaking world through his empirical analysis.

There is still no clearly accepted definition of the term 'protest' within the field of academic research, and there is also no generally accepted theoretical concept that underpins it. One approach is to distinguish between different forms of protest, including between legal and illegal forms. Another approach focuses on the various aspects of protests, differentiating between areas such as communication (internal versus external communication), cooperation (integration versus differentiation) and the way the protest is presented (performative versus media-based).

If we reduce these different forms and aspects to their basic concepts, then there would appear to be four core elements of protest. These include the conflict dimension (protest as a direct concern), the public and awareness-raising (protest as an essentially open phenomenon, accessible to all), collectivity (protest as a supra-individual concern) and, finally, direct action (construction of the protest in and through action).

Taking these core elements into account, Dieter Rucht defines a protest event as a 'collective, public action by non-state actors who articulate some form of critique or dissent together with societal or political demands'. In this respect, protest is seen as an interac-

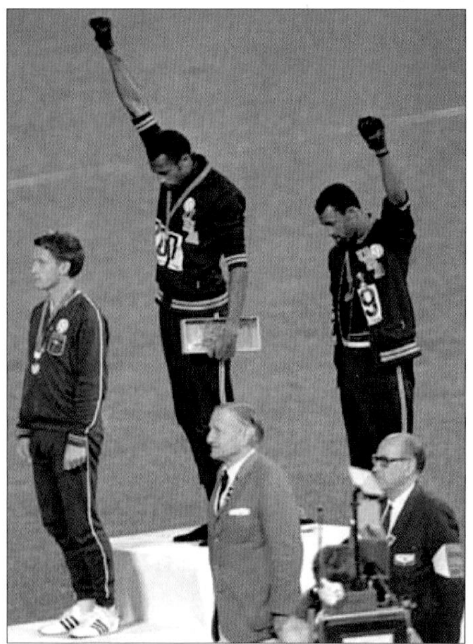

tive process between the protesters and the public – a system of action and reaction – as well as the term for an activity that advocates against something (an expression of dissent), while proposing an alternative. This kind of definition applies particularly well to sports-related protests, as the field of play as well as the grandstands in the stadium represent both the public and collectivity, and the often emotionally-charged atmosphere, conveyed by the media encourages both direct action and controversy. To this extent, (elite) sport provides the ideal stage for protests.

If we accept this particular understanding of what a protest is, then it makes sense to examine more closely the incidence, nature and form of protests, the actors involved, the specific subject matter and mobilisation processes, and the temporal and geographical dimensions of these protests.

The methodology applied to this kind of study, known as protest event analysis, does not necessarily cover every single type and incidence of social protest, but it does encompass a relatively wide range of different forms of protest, including street demonstrations, blockades, sit-ins, strikes, petitions, boycotts and attacks.

Four types of protest

One of the strengths of protest event analysis is that it is able to draw conclusions based on the range of different activities involved in protests as well as categorising the different forms of protest involved. Rucht identified four different types of protest that are relevant to this discussion on the relationship between sport and protest: the appeal protest (e.g. open letters), the judicial protest (e.g. complaints before a court), the demonstrative protest (e.g. protest marches), the confrontational protest (e.g. sit-in blockades) and the violent protest (e.g. damage to property or injury to people). There have been many examples of sport being used for the benefit of interests not actually related to sport, but in the following cases I would like to look at examples of protest involving the world of sport itself.

On 29 November 2015, 51.6 percent of the people of Hamburg who took part voted against the city's proposed application to host the summer Olympic Games in 2024. This result, based on a turnout of 50.2 percent, marked the end of a months-long debate in the Hanseatic city about the pros and cons of hosting one of the world's most important sports events.

While those in favour focused on the extensive municipal development and marketing programme that they believed would improve the city's image, provide new sports facilities and attract more tourists, those against were concerned about unresolved funding questions and potential debts. The opponents also pointed to the potential disruption to the lives of local people caused by building works, the gentrification process and concerns about the demands of IOC officials, as well as the possible disadvantages to smaller clubs and mass sport in general.

Under the banner of 'NOlympiaHamburg', the opponents of the Olympic bid undertook a wide range of activities that can, in the broadest sense, be defined as appeal protests. These included gathering signatures and creating petitions. The media can play a key role in such circumstances, as it has the real ability to influence people's opinions, especially when it comes to sport. What is interesting in the Hamburg example is that the classic media outlets, i.e. radio, TV and print media, tended to be generally in favour

While those in favour focused on the comprehensive municipal development and marketing programme that they believed would improve the city's image, provide new sports facilities and attract more tourists, those against were concerned about unresolved funding questions and potential debts.

of the Olympic bid, while those opposed to the bid relied heavily on the internet and social media.

Of the six local political parties, only Die Linke (The Left) voted against the bid, while the majority of members of the other parties, supported by the municipal government and the German Olympic Sports Federation (DOSB), voted in favour and supported the Hamburg 2024 bid committee's major Fire and Flames campaign involving advertising posters and a whole series of information events.

The protest movement in Hamburg was based on a broad but heterogeneous coalition of opponents to the bid, including academics, union members, environmentalists and city planners. They expressed their protest on the streets and particularly online, on Facebook, Twitter and on blogs and websites such as 'NOlympia Hamburg – Etwas Besseres als Olympia' and 'fairspielen.de'.

Their activities included quoting critical academic studies and posting online arguments against the poster campaign. The main goal was to try to counter the city administration's aim of trying to influence the referendum, which had been called to give the bid some legitimacy following a change to the local constitution. The battle of ideas and the attempts to win over public opinion was also reflected in the activities of the public initiative known as 'Stop Olympia', which acted largely independently of the NOlympia Hamburg campaign and which managed to gather 13,000 signatures in the run-up to the referendum, with a view to calling for another referendum to be held if a further bid were to be considered. For its part, the Hamburg initiative 'Argumente für ein NEIN zu Olympia' [Arguments for saying NO to the Olympic Games] focused exclusively on the referendum itself.

When assessing the range of different activities available to the protestors, the use of social media would appear to be particularly significant. While it is true that local opposition to the bid had been clearly expressed at a symposium in the Millerntor Stadium and that a NOlympia banner was in evidence during HSV games, the internet was still used as the main platform for the protest. The online use of the word 'NO' next to the coloured Olympic rings became the most potent symbol of the protest movement.

Just how significant and effective this kind of appeal protest can be in connection with sport is evidenced by the fact that in the past there had been two similar protests in Bavaria. In contrast to the proposed bid to host the 2022 Winter Olympic Games – which was abandoned following a negative vote by the people of Munich in October 2013 – supporters of a similar bid in Garmisch-Partenkirchen had the upper hand in the referendum that was held in spring 2011.

Judicial protest

A very different type of sports-related protest involves going down the legal route and taking advantage of the judicial process. This type of action is probably most closely linked in the public's mind with the name of Jean Marc Bosman, who obtained a decision from the European Court of Justice in 1995. This did away with the existing requirement for a transfer fee to be paid before a professional footballer could move to another club, while at the same time removing restrictions on foreign players with EU citizenship.

A current example of a judicial protest is the case of the speed skater Claudia Pechstein, which has a number of legal dimensions. It all started with the results of a blood test taken by Claudia Pechstein. These led to her being indirectly accused of blood doping by the International Ice Skating Union (ISU) and suspended from the sport. Pechstein appealed to the Court of Arbitration for Sport in Lausanne in protest against the decision. However, as the CAS ruled in favour of the ISU, Pechstein decided to take wider legal action and instigated proceedings in a number of national courts, in which she lodged complaints against being banned from taking part in the Olympic Games.

Further proceedings are currently pending in the Federal Court on a key matter of principle. Pechstein is not only protesting against her own ban, but is also seeking a landmark decision on the future role of sport courts of arbitration and the obligation for sportsmen and women to have disputes settled by such courts of arbitration up to and including the CAS. Such a decision could have a profound impact on the very autonomy of different sports and the self-organisation of the various associations involved. The costs of Claudia Pechstein's legal proceedings have been met by donations from members of the public and by warranties from the Police Union and the FIFPRO Europe sports union. As a 'sports union', the latter has a particular interest in seeing athletes being placed in a much stronger legal position when dealing with their respective associations.

This kind of judicial protest is not that common in terms of the actual number of cases and generally lacks the necessary collective framework or direct action of other forms of protest. Often this kind of protest only arises indirectly due to the support of sports unions.

Emma Green's painted nails

In terms of quantity, the most significant form of protest in sport is the demonstrative protest. During the unofficial Olympic Games in Athens in 1906, Peter O'Connor, the Irish silver medallist in the long jump, climbed a flagpole and attached the Irish flag. He was protesting against the rule that said he had to compete under the British flag because, at that time, non-independent Ireland did not have its own Olympic committee.

Afro-American athletes Tommie Smith and John Carlos, who came first and third in the 200 metres at the 1968 Olympic Games, are now firmly established in the collective memory. They both turned up to the medal ceremony wearing black socks and no shoes. Once on the podium, both Smith and Carlos raised a black-gloved fist as a symbol of the Black Power movement. This symbo-

The IAAF, the world's athletics governing body, initially stated that she had the right to freedom of speech, but it withdrew this statement under pressure from the Russian government.

lic protest quickly gained in popularity and a number of different variations on it have subsequently been seen within the world of sport.

Another good example of the range of actions that are currently used in demonstrative sport protests is provided by top Swedish high jumper Emma Green. She competed in the qualifying rounds of the 2013 Athletics World Championships in Moscow with her nails painted in rainbow shades. This was a fairly low-key protest against Russia's discrimination against homosexuals. She was trying to draw attention to current political developments and anti-gay laws in Russia, the country that was due to host the upcoming Winter Olympics.

The IAAF, the world's athletics governing body, initially stated that she had the right to freedom of speech, but it withdrew this statement under pressure from the Russian government. The athlete was told she could not take part in the final with her fingernails painted in this provocative way. Green gave in and made her later jumps with her nails painted red. This protest – and the way it was settled – can be seen as typical of current types of action in sport, because it shows how athletes have to take a stance in the face of changing media structures and the public's heightened awareness of human rights issues.

On the other hand the sports associations only allow protests to be articulated within a very narrow framework, so there is a fine line between the right to free speech and Article 50.3 of the IOC Charter, which states: 'No kind of demonstration or political, religious or racial propaganda is permitted in any Olympic sites, venues or other areas.' When we think of the fact that mega sports events will in future be held in the economically booming, theoretically democratic yet at the same time complicated BRICS countries, we are faced with the prospect of these tensions being demonstrated in stadiums in the near future, and we will see athletes becoming involved in new and ever more creative forms of protest.

In Germany, former professional footballer Markus Babbel took over from Armin Veh as head coach of VfB Stuttgart in November 2008 (despite not holding a coaching qualification). Under Veh, Stuttgart had won the German title and made good progress in the Champions League. But the 2009/2010 season started badly, with the club going seven games without a win. After VfB Stuttgart drew 1-1 with VfL Bochum on 5 December 2009, Stuttgart fans mounted a huge protest, which could be categorised as a confrontational protest. It included spontaneous demonstrations, blockades, occupations, verbal violence and minor damage, such as that caused by throwing a bag of paint.

Even before the game against Bochum kicked off, around 100 Stuttgart fans had expressed their dissatisfaction via a sit-in, preventing the team bus from accessing the stadium. Things escalated after the game ended in a draw, and a section of Stuttgart fans vented their anger on the players and particularly on their manager. Some 3,000 mainly young fans laid siege to the club's offices, running riot and hurling abuse that even included death threats.

The next day the VfB Stuttgart board gave in to the pressure and fired Markus Babbel, whose job they had guaranteed just one week earlier. The protests in Stuttgart

attracted particular attention as a sign of an increasingly clear trend towards the use of sit-ins and threats to influence the club's policies. This was all played out against the background of the suicide of German national goalkeeper Robert Enke the previous month, who killed himself as a result of depression.

The club and association boards, along with the fans, vowed that such protests would not happen again, but this was not to last. Subsequent years saw similar confrontational protests, though never on the scale experienced in other European countries, such as Italy. At the game between CFC Genoa and Siena in April 2012 around 70 Ultras stopped the game for 45 minutes by throwing fireworks and smoke bombs, as a protest against the 0:4 score. The Ultras then blocked access to the players' tunnel. it was only possible to continue the game after most of the Genoa players complied with the Ultras' demands that they take off their shirts. Once again, the club's manager was fired the following day.

Football violence in Egypt

The close and dangerous relationship between sport and politics was highlighted during the riots that broke out at a key game in the Egyptian football league between Al-Masry from Port Said and their rivals Al-Ahly from Cairo on 1 February 2012. This was a particularly violent protest in the history of sport. Even before the match began, there had been pitch invasions and fighting.

After the final whistle and an Al-Masry victory, their fans once again stormed the pitch, the opposition stand and attacked opposing players and fans. Al-Masry's fans were extremely violent and even used weapons that they had brought with them to the stadium. 74 Al-Ahly fans were killed and some of the players were also injured.

The escalation of violence was explained by the fact that Al-Masry had specifically brought in thugs, while the police stood by and watched. This inaction was explained as retaliation on the part of the police against the Al-Ahly Ultras and young fans who had played a key role in earlier protests on Cairo's Tahrir Square against the authoritarian Egyptian regime and President Hosni Mubarak.

These violent events in Egypt had a major and lasting impact. Al-Masry was banned from the Egyptian Football Association for two years, and the stadium in Port Said was closed for three years. The whole Egyptian league was shut down for a year and first division matches were subject to a crowd ban for many years. In subsequent court proceedings, 21 mainly young defendants were sentenced to death. These death sentences led to more violent protests in Port Said. Another

Football tends to be very politically charged, particularly in countries with authoritarian regimes. It also provides an outlet for fans who are critical of the regime to articulate their opposition in protests that are generally only indirectly related to sport.

32 people lost their lives, and there followed weeks of unrest.

The restrictions were relaxed at the end of 2014, but in February 2015 more football riots broke out in Egypt. The exact circumstances remain unclear, but at one of the few games that was open to the public, young fans of the Cairo team Zamalek – who had also played a key role in the Egyptian revolution – were killed at the entrance to the stadium. Violent protests in sport may still be an exception, and indeed are becoming rare in Western countries, but they are happening more often in football. Football tends to be very politically charged, particularly in countries with authoritarian regimes. It also provides an outlet for fans who are critical of the regime to articulate their opposition in protests that are generally only indirectly related to sport.

The brief examples outlined here demonstrate the increasing prevalence and complexity of protests relating to sport. In view of the attention that sport attracts, we cannot expect this trend to change. Quite the opposite in fact, as the range of actions and creativity of sporting protests seem to have no limits. The demonstrative form of protest is central. Demonstrative protests can generally be organised fairly cheaply and spontaneously, as when Emma Green and other athletes protested against Russian homophobia. Demonstrative protests have strong symbolic power, are highly visible and can be easily reported by the media. While these protests tend to be fairly understated because of the limits set by the players and athletes' associations, other types of protest have no limits. It is common to turn away from the podium or refuse to shake hands – as exemplified by César Luis Menotti with regard to the military junta after Argentina's victory in the 1978 World Cup – and this kind of protest will still happen in sports arenas in future, but new variations have developed and will continue to develop.

Whether they are protests that use sport as a medium or whether they are protests that relate directly to sport is of secondary importance. Sport will always have a political dimension and will always provide a stage for protests. In principle, this should be neither condemned nor welcomed. As long as protests do not turn into a knockabout comedy that compromises the integrity of sport and causes it permanent damage; as long as protests hold a mirror up to the world of sport or teach a lesson by highlighting negative developments, then sport and protest will continue to be mentioned in the same breath and continue to share a stage.

Jürgen Mittag is Professor of Sports Policy at the German Sport University in Cologne and Head of the Institute of European Sport Development and Leisure Studies. Since 2011 he has held a Jean Monnet Chair (to promote teaching, research and the study of European integration in universities). He has also conducted research or held guest professorships in Florence (European University Institute), Brussels (TEPSA), Paris (Sciences Po), Istanbul (Bosphorus University) and Shanghai (SUS). His current areas of research include: European integration and political systems from a comparative perspective, key developments in work and leisure, tourism, social policy, political parties, trade unions, worker movements, associations, clubs and social movements, and democracy.

Significance in action Sport reduces the complexity of modern society to tangible images. It uses spectacle to realise the displaced physical and material aspects of society. Recreational sport is now a separate area that has developed rapidly over recent decades and become bound up with pop culture. It provides the perfect public setting for highlighting social distinctions. If we want to know more about society, we need to look at sport. *By Thomas Alkemeyer*

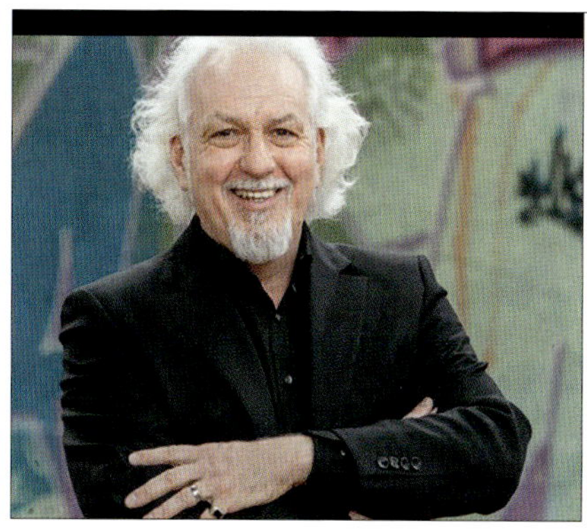

Our relationships with the world and ourselves are communicated materially and symbolically, for example through artefacts such as tools, language and images. In the words of American anthropologist Clifford Geertz, the 'webs of significance he himself has spun' that communicate these relationships are generally referred to as culture. They are created through an interplay of linguistic, discursive and 'unspoken' physical and gestural practices such as working, playing and doing sport. In this context, human physical movements go further and are different to simple physical performance or changes of location. They really mean something, they are significance in action.

In the practice of sport, the movements of the human body are framed and formatted in a particular way. This is particularly obvious in organised sport. The places where it is played out, its courts, halls and stadiums, salvage movement from the river of day-to-day life and give it its own specific form and meaning for each type of sport through the material and symbolic arrangements of running tracks, playing fields, sports equipment, codes and regulations. These arrangements were a prerequisite for the emergence of particular kinds of movement, such as the Fosbury Flop, the modern high jump technique named after American athlete Dick Fosbury.

In this respect, types of movement in sport are independent from types of movement in daily life. However, I will argue that this autonomy is relative. Because the dynamic configurations of movement and play that are revealed in the practice of sport always maintain a link to their historically changing social contexts.

In this way, organised (Olympic) competitive sport (to some extent), embodies and makes visible the characteristic motifs of modern society, such as the 'triumph of performance', as German political scientist Christian Graf von Krockow describes the idea of fair competition, the introduction of the constitution of the subject in competition with others, and the ideal of a body that has an infinite capacity to improve; and it does this more comprehensively, clearly and convincingly than any other cultural system of symbols.

From this perspective, sport creates a system of significance by means of moving the human body, revealing a specific image of society. Through this function it has undoubtedly made its own special contribution to disseminating and consolidating this image in the normal practices, consciousness, emotions and feelings of the subjects.

In this way, sport is more than just a mirror of society. It does not reflect society, but allows it to be seen from a particular perspective – and in this way it implicitly contests other perspectives. For example, behind the visible embodiment of official equality at the start of a sporting competition, any kind of real inequality disappears, which arises from different training conditions and the unequal distribution of economic and scientific resources.

Return of the displaced

At the same time, it is not enough to simply describe competitive sport as an affirmative cultural system. As a physical form of social self presentation it also has a reflexive dimension. In sport, modern society is in a way being overtaken by that unavoidable physicality of the social, whose disciplining, denigration and displacement was a sine qua non of its own self-image. We can simply call it the return of the displaced. Viewed this way, the systems of significance embodied in sport communicate two contradictory aspects of modernism: the rationality of calculation, regulated social processes and the technological possibility of optimising everything living with the romantic quest for physical activity and direct experience, for passion and sensual stimulation. Finally, it is the presence of conflicting

powers in one happening, often played out on a stage in front of an audience, that underlies the popularity, affective energy and attraction of competitive sport.

Competitive sport is the prototype of modern sport. It is an invention of the 19th-century. Its protagonists, such as the father of the modern Olympics, Pierre de Coubertin, consciously propagated it in contrast to older models of physical education, such as traditional German methods of physical training and Swedish light gymnastics. Coubertin argued that competitive sport was much more suited to the conditions of modern life, saying that physical education and gymnastics were too stiff and static. In contrast, competitive sports were dynamic in their 'purity' and time pressures, and reflected the competitive nature of fast-paced modern life in industrialised societies. He believed competitive sport was particularly suited to shaping masculine character, providing the right conditions for men to help themselves and achieve.

Coubertin's role model was the athletic education given in English public schools and universities such as Eton, Harrow, Oxford, Cambridge and Rugby. These educational establishments were founded in the 17th century to educate the lower classes, but after the 19th century they became the preserve of the sons of the upper class. They became institutions that educated the leaders of the future. Their educational methods focused on building the character of these future rulers. Competitive athletics was the incarnation of a particular set of values espoused by the middle and upper classes.

In this context, Olympic athletes embody the ideal subject of industrial modernity:

a masculine self that takes on the best and strongest opponents from around the world in the insecure context of competition, and in this way constitutes it.

The ceremonies of the Olympic Games allow this ideal subject to be symbolically elevated and ritually celebrated. The world fairs were good examples of this: they celebrated a belief in civilisation based on science, technology and industrial progress by means of elaborate exhibitions. The products of new technologies such as telephones, lightbulbs, lifts, machine guns, rotary presses, cameras, and lawnmowers were displayed using elaborate historical decorations, and artistically illuminated. They were given sentimental names such as The Invincible, The Wondrous and The Favourite. The audience approached the products displayed on altar-like pedestals as if part of a sacred rite. Coubertin was fascinated by these displays, which turned modernity and mythology into a cult of progress. In 'his' Olympic Games it was the athletes who took the place of these high-tech products – as living, high-performance machines with a human face.

The places where it is played out, its courts, halls and stadiums, salvage movement from the river of day-to-day life and give it its own specific form and meaning for each type of sport through the material and symbolic arrangements of running tracks, playing fields, sports equipment, codes and regulations.

Indicator of social change

As a cultural form of social self-presentation, sport is changing along with the society that it is part of. This makes it an indicator of social change. For example, some time ago I joined with philosophers, psychologists, sociologists, and experts in sport and education (Gunter Gebauer, Uwe Flick, Bernhard Boschert, Robert Schmidt) to look at the development of new, risky sports such as skateboarding, parkour and free climbing from this perspective as part of Berlin University's special Cultures of the Performative research programme. These new types of extreme sports no longer represent modern ideas of official equality, regulated competition and objective measurements of performance and improvements in performance.

It is noticeable that this kind of gliding, rolling, jumping, flying, and climbing is consciously done without safety measures. The underlying theme of these sports is letting go, Their proponents deliberately place themselves in unsafe situations. For a time they relinquish their habitual familiarity with the world and dramatise this renunciation in what are often spectacular ways. The meanings and values that they create and present are very different to those of competitive Olympic sport.

From an engaged, internal perspective, these practices may be a performative critique of the standardisation of behaviour in day-to-day life. The spectacular renunciation of normal safety measures and the 'Gesamtgestus' of a deregulated present-day society can be deciphered from the perspective of a secondary observer. It enjoins but also enables its members to push the boundaries of normality, take risks and constantly reinvent themselves. From this perspective, the ideal subject of this new, 'liquid modernity' (a term coined by sociologist Zygmunt Bauman) is no longer the Olympic athlete but the (still predominantly male) players who are permanently testing their limits, creatively reinventing themselves, and seeking out intense experiences.

'Gesamtgestus' is a term used by Bertolt Brecht in this theatrical theory, meaning the overall purpose, point, and character of a production. For cultural sociologists, it is interesting in its embodied forms in movement, in that Brecht only 'vaguely' understood the expression to be defined that revealed the 'attitude of an era'. Through the looking-glass of this concept, the movements of surfing and gliding can be understood as cultural articulations in which the structures that halt and bind neo-liberal liquefaction are given physical shape and made tangible.

Zero Drag

In this respect, Californian sociologist Arlie Hochschild produced a study on changes to the relationship between work and leisure time in the 1990s, in which she wrote: 'Since 1997, a new term – "zero drag" - has begun quietly circulating in Silicon Valley [...]. Originally it meant the frictionless movement of a physical body like a skate or bicycle. Then it was applied to employees who, regardless of financial incentives, easily gave up one job for another. More recently it has come to mean "unattached" or "unobligated". A dot.com employer might comment approvingly of an employee, "He's zero drag", meaning that he's available to take on extra assignments, respond to emergency calls or relocate at any time.'

In as much as representations and performances give a recognisable shape and meaning to that which they represent and present, they are part of the production of that which is represented and presented. So cultural presentations of sport are not only indicators of social change but also have their own constitutive significance for the organisation of modern society. In their physical practices, forms of movement and fashionable elements, their music and equipment, we find that milieus, sub-cultures and scenes not only present their views of the world and themselves but actually create them.

Recreational sport is now a separate area that has developed rapidly over recent decades and become bound up with pop culture. It provides the perfect public setting for highlighting social distinctions. It is a high-profile

Their proponents deliberately place themselves in unsafe situations. For a time they relinquish their habitual familiarity with the world and dramatise this renunciation in what are often spectacular ways.

place for the work of unending social representation. It is used by players in joint forms of movement and styles to articulate a shared attitude and create a joint identity that distinguishes them from others.

Through joint practice, individuals reveal themselves as a social group or collective subject, whose fiction of unity becomes real in an incarnated essence. If we want to learn something about how this collective views itself and the world, then we need to not only listen to what they say but also look at their physical manifestations.

Studying such collectives that are generally created through the medium of physical exercise can sharpen our focus on the fact that other groups and social entities also constitute a large part of our physical representation work, in movements, attitudes and gestures. This opens the door to a sociology that is not only based on linguistic expression in order to uncover social self images and systems of values and knowledge, but that also takes into account those 'unspoken' physical performances that articulate unconscious attitudes, knowledge and views of the world.

Thomas Alkemeyer is Professor of Sociology and Sports Sociology at the University of Oldenburg.

Zest for life, creativity and less is more Every age has had its people who push the limits. Today such individuals become an anachronism when they voluntarily go to places where survival is simply impossible. The challenges are shrinking with the advances of technology and growing with the destruction of the environment. But apart from how to assess risks, there is something else that 'ordinary people' can learn from mountaineers: how to do without. *By Reinhold Messner*

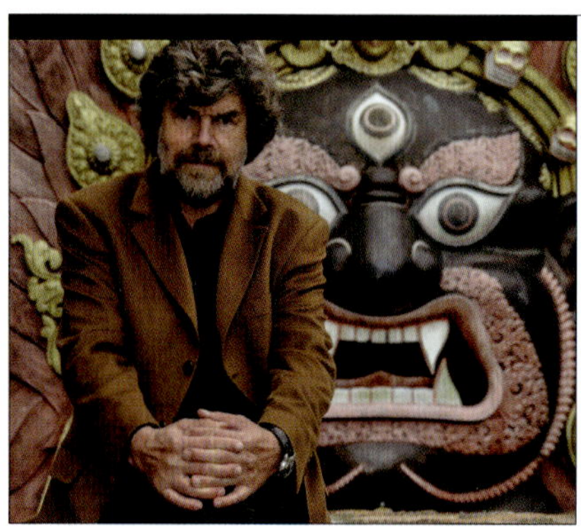

What I do is not intrinsically necessary. But it is possible. I'm happy with what I have chosen to do with my life. After all, life is about expressing yourself, making full use of your skills and experiencing what it means to be human. Exhausting our creativity is the possibility par excellence. Everything that we bring to the world – meaning, values, joy – is what makes us who we are. The greatest skill that humans possess is the ability to give meaning and purpose to life. I am not successful because I am particularly strong, persistent or daring, but because I ensure that my actions are meaningful. So it is my many failures rather than my successes that have made me who I am today. And I attribute the fact that I am still alive today to a certain amount of luck. I'm not perfect. I've made my share of mistakes. I'm human. And because I'm human, my successes, which are as much a part of my stock of life experiences as my failures, can also be of value. For me and for others.

If I were physically or psychologically stronger than other people, if I had greater endurance and were better able to endure hardship, then I know this would be of little use to them. I am not what was referred to in Greek mythology as a hero. For a hero would be somebody who stood above ordinary people, invulnerable, incomparable and therefore uninteresting. My intention here is not to try to explain why I climb mountains or how I became semi-nomadic, wandering between the high mountains and the polar deserts. What I want to talk about is how I did it, and how I want to carry on doing it. It's not about technical skills, but the demands that I make of myself.

How do I tackle a mountain? How do I approach a vast desert? How do I behave towards myself, nature, my partners? How you climb, how you keep yourself safe – this is all part of the climber's stock-in-trade, but it can never be considered the secret to success. I don't want to suggest that I am the only one who can do what others have not yet done. I would even go as far as to suggest that most people of an appropriate age, given the right experience and training, could have climbed Mount Everest or walked across Antarctica. If they had been driven by the same burning desire, the same obsession as me. But fortunately other people wanted, and still want, something different.

My world is vertical and horizontal. Summits – high and pointed, like arrow heads – for concentration, and flatlands for losing myself. The corresponding landscapes are some of the most magical on this planet. But they are not where success is found. And they are not the places where I live my life. I am only periodically there, really there, and successes come in the same way as the total when adding up. It all starts with a daydream. Out of this grows an idea. And when I focus on this idea, and work on it for weeks, months or years, it turns into a goal.

A quiet determination deep within me sparks the action. Every climb begins in your head. The mountain is just the physical manifestation. Identifying completely with a single goal means being the goal. Everyone can imagine a mountain: it has a definite shape. For children in particular, mountains

The reason I am successful is not because I am particularly strong, persistent or daring, but because I ensure that my actions are meaningful. For this reason, it is my many failures rather than my successes that have made me who I am today.

consist of clean lines that rise up to meet at the summit. For children, it is normal that I want to climb mountains. The goal is clearly visible, the motivation is a given.

However, the history of mountaineering tells us this was not always so. Man started climbing mountains – even high mountains – 5,000 years ago, but then it was a matter to survival. Modern climbing as an end in itself started around 200 years ago. It grew out of curiosity and as a balancing mechanism in the early days of industrial society. People wanted to know what it looked like up there, what the temperatures were like. They wanted to climb ever higher, try ever more difficult routes. They eventually reached the summits of the world's highest mountains and climbed the most difficult rock faces. Mountaineering gradually shifted from being an outdoor, adventurous sport to being another sport that involved records and showmanship.

Over the last 20 to 30 years, I have tried to restore excitement and adventure to mountaineering by going back to basics. But without success. I have deliberately avoided taking advantage of the superiority that man has gained thanks to modern technology and techniques in order to promote human capabilities and to face up to my own weaknesses and fears. And yet, the mountain is increasingly seen as a piece of sports equipment. We have become risk-averse, obsessed with records. How will I ever understand fear as being the flipside of courage if there is no danger? There is no courage without fear. The idea of the fearless hero is a fantasy. A hero who has no fear needs no courage.

Climbers who only want to climb faster or on more difficult routes allow the path to the record to be secured and prepared. How does this leave room for doubt, for experience? Such climbers know neither of these. They are sterile, one-dimensional, boring. For me, mountaineering is not about 'conquering' any old peak. Who is it for?

Alpinism as a form of conquest

In the same way that we need to bring an end to every form of colonialism, we also need to stop pursuing the idea of alpinism as a form of conquest. It can no longer be justified. For me, it's all about the experience. Every wild landscape, high, forbidding mountain, and desert in the external world has its counterpart within me. The higher the mountain in front of me, the greater the doubts and fears I feel within. Huge mountains are like the yawning chasms within that we can so easily fall into.

And yet the goal of mountaineering is quite simple: the summit is up there. You can see it. It is usually marked on the map. I can study it at first hand or with the help of pictures. It requires little imagination to work out where the problems lie on a mountain. K2, the second highest mountain in the world, is a massive pyramid, and yet it can still be climbed. But it will never be overrun. You can't simply decide to climb it one day, set off the next day and reach the summit on day three. It takes a great deal of preparation to generate the kind of energy that will carry us to the summit. Every mountain climb starts before you set off and the last step you take onto the summit depends on the first step you take towards that goal.

A huge amount of momentum is required to make those last, hugely demanding, steps to the summit. This is not generated simply by the desire for recognition. Ambition or victory medals also fail to provide the necessary motivation when on the mountain. Real motivation comes from passion. When I do what I do with true passion, when my actions reflect my very being, then I am strong. The longer I have worked towards achieving my goal (even if I may initially have harboured doubts about succeeding), the more energy I have invested in taking the first step, the more motivation I can call on later. What normally happens is that I uncover a possibility. It represents the start of a mental game.

Where the seed of this possibility comes from is of secondary importance (it may come from a conversation, looking at a picture, reading a story about some adventure). Suddenly I have an idea. So pushing the limits begins in my head. Then I carry the idea around with me for a long time. The idea starts to grow, I gradually feel the need to turn this idea into reality. And then it is born. The idea turns into a daydream and the daydream becomes real. Now I need to finance the undertaking. I need equipment, logistics, partners. Once the adventure starts, everything has to be right. Of course I can sort out any (small) glitches that may have occurred during the preparations when I get there. Pieces of equipment can be repaired. But often it is the small mistakes that lead to failure. When you're pushing the limits, lack of fitness or a problem with your equipment can be fatal.

I have not always been 'successful' during my life at the limits. And I've learned more from my failed expeditions than from my successful ones. With one caveat: if I had failed with my first three expeditions, I would have been forced to give up for financial reasons. So I would have failed at pushing the limits. Before 1975, I didn't have many critics. But when I started questioning the accepted 'rules' of high-altitude mountaineering and breaking taboos, suddenly lots of people thought my actions were unacceptable.

But I carried on regardless. I was fascinated by new things: doing things that had never been done; stepping outside the box; going further than anyone else had done in the past or was doing at that time. I knew how others had done things, but my first step was to take things further, to develop a new style. And this style revolutionised mountaineering. Not just because my type of expedition was cheaper; it was also lighter, faster, safer. If there are only two of you exposing yourselves to the dangers of high altitudes, the thin air, avalanches and rock falls, then only two of you can die. Risk is an intrinsic

I define pushing the limits as attempting something extraordinary that is self-organised and adapted to the individual, and that takes place in wilderness that is as untouched as possible, with all its attendant dangers. As every corner of the world is now accessible with the help of modern technology, pushing the limits increasingly means doing without modern technological aids.

part of mountaineering. But I never climb in order to die. This is why you need the 'discipline of risk' as a counterbalance to ambition. Discipline of risk means vigilance, preparation, training, self-control, restraint.

My success is based on the Prussian quality of discipline, which comes from within. Of course it also requires a dash of creativity and a zest for life, l'arte del vivere. As a South Tyrolean, I am more than familiar with the Mediterranean way of living. But without discipline, I will never achieve my goals. They are a death trap unless I am prepared to make sacrifices. Seemingly impossible actions fuel my imagination, but I will not achieve my goals without ambition and discipline.

It doesn't matter what I'm doing, how high the mountain, how vast the desert I am confronted with. It is the intensity of the confrontation that matters. Absolute intensity requires a certain amount of obsession. I realise that the word obsession has something of a negative connotation. But I'm a fan of obsession. It is impossible to achieve extremely difficult goals without fanaticism – no matter how constricting it might be. For me, vertical rock faces and horizontal polar wastes are equally fascinating. They demand absolutely everything, though in different ways. When climbing, I am totally concentrated. I have to concentrate on holds and steps, on my crampons, on the ice axe that I strike into the ice at a particular spot. One false move, one loose hold can mean a fall, even death. But when I'm trekking across the ice, when I simply keep moving on for weeks and months on end, I lose myself in time and space. After a time, moving forward becomes the reality of my day-to-day existence, and this is when the void starts to open. Suddenly there is room for new perspectives. Your imagination runs wild. It is no longer concentration and willpower that drive you forward but your wandering mind.

So climbing is an exercise in concentration. When I'm making a difficult move, I am nothing but my fingers and toes. There's no room in my head for playing games, fantasies, external stimulation. But polar expeditions, life in the ice wilderness, is like meditation. It creates a void inside. There are no distractions. There is nothing but the white expanse all around; there are no sounds, there is not even a rock; the horizon broadens because it recedes with every step. Thoughts become clear. Suddenly I am filled with new energy, ideas and strength from without. I observe myself from a distance. And it is when you have distance from yourself that you can make important decisions. I have never been able to think as deeply or clearly as when I was walking across Antarctica. Much more deeply than in the city, where my thinking is hemmed in by houses, rules, regulations, conventions. More deeply than in the Alps, where the world is framed by the mountains. I am becoming less and less interested in how high I can climb or how far I can walk. The chasms of my soul, the feeling of being lost in the solitude are what spark my curiosity. I want to put ideas into practice and find out what happens to us and between us when we are pushing the limits. When there is significant danger or we are alone for a long time, the masks start to fall away. According to this perspective, failure is as important as success. Failure has its drawbacks, especially from a financial point of view, but from a human perspective it brings nothing but benefits. It makes us more human. All too often, success goes hand-in-hand with dehumanisation.

If there is one thing that is basically pointless, it is my chosen activity. So it is difficult to justify my achievements. I do not make any moral claims. I leave the question of whether adventure is 'healthy' to the gods. I am concerned with performance as an end in itself, with actions that go beyond ethical norms. I don't think of myself as a 'sensible' person, and my reflections on adventure and alpinism are as important as my actions. It's just that both are possible – and for me sometimes compulsory. I choose to do what others dismiss as nonsensical. But I don't walk and climb as a way of countering prejudice. There wouldn't be much appeal in that. And I didn't climb the world's highest mountains to draw attention to environmental issues.

When I crossed the South Pole, my first priority was not to demonstrate in favour of an 'Antarctic World Park'. For me, the 'conquest of the pointless' was and remains all about a game that I like to refer to as 'pushing the limits': deliberately taking yourself to the limits of your capabilities and existence, taking one more step without dying in the process. I've played this game for 30 years now – in the vertical and the horizontal, at altitude and in vast expanses. The goals have become ever more challenging. The earth does in fact have an end; it peaks at the summit of the world's highest mountain. But in terms of breadth, there is never an end in sight. If I went around the world I would arrive nowhere and keep on returning,

For me, my future began during my childhood. In South Tyrol, in the Villnöss Valley. When I was growing up in a narrow, steep mountain valley at the foot of the Geisler range in the Dolomites, I could only ever see a thin sliver of sky. The clouds seemed to come from nowhere and disappear into nothingness. As a child, I often asked myself where these clouds came from and where they went to. At the age of 5 I climbed a 3,000-metre peak for the first time. Up there, I quickly realised that the world was bigger than what I could see from home. The clouds disappeared behind a far-off horizon. By the time I was 15, I was obsessed with rock climbing, and then I ventured out onto the ice. By the time I was 25 I could climb what were then the toughest ice and rock routes in the Alps – solo, and without a rope. By choosing not to use bolts and protection, I was once again making mountain climbing an uncertain activity that provided the scope to improve one's abilities. This sparked a new wave a free climbing. An expedition to the Andes in South America fuelled my enthusiasm and I was keen to go a step further, a step higher.

In 1970 I was invited to take part in an expedition to Nanga Parbat. The fascination for me was not just the mountain. It was the Rupal Face. At almost 5,000 metres, this southern face of Nanga Parbat begins where the North Face of the Eiger ends. The summit is in the Death Zone, a place where the

I have never been able to think as deeply or clearly as when I was walking across Antarctica. Much more deeply than in the city, where my thinking is hemmed in by houses, rules, regulations, conventions.

amount of oxygen in the air is so low that humans struggle to perform. Would my instincts, my abilities be up to the task of surviving up there? At that time, I knew little about high-altitude climbing. And I knew even less about the body's refusal to perform when faced with a lack of oxygen, or about how concentration and willpower dwindle at high altitude. The Rupal Face on Nanga Parbat had been attempted before, without success. Within climbing circles it was know as the Himalayan 'problem'. Many people considered it to be unclimbable. But our expedition succeeded after 40 days of 'work'. But what a price we paid! My brother Günther died and I suffered severe frostbite. Some of my toes and fingertips had to be amputated, leaving me an invalid. I had to learn to walk again. Thanks to a great deal of perseverence and autogenic training, I was eventually able to regain my former levels of fitness. I decided to pursue a new goal: pushing the limits at high altitudes, where endurance, instinct and creativity would count for more than simple climbing ability. I wanted to attain some real-life utopias again.

Nature is chaos and order

When climbing, I have often experienced visions of the future. Their origins are to be found in the past. This requires a knowledge of climbing history, memories of all those who have died during their adventures. Mountaineering has always been dangerous. Only fools try to climb the highest mountains on earth armed with the belief that they

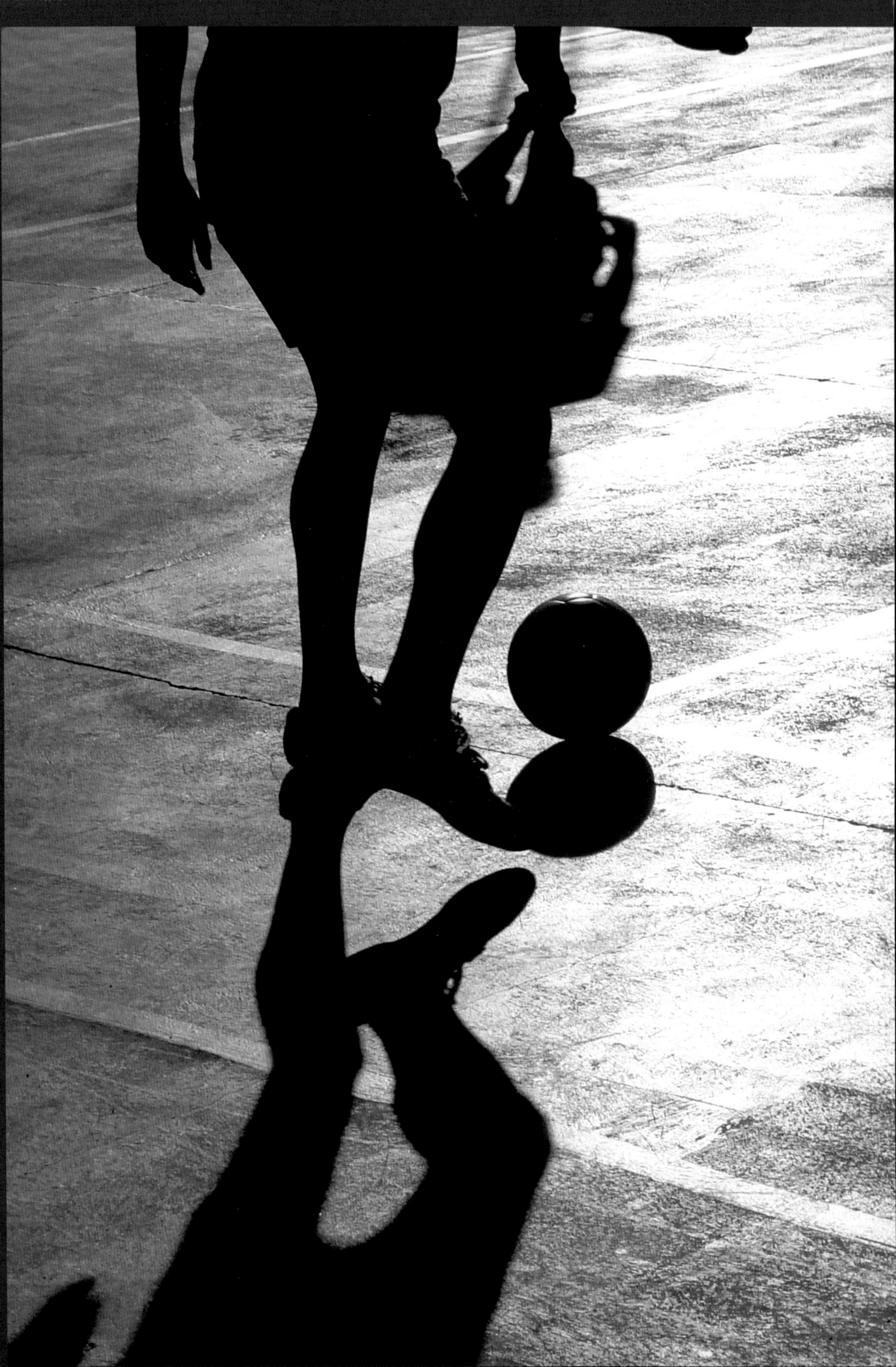

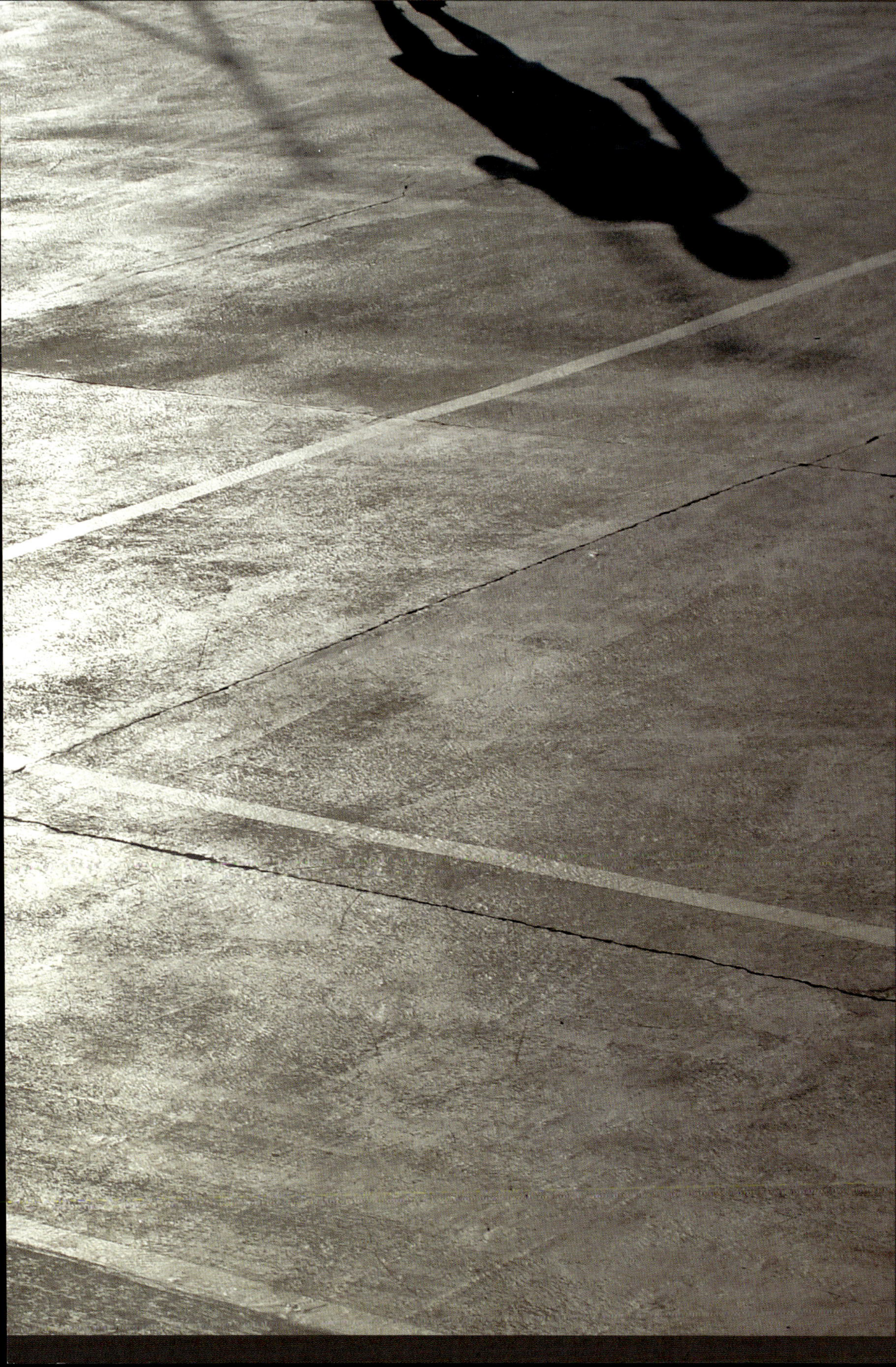

cannot die. Nature is both chaos and order. No-one is so experienced, so good, so strong, that nothing can happen to them. My kind of mountaineering is all about the experience, pushing the limits, survival. These things can't always be neatly organised. It is only by respecting the high mountains, safe in the knowledge that your next step could be your last, that it is possible to justify pushing your particular limits. I can only dare to take the next step once I have internalised the last one. The deeply religious inhabitants of Tibet often lead semi-nomadic lives in a hostile highland region. They don't climb mountains of their own volition. They stick to the mountain pastures and traverse 5,000 to 6,000-metre passes. At the top of every pass, they call out 'Lhagyelo', which means something like: 'the gods are merciful'. If I equate the gods to the forces of nature – as is also the case in Lamaistic traditions – then I am internalising the attitudes of these mountain-dwellers. Our understanding of nature is identical. We subordinate ourselves to her.

It is only when the gods (as forces of nature) are merciful that we as humans can survive the dance. The forces of nature, which also exist within us, are stronger than we are. The world, the earth, will always be capable of cleansing and healing itself. We can't. Nature doesn't need humans, but we definitely need nature. It is only in this context that ecology can be fully understood. As humans, we need to recognise that any mistakes made in the interplay between man and nature are down to humans, as the earth is simply there and does not make mistakes.

Five years after the tragedy on Nanga Parbat, my first eight-thousander, I took a fateful step on Hidden Peak (Gasherbrum I, 8,068 m) in Pakistan, a step that was destined to revolutionise high-altitude mountaineering. Prior to 1975, it had only been

climbed once before (in 1958). I didn't just want to make a second ascent via the north face, a new, difficult route. For me, it was all about style. At the time, my logistical approach – two men, a base camp and no other outside help – was considered to be totally impractical for climbing an eight-thousander in the Himalayas or Karakorum. And yet this independent climbing approach had been practised in the Alps for a hundred years. I didn't want to turn up at base camp with hundreds of porters, move tons of material or lead an army of Sherpas in order to 'conquer' a summit. I wanted to garner experiences with just one companion. Climbing an eight-thousander under your own steam means more commitment, more exposure, more risk. Possibly even failure. Peter Habeler and I arrived at the foot of the mountain with 200 kg of gear – a tenth of the amount the smallest expedition to an eight-thousander had so far carried (Broad Peak, 1957). We stayed there for two weeks. We spent our time in the Gasherbrum valley studying 'our face' through binoculars, looking for the best possible line of attack. Once we had become acclimatised we were ready to make an attempt on the mountain. My climbing partner Peter Habeler was a mountain guide who was capable of fast, sustained climbing. I had included him in my plans at the last minute, but he was someone I knew I could trust on the mountain. I invited him because he was one of the most intuitive mountaineers in Europe. I saw him as an equal partner in every respect. Rights and obligations were also split equally between us. We carried enough equipment, fuel and food for about a week and a small tent.

We left the rope behind at the 6,000- metre mark. It would have been too big a burden, in terms of both weight and the time required to use it to secure us properly. So up we went over the steep rocks, unsecured, each of us climbing for himself. With every step we moved further and further from civilisation, safety, other people. Neither of us gave any orders. We made the final climb in silence and symbiosis. After three days we finally stood on the summit in the most amazing conditions. High above the world, we looked around us. The fact that we had come this far was down to the excellent way we had worked together. We were both aware of each other's presence but had no need to talk. Two days later we were back in base camp. We held the key to changing high altitude mountaineering forever.

This new style was elegant, fast, fair. The trip had been more exciting than any major expedition. And the costs were much lower than they would have been for a traditional expedition. This form of mountaineering was much more appropriate to the natural struggle between man and mountain than

The risks associated with pushing the limits (climbing Everest, travelling to the North Pole, crossing the Sahara) are frequently overestimated by laymen. And yet they underestimate the genuine threats (heart attacks, environmental disasters, the dangers associated with driving) that could actually impact them.

the kind of material warfare conducted during the era of alpinism as a form of conquest.

Now that mountaineering is no longer about conquering mountains, scientific research or planting a flag on the summit, but all about pitting yourself against a hostile environment, the alpine style of climbing is more relevant than ever. I have had many critics since that time, who argued that my style of planning would only work on the 'small eight-thousanders'. According to them, the five highest mountains, the 'big eight-thousanders' – and Mount Everest in particular – could only be climbed with the use of oxygen. If I had to drag oxygen equipment, masks and heavy steel cylinders up these mountains in order to reach the summit, I would need whole armies of porters to help me.

And armies of porters need fixed ropes and high camps. So we would be right back where we started with the old 'classic expeditions'. In those days, a climber generally needed six to seven cylinders of oxygen to reach the summit of Everest. With each cylinder weighing around 6 kg, this amounts to 40 kg of oxygen equipment. A solo climber carrying this kind of weight, in addition to a tent, food and sleeping bag, would have had no chance of reaching the summit. This meant that Mount Everest could only be climbed alpine-style without using oxygen. But 'Everest without oxygen' was the last taboo. It is not possible to sustain human life for a long period of time on the world's highest mountains. This was the problem. The apparent contradiction between the fact that these high mountains are completely hostile to human life – nobody can survive up there for any period of time without the help of technology – and my idea of trying to climb them without that technology, is something that motivated me to want to succeed.

My plan to climb Everest, initially without the use of supplemental oxygen, then alpine-style and finally, and ideally, solo, was something that grew in spurts.

Zest for life generates energy

In 1978 I set out to climb Everest for the first time without oxygen as part of an Austrian expedition, and I was once again accompanied by Peter Habeler. The remaining members of the expedition led by Wolfgang Nairz intended to climb with the help of oxygen equipment. My first attempt to reach the summit came to an untimely end on the South Col when I was driven back by a storm. Peter had already given up, as he thought there was no chance of reaching the summit without oxygen. After a long rest at base camp, we climbed up again two weeks later, and, on 8 May, made another summit attempt. Metre by metre we climbed upwards. Relatively quickly to begin with, and then desperately slowly towards the end. We needed a whole hour to gain the last 50 metres of altitude.

The slower we moved, the higher the mountain grew and the more our willpower dwindled. With every metre of height gain, our bodies' willingness to perform diminished. It started to evaporate, like our motivation, our endurance, our strength, our hope. The lack of oxygen at high altitudes turns the performance principle on its head. The longer it takes, the more helpless you become. There is still enough sugar circulating in your blood but your brain is not receiving the energy it needs. There simply isn't enough oxygen, and without oxygen there is no combustion. It's like living in an air pocket where your life energy is slowly draining away. The years we had spent imagining this potential problem is what proved to be the key to our success.

We knew that speed and the ability to suffer were what would allow us to pull through. The motivation that had grown inside us in the run-up to the expedition – a kind of superhuman desire to succeed – is what ultimately allowed us to combat the doubt in our minds and the fatigue in our bodies and to keep climbing higher. We obstinately refused to lose hope as we tackled the seemingly unending summit ridge that towered above us at 8,800 metres. We had to get there! And we did. As I knew we would. We sat on the summit as if it was something quite normal.

We had devoted ourselves to creating a real-life utopia and suddenly we had succeeded, it was real. Belief can move mountains. As we climbed down, I knew that we had smashed one of the last taboos in mountaineering. But that wasn't what interested me. Now the foundations were in place to go one step further: it was now possible to climb all of the world's mountains without oxygen; and we had proven that Mount Everest could also be climbed solo. Having said that, I would not have had the courage to attempt a solo ascent of Mount Everest straight away. I would have been eaten up by fear. And after our success, I fell into a kind of black hole of disappointment. The vision that had consumed me for so long had suddenly become reality. As a utopia, it was dead. And with it, the enthusiasm, concentration and motivation that had been bound up with this unattained summit.

I needed a new idea that could also turn into a real-life utopia. And I understood that pushing the limits of human performance is only possible for those who take the first step. Barriers can be broken one step at a time. If I know that A and B are possible, then I can make C happen too.

My new real-life utopia was a solo ascent of Mount Everest. Before 1978, nobody had ever solo climbed an eight-thousander from base camp to summit. A few weeks after the Everest ascent I attempted to solo climb one of the smaller eight-thousanders – of course without oxygen. Carrying a 15 kg rucksack, it took me three days to climb a new route to the summit of Nanga Parbat and then to descend by a different route. Despite some unexpected difficulties – an earthquake during the ascent damaged some of the route I'd already climbed, while a snowstorm trapped me at 7,400 metres during the descent – I got back down the mountain not too much the worse for wear.

Now I was ready for the final step: solo to the top of the world! These two experiences – Mount Everest without oxygen and Nanga Parbat solo – gave me the psychological strength, confidence and experience that I needed to make a solo attempt on the world's highest mountain. In 1980, the Chinese government gave me a permit to climb Everest for the second time. This time from the nort-

hern side, from Tibet. Up to around 7,000 metres, there were no real problems. But above that there was too much snow. I waited for a break in the monsoon, then tried again. The first real problem I encountered was a crevasse just below the North Col. I was hoping to carefully cross this lateral crevasse, which was very difficult to make out.

I was trying to dig my ice axe into the steep snow face on the mountain side of the crevasse, when my valley-side foot slipped. I fell 8 metres into a hole, an A-shaped fissure. Fortunately, I landed uninjured on a snow bridge. Shaking, I looked up. There didn't seem to be any way out. All I could see were the stars twinkling through a hole the size of a tree trunk. I was trapped. Buried alive in the ice. The crevasse got wider as it went further down, the abyss that opened beneath me was fathomless. I couldn't climb out by placing one foot on each wall of the crevasse. So what should I do? Fortunately – after I'd promised myself that I would give up and go home if I ever got out of the crevasse alive – I found a system of caves and a kind of ramp inside the crevasse that I could use to climb out. Once I was back out in the open, I continued to climb upwards. I had forgotten or suppressed my intention of giving up. As though in a trance, as if programmed to reach the summit, I returned to the gaping hole I had fallen into and this time crossed it carefully. I climbed quickly up to the North Col and then on to the North Ridge. I managed 1,400 vertical metres of climbing that day. I'd internalised the route to such an extent before I set off that I now felt compelled to see the climb through. I'd carried the idea

205

of this ascent around with me for two years, so I had no choice but to carry on. Only by continuing upwards could I clearly identify with my goal, my idea.

The snow conditions on the North Ridge of Mount Everest became more difficult. On the second day, I only managed 400 vertical metres of climbing, partly because I was also traversing the North Face. Progress was too slow. Doubts started to creep in. The weather was also getting worse. But on the third day, after climbing up steep steps and gullies and crossing snowfields, I eventually reached the highest point. With my last ounce of strength. It was late and I was so exhausted that I barely looked around, took pictures or reflected on what I'd achieved. I just sat there and rested. My mind was a blank, I even forgot where I was. After an hour, I gathered the strength to stand up.

Two days later I was back at base camp. It was only when I got back down that the emotions hit me. It wasn't the joy of climbing Mount Everest solo. It was the feeling of having found my way back to life – to other people, the first plant life, insects, flowing water. I hadn't missed all these living things when I was up on the mountain. It was only now that I started to appreciate the sheer unadulterated hostility of the environment in which I had battled against madness and despair for five long days. I had spent five days alone in a totally dead and frozen world. It was always exhausting and dangerous, often desperate. I slept up there like a bird: constantly alert and ready to move, constantly on my guard. And yet it was returning to the land of the living that shook me to my core. Even though I was more exhausted than I had ever been in my entire life. I could not have coped with another minute of effort, of being alone in this hostile environment.

A few years later, in 1986, I stood on the summit of Lhotse, a mountain just to the south of Mount Everest. It was my fourteenth eight-thousander. I'd actually climbed some of the 14 highest mountains in the world twice. Offers to do lectures and advertising were flooding in. In material terms, I could have lived off my mountain successes for the rest of my life. But I couldn't have lived off them spiritually. Past achievements and successes are not what make me feel fulfilled. Yesterday belongs in my biography. Failures and successes alike.

I see myself as a creative person who wants to express himself, move forward, seek out new challenges. So I took up a new challenge – first in my mind, then in reality – a challenge that would once again push me to my limits: crossing Antarctica on skis. I spent three years preparing for the expedition because I knew on this journey I would not be coping with extreme conditions for five days like on Everest, but for a hundred days. I had to prepare for a region that is more hostile to human life than the summit zone in the Himalayas and further from civilisation than the Taklamakan Desert in China. A place that has no flowing water, no animals, no people.

I needed an idea of what lay in store. Antarctica was first discovered around 200 years ago and then explored more fully during the 20th century. In 1986 I travelled to Mount Vinson, Antartica's highest mountain. From a technical point of view, climbing the mountain presented no real problems. But it was really cold: –50 °C. And then there were the storms. But what really made an impression on me was the view from the summit. I had never experienced such vastness. And the silence! After the climb, when I was back at the foot of the mountain, I decided that one day I would cross the Antarctic continent on foot. Back at base camp, I experimented with packing a sled. First with 80 kilos and then with 120. I tried skiing along for an hour, pulling the sled behind me. I was able to cover about 4 kilometres in this time. If I could repeat this 4 kilometers an hour for 8 hours a day, I would be able to cover around 30 kilometres per day. And if I multiplied this 30 kilometres by 100 days – including rest days – I could cover 2,800 kilometres, the distance required to do a complete overland crossing of Antarctica.

In 1911, Amundsen became the first person to reach the South Pole, using dog sleds. In the 1950s, Sir Vivian Fuchs led an expedition that completed an overland crossing of Antarctica with the help of tracked vehicles and air support. A huge undertaking that would cost hundreds of millions of dollars today. However, nobody have ever completed an overland crossing of Antarctica on foot. And nobody in their right mind would dream of such a venture in a technological age such as ours. People had set up research stations and undertaken all sorts of weird and wonderful expedition projects in Antarctica, fuelled by a firm belief in the potential offered by modern technology. My expedition flew in the face of this trend. I wanted to seek out the real Antarctica on a

When you're 40, you either have to give up being someone who pushes the limits, or actually go further than ever before.

human scale, using manpower alone. I was also becoming increasingly aware of the environmental issues surrounding Antarctica, a continent that is up to 98 percent covered by ice and holds 70 percent of the world's reserves of fresh water. When I got home, I started looking into the logistics of the undertaking. How would I get to the start of my sled journey and how would I get home again afterwards? I also needed a partner. I eventually found Arved Fuchs, a north German seaman who had traversed Greenland with dog sleds and was an expert in navigation. I have never been so beset by doubts before the start of an expedition as I was before the crossing of Antarctica. I had nightmares every night. We might suffer the fate of Captain Scott. In my dreams, I was trapped, unable to move. I was no match for the vastness, the sheer endlessness of Antarctica.

It was only when we set off that my doubts began to fade. What had been a daydream was now becoming reality. Harsh reality. We only had three months of summer months to make the crossing. The rest of the year it was too cold. As Arved Fuchs and I set off – totally unsupported – we initially made slower progress than originally planned. Much too slow. Arved navigated, I broke trail. There were no personal problems between us. Just problems with our speed. Arved wanted to spend fewer hours hauling the sleds, I wanted to spend more. In the end we agreed on six hours per day. A compromise that put us further and further behind every day.

After only three weeks, we were already 200 kilometres behind schedule. At this rate, there was little chance of us traversing the whole of Antarctica. Whenever I thought ahead, I was overcome by hopelessness. In order to try and improve our pace, we redistributed the weight on the sleds. This helped as to achieve the necessary 30 kilometres per day. And for the first time, I started to have a glimmer of hope that we might actually traverse the South Pole and reach McMurdo. After 50 days, we arrived at the South Pole. We hadn't managed to cover half of the total distance yet, but we had reached our first intermediate stop. We wanted to carry on, continuing to use the tactics we had come up with between us. The section from the South Pole to McMurdo was more difficult than the first section.

For a short time we were able to travel more quickly by using sails to harness the wind. But the wind soon dropped. We were in trouble again. Our daily progress was leaving us consistently behind schedule. Ice bridges and dry snow slowed us down. The sleds weighed more than 100 kilos. Having a bold idea and identifying with this idea means nothing if you don't have the endurance. I could only persuade Arved to keep going for longer each day by coaxing him or using tricks. In the end I just stubbornly stayed out in front, forcing him to follow, because the tent was on my sled. We had to walk 2,800 kilometres and cross 6,000 crevasses. Often in temperatures as low as – 40 °C, with the wind blowing in our faces. And always the question in our minds: were we going to make it? When we finally returned to civilisation, we no longer knew how to deal with it. Our energy was spent. The beer that we drank played havoc with our water balance. I also missed the silence, the endless peace and vastness of those three months, despite my occasional feelings of despair. Now I am planning new adventures – leading the way is addictive.

One thing is clear: I can only continue to be successful in the long-term if I'm also allowed to fail. How can I play the game if I can never lose or fail? Even if I enjoy a whole string of successes due to skill, luck or chance, I would still lose sooner or later. And I would lose touch with reality as a result. And sooner or later losing touch with reality inevitably leads to ultimate failure. As humans we all have our limitations. We all make mistakes. I see failure as a huge opportunity.

I've regularly emerged from failure with a new sense of determination and a clear vision of what I want to do. I took me 30 expeditions to climb the 14 eight-thousanders. I summited 18 times and failed 12 times. And if in the end I achieved my goal, it is also because I got back up every time I was knocked down. If I am to push the limits further than others, I have to get back up more often than others and learn to deal with failure. Defeat also helps you to become modest, wise and tolerant. Successful people are those who, more than other people, are able to pick themselves up and start again. We are all Sisyphus and shouldn't allow a fall to spoil our joy in our achievements. It is about learning from our failures and attempting to go further than last time.

My goal in life is not to accumulate as many successes as possible. Of course I celebrate my successes. Of course success breeds confidence, strength – and success. Nothing is more successful than success itself. My goal in life – in the broadest sense – is to become wiser. I don't want to be a rich or successful or famous old man (if indeed I reach old age); I want to be a wise old man.

Humans do not have an a priori profession. I know that today's society lays ever more emphasis on the need to have specific qualifications. There is a growing demand for specialists in a very small area of human activity, rather than for jacks of all trades. I'm a specialist too. These days, we live in a gigantic performance system and can't do everything. But some of us have still managed to get by without learning a particular profession. I think we are lucky. I don't work in a particular profession, or at least not in the profession that I studied for or should have studied for (surveyor, civil engineer, architect). I live. I do what I do best. I have also constantly changed the way I push the limits and the appraisal that goes with it. In fact I would argue that I currently have half a dozen different professions: author, public speaker, photographer, alpine farmer, filmmaker, incentive group guide.

But my principal activity – pushing the limits – is not included on this list. It doesn't bring in money. It is my calling. Just as animals and plants have no profession, humans also have no a priori profession. I'm not trying to suggest that this approach to life is the only one. Quite the opposite, I accept the idea of education, training, specialisation. But only as a necessary evil. It is necessary because the world is becoming more densely populated and more specialised than ever. But today's career paths are not set in stone. We Europeans are not as flexible as other societies. In the USA, for example, people seem to change their professions as often as

they change their shirts. Americans place a premium on income, success and ambition, but in Central Europe ambition tends to be viewed as a negative trait. Yet most people are ambitious. And so they should be. Ambition is an essential part of motivation. I can only perform at the top of my game if I pursue my ambitions and do what I'm good at. I may not be equally satisfied, fulfilled or happy with everything at every point in my life, so it makes sense at some time or another to change from activity A to activity B. I've already changed horses a couple of times during my career as someone who pushes the limits. I started out as a young, ambitous rock climber who wanted to climb harder routes than everybody else. Then I became a high-altitude mountaineer, who managed to climb all 14 eight-thousanders, and finally someone who trekked across deserts and icy wastes.

As you get older, your speed and agility tends to drop off, so these days I try to make the best use of my endurance, mental and physical strength and experience. It's possible that I will change direction for a third or fourth time. Every time I do this, my teams get younger. Not just for practical reasons – most of my previous partners eventually returned to more normal career paths – but also because I am drawn to young people.

I've always associated my changes of direction with a sense of rejuvenation. Every time I have tried something new, I have talked to young experts who are obsessed with that particular field in order to go one step further than before. In itself, playing is a form of rejuvenation. Changing direction

As humans we all have our limitations. We all make mistakes. I see failure as a huge opportunity.

is like a rejuvenation treatment. They are two good ways for me to move forward. I don't view moving forward as a demand that is imposed upon me from above. It's a demand I impose on myself. On this earth, people are not subject to 'higher' demands, other than our responsibility for family and friends (who in turn make their own choices) and our shared responsibility for the community as a whole. But we have the right to choose what we do with our lives, to set ourselves challenges. I have regularly exposed people who talk endlessly of ideals as being people who have a sense of entitlement. They hide the wanton demands they impose on others behind their moral code, behind the shield of idealism that they carry in front of them. It is the demands that are important to them, not what they actually do. It's all about them.

I've found that the latent discontent felt by so many people in today's performance-oriented society is most pronounced in those who like to extol the virtues of idealism, altruism and subordination. Their lives are determined by others. Their idealism is the product of a hunger for recognition. Their altruism is an excuse. Subordination is a game of hide and seek. They are fundamentally opposed to the idea of placing demands on themselves. I believe that the only way to remove the discontent that pervades the rich industrialised nations is for individuals to have the courage to pursue their own dreams. I believe every one of us has individual abilities that predestine us to achieve certain things. And we are driven to do these things. If only we would allow ourselves to go down that path! Unfortunately, only a few of us are prepared to do so. Fear prevents many people from taking control of their own lives. Fate is often described as an external force over which we have no control. I like to think of fate as the destiny that allows us to be our-

selves. Every single person is their own fate. Everyone has their own path. There are as many paths as there are people. When young people ask me what they need to do to push the limits like me, I always tell them they should not simply follow in my footsteps. My path cannot be their path; they have to seek their own way forward.

I don't believe I was born for a 'higher purpose'. People are born with everything they need to be human; with all the abilities and opportunities to understand their own being and recognise their limits. No more, no less. I try to live my life with a heightened sense of personal consciousness so that I do not impinge on others. This helps me to feel balanced, content, and at peace. In my experience, people tend to be hostile and aggressive when they cannot live their lives; when they suppress their feelings, their fears, their dreams; when their sense of who they really are is grafted onto them by others. This doesn't mean my approach justifies everything. There are so many humans living on such a small planet that I am simply amazed at how well we are able to block out major dangers: from global environmental threats (the disappearing ozone layer, reactor accidents, rapid climate change) to major social problems (overpopulation in Asia and Africa, mass migration).

It's almost as if there is a whole reassurance industry at work to suppress the facts and people's concerns about these issues. Apart from a few environmentalists and scientists, it seems only frightened children are asking whether the planet can still be saved. Amongst politicians, where are the individuals who are capable of tackling these ecological issues in the same way that Europe's social problems were tackled at the beginning of the last century? People only start to become really afraid when it is a matter of life and death. Only then do they start to ask questions. My repeated attempts to push the limits of human endeavour are all about the thrill of fear, in as much as the mind vacillates between the extremes of pleasure and fear. Like risk, fear is part of pushing the boundaries. It signals the presence of real danger. The more sensitive I am to it, the better I can prevent, avoid or tackle such dangers. I've never had a problem with fear.

I'm never more aware of our progressive alienation from the natural world than when I'm out in the wilds and am enveloped by a sense of peace and harmony. Like images, insights appear out of nowhere. I often have the feeling of knowing without thinking. When I am out there, my subconscious seems to become keener than usual. It is like being in a trance or sleepwalking. I am filled with positive thoughts and feelings. For me, this is quality of life, not a second car or the latest video player.

When I'm pushing the limits, I want to do it without planes and snowmobiles, not just because of pollution, but because of the

When it comes to global threats, we seem to be happy to simply stick our heads in the sand. Humankind is at risk more than ever before. The looming environmental disasters will be deadlier than rockfalls or avalanches.

game. I set my own rules! If we all decided to leave the car behind this weekend and go for a walk instead; if we switched off the TV occasionally, switched off our phones, then we could all start to appreciate the value of silence, harmony and peace. Wouldn't that improve our quality of life? Maximising profits cannot simply mean that we have to want more of everything. It has taken the Earth millions of years to store up the energy that we consume in 100 years. We don't use the yields to develop new forms of energy; we just consume them. And they are gone forever. We have achieved a standard of living that is probably the highest that humankind has ever achieved. And of course our system is still functioning. From a purely economic perspective, you could even say it functions very well. But if we cannot learn to do without of our own volition, one day it will be forced upon us.

The principle of doing without is a fundamental prerequisite for success. Knowing precisely what I can do without and in what quantities is an art that outsiders can perhaps appreciate, but it is difficult to learn. If my attempts to push the limits engender admiration among laymen, it is in part because we all suspect that doing without – and especially doing without material things – is something that is set to become a part of everyday life for humans. Our bodies, our most important common denominators, have remained largely unchanged. So anyone who is attempting to consistently push the boundaries of what is possible with the help of fewer and fewer external aids is pointing the way to the future.

Today, people who are pushing the limits are defined less by the goals they have set themselves than by their ability to consistently minimise the use of external aids and technology. I am not fundamentally opposed to technology. Without technology humans wouldn't be able to live on Earth in such huge numbers. And in the rich industrialised nations we would not be having such comfortable lives. But I choose not to take advantage of it (or only to a limited extent) when my activities are essentially pointless. My attempts to push the limits are pointless. I am someone who pushes the limits and does without, and I believe this is the only way forward. A company can only be considered futuristic if it operates in an environmentally-friendly, energy-saving and humane way. I therefore expect huge demands to be put on companies in environmental and human terms.

When it comes to global threats, we seem to be happy to simply stick our heads in the sand. Humankind is at risk more than ever before. The looming environmental disasters will be deadlier than rockfalls and avalanches. Not for one person, but for millions, even billions of people. It is our duty to make people aware of these dangers, but also to try to mitigate them on a global scale. This means moving huge mountains. Apart from how to assess risk, there is something else that 'ordinary people' can learn from mountaineers: how to do without. Voluntarily reducing our needs is now the order of the day. Governments are clearly incapable of emulating the actions of the founders of religions. They lack vision. We don't need new religions or sects, but we do need strong personalities who embody and provide an example of contemporary ways of living. We all face the challenge of ensuring that humankind can continue to live for a little longer in peace and relative health. We need vision and leadership. On a global scale. It's too late for defensive thinking.

What we need now is creativity, and not just picking holes in other ideas. It's time to sweep away fixed hierarchies! Individuals who are chosen as leaders or are prepared to take on the mantle of leadership automatically take on more wide-ranging responsibility. They speak on behalf of others as representatives of a group and as part of a greater whole. They embody the corporate culture and are the foundations upon which a conglomerate is built, a conglomerate I like to think of as particular global ethics. If we are to achieve a different type of culture with the demise of power politics, then the leaders of tomorrow will need to be capable of inspiring people to turn their backs on old habits. When we look at the major problems facing our planet, it is not going to be statistics and slogans that help us to find the best solutions.

In our multipolar world, good intentions tend to fall at the hurdle of economic realities. The climate debate is leading us inexorably towards the extinction of species and increased social tension. The energy debate is all about raw materials and better technology. Everyone wants to do something, but no-one knows what. Our commitment to climate consensus and the competition for resources is numbing us to the problems. It is difficult to take danger seriously unless it is experienced at first hand. Are we willing and able to adapt to different environmental conditions and other requirements in the way we conduct global business? Not really. As humans, we only truly retain things that we have learnt first-hand rather than from the experiences of others. Only then do we learn to adapt and seek out new solutions. But humans have now changed the earth into a reality of their own making, and it is only by taking a holistic view that we can and must adapt to the world that we have created. Impossible? I hope not.

Once people began settling in one place it became possible to feed more mouths. And they became richer. But, in doing so, they became less creative. The best place to restore our creativity is in nature. Nature imposes inescapable conditions. Its rules cannot be manipulated and are infinitely diverse. In the world of work, many of us are increasingly losing touch with the outcome of our activities. We sit for hours at the same desk, doing the same things year in, year out. But when you're out in the wilds you experience the thrill of constantly new experiences. This creates a real sense of fulfilment. And, perhaps unconsciously, both these sensations provide us with a feeling of doing creative work and achieving something.

Being creative means daring, playing, rolling the dice. I need to be open to the unexpected, and also be prepared to lose. The basic conditions of a creative life are curiosity, action and failure. In the world of adventure, it is people who are prepared to roll the dice who break new ground. Sir Edmund Hillary, the first man to climb Mount Everest, was not meant to be the climber who would tackle the summit. But when Evans

The crime has occurred on our earth, despite knowing better, unchecked by the collective and always caused by humans.

and Bourdillon failed in their summit bid, Hillary was ready to make his attempt. He had the ideal partner in Sherpa Tenzing, who was obsessed with succeeding, and who had repeatedly failed on earlier attempts to reach the summit. Their success was not just due to the fact that their predecessors had passed on their wealth of knowledge and experience. They succeeded because they were prepared to play the game by a different set of rules. Hillary and Tensing decided to bivouac at an intermediate camp at 8,500 metres before making their summit attempt. Nobody had ever spent a night at such high altitude. But it was this decision that allowed them to reach the top.

As crazy as it might sound, chaos is actually a better prerequisite for creativity than order. Order doesn't reflect reality. Order is just wishful thinking. Classical physics likes to give us a false impression of order, but it is a superficial type of order that has been invented. Creativity provides us with insights into the laws of nature, with experiences of the social, economic and historic kind. And this is even more the case when we are thrown into that chaos – both external and internal – that is the world under its thin veneer of preconceptions. How quickly you learn to see, think and feel in a holistic way when you are being pushed to your limits in the wilds! Thinking and doing become one and both sides of your brain start to synchronise.

I want to go beyond being part of a universal, democratic and prosperous society; I want to be at the mercy of uncertainty with all its daily risks. I want to have a blank sheet of paper in front of me and have to prove myself. I do not only operate in accordance with economic models. If I still hunger for opportunities to push the limits, then it's because I want to experience life at a number of levels. I cannot imagine a life without passion, without risk. I don't want to be reduced to a timid herd animal or dumb consumer. I measure my quality of life by the quality of the challenge, not by the quantity of material things.

Dealing with chaos

Now, in the summer of 1995, I'm going to be grounded for months because I fell off the castle wall and broke my heel bone. But I haven't given up on the idea of the North Pole. I'm going to need several operations before I can even attempt to start walking again. Then I will need to get back in training to regain my former levels of endurance. But even if I continue to have difficulty walking, I'm not going to give up. Coping with new situations – illness, age, poverty – is one of the skills that you have to develop when you are dealing with chaos.

Of course, coping with these kinds of problems is never fun. But the art lies in seeking out alternatives and getting back into action. I am always prepared to seek advice from people with more experience when I am looking for new fields of endeavour. I can imagine a whole range of activities that make sense to me and that I could throw my-

self into body and soul. For the first time I am having to cope with not being involved in pushing the limits, but I am still sticking to my plans. Another dream is slowly taking root in my mind: being in a desert with just a rucksack and no map. Not knowing where I am, but finding a way through. I am no longer a 20-year-old dropout. I am no longer rejecting the state or the capitalist world. It is more a case of seeking out an existence, a preserve, a playing field that is far removed from data networks and administrative rules. I would never swap my life for someone else's. Partly because I know I can't have anything that I have not personally experienced or suffered. Even the experiences or intentions of yesterday are not enough. The radicalism of pushing the boundaries changes the way you lead your life. Life seems to be ripped apart, whatever the surroundings, and yet becomes normality. This allows me to build awareness on top of my own awareness, even when I am fully absorbed in my actions. When pushing the limits, I consciously try to take advantage of opportunities that come my way (the wind in Greenland, for example). I remain programmed for the future. Even when I play with gradually reducing the basic requirements of life – oxygen, light, warmth, water, fire, land. Despite all my self-criticism, I am basically optimistic.

It is not only those of us who push the limits who have to move away from the language of the military; we also have to move away from the planning and strategy that are part and parcel of the military metaphor. Autonomous action, situational creativity, daring to change are the foundations for a tomorrow of possibilities. We will never highlight the playful nature of our actions if we insist on using a language full of military metaphors – 'conquering a peak', 'attacking a summit'. A new spirit requires a new language.

Immersing ourselves in the wild alleviates the fear and uncertainty that besets humankind at the beginning of the third millennium, the feelings of loneliness, angst and disorientation. We are all afraid of death. Even I haven't been able to free myself of this fear. Even though I have brushed with death, and once even thought I had died. But after a kind of rebirth I began a second life. I learned a great deal from these near-death experiences. They too are part of my life story.

It is still important for me to find out whether I can continue to push my limits and experience how ambition, instinct and fear impact me at the point of no return. The competitive nature of today's society means we all have our backs against the wall. Today's environmental problems are waiting for a solution in the same way that the Western industrialised nations needed a solution to social problems in the early 20th century. And peace! We need visionaries to lead us out of our impasse. The Earth's resources are finite. Man is finite too. Only the spirit is infinite. Creativity, our 'divine attribute', is the human spirit's biggest strength. However, this 'boundlessness' of the human spirit is infinitely underused. We need to use our consciousness to open up new dimensions for survival. More than anything else, today we need to use our creativity to give meaning to our lives if we want to create a human existence that is both peaceful and viable.

But the sheer numbers of people on the planet make everything relative. Everything is getting out of balance. And yet we are still hell-bent on maximising profits. The free market economy will inevitably lead to disaster if we fail to take nature into consideration as we attempt to increase GDP. Every one of us needs to move mountains. As individuals, we need to change our way of thinking and break out of the lethargy of 'but everybody does it' attitudes in order to make life bearable for everybody – if only for a limited time. Humankind is the sum of all individuals.

Reinhold Messner is an extreme mountaineer, adventurer, author and former politician (Verdi Grüne Vërc) from South Tyrol, Italy. In 1978, together with Peter Habeler, he became the first person to climb Mount Everest without the use of supplemental oxygen and the first to climb all fourteen eight-thousanders (1970–1986, all without oxygen). He also made the first solo ascent of an eight-thousander (Nanga Parbat in 1978). In 1986, he became only the second person to climb the Seven Summits. He has also made successful crossings of Antarctica (1989/1990 with Arved Fuchs), Greenland (1993) and the Gobi Desert (2004). This article is based on his book *Berge versetzen – Das Credo eines Grenzgängers*, published in German by BLV Buchverlag.

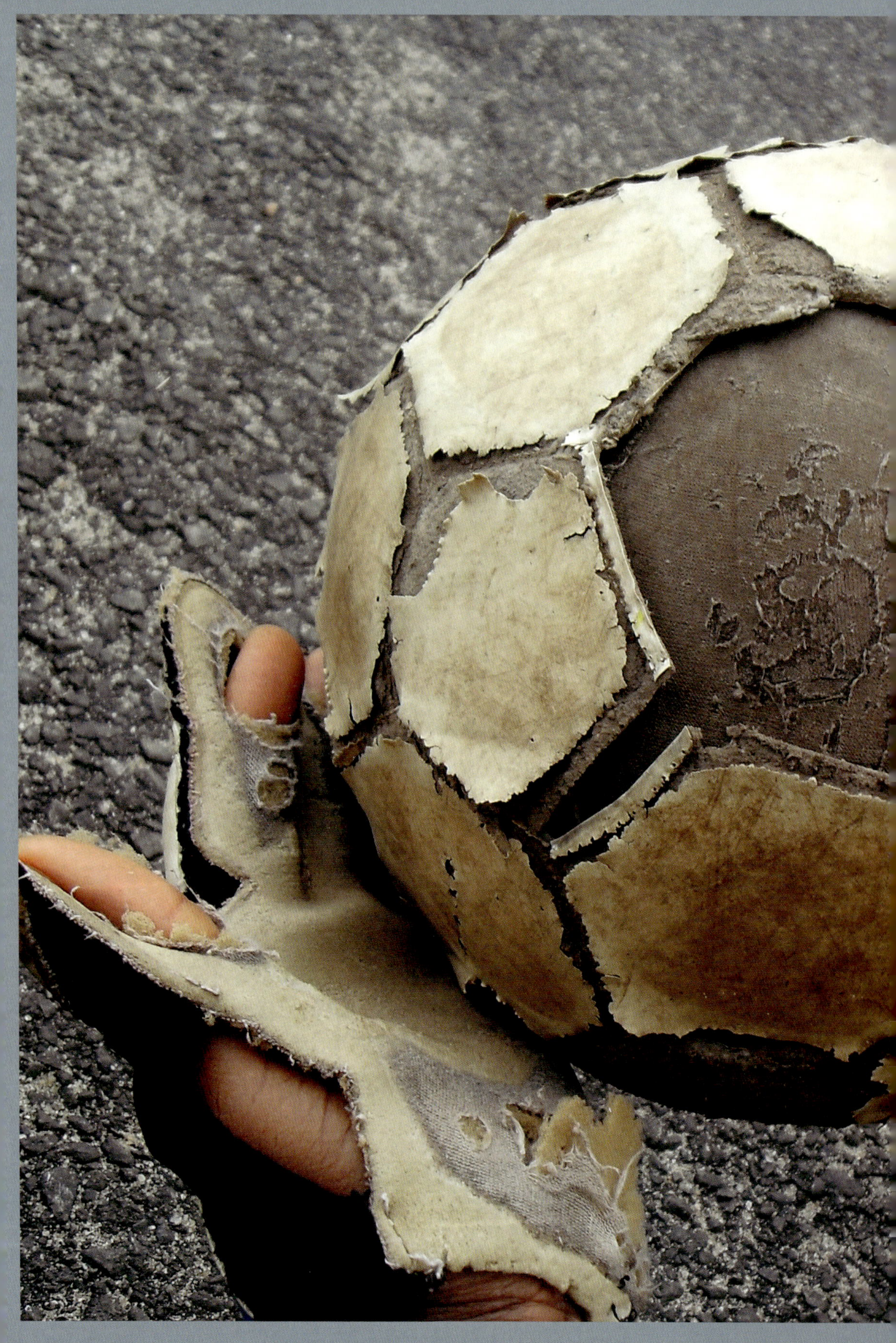

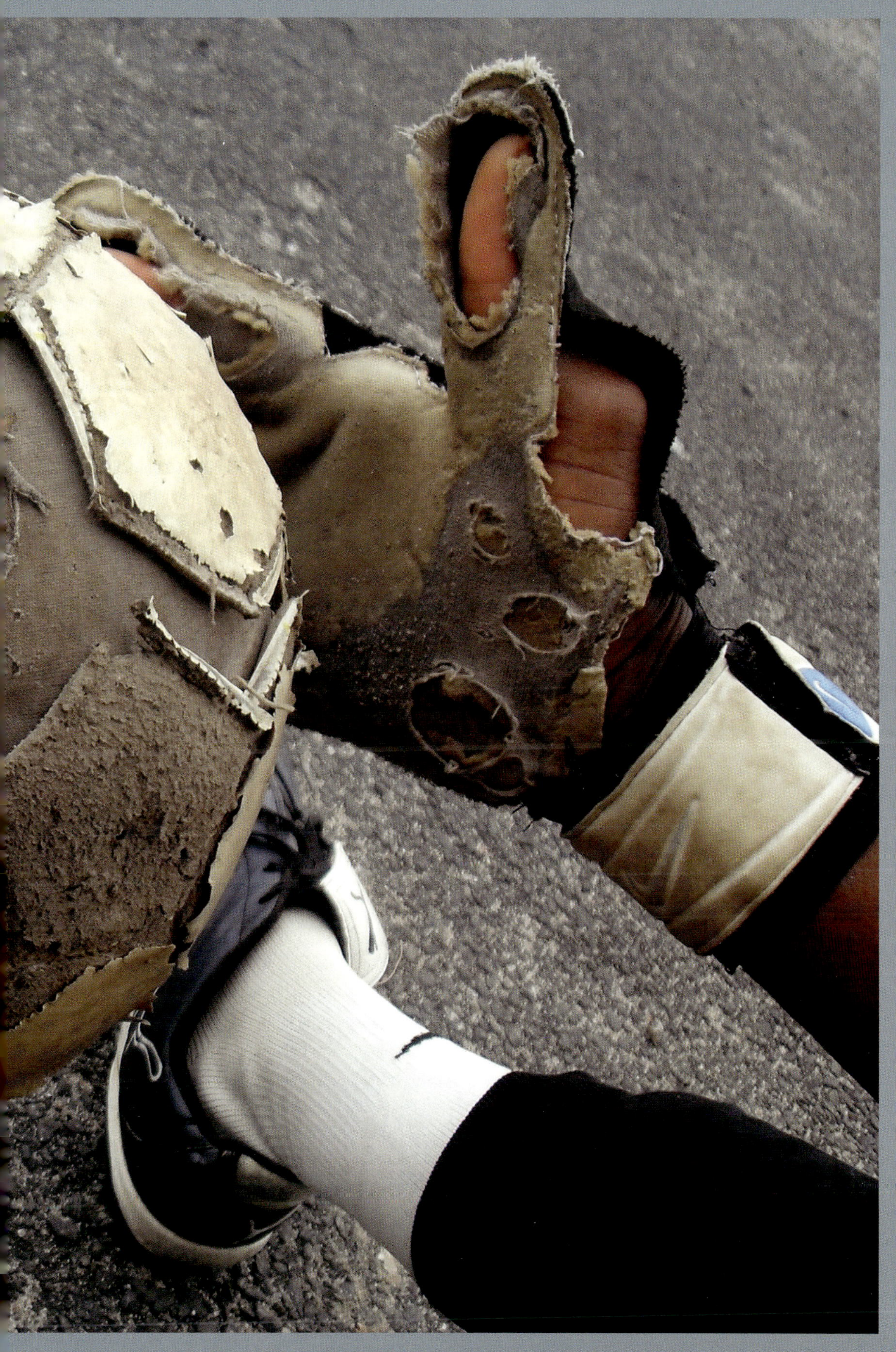

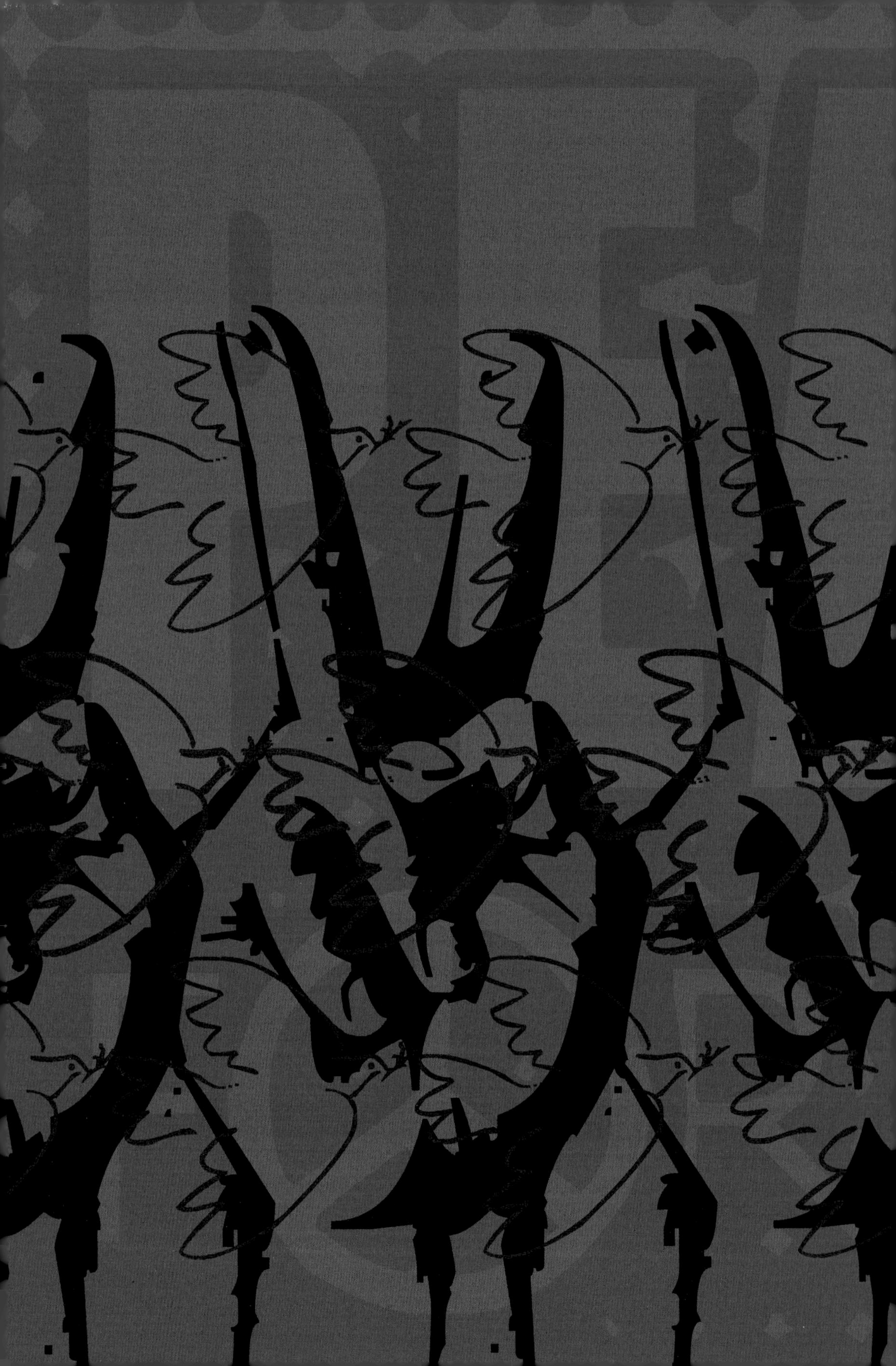

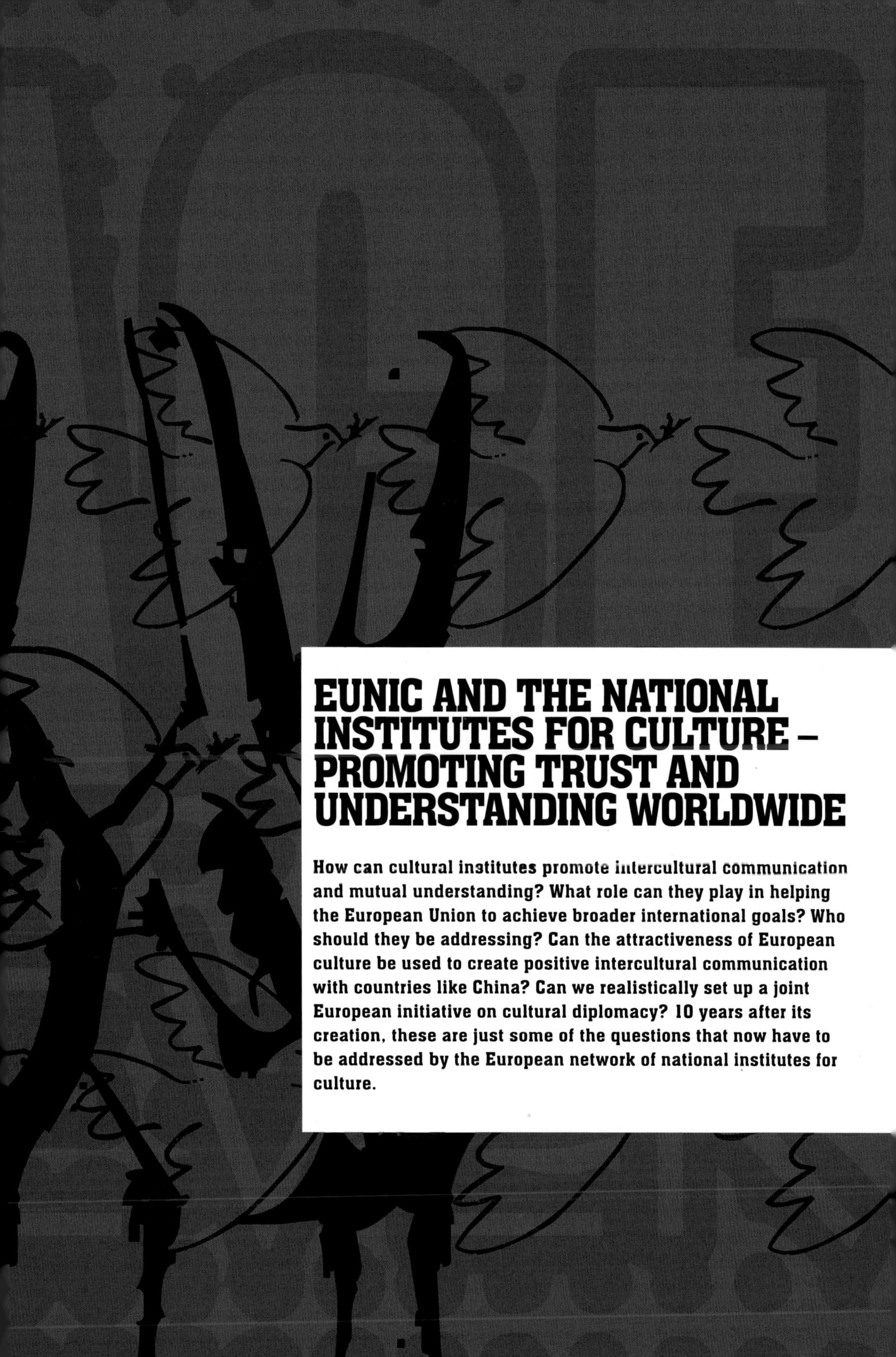

EUNIC AND THE NATIONAL INSTITUTES FOR CULTURE – PROMOTING TRUST AND UNDERSTANDING WORLDWIDE

How can cultural institutes promote intercultural communication and mutual understanding? What role can they play in helping the European Union to achieve broader international goals? Who should they be addressing? Can the attractiveness of European culture be used to create positive intercultural communication with countries like China? Can we realistically set up a joint European initiative on cultural diplomacy? 10 years after its creation, these are just some of the questions that now have to be addressed by the European network of national institutes for culture.

EUNIC, the first ten years EUNIC, the European Union National Institutes for Culture, is celebrating its tenth birthday this year. This article looks back over the last decade to assess to what extent the initial aspirations and goals of EUNIC have been realised. I should stress from the outset that this is a personal view and by no means represents the official position or views of the current Presidential team. *By Andrew Murray*

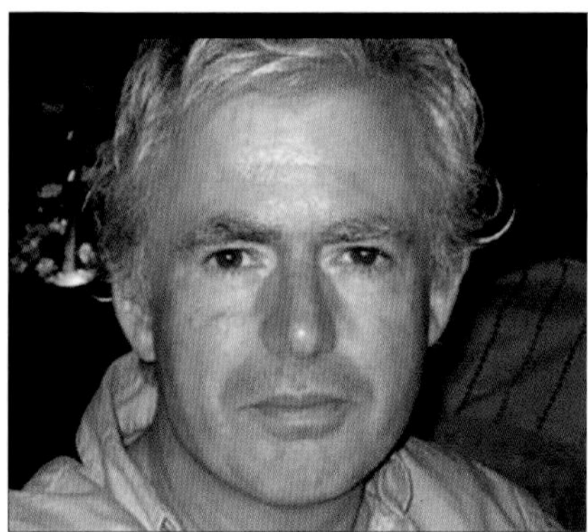

The first 'constitution' that was drafted by EUNIC dates from June 2006 and it sets out the mission of the organisation as well as the sets of actions by which this mission will be achieved.

EUNIC aims to create effective partnerships and networks between EU National Institutes for Culture in order to improve and promote cultural diversity and understanding between European societies and to strengthen international dialogue and cultural cooperation with countries outside Europe.

This will be done through:

- Discussing issues of common interest
- Sharing best practice
- Collaborating on joint projects that promote a better understanding of European culture in its diversity, both inside and outside Europe
- Acting as a partner of the European Commission in defining and implementing European cultural policy
- Undertaking joint research that will be of value to the European Commission and to other organisations (e.g. the Council of Europe) in furthering understanding of Europe-wide cultural issues
- Acting as an advocate for the value of cultural relations in promoting better international understanding and, as part of this, arguing for a strong and independent voice for the cultural sector.

This mission statement and aims were subsequently embodied in the statutes of the organisation and they still describe what the organisation stands for and what it purports to do. They are hugely ambitious goals.

Let's begin by looking at the first paragraph, EUNIC's 'mission statement'. To what extent has EUNIC created effective partnerships and networks between EU National Institutes for Culture? If we were marking EUNIC's report card then the evaluation would have to be 'some progress made but could do better'.

In 2006 the aspiration of the founding members of EUNIC was that they would engage in a variety of collaborative activities (the six detailed above starting with discussing areas of common interest) with the aim of promoting cultural diversity and understanding between European peoples and strengthening intercultural dialogue and co-operation with peoples outside Europe.

One recurrent and very difficult issue for the practitioners and academics of cultural relations and cultural diplomacy is the lack of any tools for measuring its effectiveness, other than the measurement of inputs. Thus we cannot measure whether EUNIC has in fact 'improved cultural diversity and understanding' between European societies or has 'strengthened international dialogue and

cooperation.' In 2006 no baseline studies were undertaken and there is still no agreed methodology among EUNIC members for measuring impact and outcomes.

What we can measure though are the six activities that are intended to deliver the as yet un-measurable outcomes. How has EUNIC performed with each of these?

General Assemblies

The heads of EUNIC members gather twice a year in General Assemblies; these are fora which are ideally suited to the discussion of issues of common interest and to the extent that these meetings have had on their agenda issues such as multilingualism, the cultural relationships between the EU and China, and between the EU and its Southern Neighbourhood, then we can say that they have been successful, though little common action has resulted from these discussions. The few collaborative projects that have taken place, the EU-China Dialogue, for example, six of which have taken place over the last ten years, cannot deliver evidence of significant outputs or outcomes.

Moving on to the next activity, the sharing of best practice, one would think that the General Assemblies would have been ideally suited for sharing what works and what doesn't work in cultural relations and cultural diplomacy; however, this subject has rarely if all been on the agenda. There has been some bilateral sharing of 'best practice', for example via annual meetings between the Goethe Institut and the British Council; but here again there was neither the appetite

> **One recurrent and very difficult issue for practitioners and academics of cultural relations and cultural diplomacy is the lack of any tools for measuring its effectiveness, other than the measurement of inputs.**

to learn from each other nor the mechanisms (secondments, attachments, joint seminars and workshops) in place to facilitate sharing and learning.

I have already mentioned the EU-China Dialogues, an example of collaboration at members' level of the third activity, collaboration on joint projects that promote a better understanding of European culture in its diversity. It is at the level of clusters, however, that we find most evidence of EUNIC collaborative projects.

EUNIC in 2016 has over one hundred 'clusters' around the world, usually in capital cities and half of them located in the EU. These clusters meet on a monthly or bi-monthly basis and they are led by a presidency team of a president and two vice-presidents elected from the directors of the EUNIC members with operations in that country. The growth of clusters, from a handful in 2006 to over a hundred at the time of writing, has not been the result of management directives from members' heads. It has largely been a 'bottom up process' in which members, directors and managers at local level have understood the benefits which can accrue from meeting and working together.

There is evidence that clusters do discuss issues of common interest (for example, how to deal with the local ministry of culture); and some clusters do share best practice, for example in event management. It is evidence relating to clusters' collaboration on joint projects, however, which is the most important achievement of EUNIC over the last ten years, putting to shame the lack of collaboration at headquarters and at members' level.

The most common collaborative activities carried out by EUNIC clusters have been 'stand-alone' traditional cultural diplomacy events: European Film Festivals, Literature Nights, European Days of Languages and of course Europe Days. If one was being ungenerous, these projects could be described as 'collective nation branding' but, given the mandates and missions of the majority of members, this was all that they could do.

Some clusters have managed to go beyond the 'lowest common denominator' approach and have engaged in projects that involve partnerships with local cultural actors and civil society organisations, develop links between individuals and institutions in Europe and their host countries, and have the long term aim of promoting trust and understanding. The clusters in Jordan and Tunisia have been particularly successful in this regard, but there are examples throughout the cluster network and they have become increasingly common and more ambitious.

That brings us to the fourth activity: acting as a partner of the European Commission in defining and implementing European cultural policy and acting as an advocate of the value of cultural relations. Here EUNIC members have been more successful in helping define European cultural policy in external relations than in the internal EU arena.

Culture and education are supporting competences, meaning that Member States somewhat jealously protect and preserve their control over these sectors inside the EU. The Treaty of Lisbon gave the newly minted European External Action Service a special competence in culture and EU external relations. The process of defining that competence, and the active support of the European Parliament and the Education and Culture Directorate of the European Commission, have provided EUNIC members with the opportunity to work as partners of European institutions and to help define that policy.

However it has not been EUNIC acting as EUNIC that has been responsible for the successful advocacy of the value of cultural relations in EU external relations. Instead it has been a consortium of EUNIC members, More Europe, which has been the key player, winning a contract from the European Commission; and the Preparatory Action on Culture and EU External Relations, which in 2014 provided the evidence and the arguments that have convinced the European institutions to develop a cultural relations approach to cultural diplomacy.

The creation in 2010 of More Europe, a consortium of EUNIC members (Goethe Institut, the British Council, Institut Français and the Danish Cultural Institute) with civil society organisations active in cultural policy, was in part the result of frustration felt by these EUNIC members that their ambition to become partners of the European institutions, both in defining EU cultural policy in external relations, but also in eventually implementing this policy, was being held back by the need to develop a consensus among all EUNIC members before taking action. As one of the founding members of More Europe complained at the time 'an association of 30 members is not the speedboat required to

Culture and education are supporting competences, meaning that Member States somewhat jealously protect and preserve their control over these sectors inside the EU.

respond to the policy dialogues and discussions asked for by EU institutions, rather it is an oil tanker'. EUNIC has benefited greatly from the More Europe initiative in that EUNIC is now seen by European institutions as a 'major partner' in the new emerging EU Cultural Diplomacy. This is probably the most important of all the achievements of EUNIC over the last decade, together with the creation of the network of clusters.

Activities five and six: research and advocacy, have not been priority areas for EUNIC (other than the advocacy carried out by EUNIC members under the auspices of More Europe). This is not a surprise: research in cultural relations and cultural diplomacy is in its infancy, both in academia and among EUNIC members. There is an urgent need to bridge the gap that exists between academics and practitioners so that empirical research can be undertaken into the impact and evaluation of cultural relations and cultural diplomacy. Without evidence of the efficacy of these activities there is a risk that the government funding will completely dry up or be targeted only at conventional 'nation branding'.

Before making a final assessment of EUNIC's performance as well as looking forward to the next ten years, one anomaly needs to be explained: in the following pages you will find a directory of EUNIC members, however many of these institutions are not cultural institutes, indeed several are ministries or cultural institutes in name only and are in fact government departments. How has this come about?

The institutional parents of EUNIC were the Goethe Institute and the British Council. It is no accident that these two 'arms-length' organisations insisted that participating organisations of EUNIC should 'have a degree of autonomy from their national governments' and that 'EUNIC undertakes to maintain communication with relevant organisations in those members' states that do not have national cultural institutes and are therefore not formally part of the EUNIC network'.

In 2006 the Goethe Institut and the British Council shared an understanding that their primary purpose was the building of trust between peoples through cultural relations. They believed, and I put stress on the word 'believed' since there was and still is little empirical evidence, that trust-building is more effectively done by being independent from government, having a long-term perspective and having an approach based upon the values of mutuality and reciprocity. Thus the original idea behind EUNIC was that it should not include government ministries or departments since this would mean that cultural relations could not be practised, only cultural diplomacy, that is, the utilisation of culture for the pursuit of foreign policy aims.

This idea proved to be an exclusive one: many Member States did not have cultural institutes and thus it was difficult if not impossible to claim to have full EU representation if there was not room for flexibility and compromise. In 2009 the EUNIC General Assembly in Copenhagen agreed that 'Ministries of Foreign Affairs should be excluded, except from countries which have no national cultural institutes. It was emphasi-

sed that even in these countries Ministries should be encouraged to nominate an arm's-length cultural organisation to represent the country within EUNIC'.

Since 2009 EUNIC membership has expanded to include all 28 Member States; however there has been no enthusiasm on the part of ministries to nominate an arm's-length cultural organisation in their place. We now have a mixed economy of institutions, most of whom mainly practise cultural diplomacy, and an increasingly vulnerable minority who mainly practise cultural relations (the British Council in its recent government review was told that it was funded to deliver cultural diplomacy and that the reviewer did not understand the concept of 'cultural relations').

It has been argued recently by one of the few academics (Melissa Nisbett) working in the field of cultural diplomacy that over the last ten years the arm's length approach of cultural relations has been overtaken by the 'soft power' approach of cultural diplomacy. Does the story of EUNIC provide further evidence of this transition? And what does the future hold?

EUNIC began as a small association of institutes who were 'advocates of the value of cultural relations in promoting better international understanding'. Over the last ten years it has grown into an EU institution which, like all EU institutions, has had to make changes and compromises in order to manage the diverse interests of its members. It is still a young organisation, learning how to make partnerships and how to make this amazing network deliver to its potential. This does not mean, however, that the original ethos has been abandoned or forgotten.

At the time of writing the distinction between arm's-length cultural relations and government-led cultural diplomacy is in the process of being bridged by a new definition and understanding of Cultural Diplomacy being developed by a partnership of EUNIC members and European institutions. The next EUNIC Yearbook (2017) will be based on a conference being held on 20 April 2016 in Brussels called 'A New Role for Culture in External Relations: Re-integrating Cultural Relations and Cultural Diplomacy'. The conference, and the papers it will commission and produce, will tackle the following questions:

- How can we design a new cultural diplomacy that re-integrates what have been thought of as very different approaches – governmental cultural diplomacy and non-governmental cultural relations?
- How can state actors work purposefully in the cultural sphere in such a way as to generate – earn – trust, without instrumentalising cultural expression and conversation to the point where trust ceases to be earned?
- Is there an attainable position, and an ethic, which would allow diplomacy as practised by governments and the EU to earn and consolidate widespread 'environmental' trust though cultural engagement? And can we begin to define how it might work?

I hope to be writing again in this space next year with some of the answers to these questions...

Andrew Murray is Director of EUNIC Global in Brussels.

Who we are and what we do – An overview of EUNIC members

AUSTRIA

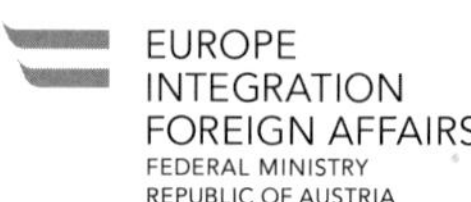

Name   Cultural Policy Directorate-General
Federal Ministry for Europe, Integration
and Foreign Affairs of the Republic of Austria
Founded 1973 (year of integration of the
International Cultural Policy Directorate-
General, Section V, in the MFA)
Head   Ambassador Teresa Indjein (Head of the
Cultural Policy Directorate General, Section V)
Address Minoritenplatz 8, 1010 Vienna, Austria
Staff   171 in the Culture Department
Website http://www.bmeia.gv.at/en/european-fo-
reign-policy/international-cultural-policy/

Mission/fields of activity
The international cultural policy pursued by the Federal
Ministry for Europe, Integration and Foreign Affairs in
collaboration with its embassies, consulates-general,
Cultural Forums, Austria Libraries and Austria Institutes
is based on clearly defined geographic and thematic
priorities, which are as follows for the period from 2015
to 2018:

Geographic priorities
Austria's neighbouring states and the Western Balkan
countries.

Thematic priorities
Film and the new media, architecture, dance, women in
art and science and Austria as a centre for dialogue

Building on these priorities, the three primary objectives
of Austrian international cultural policy are as follows:

1. Presenting Austria on the international stage as an innovative and creative nation that is historically diverse
and rich in culture and scientific know-how.
2. Contributing pro-actively to promoting the process of
European integration ('unity in diversity').
3. Making a sustainable contribution to building trust
and securing peace on a global level by launching initiatives in the field of intercultural and interreligious
dialogue.

Measures designed to achieve the objectives of Austrian-
international cultural policy:

1. Maintaining and developing efficient networks of Austrian cultural institutions abroad.
2. Implementing and/or supporting young, creative and
innovative cultural and scientific projects from Austria
abroad.
3. Implementing and supporting projects to promote
intercultural and interreligious dialogue both at home
and abroad, along with positioning Austria as a key
player in this field and building confidence and peace
at a global level.
4. Representing Austrian cultural interests in the decision-making processes of the EU and international organisations (particularly UNESCO), along with promoting
cultural initiatives launched by the EU and international organisations (especially by UNESCO) in Austria.

Global Network/infrastructure
96 embassies and consulates
29 Austrian Cultural Forums

BELGIUM

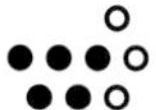

Name   WBI-Wallonie Bruxelles International
Founded 2009 as WBI, 1993 as CGRI
Head   Pascale Delcomminette
Address 2, place Sainctelette,1080 Brussels,Belgium
Staff   376
Website http://www.wbi.be/

Mission/fields of activity

The WBI is a public body that is responsible for the international relations of Wallonia-Brussels. It is the instrument for implementing the international policy of the French Community of Belgium, the Walloon Region and the French Community Commission of the Brussels-Capital Region.

Bilateral relations

The WBI is responsible for implementing these international policies. Its activities are situated in the context of bilateral relations. The objectives of these bilateral relations are as follows:

- To support the creative resources (cultural and business) of Wallonia-Brussels and contribute to the development of our regions.
- To promote the constituent parts of Wallonia-Brussels as entities authorised to act in an international capacity.
- To defend the values and interests of each part and to promote their competencies by helping each other in a spirit of cooperation.

Sector activities also exist within the framework of development co-operation, human rights, health and social affairs, the environment, youth exchanges, education and training, higher education and scientific research, and culture.

Multilateral relations

The activities of WBI in the field of multilateral relations means the federated entities in question are represented in various bodies and they can participate in specific European, francophone or international projects and programmes.

These multilateral relations concern activities in the following 4 fields:
- European integration
- Cross-border and interregional aspects of Europe
- Francophonie
- Worldwide multilateral co-operation.

Global network/infrastructure

17 offices and 2 cultural centres (Paris and Kinshasa), but active in 70 countries through cooperation agreements and activities.

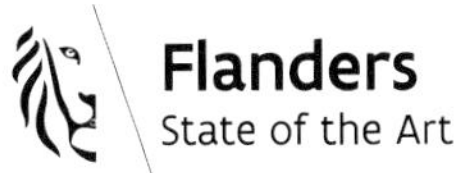

Flanders
State of the Art

Name   Flanders Department of Foreign Affairs
Departement Internationaal Vlaanderen
Founded 2006
Head   Koen Verlaeckt, Secretary General
Address   Boudewijnlaan 30, P.O. box 80, B-1000 Brussels
Staff   186
Website   http://www.vlaanderen.be/int

Mission/fields of activity

The Flanders Department of Foreign Affairs prepares the international policy of the Government of Flanders. According to the Belgian constitution, Flanders exerts a broad range of policy competences both domestically and internationally (including culture, education and media policy). This provides Flanders with a unique position in the world, entitling it to its own diplomatic representation abroad and the power to conclude international treaties and cooperation agreements.

More specifically, the Department's activities focus on foreign policy, development cooperation (in southern Africa), international trade and tourism policy. Over recent years the Department has been paying more attention to economic, cultural and science diplomacy as powerful instruments for safeguarding and expanding our interests abroad and for our international branding as a state-of-the-art region in the heart of Europe.

Global network/infrastructure

The Department operates a network of 11 permanent diplomatic representations, based in The Hague, London, Paris, Berlin, Vienna, Warsaw, Madrid, Pretoria, New York, Geneva and Brussels (EU). A 12th representation will open before 2019.

The Government of Flanders also funds cultural institutes in The Netherlands (De Brakke Grond, Amsterdam) and Japan (Flanders Center, Osaka).

BULGARIA

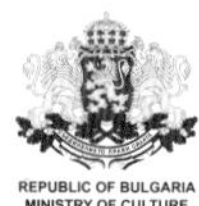

REPUBLIC OF BULGARIA
MINISTRY OF CULTURE

Name Ministry of Culture of the Republic of Bulgaria
Министерство на културата
на Република България

Bulgarian Cultural Institutes Abroad are state cultural institutes that are methodically and financially managed by the Ministry of Culture. They create and implement their activities on the basis of signed bilateral intergovernmental agreements that regulate their legal status and working conditions.

Founded 1954 (Ministry of Culture)
Head Minister Vezhdi Rashidov
Address 17, Al. Stamboliiski Blvd., Sofia, Bulgaria
Staff 150 employees in the Ministry of Culture
32 permanent employees total staff
in BCIs abroad
20-30 staff on temporary contracts
Website http://mc.government.bg/page.php?p=285&s=317&sp=318&t=0&z=0

Mission/fields of activity

Our aims are as follows:

- To represent the overall image of Bulgaria as a modern democratic state by providing extensive information about its culture, history, society and politics.
- To promote international cultural cooperation and intercultural dialogue.
- To expand the presence and influence of Bulgarian culture.
- To develop programmes and activities to promote an active European civil society.

General activities

- Building, developing and enhancing the activities of the Bulgarian Cultural Institute abroad.
- Conducting a comprehensive policy for the presentation of Bulgarian culture in accordance with the specificities of the host country and in accordance with the bilateral agreement regulating the activities and functions of the Bulgarian Cultural Institute.
- The presentation of Bulgarian artists, art collectives and cultural products.
- Facilitating the realisation of Bulgarian artists and cultural products on the international cultural market.
- Organising and running representative one-off events and series of events that represent contemporary Bulgarian culture: individually and in cooperation with host country institutions.
- Cooperating to realise other representative performances of Bulgarian culture abroad.
- Implementing an information policy to promote the achievements of Bulgarian culture and arts and Bulgaria as a whole.

Specific activities

- Programmes and events in the following areas:
- Culture – theatre and musical performances, exhibitions, film screenings, literary readings, workshops.
- Conferences and discussions – conferences, round tables, seminars, debates, artist talks.
- Education and culture – courses in Bulgarian language and folklore, information on student exchanges, training for children in the arts.
- Cultural tourism – organisation and participation in tourism fairs, distribution of promotion materials about cultural tourism in Bulgaria and the tourism sector in the country.
- Cooperation and participation in the Network of European Union National Institutes for Culture (EUNIC).
- Implementation of bilateral cultural cooperation programmes.
- Joint events with other countries that do not have cultural institutes in the respective country.
- Social media, information and promotion – maintaining the website of the institute, organisation of press conferences and briefings related to the activities of the institute, maintaining contacts with local electronic and print media.

Global network/infrastructure

11 offices in 11 countries

CROATIA

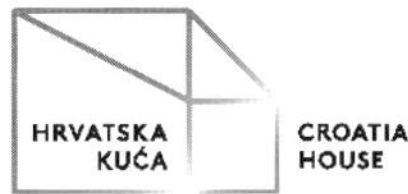

Name   Fondation Croatia House
Hrvatska kuća
Founded 2014
Head   Sandra Sekulic
Address Trg Nikole Šubića Zrinskoga 7–8
10 000 Zagreb, Croatia
Website http://www.mvep.hr/hr/posebni-projekti/hrvatska-kuca/
http://www.min-kulture.hr/default.aspx?id=10864

Mission/fields of activity

The Foundation Croatia House was established to promote Croatian culture, art, history, the Croatian language and cultural heritage abroad. It has been founded to coordinate all activities for the promotion of Croatian culture through diplomatic and consular offices and cultural centres. Since its establishment in 2014 the Foundation has carried out more than 200 projects in almost 50 countries. In order to achieve its aims, the Foundation funds a programmes and activities abroad to promote the wealth of Croatian culture, art and cultural heritage. The Foundation promotes the work of contemporary Croatian artists, contributes to learning about Croatia, promotes international cultural cooperation, and encourages the artistic creation and cultural activities of Croats outside Croatia.Beside its own programmes and activities, the Foundation cooperates at regional and international level and encourages other forms of action to achieve the aims of the Foundation.

Global network/infrastructure

1 office in Zagreb, Croatia (+ diplomatic and consular missions around the world)

CYPRUS

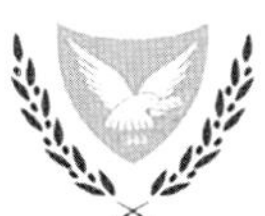

Name   The Cultural Services of the Ministry of Education and Culture of the Republic of Cyprus
Πολιτιστικές Υπηρεσίες του Υπουργείου Παιδείας
και Πολιτισμού της Κύπρου
Ministry of Education and Culture of the Republic of Cyprus
Founded 1965
Head   Head of EUNIC for Cyprus: Director of Cultural Services – Pavlos Paraskevas
The Minister of Education and Culture of the Republic of Cyprus is Costas Kadis
Address The Cultural Services
Ministry of Education and Culture of the Republic of Cyprus
Ifigeneias 17, Nicosia 2007, Cyprus
Staff   2
Website http://www.moec.gov.cy/

Mission/fields of activity

Cultural Services is the main exponent of the cultural policy of the state with regard to contemporary culture. The Department plays a vital role in shaping the cultural image of the country by being responsible for the development of arts and letters in Cyprus, informing the public about cultural events and its participation in them, and promoting the achievements of our cultural activities abroad. Fields of activity include the following:

- Culture
- Letters
- European Affairs
- Council of Europe
- UNESCO
- Cinema
- Theatre
- Music
- Dance
- Visual Arts
- Popular Culture/Cultural Heritage

CZECH REPUBLIC

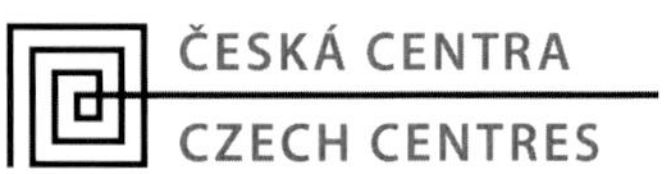

ČESKÁ CENTRA
CZECH CENTRES

Name   Czech Centres
Česká centra
Founded The Czechoslovak Cultural Institute was created shortly after WW II, in 1949 (first centres were founded in Warsaw and Sofia). After Czechoslovakia's split into the Czech Republic and Slovakia, Czech Centres were created in 1993 as a direct successor organisation, under the name 'Administration of cultural facilities abroad'. Since this name was not very appealing, the organisation was renamed the 'Administration of Czech Centres' in 1999. In 2004, a new name was introduced: 'Czech Centres'.
Head   Zdeněk Lyčka
Address   Václavské nám. 816/49
110 00 Prague 1, Czech Republic
Staff   Permanent: 87
Temporary: 43
Website   http://www.czechcentres.cz/

Mission/fields of activity

Czech Centres is an agency of the Ministry of Foreign Affairs of the Czech Republic, established to promote the Czech Republic around the world. The network is an active public diplomacy instrument of the Czech Republic's foreign policy.

We believe that the best promotion is successful cooperation; therefore our activities are based on partnerships. We mostly work through bilateral and multilateral projects. We prefer multilateral international cooperation wherever possible, and we always work with local partners and with reference to local 'hot topics'.
Every year we organise, co-organise or participate in more than two thousand projects. Our key activities deal with all fields of culture (arts in all forms), science, innovation, tourism, business, and language (including language courses). We collaborate with leading Czech and foreign experts, curators, shows and competitions, arts and cultural organisations, universities, non-governmental and expatriate organisations, galleries, theatres, festivals, music clubs, museums, and the media.

A few examples of our activities

- Film festivals
- Urban and architecture festivals
- Debates on the arts in politics and politics in the arts
- Dance theatre showcased in festivals
- Literature/translation competitions
- Language courses
- Art exhibitions
- Design fairs

Global network/infrastructure

22 offices in 20 countries

DENMARK

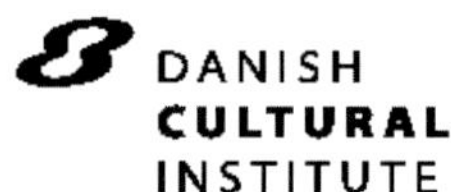

DANISH
CULTURAL
INSTITUTE

Name   The Danish Cultural Institute
Det Danske Kulturinstitut
Founded 1940
Head   Michael Metz Mørch
Address   Vartov, Farvergade 27 L, 2. SAL
DK-1463 København K, Denmark
Staff   45
Website   http://www.dankultur.dk

Mission/fields of activity

The Danish Cultural Institute promotes dialogue and understanding across cultural differences and national borders. Our work is founded on a broad conceptual platform that embraces art, culture and society; areas that unite people across cultures, promote international understanding and facilitate intercultural communication.

We focus on:

- Co-creation and innovation
- Children & young people
- Sustainability and welfare

The Danish Cultural Institute facilitates networks and strengthens collaboration between Danish and international artists, cultural institutions, education, research and the business community. Using culture as a common starting point, we create platforms for knowledge-sharing, exchanging ideas and experiences and lasting cultural relations.

These activities are diverse – from concerts to exhibitions; workshops and conferences to field trips and study

tours; from performance to film and media ; from urban interventions and arts/culture education to other forms of crossover ; and in some countries, Danish courses.
In this way culture plays an active role in daily life, providing personal experiences for one and all.

Global network/infrastructure
7 offices, including one centre, covering China, Russia, Brazil, Benelux/Germany, Poland, the Baltic States and other collaboration in Europe and the rest of the world. Offices covering Turkey and India are to be opened.

ESTONIA

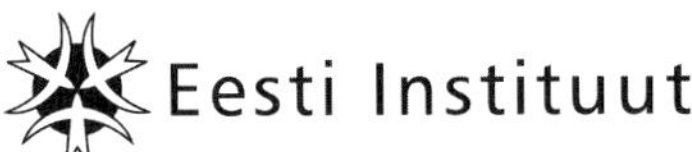 Eesti Instituut

Name	Estonian Institute
	Eesti Instituut
Founded	1989
Head	Karlo Funk
Address	Estonian Institute, Suur-Karja 14
	10140 Tallinn, Estonia
Staff	14
Website	http://www.estinst.ee/

Mission/fields of activity
The Estonian Institute promotes Estonian culture, develops cultural relations and coordinates teaching of the Estonian language around the world.

Over the years the Institute has published dozens of information booklets and periodicals, established web platforms, organised festivals, exhibitions, conferences and seminars. With offices in Helsinki and Budapest, the Institute actively promotes cultural exchange in Europe. The Institute acts as a cultural gateway and cooperation partner in Estonia.

Global network/infrastructure
3 offices in 3 countries

FINLAND

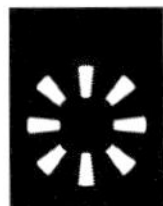

Suomen kulttuuri- ja tiedeinstituutit ry
Finlands kultur- och vetenskapsinstitut rf
The Finnish Cultural and Academic Institutes

Name	The Finnish Cultural and Academic Institutes
	Suomen kultturi – ja tiedeinstituutit
	Finlands kultur – och vetenskapsinstitut
Founded	1954
Head	Tove Ekman
Address	Suomen Kulttuuri- Ja Tiedeinstituutit Ry
	Kalliolinnantie 4 (1. KRS), 00140 Helsinki, Finland
Staff	132
Website	http://instituutit.fi/

Mission/fields of activity
The Finnish cultural and academic institutes are :
- Non-governmental bodies promoting co-operation between Finnish and international cultural and academic organisations and professionals.
- Innovative and cost-effective expert organisations that boost Finland's global visibility.
- Independent non-profit organisations. maintained by a private foundation or fund

The mission of the institutes is to :
- Promote international mobility and co-operation in the arts, culture, science and research.
- Provide information on Finnish culture, arts, science and research.
- Organise seminars, exhibitions and other events.
- Run residency programmes for artists and researchers.
- Conduct academic research.
- Implement projects relating to cultural and education exports.
- Offer Finnish language courses.

Global network/infrastructure
17 offices in 16 countries
The institutes are independent non-profit organisations maintained by private foundations or funds. They receive basic funding from the Ministry of Education and Culture in Finland, each institute submitting their own application annually to the ministry. The institutes receive additional project funding from various sources such as private foundations and companies and from other Finnish and foreign partners.

FRANCE

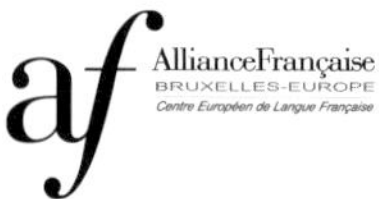

Name Fondation Alliance française
Founded July 2007 in Paris
Head Jérôme Clément, President
Address 101 boulevard Raspail, 75006 Paris, France
Staff 14 people in the HQ
Website http://www.fondation-alliancefr.org/

Mission/fields of activity

The Fondation Alliance Française is the hub of the Alliances Françaises around the world and serves the entire network of Alliances Françaises.

Alliance Française is the largest cultural network in the world with more than 800 associations in 133 countries. Every year more than 500,000 people French at the Alliance Française and more than 6 million people participate in its cultural activities.

The mission of the Alliance Française is to encourage and develop knowledge of the French language and French and Francophone cultures, to enhance cultural diversity and to foster cultural, intellectual and artistic exchanges between the country where it is implemented and France and the French-speaking countries. Each Alliance Française is governed locally and operated as an independent, non-profit, non-political, non-discriminatory organisation.

Global network/infrastructure

800 associations in 133 countries.

INSTITUT FRANÇAIS

Name Institut Français
Founded 2010
Head Bruno Foucher, Executive Chairman
Anne Tallineau, Chief Executive Officer
Address Institut français, 8 - 14 Rue du Capitaine Scott, 75015 Paris, France
Staff 140 people
Website www.institutfrancais.com

Mission/fields of activity

The Institut Français is the agency responsible for the conduct of France's external cultural action. Under the supervision of the Ministry of Foreign Affairs, its role is to help to promote French culture abroad through greater dialogue with foreign cultures, while responding to the needs of France via a policy of listening, partnership and openness to other cultures. The Institut Français replaces the Culturesfrance association, with the legal status of a 'public industrial and commercial undertaking'.

The Ministry of Foreign Affairs has transferred a number of new missions to the Institut Français in addition to those performed by Culturesfrance in the field of cultural exchanges and welcoming foreign cultures to France. Among these new activities are promoting the French language, thought and knowledge, as well as training the staff of the French cultural network. The Institut Français upholds freedom of expression and diversity in today's globalised world, while at the same time asserting its capabilities and expertise in the promotion of French culture worldwide. It is instrumental in projecting France's influence and cooperative activities, and as a centre of expertise and advice.

Furthermore, the Institut Français has a central role to play in addressing today's digital challenges. The Internet and social networks are transforming the way in which culture is disseminated. The Institut Français will be adopting these technologies to turn them into a channel for advancing French influence.

Global network/infrastructure

1 office in Paris

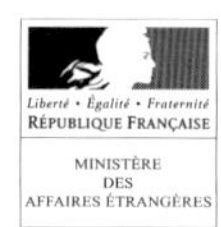

Name French Ministry of Foreign Affairs.
Directorate-General for Global Affairs, Culture, Education and International Development
Head Anne-Marie DESCÔTES (Director-General: Directorate-General for Global Affairs, Culture, Education and International Development)
Directorate for Culture, Education, Research and the Network
Anne GRILLO (Director)
Pierre LANAPATS (Deputy Director)

Address 27, rue de la Convention, CS 91533 – 75732 Paris cedex 15
Website http://www.diplomatie.gouv.fr

Mission/fields of activity

This department defines and implements the actions of France on global issues, sustainable development, international cooperation, political influence and major sectorial policies, particularly in the context of multilateral fora within its fields of competence. This activity is realised in conjunction with the relevant authorities and in partnership with all international organisations and stakeholders.Moreover, it contributes to the coordination by the Ministry of measures to enhance the international attractiveness of France. It promotes French expertise abroad on these issues.

Global network/infrastructure

161 services of cooperation and cultural action including 98 Instituts Français around the world.

GERMANY

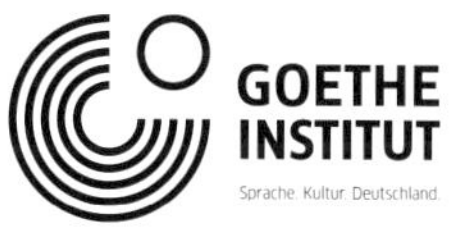

Name Goethe-Institut
Founded 1951
Head Klaus-Dieter Lehmann (President)
Johannes Ebert (Secretary General)
Address Dachauer Str. 122, 80637 München, Germany
Staff 3,500 worldwide (2014)
Website https://www.goethe.de

Mission/fields of activity

The Goethe-Institut is the cultural institute of the Federal Republic of Germany with a global reach. We promote knowledge of German abroad, encourage international cultural exchange and convey a comprehensive image of Germany.

For over sixty years we have provided access to the German language and culture and have worked towards mutual dialogue with the civil societies of our host countries, thus creating lasting trust in our nation. The work of the Goethe-Institut is supported by Germany's Foreign Office and is carried out independently without any political party affiliations. The institute generates about one third of its budget on its own through language courses and examinations. At present, the Goethe-Institut operates 159 institutes in 98 countries, 12 of them in Germany. The Goethe-Institut's ties with partner institutions in many other places give it about 1,000 points of contact around the world.

Global network/infrastructure

159 institutes in 98 countries, 12 of them in Germany

ifa Institut für Auslandsbeziehungen

Name ifa (Institut für Auslandsbeziehungen)
Founded 1917
Chair Ronald Grätz – Secretary General
(Appointed by the Executive Committee)
Address ifa (Institut für Auslandsbeziehungen)
Charlottenplatz 17,70173 Stuttgart, Germany
Staff 123 permanent employees (plus freelance, temporary and project staff)
Website http://www.ifa.de/

Mission/fields of activity

ifa (Institut für Auslandsbeziehungen) is committed to promoting peace, cultural exchange and opportunities for encounter. Its programmes, exhibitions, publications and sponsorship help to shape Germany's foreign cultural policy.

ifa showcases and disseminates 20th and 21st-century German art, architecture and design with exhibitions around the world. It supports international exhibition projects and coordinates Germany's contribution to the Venice Biennale. The ifa Galleries in Stuttgart and Berlin display art and architecture from Africa, Asia, Latin America and Eastern Europe.

ifa supports intercultural learning and civil society structures with its funding, exchange and placement programmes, for example in predominantly Muslim countries in the Middle East and Central/East/South-East Europe. It supports peace projects in conflict-torn regions as part of its civil conflict resolution programme. ifa organises discussion events and research projects to accompany developments in international politics. The

Foreign Cultural and Educational Policy (FCEP) Library, KULTURAUSTAUSCH (the magazine for global perspectives), and the online portals are key forums for information on FCEP in Germany.

Current EUNIC activities
ifa is a member of EUNIC, and as part of its Culture and Foreign Policy research programme it organises an annual public conference for the network in Brussels. It publishes the Culture Report/EUNIC Yearbook in partnership with Steidl Verlag and is an active member of the EUNIC clusters in Stuttgart and Berlin.

Global network/infrastructure
ifa is based in Europe but is active around the world. It has a branch in Berlin (offices and ifa Gallery) and its headquarters are in Stuttgart (offices, German school, ifa Academy, ifa Gallery and ifa Library). It draws on a global network of experts, collaborators and alumni from politics, civil society, culture, the arts, media and academia. It focuses on developing countries and countries in transition, such as the Eastern Partnership countries, Muslim countries, Central Eastern Europe, South-East Europe and the Commonwealth of Independent States.

GREECE

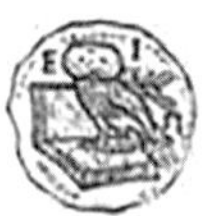

Name	Hellenic Foundation for Culture
	Ελληνικό Ίδρυμα Πολιτισμού
Founded	1992
Head	Konstantinos Tsoukalas (President)
Address	50, Stratigou Kallari St., GR - 154 52 Athens, Greece
Staff	Headquarters: 20
Branches (overall): 25	
Website	http://hfc-worldwide.org/

Mission/fields of activity
The aim of the Hellenic Foundation for Culture is to promote Hellenic culture and disseminate the Greek language all over the world, and also to encourage intercultural relations and bilateral cooperation in the field of culture. Since it was founded in 1992, the HFC has opened branches in Odessa, Alexandria and Berlin. It operates offices with representatives in London, Vienna, Brussels and Washington. During the period 2007-2009, the HFC founded Centres of Hellenic Culture in Trieste, Belgrade, Bucharest, Tirana, and Sofia and in 2015 established another in Nicosia. The Foundation offers Greek language courses, organises cultural events and movie screenings, lectures, exhibitions and concerts, publishes books and operates lending libraries in its branches, which are open to the public.

Global network/infrastructure
12 offices and centres in 12 countries (including the headquarters in Greece)

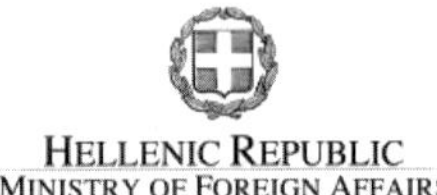

Name	Hellenic Republic Ministry of Foreign Affairs
	Ελληνική Δημοκρατία Υπουργείο Εξωτερικών
Founded	1863
Head	Nikolaos Kotzias
Address	1, Vasilissis Sofias Ave. 106 71, Athens, Greece
Staff	1777 (2215 incl. local staff)
Website	http://www.mfa.gr/

Mission/fields of activity
The Ministry of Foreign Affairs (MFA) is in charge of diplomacy and foreign policy with respect to the country's bilateral relations, as well as its relations with the EU and international organisations. The MFA forges and supports a wide range of bilateral relations with neighbouring and distant countries alike, plays an active part in all negotiations and decisions concerning the policies of organisations such as the UN, UNESCO, and NATO, and is working towards the deepening and integration of the EU, participating actively in all of the Union's organs and institutions.

Cultural diplomacy
The MFA attaches particular importance to cultural diplomacy as a quintessential tool for approaching peoples and exercising foreign policy. The universality of Hellenic Culture is the connective tissue in the quest for common origins and historical ties with other countries, while intercultural dialogue contributes to international peace and cooperation. Agreements and bilateral educational and cultural programmes with third countries are a fundamental institutional tool. The various cultural

events organised by our embassies and consulates contribute to cultural exchanges and the promotion of all forms of classical and modern Greek culture. On a multilateral level, and particularly in the context of international organisations, Greek cultural diplomacy is aimed at highlighting, promoting and utilising a universal value system for interstate relations.

Educational diplomacy

The aim of Greek educational diplomacy is to create synergies between culture, education and economy, utilising the services of educational institutions abroad (e.g Departments of Greek in various foreign universities), or the facilities of select Greek agencies located in areas of particular natural, historical and cultural value (e.g., the European Cultural Centre of Delphi, the International Olympic Academy). Educational/scientific attendees are hosted for specialist programmes in a variety of fields (e.g. architecture, classical studies, Olympism, medicine).

Global network/infrastructure

84 embassies
113 consulates
Permanent representations, liaison offices and trade offices

HUNGARY

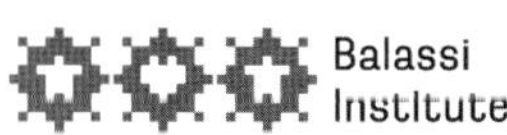 Balassi
Institute

Name	Balassi Institute
	Balassi Intézet
Founded	2007
Head	Judit Hammerstein
Address	Somlói út 51, 1016 Budapest, Hungary
Staff	170
Website	http://www.balassiintezet.hu/en/

Mission/fields of activity

The Institute plays a key role in developing and attaining Hungary's objectives in the area of cultural diplomacy. As an organisational hub, it coordinates and directs all activities provided by Hungarian institutes abroad and supports the worldwide community of Hungarian education.

The Institute not only spreads and promotes Hungarian culture abroad, it also introduces the traditions and cultures preserved by Hungarians from outside our borders to those living in Hungary today. The Institute's uniqueness therefore lies in the content and scope of its activities, as well as in the methodology used to reach its goals.

Global network/infrastructure

24 offices in 22 countries

IRELAND

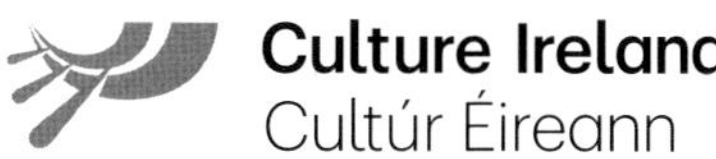 **Culture Ireland**
Cultúr Éireann

Name	Culture Ireland
	Cultúr Éireann
Founded	2005
Head	Christine Sisk
Address	Culture Ireland, Third Floor, 23 Kildare Street, Dublin 2, D02 TD30, Ireland
Staff	7
Website	http://www.cultureireland.ie/

Mission/fields of activity

Culture Ireland promotes Irish arts worldwide. It creates and supports opportunities for Irish artists and companies to present and promote their work at strategic international festivals and venues. Through showcases at key global arts events, including the Edinburgh Festivals and the Venice Biennales, Culture Ireland develops platforms to present Irish arts to international audiences. As part of its role in presenting special culture initiatives globally, Culture Ireland is presenting a year long international culture programme to commemorate the Easter Rising in 1916.

Global network/infrastructure

1 office in 1 country

ITALY

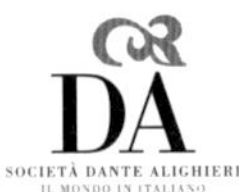

Name Società Dante Alighieri
Founded 1889
Head Andrea Riccardi
Address Piazza di Firenze, 27, 00186 Roma, Italy
Website http://ladante.it/

Mission/fields of activity

Società Dante Alighieri was founded in 1889; the mission of SDA is to promote the Italian language and culture in Italy and abroad. SDA has a global network; the local offices deliver Italian language courses and organise cultural events. PLIDA (Progetto Lingua Italiana Dante Alighieri), is one of the four Italian language certificates recognised by the Italian Ministry of Foreign Affairs and assesses language competence across an ascending scale of difficulty of six levels, from A1 to C2 (corresponding to the levels of the Common European Framework). PLIDA B2 and PLIDA C1 are recognised by the Italian Ministry of Education, University and Research as valid qualifications for applying to Italian universities. SDA is part of CLIQ, (Certificazione Lingua Italiana di Qualità), the Italian association of language testers, which guarantees quality in the process of language testing and provides general guidelines for language test design. ADA is the curricular plan of the Italian language courses of the SDA where guidelines for organising and planning courses are offered along with reference levels for teachers and directors of studies.

Every year SDA organises one-year training courses for Italian language teachers and training courses for PLIDA examiners.

Global network/infrastructure

423 offices in 60 countries

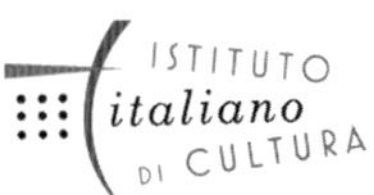

Name Istituto Italiani di Cultura of the Italian Ministry of Foreign Affairs and International Cooperation (MAECI)

Founded 1926
Head Vincenzo De Luca Director General DGSP
Address MAECI Piazzale della Farnesina, 1, 00194 Rome
Staff 1,374 in HQ and overseas including cultural officers, directors, locally hired employees, Italian language teachers.
Website http://www.esteri.it/mae/en/politica_estera/cultura/reteiic.html

Mission/fields of activity

The mission of the 83 Italian Cultural Institutes (IIC) is to promote the Italian language and culture in foreign countries. They offer opportunities to meet and establish a dialogue with Italian intellectuals and artists. The Institutes' aim is to promote the image of Italy and its culture, both classic and contemporary. This is carried out through the following activities:

- Organising events with a focus on visual arts (painting, sculpture, photography, video art), music, cinema, literature, theatre, dance, fashion, design, and architecture.
- Organising courses in Italian language and culture in accordance with the Common European Framework of Reference for Languages.
- Promoting Italian scientific culture.
- Managing an efficient network of libraries.
- Establishing contacts between Italian and foreign cultural institutions and individuals.
- Facilitating an intercultural dialogue founded on democratic principles.

Global network/infrastructure

83 offices in 59 countries

LATVIA

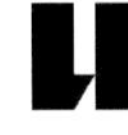

he Latvian Institute

Name Latvian Institute
Founded 1998
Head Aiva Rozenberga
Address Pils iela 21, Riga, LV-1050, Latvia
Staff 4
Website http://www.latvia.eu/

Mission/fields of activity

Promotion of Latvia's positive international recognition through:

- The creation and coordination of the identity policy of Latvia.
- Establishing and participating in local and international cooperation networks – governmental, private, non-governmental).
- Implementing activities abroad and at home to promote Latvia.

Global network/infrastructure 1 office in 1 country

LITHUANIA

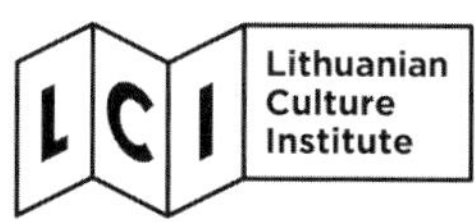

Name Lithuanian Culture Institute
Lietuvos kultūros institutas
Founded 2007
Head Aušrinė Žilinskienė
Address Z. Sierakausko g. 15, LT-03105 Vilnius, Lithuania
Staff 15
Website http://lithuanianculture.lt/http://lithuanian-culture.lt/

Mission/fields of activity

Our mission is to increase the international competitiveness of Lithuania's cultural and creative industries and contribute to the forming of a cultural climate by implementing cultural projects; and to represent Lithuanian professional art abroad effectively and constructively. Our activities are as follows:

- Organising and coordinating diverse representational Lithuanian cultural programmes abroad.
- Implementing cooperative bilateral and multilateral exchanges as well as cultural programmes in Lithuania and abroad.
- Working closely with and implementing projects of the cultural attaches of the Republic of Lithuania in foreign countries.
- Promoting Lithuanian literature abroad: consulting with and informing foreign publishers and translators

on issues concerning Lithuanian literature; organising seminars for translators and publishers; organising presentations and creative sessions of Lithuanian writers abroad; and administering a translation promotion programme.

- Organising and administering the cultural events programme at the annual Vilnius Book Fair.
- Coordinating Lithuania's participation in the Creative Europe and Citizens for Europe programmes of the European Union.
- Preparing and disseminating information about Lithuanian culture, artists and creative works.
- Producing informational publications to promote Lithuania's art and culture.

Our vision is to be an instrument for international cooperation, and an active catalyst for cultural and social initiatives in Lithuania and abroad.

Global network/infrastructure
1 office in 1 country

LUXEMBOURG

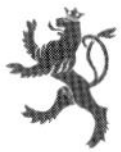

LE GOUVERNEMENT
DU GRAND-DUCHÉ DE LUXEMBOURG
Ministère des Affaires étrangères
et européennes

Name Ministry of Foreign and European Affairs of the Grand-Duchy of Luxembourg
Ministère des Affaires étrangères et européennes du Grand-Duché de Luxembourg
Founded 1936
Head Carlo Krieger (Director of Legal and Cultural Affairs)
Address 33, boulevard Roosevelt, L-2450 Luxembourg
Website http://www.gouvernement.lu/maee

Mission/fields of activity

The Department of Legal and Cultural works closely with the Ministry of Culture for the promotion of Luxembourg culture abroad by the diplomatic network of the Grand-Duchy of Luxembourg.

Global network/infrastructure
31 embassies
135 consulates

MALTA

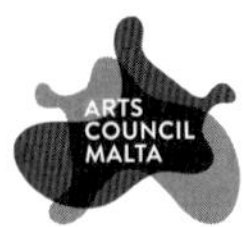

Name Arts Council Malta
Founded Arts Council Malta was created on 29 May 2015 and replaced the Maltese Council of Culture and Arts, which was founded on 15 August 2002
Head Albert Marshall
Address Arts Council Malta, Casa Scaglia 16, Mikiel Anton Vassalli Street, Valletta VLT 1311
Staff 22 people in the HQ
Website http://www.artscouncilmalta.org/

Mission/fields of activity

Arts Council Malta (ACM) is Malta's national agency for development and investment in the cultural and creative sectors.

It operates through three specific directorates. The creation and development of strategies for the sector falls under the Strategy Directorate. The Directorate is built on five strategic focal points which include: internationalisation, business development, research, education and training, diversity and communities. These points run through the council's national strategy for the cultural and creative sectors and inform its funding programmes. Festivals fall under their own distinct directorate, whose role is to focus on the management and development of the diverse festivals portfolio of the Council. With a brief which ranges from ensuring that the development of festivals is built on solid ground to issues such as audience development and cultural participation, this directorate also aims to create a partnership with existing festivals, with a view to eventually increasing the number of festivals in the calendar.

The third directorate – Corporate Affairs – provides all the support services for the effective and efficient functioning of the other two directorates and the Public Cultural Organisations.

In recent years, the cultural and creative sectors in Malta have been going through an exciting period of growth and change which have brought about corresponding challenges for the sector. With events such as the IFACCA World Summit happening in Valletta in 2016, the Maltese Presidency of the Council of the European Union in 2017 and Valletta as the European Capital of Culture in 2018, a reorganised and effective Arts Council Malta is poised to be a major player in what promises to be one of the most energetic and bristling sectors in Malta in the years to come.

Global network/infrastructure

2 offices: one in Valletta and one in New York.

THE NETHERLANDS

DutchCulture
centre for international cooperation

Name DutchCulture
Founded 2013 (as a merger of SICA, TransArtists and MEDIA Desk Netherlands)
Head Cees de Graaff
Address Herengracht 474, 1017 CA Amsterdam The Netherlands
Staff 34 (23 full-time employees)
Website www.dutchculture.nl

Mission/fields of activity

DutchCulture promotes international cultural cooperation. We advise, coordinate and produce programmes worldwide. With information and expertise DutchCulture supports international cooperation of the cultural sector and the Dutch diplomatic representations abroad. Every day we work to increase the visibility of the cultural capital of the Netherlands. The successful international cultural cooperation of our primary target groups and our partners is the critical success factor of DutchCulture.

DutchCulture is convinced that cultural cooperation will contribute to more equal and just international relations and, ultimately, a better world. In a complex world in which we are increasingly dependent on each other it is necessary to meet, share knowledge and collaborate with reciprocity as a starting point. Arts and culture can increase our curiosity about one another, inspire and challenge us to look across borders.

Artists and creatives know where to find each other worldwide. Yet successful international cultural cooperation is not always, nor everywhere, a given. DutchCulture has specific knowledge about countries, regions, themes and skills to help professionals in the Dutch cultural and diplomatic field on their way to realising their international ambitions. We provide access to a large international network, reliable information and expertise on certain regions and knowledge of global trends.

As a platform for sharing information and knowledge, DutchCulture contributes to the high visibility of international activities to culture professionals, international networks and the wider audience in the Netherlands. In addition, DutchCulture helps international partners connect with the right organisations and interesting partners in the Netherlands, and in that way we provide opportunities for international activities.

Global network/infrastructure
1 office in the Netherlands. Cultural representation of the Netherlands mainly goes through the network of diplomatic representations.

POLAND

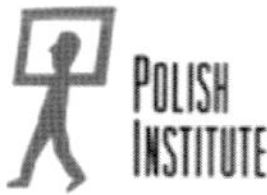

Name	Polish Institutes
	Instytuty Polskie
Founded	1939
Address	Ministry of Foreign Affairs, Department of Public and Cultural Diplomacy, al. J. Ch. Szucha 23 ; 00-580 Warsaw, Poland
Staff	6-8 people per Institute
Website	http://www.msz.gov.pl/en/p/msz_en/foreign_policy/public_diplomacy/polish_institutes/polish_institutes

Mission/fields of activity
The Polish Institutes exist to ensure that Polish culture has a presence and is appreciated around the world. They achieve this through public cultural events, pinpointing the most effective spheres, formats and topics for promoting Poland, giving it international recognition and a competitive advantage. By making successful use of these opportunities, they enhance Poland's political, economic and cultural position, building a positive image of Poland worldwide through their day-to-day work.

The Polish Institutes are run by the Ministry of Foreign Affairs. Their primary task is to promote Polish culture and foster better knowledge and understanding of Polish history and national heritage, as well as to support international cooperation in culture, education, science and social life. In many places, the Polish Institutes also act as the cultural and scientific affairs sections of Polish Embassies.

The Polish Institutes are centres for the advancement of knowledge about Poland through promotional and educational activities, ensuring the participation of Poland in local cultural life. The main task of the Polish Institutes is to introduce Polish culture to key actors in the countries in which they operate, ensure significant Polish involvement in international events, and establish long-lasting relations between Polish and foreign partners who are actively committed to international cultural exchange.

Global network/infrastructure
24 offices in 21 countries

PORTUGAL

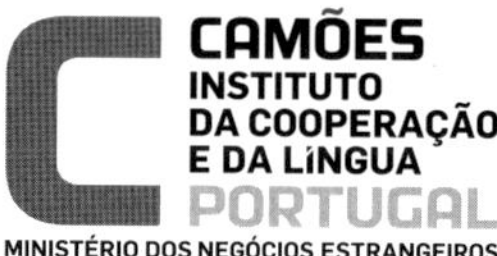

Name	Institute for Cooperation and Language, Camões, I.P.
	Instituto da Cooperação e da Língua, Camões, I.P.
Founded	1992
Head	Ana Paula Laborinho
Address	Avenida da Liberdade 270, 1250-149 Lisboa Portugal
Staff	550 (including 377 teachers - data2015)
Website	http://www.instituto-camoes.pt/

Mission/fields of activity
The main mission of Camões – Institute for Cooperation and Language, I.P, in short Camões, I.P., is to coordinate with the Ministry of Foreign Affairs to implement foreign policy mandates such as cooperation or humanitarian assistance, and the expansion and promotion of the Portuguese language and culture abroad.
The mission of Camões, I.P. is to propose and implement

Portuguese cooperation policy, coordinate activities undertaken by other public entities involved in implementing that policy, propose and implement the educational policy, disseminate Portuguese language and culture in foreign universities, and to manage the foreign Portuguese teaching network at primary and secondary levels.

Global network/infrastructure
Camões, I.P. operates in 84 countries with 69 language centres and 19 cultural centres all around the world, although their presence is mainly concentrated in Europe and Africa. It works in partnership with over 300 universities, as well as with other international organisations The main geographical priorities are Portuguese-speaking African Countries and East Timor, Sub-Saharan Africa, the Ibero-American states, the Maghreb and the Middle East region.

ROMANIA

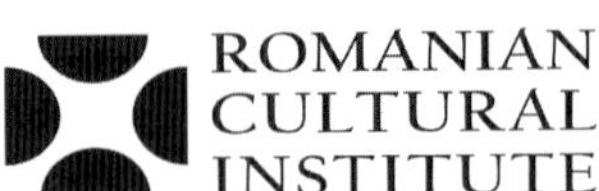
ROMANIAN CULTURAL INSTITUTE

Name	Romanian Cultural Institute
	Institutul Cultural Român
Founded	2003
Head	Radu BOROIANU,
	President since April 2015
Address	38 Aleea Alexandru, sector 1, 011824,
	Bucharest, Romania
Staff	Around 184 in the headquarters, of which 6
	are involved in EUNIC projects;
	Around 122 in our 19 branches worldwide
Website	http://www.icr.ro

Mission/fields of activity
The Romanian Cultural Institute's mission lies in representing, protecting and promoting national culture and civilisation in Romania and abroad, the major goal being to increase the visibility, prestige and knowledge of Romanian values in today's world by actively promoting openness to other cultures of the world. The Romanian Cultural Institute aims to facilitate dialogue and collaboration between Romanian cultural and scientific communities and worldwide partners.
The RCI's main preoccupations are the promotion of

prospective artists, collaboration with influential cultural media in different countries, and ensuring Romania's participation in major international events (book fairs, festivals, conferences, etc). The Romanian Cultural Institute encourages innovative initiatives and original creations, and supports authors financially through open competitions, with independent panels of judges making their decisions based on the value of the projects submitted.

In order to allow the Romanian Cultural Institute to fulfil its role as a global player in increasing the visibility, prestige and knowledge of national culture and civilisation, we have created several subsidiaries in major cities around the world (Paris, New York, Vienna, London, etc.), leading to its gradual transformation into an international player.

Global network/ infrastructure
The Romanian Cultural Institutes have their headquarters in Bucharest and have another 19 branches worldwide (in 18 countries, including the United States and China). It is represented by its branches in 22 EUNIC clusters and by Ministry of Foreign Affairs diplomatic missions in another 16 EUNIC clusters.

SLOVAK REPUBLIC

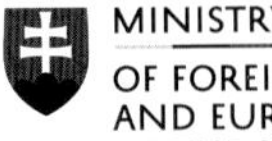
MINISTRY OF FOREIGN AND EUROPEAN AFFAIRS OF THE SLOVAK REPUBLIC

Name	Ministry of Foreign and European
	Affairs of the Slovak Republic
	Ministerstvo zahraničných vecí a európskych
	záležitostí slovenský republiky
Founded	1993
Head	Director, Department of Cultural Diplomacy
Address	Hlboká cesta 2, 33 36 Bratislava
Website	https://www.mzv.sk

Mission/fields of activity
The Department of Cultural Diplomacy is part of the Minister Section of the Ministry of Foreign and European Affairs of the Slovak Republic. Slovakia emphasises the importance of cultural diplomacy as a tool for building international relations.
The Department of Cultural Diplomacy directs the me-

thodological aspects of the cultural activities of the Slovak Institutes abroad. The Slovak institutes represent the institutional basis for the presentation of Slovak art and culture in foreign countries. Their mission is to raise awareness of culture and the arts, education, science and tourism.

Another important role is to cooperate on a bilateral and multilateral basis with different platforms with a view to promoting Slovak culture abroad and building respectful recognition of national heritage and cultural diversity. One of the main goals is to establish partnerships among other nations, mainly with V4 countries, EUNIC, ASEF (Asia-Europe Foundation), PCCE (Platform Culture Central Europe member states), etc.

The Department of Cultural Diplomacy cooperates with the Ministry of Education, Science, Research and Sport of the Slovak Republic in the field of education and science. Cooperation is also created with the Ministry of Culture of the Slovak Republic to support the role of artists abroad. The Department of Cultural Diplomacy is also the coordinator for the intergovernmental bilateral agreements on cooperation in the field of culture, education, science, research and sport and the Joint Committees set up on this basis.

Global network/infrastructure
8 Slovak Institutes in 8 countries

SLOVENIA

REPUBLIC OF SLOVENIA
MINISTRY OF CULTURE

Name   Republika Slovenija Ministrstvo za Kulturo
Republic of Slovenia Ministry of Culture
Founded 1993
Head   Katarina Culiberg (Head of the Office of European Affairs and International Cooperation)
Address Maistrova 10, 1000 Ljubljana, Slovenia
Website http://www.arhiv.mk.gov.si/

Mission/fields of activity

The Office for European Affairs and International Cooperation of the Ministry of Culture fosters and facilitates international cooperation in the field of culture with the aim of promoting Slovene culture at bilateral, multilateral and regional levels.

The office cooperates in the preparation of international framework agreements and programmes, preparing inter-ministerial bilateral cooperation programmes and strategies and supervising and monitoring their execution. It directs Slovene international cooperation in multilateral international organisations, other multilateral connections (UNESCO) and regional initiatives.

The office advances and prepares promotional strategy for Slovene culture in cooperation with other ministries, diplomatic/consular representatives, cultural institutions and other organisations. It cooperates on a regular basis with the Ministry of Foreign Affairs and with the SPIRIT Slovenia Public Agency on cultural tourism issues.

There are annual open calls for Slovenian artists, translators, critics, curators and researchers in the field of arts and culture to compete for a one-month residency in the New York, Berlin, London and Vienna apartments offered by the Ministry of Culture. A special committee of experts from various disciplines evaluates the applications and proposes the final selection to the Minister. The European Affairs and International Cooperation Service also monitors the programme of the Slovenian Culture and Information Centre, Vienna.

Since 2011 special funding can be acquired from the Ministry of Culture and the Ministry of Foreign Affairs for selected cultural events organised by the Slovene embassies and consulates around the world. The embassies propose the projects they would like to support, and the final selection is made by the Ministries Commission.

SPAIN

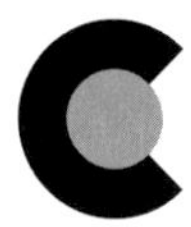

aecid

Name AECID-Agencia Española de Cooperación
Internacional para el Desarrollo
Spanish Agency for International
Development Cooperation
Founded 1988
Head Jesús Manuel Gracia Aldaz, President
Address Avenida de los Reyes Católicos, 4
28040 Madrid, Spain
Staff 1,073
Website http://www.aecid.es

Mission/fields of activity

The mission of the Spanish Agency for International
Development Cooperation is to foster, manage and
implement Spain's development cooperation policies,
aimed at the fight against poverty and sustainable development of developing countries. It also coordinates
the promotion and development of Spain's cultural and
scientific relations and cooperation.

Fields of activity

International Development Cooperation
Cultural and Scientific Relations
Cultural and Scientific Cooperation

Global network/infrastructure

32 Technical Cooperation Offices in 32 countries, 13
Cultural Centres and 6 Associate Cultural Centres in 16
countries
4 Training Centres in 4 countries

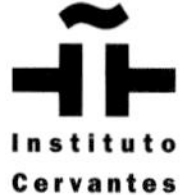

Instituto Cervantes

Name Instituto Cervantes
Founded 1991. Instituto Cervantes brought together
a number of separate cultural networks that Spain had
been operating since the 1940s.
Head Víctor García de la Concha, Director
(President); Rafael Rodríguez-Ponga,
Secretary General (CEO)
Address Calle de Alcalá, 49, 28014 Madrid, Spain
Staff 1,000 on its payroll and as many
contract workers.
Website http://www.cervantes.es

Mission/fields of activity

Spain's public institution for the international advancement, alongside all Spanish-speaking countries, of the
language and culture they all share. It has a worldwide
network of centres – self or jointly managed and collaborative – that allows it to effectively operate on all five
continents. The Instituto Cervantes Institute also caters
for the global community of professionals linked to Spain
by means of an online resource centre, the Cervantes
Virtual Centre.

In its efforts to promote international cultural relations,
the Instituto Cervantes partners with countless public
and private entities, both Spanish and foreign.Attached
to the Ministry of Foreign Affairs and Cooperation, the
Instituto Cervantes is an instrument of cultural diplomacy. It contributes to building relations of trust and understanding with civil society in all the countries where it
operates.

In pursuance of its main objectives, it performs a wide
variety of activities: public events, seminars and international conferences that advocate for culture; participation in educational and cultural international networks;
creation of both traditional and online libraries; and the
definition and establishment of standards in all fields
related to learning Spanish: curriculum, content, teacher
training, certification of proficiency and quality control
and accreditation of teaching entities, be they private or
public, Spanish or foreign.

Global network/infrastructure

76 centres that Instituto Cervantes operates itself, 15
centres jointly managed with a partner organisation and
1000-odd collaborative centres.

SWEDEN

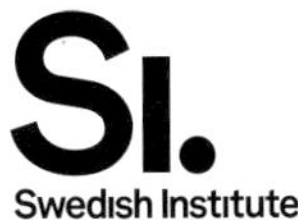

Swedish Institute.

Name	Swedish Institute
	Svenska institutet
Founded	1945
Head	Annika Rembe
Address	Slottsbacken 10, Box 7434, 103 91 Stockholm
Staff	140
Website	https://si.se/

Mission/fields of activity The Swedish Institute (SI) promotes interest and confidence in Sweden around the world. The SI seeks to establish cooperation and lasting relations with other countries through strategic communication and exchange in different fields. Our activities span fields such as culture, society, research, higher education, business, innovation, democracy and global development.

Our work with Sweden's image abroad and our activities in international development cooperation go hand in hand. The overarching objective is to create mutual relationships with other countries around the world. Our support for Swedish language instruction at foreign universities also fits into this common agenda.

Global network/infrastructure
3 offices in 2 countries

UNITED KINGDOM

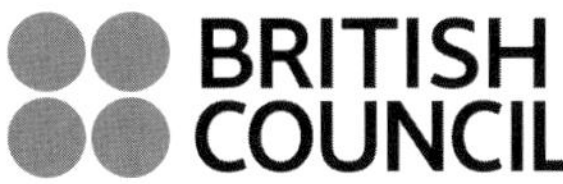

Name	British Council
Founded	1934
Head	Sir Ciárán Devane
Address	British Council
	10 Spring Gardens, London SW1A 2BN, United Kingdom
Staff	8,500+
Website	https://www.britishcouncil.org/

Mission/fields of activity
Founded in 1934 under the name 'British Committee for Relations with Other Countries', the British Council is now headed by Chief Executive Sir Ciarán Devane, appointed by the Board of Trustees with prior approval of the Foreign Secretary.

The founding purpose of the British Council was to create a friendly understanding and knowledge between the people of the UK and other countries; this remains its mission to this day.

Intercultural dialogue is embedded in the British Council's mandate. Through its work on English language teaching, Arts, and Education and Society, the British Council builds links between UK people and institutions and those around the world. It makes a positive contribution to the countries it works with and helps to create trust, foster social change, and lay foundations for prosperity and security around the world.

Global network/infrastructure
191 offices in 110 countries

EUNIC – The next ten years

EUNIC is now marking, in 2016, its 10th anniversary. Its creation in 2006 was the result of a clear perception among a small number of European Union (EU) Member States' national institutes for culture of the need to closely cooperate with each other and with EU institutions. The British Council and Goethe Institut had the vision of setting this network on the right track. *By Rafael Rodríguez-Ponga*

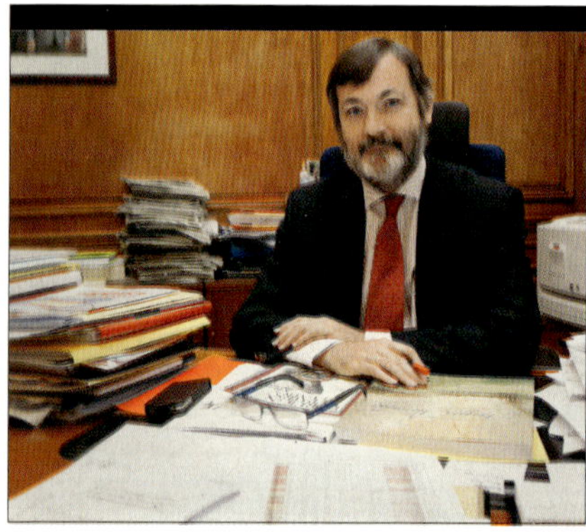

The main results achieved over the past ten years enable us to look ahead with confidence. EUNIC today brings together 35 organisations, either state arm's-length cultural institutes or other governmental bodies. Some ministries of foreign affairs are also members of EUNIC, but only to the extent that, within their national organisational structures, they are tasked with international cultural relations and cultural promotion, beyond the traditional responsibilities associated with the job of cultural counsellor. It is also worth noting that two of our 35 members are private: the Fondation Alliance Française and Società Dante Alighieri.

Today, after the admission of the Malta Arts Council in the General Assembly held in Madrid in June 2015, EUNIC brings together members from all the 28 Member States. Cooperation has brought with it a growing alignment on fundamental issues. Many member organisations are today increasingly sceptical of the traditional paradigm of their activity, based on the unilateral projection of national culture on foreign audiences, both inside and outside the EU.

The Preparatory Action document (2014) has highlighted the extent to which this default strategy of most national institutes of culture, consisting of the mere presentation of national culture, quite often fails to address the key impulse that makes people in third countries keen to get closer to Europe's cultural wealth, namely, the expectation to participate in it and to benefit from it for personal or social improvement.

Global and local levels

EUNIC works on two levels. Firstly, at global level, with an international network built upon an association registered under Belgian law, with a Board of Directors, a General Assembly, a Strategy Group and its head office in Brussels (EUNIC Global Office), led by a director. And secondly, at local level, in every country or city where more than three of our member organisations have branches that work together in EUNIC clusters.

Today, EUNIC's international network consists of 100 clusters all around the world. Some of them have already achieved a high degree of operational maturity and collaborate effectively with high-profile local entities and with the EU delegation. This is the case with the clusters in Jordan and Tunisia. Both manage major service contracts for the EU. It is to be noted that quite often EUNIC members work together much more easily at local level than at headquarters level.

In spite of the progress made, enhanced coordination and effective sharing of know-

Many member organisations are today increasingly sceptical of the traditional paradigm of their activity based on the unilateral projection of national culture on foreign audiences, both inside and outside the EU.

ledge, information, expertise and resources among member organisations remains a key challenge for EUNIC. When put together, the institutional tools that the EU and Member States use for external cultural action still provide a disheartening picture of disunity. EU external actions in the field of culture will only be effective if they are aligned with those of Member States. It is worth remembering that the main roles and responsibilities in everything related to culture lie with Member States. It is up to them to decide how they exercise those responsibilities in the domestic sphere and to what extent they are ready to share them, and how, at EU level. The Lisbon Treaty recognises this by granting the EU the role of supporting the efforts undertaken by Member States in accordance with the principle of subsidiarity.

Recent achievements

It is probably not an overstatement to say that EUNIC has achieved more over the last fifteen months than in the ten years since its creation in 2006. If those years have allowed member organisations to know each other better, to build mutual trust and to have a better understanding of their shared interests, the past few months have been marked by a sustained effort to reconcile the network to its stated objectives and increase its operational capacities. There is no doubt that the EU's fresh resolve to bring forward an effective European cultural strategy in the external field is acting as a spur to EUNIC in the current phase of its development. Moreover, the financial support that the European Commission has given to the strengthening of the network since 2015 is now fundamental. The assessment of the initial phase of our three-year Crossroads for Culture (CXC) project, funded by the Creative Europe programme, is extremely positive.

After a lengthy period of internal consultations, conducted in a 'bottom-up' approach, EUNIC adopted a clear strategic framework at the winter meeting of its General Assembly in Brussels in December 2015. The new overall direction of the network brings together inputs from planners and strategists in member organisations and from the presidents of numerous clusters.

Ambitious target

By 2025, EUNIC has set itself the ambitious target of more effectively combining the capabilities, expertise, international network and international portfolio of partners of each of its members, and as a result being recognised, in the fields of cultural diplomacy and cultural relations, as the partner of choice by governments, the EU and other international organisations. To this end, over the next few years EUNIC will focus its work on a series of strategic areas, namely, research and advocacy, knowledge-sharing and improvement of operational capacities, and the design and delivery of international projects in a limited number of thematic areas and priority clusters outside the EU. In order to avoid delays and departures, both EUNIC's permanent office in Brussels (Global Of-

It is probably not an overstatement to say that EUNIC has achieved more over the last fifteen months than in the ten years since its creation in 2006.

fice) and member organisations have now set out their commitments in annual operating plans, whose performance will be reviewed by the General Assembly at its next meeting in June 2016 in Copenhagen.

EUNIC is part of the consortium, composed mostly of member organisations of the network, to which the European Commission has awarded a service contract for the establishment of a Cultural Diplomacy Platform under the Partnership Instrument (PI). The PI is a financial instrument specifically designed to circumvent the limitations of the other instruments whereby the EU funds its external action, to foster engagement with its strategic partners, and to give the EU the ability to act on the international scene as a global player.

One of the four key objectives of the PI is to improve the knowledge and visibility of both the EU and the role it plays in the world through actions of public diplomacy (cultural diplomacy is a component of public diplomacy). EUNIC and its clusters are closely following a number of public diplomacy programmes that the EU plans to implement in various countries and regions under PI tenders. Clusters examine the conditions laid down by the various EU delegations, gather the necessary capacities to provide the required services and bid for the contract. By doing this, EUNIC offers its extensive expertise to assist the EU in the effective implementation of its public diplomacy strategy.

The EUNIC cluster fund

The EUNIC cluster fund – the mechanism whereby EUNIC's Global Office transfers funds to clusters – is under evaluation and will soon be reformulated and aligned with the three strategic goals adopted in December 2015. Member organisations still have a long way to go in terms of internal advocacy to achieve an effective alignment between them. The profile of EUNIC's focal points in each of them is being reinforced to ensure compliance with this goal.

In the field of external advocacy, EUNIC remains in line with More Europe, a grouping of some of its members and civil society organisations, whose main purpose is to raise awareness of the value of culture in EU external relations. During the second half of 2016 EUNIC will carry out the first phase of a review of its governance structure, covering issues such as governing bodies, decision-making processes, membership, and the legal status of clusters. The status of associate members or non-full members is still an open question.

The growing strategic alignment between the EU and EUNIC is becoming more and more apparent. Since June 2014, when a consortium, largely composed of members of EUNIC, made public the Preparatory Action report on culture in the EU's external relations, which had been commissioned by the European Commission on the European Parliament's (EP) initiative, there has been a number of gestures that amount to a recognition of culture being one of the greatest assets of the EU's external action and of the need to team up if that asset is to be rightly used.

The Work Plan for Culture (2015-2018) approved by the Council at the level of ministers of education and culture at the end of 2014; the joint meeting of the PE Committees on Foreign Affairs and Culture and Education in March 2015 to evaluate compliance with the recommendations of the Preparatory Action; the conference titled Culture and Development: Towards A More Strategic Approach to Cultural Policies in the EU's External Relations, organised by the Luxembourg presidency of the EU Council in September 2015; the conclusions adopted by the Council of Ministers in November 2015 on culture in the EU's external relations; or the recent report 'European Cultural Institutes Abroad' commissioned by the EP that contains highly practical recommendations to achieve a better alignment in terms of strategies and resources between the EU and Member States in the field of culture in external relations.

Joint communication

All these developments bear witness to the increasing attention that the issue is getting from political and opinion leaders. The European Commission (specifically the

By 2025, EUNIC has set itself the ambitious target of more effectively combining the capabilities, expertise, international network and international portfolio of partners of each of its members.

three DGs Education and Culture, International Cooperation and Development, and Neighbourhood and Enlargement Negotiations) and the European External Action Service are expected to make public a joint communication that will drive forward the EU's external relations and cultural strategy and will also recognise the crucial role that EUNIC must play in it.

It might be now useful to make some closing remarks of a more general nature. The current international environment, in which force and intimidation are often less effective than persuasion, is clearly advantageous to the EU, whose foreign policy is closely associated with cooperation and civil collaborative networks. Furthermore, whereas governments face growing difficulties in getting practical results in terms of influence and relevance by using traditional diplomatic instruments, emerging states and non-state actors now have increasing influence in the field of foreign policy, thanks to the ongoing technological revolution.

If it is keen to ensure a prominent role in the increasingly charged global political agenda and preserve its ability to shape the international environment in accordance with its values and principles, then the EU must be clearly aware of its soft power resources and learn to use them in a thorough way.

As became quite clear during the run-up to the 2005 UNESCO Convention for the Protection and Promotion of the Diversity of Cultural Expressions, 'unity in diversity' is both at the very essence of the EU and one of its main assets. On the one hand, the general perception of the EU beyond its external borders is almost invariably associated with an immense historical and artistic heritage, rich traditions, excellent education, major sporting achievements and an inexhaustible wealth of creativity and talent. On the other hand, the EU is a unique international construction that enables the peaceful and prosperous coexistence of peoples with different cultural and historical backgrounds that have agreed on a number of principles and practices to effectively comply with them.

Largely by its successful implementation in the EU, these principles are now generally regarded as having an almost universal authority. In a word, since the EU is an exceptional 'democracy of cultures', individuals and civil society from third countries

If it is keen to ensure a prominent role in the increasingly charged global political agenda and preserve its ability to shape the international environment in accordance with its values and principles, then the EU must be clearly aware of its soft power resources and learn to use them in a thorough way.

feel, almost without exception, favourably disposed to it.

good use of this precious foreign policy asset. In this way it actively supports EU efforts to make trust and mutual understanding the backbone of international relations.

Since presidents and members of the presidential board of EUNIC are not paid any allowances for their dedication to the network, I would like to express my gratitude to all previous presidents and members of the Board of Directors. To a large extent, EUNIC is the result of the time, energy and inspiration they have brought with them.

Ten years from now, when we will be marking its 20th anniversary, EUNIC will certainly be a key part of the cooperative environment that the EU and Member States are now building in order to make

Rafael Rodríguez-Ponga is Secretary-General of the Instituto Cervantes and President of EUNIC.

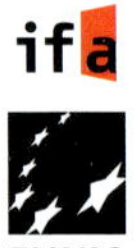

Culture Report EUNIC Yearbook 2016

Published by: EUNIC (European National Institutes for Culture) and Institut
für Auslandsbeziehungen e.V. (ifa)

Project editors: William Billows, Sebastian Körber
Editor, English edition: Gill McKay
Editorial assistance: Andrew Murray
Graphic design: Eberhard Wolf
Translation: Neil McKay, Gill McKay

ifa address: Charlottenplatz 17, 70173 Stuttgart

The views expressed are those of the respective authors.

Photo credits, photo spread:
Streetfootballworld
Centro de Educacion y Desarrollo Comunitario
Spirit of Soccer
Kick4Life
Grassroot Soccer

Photos of authors:
P. 104: Isolde Ohlbaum, P. 113: Em-J Staples, P. 169 Carolin Seeliger

First edition 2016

© 2016 the photographers
© 2016 the authors for the contributions
© 2016 the publishers: Steidl Verlag, for this edition
Image processing: Steidl's digital darkroom

Production and printing:
Steidl, Göttingen
Steidl
Düstere Str. 4 / 37073 Göttingen
Tel. +49 551 49 60 60 / Fax +49 551 49 60 649
mail@steidl.de
steidl.de

ISBN 978-3-95829-198-0
Printed in Germany by Steidl